A Devotional Study of
Matthew and Mark

Your King
and
My Servant

Warren Henderson

Your King and My Servant – A Devotional Study of Matthew and Mark

By Warren Henderson
Copyright © 2025

Cover Design: Ben Bredeweg
Editing/Proofreading: David Lindstrom, Dan Macy

Published by Warren A. Henderson
1025 Iron Cap Dr.
Stevensville, MT 59870

Perfect Bound ISBN: 978-1-939770-76-9
eBook ISBN: 978-1-939770-77-6

ORDERING INFORMATION:
Copies of *Your King and My Servant*
are available through various online retailers
worldwide.

Table of Contents

The Cover

Angelic beings testify of God's greatness (Ps. 103:20-22). These include cherubim, seraphim, and the four living creatures in heaven who reflect various glories of Christ while concealing their own intrinsic beauty with their wings. For example, the faces of these powerful creatures depict Christ as exemplified in each of the four Gospels. The *lion* is the king of the beasts, which reflects Matthew's perspective of Christ as being the legitimate King to sit on David's throne. The *ox*, as a beast of burden, is harnessed for the rigors of serving, and pictures Mark's presentation of Christ as Jehovah's lowly Servant. The face of the *man* portrays Luke's theme of the Lord's humanity. Lastly, the *eagle* flies high above all the other creatures to declare Christ's deity, which is John's theme.

An Overview of the Gospels

What Does "Gospel" Mean?

The word "gospel" is found 101 times in the New Testament. In the original language, the noun form *euaggelion* simply means "a good message," while the verb form *euaggelizo* refers to "announcing the good news," or "to evangelize." The gospel message is good news from heaven to all humanity. The good news is that, through Christ, God's peace would come to mankind, or as the angelic host declared to the bewildered shepherds near Bethlehem so long ago, *"Glory to God in the highest, and on earth peace, goodwill toward men!"* (Luke 2:14).

As one examines the four Gospels (Matthew, Mark, Luke, and John), it is quickly observed that deliberate variations, exclusions, and inclusions of content exist within each account. There are different styles of language and arrangement of subjects. The Spirit of God obviously never intended for there to be a multiplication of narratives, but rather a necessity for variation. Likewise, the Holy Spirit made no attempt to convey a complete biography of the Lord's life, for lengthy gaps of personal history are apparent.

A brief breakdown of the content matter within the four Gospels will clearly demonstrate this point. Of the eighty-nine chapters in the four accounts, eighty-five pertain to the Lord's last three years on earth, and twenty-eight of these focus solely on His final week of ministry, His crucifixion, and His resurrection. Therefore, roughly one-third of the four Gospels is devoted to the specific details surrounding the events of Calvary. The Gospel focus is a Person, not a biography of a person. The Gospels contain both the wisdom of God in sacred expression and what the Father longs for us to appreciate – the profound excellencies of His Son. C. I. Scofield summarizes the main purpose of the four Gospels:

> The four Gospels record the eternal being, human ancestry, birth, life and ministry, death, resurrection, and ascension of Jesus the Christ, Son of God and Son of Man. Taken together, they set forth, not a biography but a Person. ... The four Gospels, though designedly incomplete as a

1

story, are complete as a revelation. We may not know everything that Jesus did, but we may know Him. In four great narratives, each of which in some respects supplements the other three, we have Jesus Christ Himself.[1]

God's written "good news" to mankind is presented from the four unique vantage points of Christ found in Matthew, Mark, Luke, and John. Many have tried in vain to fully harmonize these Gospel accounts, but they cannot be fully harmonized; each Gospel stands alone as an inspired testimony of a unique theme of Christ's life and ministry. On this subject, Samuel Ridout remarks as follows:

> Had God intended that we should have but one narrative, He would have given us the record of the life of our Lord in that form. Our attention, therefore, should be directed to each separate Gospel to ascertain, as far as we may, its general character, its main theme, its point of view, the manner in which it presents our Lord.[2]

Clearly, the intended purpose and distinct content of each of the four Gospels must be understood to better appreciate what God has *spoken unto us by* [His] *Son* (Heb. 1:2). Matthew and Luke do not strive to record events in sequence, but in accordance with their associated themes of royalty and humanity, respectively. For this cause, miracles, discourses, events, and related facts are grouped together to ensure the fullest development of the deliberate theme of the Holy Spirit. Mark provides the most concise and most chronologically accurate Gospel account; He is upholding the "doings" of the Lord. John would be the next most chronological account of the Lord's ministry but is characterized by vast gaps in the life of Christ. In summary, it is the differences within the Gospels that call our attention to topical truths.

Matthew and John were personally discipled by Christ, while Mark and Luke were not. God employed quite a variety of writers and styles to portray His Son to the world. Two were apostles; one was a Gentile believer, and one a later Jewish convert to Christ. One of the apostles and one of the non-apostles recorded events as they occurred, while the remaining two organized events to affirm their presentation of Christ.

The unique Gospel themes preclude a full harmony of facts but serve as an invitation to appreciate the distinct glories of Christ's holy character, divine essence, and selfless ministry. As one slowly rotates a prism immersed in white light, various colors are refracted through the prism, such that the color one perceives will depend upon the viewpoint from which one gazes upon the prism. Same prism, same light, but distinctions in radiance are observed from various on-looking positions. As we view the Lord Jesus Christ by the light of divine revelation, we learn to appreciate the fullness of His matchless splendor from the diverse Gospel illuminations. The Son is altogether lovely, as the Father fittingly proclaims to us through the four Gospel records.

The Gospel Themes

One of the most beautiful panoramic views of the differing vantage points of Christ is seen in the Gospel message itself. There is but one Gospel message, yet each writer highlights varying aspects of the Gospel as it directly relates to his associated theme.

Matthew's authority theme stresses "repentance" eleven times, but only three times does he speak of the necessity to believe in the Lord Jesus (e.g., Matt. 4:17). In fact, in Matthew, the Lord spends more time criticizing the Jews for not believing John's message of repentance than for not believing on Him.

Mark stresses the need to both repent and to believe in Christ to be saved, but there is clearly a heavier focus on believing (e.g., Mark 1:14-15). He speaks of believing in Christ nearly a dozen times and of the necessity to repent only four times. As Christ is not lauding His kingly authority in Mark, repentance is of a secondary emphasis. Accordingly, it would require real faith to believe on a lowly Servant for salvation.

Luke speaks of believing in the Lord five times but addresses the matter of repentance fourteen times. The beloved physician instead employs terms in his Gospel which appeal to human need and suffering, such as "perishing" (Luke 13:3, 5). "Perishing" speaks of dying, and Luke speaks of it more often than the other gospel writers. On behalf of Christ, Luke petitions the sick, the suffering, and the brokenhearted hurting under the effects of sin. The Lord feels our painful infirmities caused by sin. He desires to save the sinner from eternal judgment and to relieve the agonizing aftermath of sin.

John's Gospel expresses the heavenly perspective of the gospel message. While Matthew and Luke stress repentance, for one must acknowledge their sins before salvation can be obtained, John simply declares the overall spiritual situation: In God is life, and apart from God is death (John 1:3-4). Speaking of Christ, John writes: *"All things were*

3

made by Him"; John stresses the fact that man is spiritually dead and must be born again (John 3:3) and made alive (John 5:21). How is this accomplished? By believing (John 3:16, 3:36, 5:24). Consequently, the words "repent" and "forgive" are not found in John's account, but the matter of believing is emphasized ninety-nine times! Man is dead in the world. Eternal life is only in Christ.

Why Four Gospel Accounts?

But why did God choose to reveal His Son to us through four gospels? Why not use seven, the number of perfection, instead of four? In Scripture, the number "four" is the number of *earthly order*, as created by God. For example, on earth we observe four seasons, four directions, four divisions of day, four phases of the moon, four realms of life (on the earth, under the earth, in the heaven, or in the sea), and four divisions of humanity (kindred, people, tongue, and nation).

How does *four* then relate to God's presentation of His Son to humanity? When the Son exited the dimensionless and timeless realm of majesty on high and descended to the earth, He willingly placed Himself under earthly order. As a man, He became subject to the natural laws of creation, even though, as God, He still maintained the order of all things (Col. 1:17). Consequently, the Lord never invoked the blessings of His deity to satisfy His humanity beyond the normal scope in which all humanity experiences the daily blessings of God.

Many other means are employed in Scripture to convey relevance to the Lord's condescending journey to earth for the sole purpose of suffering death, that mankind might have an opportunity to be restored to a holy God. For example, the Lord Jesus referred to Himself more often by the title "Son of Man" than by the title "Son of God." In so doing, He was not calling attention to His divine essence but to His lowly position and ministry on earth. The Spirit of God, throughout the Bible, consistently represents the glories of the Son, while being *earthly-connected*, by employing the number *four*. Hence, the four Gospels uphold the brilliancy of the Lord from different perspectives and to varying audiences. The following table summarizes these distinctions.

Gospel	Matthew	Mark	Luke	John
Perspective	King	Servant	Humanity	Deity
Audience	Jewish	Roman	Greek	The World

The Father provided perfect representation of His Son through four unique vantage points of His greatness. *Four* is the number pertaining to earthly order. It is the best number to declare the "good news" message – the goodness of God to mankind. The Son willingly laid aside His outshining glory and departed from His celestial home. He became subject to creation order and took the place upon an accursed tree for every man, woman, and child that would ever live. There, rejected and abandoned, the billows and waves of divine judgment broke upon the Savior as every human sin was judicially accounted for. As a result of Christ's finished work, man now has the wonderful opportunity to be forgiven, redeemed, justified, and eternally restored to God. The Gospel of Jesus Christ, from every viewpoint, is "good news" indeed!

Christ's Regional Ministries

It seems likely that Christ's baptism and the subsequent forty days of testing by the devil occurred in late Summer or early Fall of 26 A.D. (this assumes the traditional date of 30 A.D. for Christ's crucifixion). John the baptizer, Christ's forerunner, had already been calling Israel to repentance for some time (perhaps one to two years) when Christ was water baptized and then anointed by the Holy Spirit. After the first cleansing of the temple at Passover (John 2:13-22), Christ departed Jerusalem through Samaria and returned to Galilee (John 4). At this juncture (the Spring of 27 A.D.), an approximate two-year ministry began throughout Galilee. Capernaum was the Lord's home base of operation during this time.

In the Spring of 29 A.D., the Lord moved His ministry to the region of Decapolis, east of the Sea of Galilee. This was a time of specialized ministry for His disciples, some of which were permitted to witness His transfiguration and see Moses and Elijah attending to Him.

The ministry in Decapolis concluded with the Lord's return to Jerusalem for the Feast of Tabernacles in the Fall of 29 A.D. (John 7:1-8:11). For the next three months, the Lord and His disciples traveled throughout Judea spreading the Kingdom gospel message (Luke 10:1-17). This ministry concluded with the Feast of Dedication (called *Hanukkah* today) in December of that year (John 10:22-39).

Map of Christ's Regional Ministries:
Galilee, Decapolis, Judea, Perea, and Jerusalem

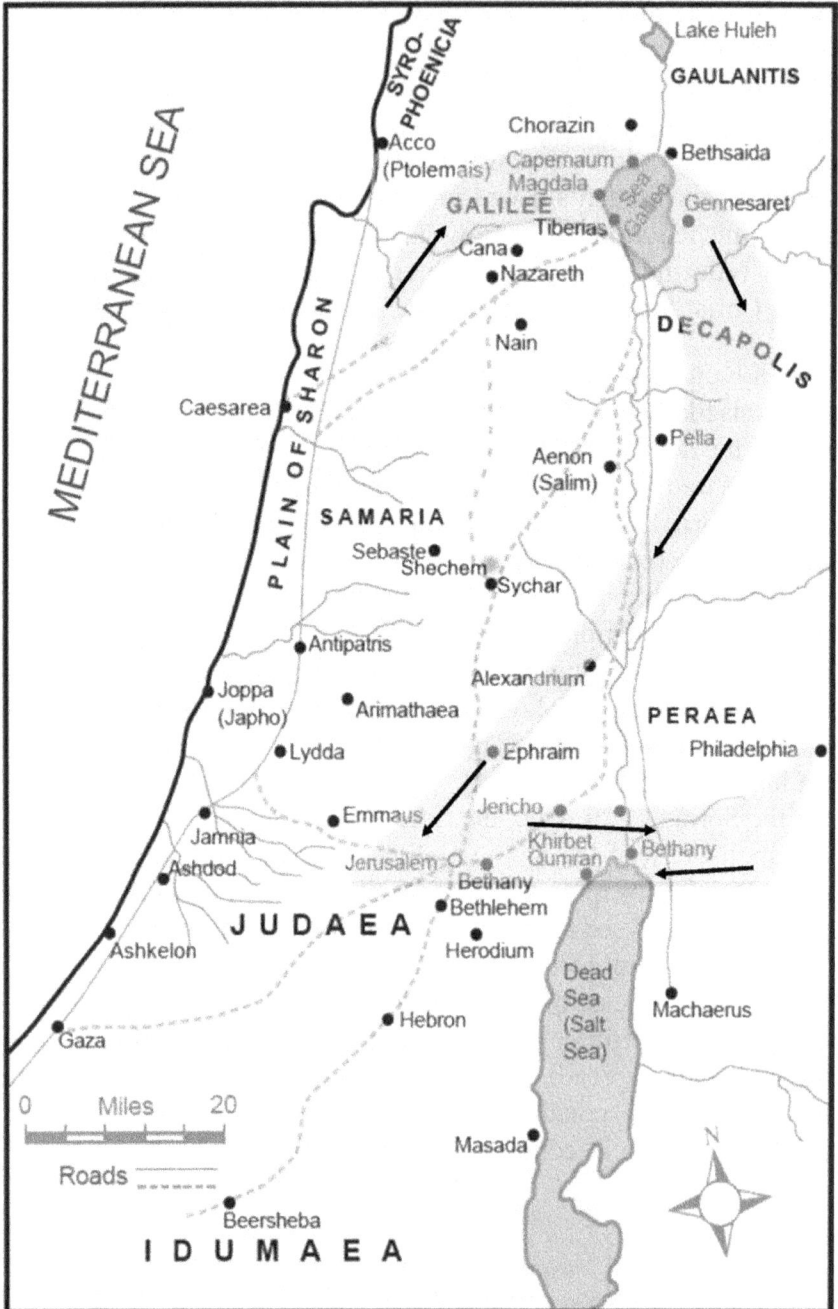

The Lord and His disciples spent the next four months mainly in Perea, where John had previously baptized those repenting of their sins (John 10:40-42). It is during the Judean and Perean ministries that the Lord's parable-telling kicked into overdrive. Most of the parables He told occurred during these final months of His earthly sojourn.

Christ and His disciples departed Perea and traveled to Bethany, near Jerusalem, just prior to the Passover feast in 30 A.D. It is at this time that the Lord raises His friend Lazarus from the dead (John 11). This miracle is followed by His triumphal entry into Jerusalem on the colt of a donkey on what is commonly referred to as *Palm Sunday* (John 12:1-19).

The final week of the Lord's ministry on earth was spent confronting stubborn Jewish attitudes and promising reward to those found faithful when He returned to establish His kingdom. The culmination of Christ's earthly ministry then occurred in Jerusalem: His suffering and death at Calvary, and His resurrection from a garden tomb three days later.

The number "2" superimposed on the adjacent map of Israel nicely summarizes the movements of our Lord and His disciples while they sought the lost sheep of Israel in a three-plus-year gospel campaign. The base of the "2" is bi-directional, as the Lord returned from Perea (or Peraea) to Jerusalem the final week of His earthly sojourn.

The Parables

The Lord's parables are one of the most mystifying aspects of His ministry. These parables are often perplexing, cryptic, and hard to understand. The Lord told parables in response to questions, self-righteous attitudes, pious murmurings, or as a means of engaging an audience to think about spiritual matters more deeply. On some occasions, the subject matter was so vast that the Lord strung several parables together in addressing His listeners, but at other times, a single allegory sufficed.

If studied individually, Christ's parables seem to address a wide range of subjects and have an equally vast intended purpose. Yet, stepping back from the intrinsic value of each story to a panoramic view, the Lord's parable ministry reveals some interesting patterns. For example, the gospel accounts indicate that the Lord told no parables for perhaps a year and a half after His baptism. Furthermore, the Lord spoke only fourteen parables by the close of the Galilean Ministry and eight of these were told on the same day. It was not uncommon for several months to pass without any parables being communicated or for several to be spoken all at once. All the parables seem to be spoken on only fifteen different occasions, with fifteen parables spoken on two occasions. It is also observed that nearly two-thirds of the parables were disclosed in the final eight months of the Lord's earthly ministry. Arthur Pink affords a concise definition of a parable:

> What is a parable? The word "parable" means to "cast alongside." The popular definition of Christ's parables is that they were earthly stories with a heavenly meaning. How man gets things upside down! The truth is that His parables were heavenly stories with an earthly meaning, having to do with His earthly people, in earthly connections.[3]

The Lord used a story format to align a spiritual truth beside a common everyday activity the people could relate to, such as sowing seed, using a dragnet for fishing, or watching birds feed in a mustard tree. Perhaps the simplest definition of a "parable" is "a heavenly story with an earthly meaning."

Why did the Lord speak in parables? The Lord Jesus intentionally spoke in parables to reveal truth, but in a partially veiled manner. The parables were not just enjoyable stories but served as a test to the hearers. The casual onlooker, the "window shopper," would hear and not understand, nor would he or she desire any more insight concerning the parable – "thanks for the good story." But those longing to understand the spiritual significance of the parable would seek the Lord for further instruction (e.g., Mark 4:10-12); those who merely enjoyed the story would go their own way. Often it was only the Lord's disciples who sought to learn the deeper meaning of His stories. By design, then, a parable is concealed truth that tests the heart of each one listening to it.

As the Lord neared Calvary, the meaning of His stories became more obvious. While speaking parables in Jerusalem on the Tuesday before His death, even the Pharisees understood that He was speaking of them.

Christ's Parables

Matthew labors in his account to validate Jesus Christ as the Jewish Messiah. Mark focuses on the busy life of Christ in doing miracles and ministering to the brokenhearted and the down-and-outers. Mark depicts Christ ministering to God's chosen people, while Matthew reveals Christ as testing Israel. Matthew upholds the kingly assertion in his Gospel, while Luke is careful not to distract from the humanity of Christ and the social appeal of the Savior. Mark contains only four parables, whereas Matthew and Luke contain many more.

Matthew meticulously demonstrates that Christ is the culmination of Old Testament prophecies. In contrast, John affirms the deity of Christ in his account and, therefore, repeatedly connects Christ to the completion of Old Testament "types." Interestingly, the word "parable" is found thirty-two times in the four Gospels, but only once in John.

The Greek word rendered "parable" in John 10:6 is *paroimia*, literally meaning "a proverb" or a "figure of speech." J. H. Thayer defines it this way: "a saying out of the usual course or deviating from the usual manner of speaking ... any dark saying which shadows forth some didactic truth, especially a symbolic or figurative saying."[4] The normal Greek word used thirty-one times in the synoptic Gospels is *parabole*, meaning "a similitude implied by a fictitious narrative."[5] The Lord articulated the importance of Himself as the Good Shepherd in John 10; this was not an application-enriched story to prompt the listener to action. Technically then, there are no parables within the Gospel of John.

As the Lord approached the cross, the parable veil thinned, and the meaning of His stories became more obvious, even to the dissident. While speaking parables in Jerusalem on the Tuesday before His death, even the Pharisees understood that He was speaking of them. In general, the parables can be organized into four main subjects, with each compilation of parables leading to the next in a nearly chronological fashion. These are: "Mysteries of the Kingdom" parables, "Salvation and the Evidence of Salvation" parables, "The Second Coming and Jewish Attitudes" parables, and "Reward for Faithful" parables.

In the eight "Mysteries of the Kingdom" parables, the Lord reveals a chronology of events that would characterize the "kingdom of heaven" from His first advent (a seed-sowing mission) until His return to rule the world in peace. Satan is busy in the first four parables undermining the kingdom of heaven. In these parables, Satan is seen attacking the gospel message, trying to neutralize the influence of believers on earth, corrupting church leadership, order, and structure, and finally, promoting false doctrine within the Church. However, in the last three parables, Satan is absent, and God demonstrates His fathomless grace in saving sinners. Christ paid the great price for the hidden treasure (yet unrestored Israel) and the pearl (the Church) and extends blessing to those Gentiles not bowing to the Antichrist during the Tribulation.

In the second group of parables, the Lord focuses on important aspects of salvation, such as not mixing the law with grace and the necessity of repentance to receive salvation. Then several parables reinforce the "practice" of the believer once his "position" in Christ is secure (forgiving, giving, obeying, and loving each other and the Lord).

The remaining parables largely focus on the Lord's Second Advent and were mainly told in the final three or four months of the Lord's ministry on earth. Part of these parables focus on religious pride and Jewish rejection of the Lord and the consequences of that rejection, while others emphasize rewards for the faithful when the Lord comes into His Kingdom, including: faithfulness to the opportunities we are given to serve (the parable of the Laborers), abilities given to serve (the parable of the Talents), and using what God makes available to us to serve (the parable of the Pounds).

This is a summary of the parables that Christ told:

The Mysteries of the Kingdom

Parable Title	Reference
The Sower and the Soils	Matt. 13:5-8; Mark 4:3-8; Luke 8:5-8
The Tares	Matt. 13:24-30
The Mustard Seed	Matt. 13:31-32; Mark 4:30-32; Lk. 13:18-19
The Leaven and the Woman	Matt. 13:33; Luke 13:20-21
The Hidden Treasure	Matt. 13:44
The Pearl of Great Price	Matt. 13:45-46
The Dragnet	Matt. 13:47-50
Mysterious Growth	Mark 4:26-29

Salvation and Evidence of Salvation

Parable Title	Reference
The New Cloth/New Wineskin	Matt. 9:16-17
The Two Houses	Matt. 7:24-27; Luke 6:47-49
The Two Debtors	Luke 7:41-43
The Unforgiving Servant	Matt. 18:23-25
The Good Samaritan	Luke 10:25-37
Friend at Midnight/Fatherhood	Luke 11:5-8
The Rich Fool	Luke 12:16-21
The Great Supper	Luke 14:15-24
The Unfinished Tower/King's Rash War/Salt	Luke 14:28-33
The Lost Sheep	Matt. 18:12-14; Luke 15:4-7
The Lost Coin	Luke 15:8-10
The Lost Son	Luke 15:11-32

The Second Coming and Jewish Attitudes

Parable Title	Reference
The Rude Children	Luke 7:31-35
The Barren Fig Tree	Luke 13:6-9
The Unjust Judge	Luke 18:1-8
The Pharisee & the Tax Collector	Luke 18:9-14
The Two Sons	Matt. 21:28-32
The Landowner & Vinedressers	Matt. 21:33-46; Mark 12:1-12; Lk. 20:9-19
The Marriage Feast	Matt. 22:1-14
The Ten Virgins	Matt. 25:1-13
The Doorkeeper	Mark 13:34-37

Reward for the Faithful

Parable Title	Reference
The Shrewd Manager	Luke 16:1-9
The Servants' Reward	Luke 17:7-10
The Workers in the Vineyard	Matt. 20:1-16
The Minas (Pounds)	Luke 19:11-27
The Two Servants	Matt. 24:45-51; Luke 12:42-48
The Talents	Matt. 25:14-30

Christ's Miracles

Paul acknowledges the natural propensity of the Jewish people to be guided by sight rather than faith, *"For the Jews require a sign, and the Greeks seek after wisdom"* (1 Cor. 1:22). The Lord Jesus said, *"This is an evil generation, they seek a sign"* (Luke 11:29). The Lord performed ample miracles while on earth, yet the Jews did not believe that He was the Messiah and, in fact, crucified Him. Peter determinedly proclaimed this point at Pentecost (the first day of the Church Age; Acts 2:22-24).

The word "miracle" is not found in Matthew's Gospel; rather, the miracles that the Lord performed are referred to as "signs." Signs of what? The signs witnessed by Israel were irrefutable evidence proving that Christ was who He claimed to be – the Messiah. The Lord's preaching and signs composed the kingdom message to the Jews. Though the signs provided proof that Jesus was the Christ, they would prove insufficient to cause the people to trust the Messiah for salvation. *"Without faith it is impossible to please Him* [God]*"* (Heb. 11:6), and faith requires the soul to venture beyond what the senses can verify.

Apparently, only a fraction of Christ's total number of miracles were written down for our appreciation. Mark notes, *"For He healed many, so that as many as had afflictions pressed about Him to touch Him"* (Mark 3:10). What types of miracles did the Lord perform?

Miracles of Physical Healing. Included are healings of fever (2), blindness (4), hemorrhage (1), dropsy (1), leprosy (2), paralysis (4), deaf-mute (1), and severed body parts (1).

Miracles of Resurrection. Only three resurrections were recorded in the Old Testament; Elijah and Elisha are associated with these. The Lord raised three people from the dead during His ministry on earth, then effected His own resurrection also (John 10:17-18). The Lord Jesus was the seventh and, thus, the perfect resurrection of the Bible.

Miracles Removing Demon Possession. The Lord is recorded seven different times as driving out demons from the host they possessed. This always resulted in emotional and physical healing.

Miracles Defying Earthly Physics. Besides miracles that brought personal healing, the Lord Jesus performed supernatural feats to demonstrate His power over creation. Twice He calmed a raging storm by a simple command (Matt. 8:27). Water became His sidewalk for crossing the Sea of Galilee and for Peter's brief excursion as well. Directly after this event, the Lord instantaneously moved their boat a great distance across the sea to arrive at Capernaum (John 6:15-21).

Miracles Related to Plant and Animal Life. Though the Lord had no tax liability, He graciously agreed to pay taxes to not stumble the unsaved. For this reason, and for this purpose only, Peter received the money via the mouth of a fish (Matt. 17:27). On two different occasions, the Lord commanded fishermen to drop their nets for a great draught of fish (Luke 5; John 21). Near the end of the Lord's ministry, to demonstrate His disgust for fruitless Israel, He cursed a fig tree. The disciples noted how quickly it was completely withered (Matt. 21:20).

Miracles Related to Food and Drink. On two different occasions, the Lord took a few fish and loaves of bread and multiplied them to feed thousands of people to their fill. In so doing, He demonstrated that He was the Master of quantity. The Lord's first miracle, turning water into the best wine, also confirmed that He is the Master of quality also.

Matthew

Matthew Overview

Author

Matthew, also called Levi, was a Jew who collected taxes in Capernaum (9:9) for the Roman government and therefore was despised by the Jewish community. Tax collectors were usually well-off because they collected more from the people than their tax obligation. Matthew was likely the wealthiest of the disciples called into ministry. Luke informs us that Matthew could afford to host a great banquet with a large crowd in attendance (Luke 5:29).

Mark and Luke do not specifically state that Levi is Matthew, but his call to ministry is identical to that of Matthew in Matthew's gospel. He may have been disowned by his parents, as he does not mention the identity of his father when listing himself along with the other eleven disciples (10:3). However, when Mark and Luke list the twelve disciples, Alphaeus is stated as being Levi's (Matthew's) father (Mark 2:14; Luke 5:27).

Date

Church Tradition says that Matthew preached about fifteen years in Palestine and then left to evangelize in foreign lands. It is generally believed that before he departed, he left a first draft of his Gospel in Aramaic. This would have been approximately 45 A.D. Matthew later made a Greek edition for wider use in 50 to 55 A.D. or perhaps even later, but not after the destruction of Jerusalem in 70 A.D. (Matt. 4:5, 27:53). Five early church fathers indicate that Matthew first wrote his work in Aramaic and later in Greek: Papias (80-155 A.D.), Irenaeus (130-202 A.D.), Origen (185-254 A.D.), Eusebius (fourth century A.D.) and Jerome (sixth century A.D.).[6] The original Aramaic work may have been merely "The Sayings of Jesus," while the full work was later written in Greek.

Why Is Matthew's Gospel First?

Why is Matthew the first book of the New Testament? The opening sentence both introduces the theme of Matthew and answers this question: *"The book of the generation of Jesus Christ, the Son of David, the Son of Abraham."* The principal topic is the direct fulfillment of the Davidic and Abrahamic covenants through Christ. These were unilateral covenants that God had made with David and Abraham but never had been completely fulfilled. For the Jews, the hope of permanent royalty from *a man after God's own heart* and the acquisition of blessing promised to *the friend of God* were paramount.

The genealogies of Matthew 1 served as proof to the Jews that Jesus, through Joseph, was a direct descendant of David and, thus, the legal and rightful heir to David's throne. As to not distract from his theme of covenant fulfillment, Matthew begins with Abraham, not Adam, in rendering Christ's genealogy. Luke's genealogy of Christ, however, is for a different purpose. Luke upholds Christ as the "Son of Man," or more specifically, the "Son of Adam." In so doing, Luke shows Christ to be the "Last Adam," God's replacement representative of righteousness and the literal fulfillment of the prophesied Messiah being derived from the "seed of a woman" (Gen. 3:15-16). God thought it critical for mankind to understand that the Messiah would not be of the seed of fallen man, yet His royal lineage would be established through a man, Joseph, back to Solomon and finally David. The two genealogies accomplish this: Luke focuses our attention upon the Lord's humanity derived from Mary by the power of the Holy Spirit, while Matthew demonstrates Christ's official authority through Joseph.

The last book in the Hebrew Bible is *Chronicles*, which is 1 and 2 Chronicles in our Bibles. Hence, the Hebrew Bible concludes with genealogies from Adam to the point in time in which God invoked 400 years of silence concerning His rebellious covenant people. This prophetic hush was broken with the announcement of the Savior's coming to earth. In Matthew 1, the genealogies pick up again after the centuries of silence and lead the Jews to their predicted Messiah, the Lord Jesus Christ. He would be the literal fulfillment of God's promise to David of an everlasting throne (2 Sam. 7:13). Matthew completes what Chronicles only partially disclosed and bridges the remaining gap between the first Adam and the last Adam, who would restore righteousness and rule forever.

Matthew's Divisions

When Christ walked upon the earth, the Jews had been without their own king for more than six centuries. Four different Gentile empires had ruled over them during that time, most of them cruelly. The Jews longed to be liberated from Roman oppression and to be a self-governing nation again. From this political ideology, the prophesied Messiah was coveted, but from a spiritual sense, the heart of the people had drifted far from God over the centuries of exile and silence. The *"feasts of Jehovah"* had become the *"feasts of the Jews."* The legalistic traditions of the Pharisees controlled the people harshly and perverted the clear teachings of the Mosaic Law. Their oral laws had declared it wrong to serve others or to do good deeds on the Sabbath day and upheld that it was more honorable to give money to God than to use it for the proper care of aged parents. So, when their long-awaited Messiah did arrive, His message of repentance and spiritual transformation was not only unwelcome but flatly rejected – it was not what the Jews wanted, but it was exactly what they needed.

Often Scripture provides its own outline of a particular passage or book. The phrase *"from that time,"* found only twice in Matthew's Gospel (4:17 and 16:21), properly divides the book into three main sections: *"From that time ... Repent for the Kingdom of heaven is at hand"* (Matt. 4:17). *"From that time forth began Jesus to show unto His disciples, how that He must...suffer"* (Matt. 16:21). Accordingly, Matthew 1:1 – 4:16 forms an introduction, while Matthew 4:17 – 16:20 presents the Jewish Messiah, and Matthew 16:21 – 28:20 records the rejection of the Jewish Messiah. The last section begins after Peter's confession of Jesus as Christ and the Son of God and just prior to the Lord's transfiguration. Matthew records that the Lord informed His disciples of His future suffering, death, and resurrection at this time.

After being anointed by the Holy Spirit, the Lord labored in Galilee for about two years, then in Decapolis for six months, in Judea for three months, and then withdrew to Perea for the final four months, prior to returning to Jerusalem for the Passover and crucifixion. Hence, Matthew 4:17-16:20 covers nearly two and a half years of history, while the last section in Matthew (16:21-28:20) spans the final seven or eight months of the Lord's sojourn on earth.

Matthew's Spirit of Prophecy

Matthew labors in his Gospel account to validate Jesus Christ as the Jewish Messiah – He was born of the Jews and for the Jews. He frequently quotes Old Testament prophecies to show that Jesus Christ literally fulfilled them. Where John repeatedly connects Christ to the completion of Old Testament "types," Matthew meticulously demonstrates that Christ is the culmination of prophecy, or as John would later write, *"For the testimony of Jesus is the spirit of prophecy"* (Rev. 19:10). Bible prophecy finds its center in the Lord Jesus Christ.

Because Matthew directly relates Jesus Christ to Old Testament declarations, the word "fulfilled" appears sixteen times in his Gospel. Fourteen of these references are clearly messianic, compared to eight in Mark, Luke, and John combined. It is noted that well over one hundred first-advent prophecies concerning the Messiah are found in the Old Testament and that Jesus Christ fulfilled them all. The statistical probability of such a feat is astronomically impossible, but not for God's chosen Son.

Matthew's Two Witnesses

Under the Mosaic Law, at least two witnesses were required to substantiate a legal claim or allegation (Deut. 19:15). While offering instructions on how to reconcile an offense with a brother, the Lord acknowledged the importance of two witnesses to confirm the truth. *"But if he will not hear, take with you one or two more, that 'by the mouth of two or three witnesses every word may be established'"* (Matt. 18:16). Matthew is the only Gospel writer to record these statements of Christ.

As Matthew is mainly addressing a Jewish audience, he is conscious of this legal regulation in his writing. Though the other Gospel writers neglect this detail, he often identifies the existence of *two* witnesses to legally substantiate important events of the Lord's life.

Matthew records that there were:

two demon-possessed individuals cured by Christ in the country of the Gergesenes (Matt. 8:28);

two blind men healed by Christ near Nazareth (Matt. 9:27);

two of John's disciples who came to inquire of Jesus (Matt. 11:2);

two blind men healed by Christ leaving Jericho (Matt. 20:30); one was Bartimaeus (Mark 10:46);

two false witnesses at His trial (Matt. 26:60);

two Gentile witnesses of nobility attesting to His innocence. (Both Pilate and his wife declared Christ was a righteous man; 27:19, 24.)

Matthew's focus on *two* witnesses is unique, for none of the other Gospel writers were compelled by the Holy Spirit to record the above details. Through compliance of the Law, Matthew shows us that there was ample and adequate testimony of Christ's ministry.

Matthew's Mountains

Symbolically speaking, mountains refer to "kingdoms" in Scripture (e.g., Isa. 2:1; Jer. 51:25; Mic. 4:1). Daniel invokes this imagery to speak of the Lord Jesus coming into His kingdom after all Gentile powers had been judged (Dan. 2:44-45). Daniel describes King Nebuchadnezzar's secret dream to him as being a tall image composed of various metals. Suddenly, a stone from heaven struck the image in the feet and caused it to fall and crumble into powder. The wind blew away the debris, then the stone grew to become a glorious mountain.

Daniel explains that the image is a blueprint of five world empires that would be permitted to rule over God's covenant people from that timeframe forward. Each of these kingdoms would exist before Christ's return to establish His own kingdom on earth: Babylon, under Nebuchadnezzar's leadership was the head of gold; the Medes and Persians were the chest and arms of silver; the bronze torso and thighs represented the Greeks; the two iron legs, the Roman empire; and the ten toes of clay and iron, the final Gentile empire rising out of the old Roman Empire and controlled by the Antichrist.

The stone that was not cut with human hands (an expression of deity) and that came down from heaven to strike the image in the feet represents Christ's Second Advent to earth. At that time, He will wipe out the Antichrist and his armies (as pictured in the image's feet) and establish a worldwide kingdom of peace and righteousness (Rev. 19).

John applies this same metaphorical meaning in Revelation 17 where seven mountains are described as seven world empires, five of which had past, one was, and one was yet to come under the Antichrist. The Egyptian and Assyrian empires preceded the Babylonian empire.

Matthew, upholding the nobility of Christ, references mountains to signify His forthcoming earthly kingdom. Though all the Gospels record the Lord venturing up and down mountains during His ministry, the other writers, for the most part, do not apply the symbolic representation during key events as Matthew does. Examples include: the Sermon on the Mount (Matt. 5-7), but no mention in the other three Gospels; the transfiguration (on a high mount; Matt. 17:1), but no mention in John; the Olivet Discourse (Matt. 24:3), but no mention in Luke or John; the Galilee Commission (Matt. 28:16), but no mention in the other Gospels.

Matthew's Ministering Angels

Angels are rarely mentioned in Mark and John, but Matthew and Luke refer to them 43 times, yet from different viewpoints. In general, Matthew refers to these spiritual beings as messengers of God (mainly communicating through dreams) and as subordinates doing the Lord's bidding. Luke emphasizes their various ministries, including praising God, being His messengers, and being witnesses to His earthly operations. Perhaps Mark does not refer much to the ministry of angels because the ministry of the humble Servant of Jehovah is primary. In John, the Lord Jesus, the Supreme Son of God, is entrusted with all the work; no one else, not even the disciples, share in the Lord's ministry.

The authority theme of Matthew is upheld in the Lord's relationship with the angels, as He often commands their activities (e.g., 13:41, 16:27, 24:31, 25:31). Luke is the only Gospel writer to record that an angel assisted the Lord in the Garden of Gethsemane (Luke 22:43). The purpose of this visit was to "strengthen" the Lord. Luke uses *enischuo*, which means "to invigorate or make strong" to describe the ministry of the angels to Christ. Luke draws our attention to the Lord's frail humanity to demonstrate that, like us, He also was prone to weariness, thirst, hunger, emotional distress, etc. Contemplating Calvary had agitated the Lord's soul, but an entire night of prayer had quieted His heart, though it left Him physically and emotionally exhausted.

Though the "strengthening" language is consistent with Luke's "Son of Man" theme, it would be out of place in Matthew. Once in Matthew, after the forty-day period in which Satan futilely solicited the Lord to sin, we read of angels "ministering" to the Lord (Matt. 4:11). Only

Matthew records the Lord Jesus rebuking and commanding Satan to go at the end of the forty days of testing. The word translated "ministered" in Matthew is *diakoneo*, which means "to be an attendant or wait upon." It is the same word from which the church office of deacon is derived. As King, Christ commands and is waited on by subordinates.

Matthew's Righteousness

Matthew emphasizes God's righteousness in a way that substantiates mankind's inherent unrighteous state, humanity's need to be righteous, and man's natural propensity to boast of self-righteousness. Of the twenty-nine times that the words "righteous" or "righteousness" are found in the Gospels, nineteen reside in Matthew (e.g., 5:6, 10, 6:33).

The subject of righteousness unquestionably relates to Christ's legitimate claim to the throne of David, from which He will establish an endless rule of righteousness. The kingdom manifesto in Matthew 5 demands righteous subjects for this kingdom, for Christ's kingdom will be thoroughly evidenced by the righteousness of God. By such association with Him, God's holy character demands dedicated and yielded subjects. *"Be holy, for I am holy"* (1 Pet. 1:16). *"Serve God acceptably with reverence and godly fear. For our God is a consuming fire"* (Heb. 12:28-29). The Jews rejected both Christ's righteousness and His call to righteousness and are, to this day, a suffering people waiting for their Messiah. The refined Jewish nation will acknowledge Jesus Christ as Messiah at His Second Advent to the earth (Zech. 12:10). Isaiah describes Messiah's righteous ministry at that time:

> *But with righteousness He shall judge the poor, and decide with equity for the meek of the earth; He shall strike the earth with the rod of His mouth, and with the breath of His lips He shall slay the wicked. Righteousness shall be the belt of His loins, and faithfulness the belt of His waist* (Isa. 11:4-5).

The Kingdom of Heaven

The phrase "kingdom of heaven" is found thirty-two times in Matthew but nowhere else in all of Scripture. This peculiarity must be associated with the authority theme of his Gospel (i.e., Jesus Christ is the Messiah and the legitimate heir to the throne of David). The similar and associated term "kingdom of God" is applied fifty-four times in the Gospel accounts, but only appears five times in Matthew and merely twice in John. What is the significance of these phrases, and how do the two terms relate to each other?

Centuries of debate on this subject prove insufficient to answer this question fully. The terms are used interchangeably by the Lord during the Sermon on the Mount and the Lord's discussion with His disciples concerning the rich young ruler who valued his wealth above following the Lord (Matt. 19:23-24). Mark and Luke use "the kingdom of God" terminology in recording the Lord's words (Mark 10:23; Luke 18:24). These instances seem to indicate that there is minimal difference in the meaning of the terms, or perhaps, an interrelated meaning where the "kingdom of God" is a subset of the "kingdom of heaven" – the former, representing those who willingly acknowledge and submit to God's sovereignty, and the latter, all those under His rule, whether they acknowledge it or not.

Given this understanding, the "kingdom of heaven" refers to the realm of human profession in which one is given an opportunity to acknowledge God's sovereign rule or "the kingdom of God." C. I. Scofield summarizes this viewpoint:

> The kingdom of heaven is similar in many respects to the kingdom of God and is often used synonymously with it, though emphasizing certain features of divine government. When contrasted with the universal kingdom of God, the kingdom of heaven includes only men on earth, excluding angels and other creatures. The kingdom of heaven is the earthly sphere of profession as shown by the inclusion of these designated as wheat and tares, the latter of which are cast out of the kingdom (Matt. 13:41), and is compared to a net containing both the good and bad fish which are later separated (Matt. 13:47).[7]

Other commentators, such as William MacDonald, also acknowledge a realm of human profession within the kingdom of heaven, which is composed of true believers and mere professors, but see no tangible disagreement between the terms "kingdom of heaven" and "kingdom of God." He writes:

> The kingdom of heaven is the sphere in which God's rule is acknowledged. The word "heaven" is used figuratively to denote God; this is clearly shown in Daniel 4:25-26. In verse 25, Daniel said that the Most High rules in the kingdom of men. In the very next verse, he

says that Heaven rules. Thus, the kingdom of heaven announces the rule of God, which exists wherever people submit to that rule.[8]

It is important to understand that the "kingdom of heaven" and the church are not synonymous terms, for the kingdom of heaven contains both the children of God and the children of the devil, while the universal Church is only composed of true believers. Those who have believed the gospel message experience rebirth, become the children of God, and part of Christ's Church (John 1:12-13; Eph. 2:1-6).

So, why is the term "kingdom of heaven" unique to Matthew? The Jews would have been familiar with the prophet Daniel's association of "heaven" and "kingdom" terminology in declaring the scene in which the Son of Man (Christ) would return to earth from heaven to establish an everlasting dominion (Dan. 7:13-14).

Matthew's presentation of Jesus as the Jewish Messiah and Daniel's foretelling of Messiah coming from heaven to establish rightful authority over the Jews combine nicely to speak of the "kingdom of heaven" message (or offer, if you will). Would the Jews acknowledge His claim of authority over them? The term "kingdom of heaven" seems to relate to the presentation of Christ and the decision of the people to accept or reject Him as king. L. Laurenson summarizes the matter:

> The expression "Kingdom of Heaven" is found only in Matthew, and only in Matthew do we get the "Gospel of the Kingdom," and that thrice repeated (Chapters 4, 9, 24). Here was the cure for all the ills that afflicted Jehovah's land, but, alas! Israel refused the Gospel of the Kingdom then, as sinners today refuse the Gospel of Grace. And there never was grace like the grace of Christ.[9]

In the realm of human profession of God's sovereign rule, some reject God's authority over them, others extend mere "lip service" to God, but only those who sincerely believe and submit to God's Word will inherit Christ's kingdom. While the kingdom of heaven contains non-believers and wicked aspects, the true kingdom of God will have none of these things in it. Accordingly, the two terms can be used interchangeably, as long as this distinction is understood.

The Stages of God's Kingdom

There are five main stages of God's kingdom identified in Scripture. The Lord Jesus addressed three of these intervals during a parable series spoken from a boat to a large crowd gathered at the Sea of Galilee (Matt. 13:1-2). The Lord refers to the second kingdom interval in the first parable of *The Sower and the Soils* and the fourth kingdom interval in the last parable of *The Dragnet*; the third kingdom interval is referred to in the remaining parables. The five intervals of God's Kingdom are as follows:

The First Interval: The Kingdom Predicted (Dan. 2:44-45). Daniel's dream predicted that the Stone (i.e., a stone not cut with human hands, representing God's Son) would return to the earth to put down all Gentile rule and establish His kingdom that will last forever.

The Second Interval: The Kingdom at Hand (Matt. 4:17, 12:28). Both John the Baptist and the Lord Jesus announced that the kingdom had arrived. It was offered to the Jews, who largely rejected the King who offered it.

The Third Interval: The Kingdom in Interim (Acts 8:12, 19:18, 20:25). Although the King is absent, His Spirit-filled subjects are living out the kingdom's characteristics (during the Church Age) until the King literally returns to set up His kingdom on earth. The Church Age ends with *The Day of Christ*, which refers to the rapture of the Church and the subsequent evaluation of each believer's works at the *Judgment Seat of Christ*.

The Fourth Interval: The Kingdom Manifested (Rev. 19:11-20:3). During this interval, Christ will return to the earth, defeat the opposing forces, judge the Antichrist, false prophet, and those who took the mark of the beast, put Satan in the bottomless pit, and then reign over the world for a thousand years. The Jewish nation will be forever restored to God at this time. As applied in the New Testament, this interval relates to *The Day of the Lord*.

The Fifth Interval: The Eternal Kingdom (2 Pet. 1:11; 1 Cor. 15:28). Also referred to as *The Day of God* by Peter. The Son will return all things that were degraded by sin back to the Father in perfection. There will be a new heaven and a new earth which will form the *eternal state*.

Christ's kingdom was foretold in the Old Testament, announced first by John the Baptist and then Jesus Christ, but was ultimately rejected by the Jews (i.e., its spiritual aspects and its King). *The Kingdom Parables* of Matthew 13 bridge the gap between the first advent of the Lord to the earth to suffer for our sin and His second advent in which His kingdom will be established and all that is wicked will be removed.

After the Jews rejected Christ's offer of a literal, earthly, political kingdom with Him as King, the kingdom, in its spiritual sense, was then offered to the Gentiles. Consequently, today, God's kingdom rule is evident in the hearts of believers in the Church. This spiritual interim of God's kingdom will conclude at the end of the Church Age, and then the same kingdom offered to the Jews long ago will be physically established on earth at Christ's Second Advent. God's kingdom in its final phase will be the establishment of a new heaven and a new earth; this will be the eternal state of righteousness – *"that God may be all in all"* (1 Cor. 15:28).

Outline

Your King and My Servant

Matthew Chapter 1

The Son of David – the Son of Abraham (v. 1)

The order of mention in the first verse of Matthew is important: "the Son of David," then "the Son of Abraham." Normally, when these two chief patriarchs of Jewish history are mentioned, Abraham is referred to first, for he walked upon the earth more than a thousand years before David was born. The order arranged by Matthew, however, introduces us to the "authority" theme of his Gospel. And who better than Matthew, a Jewish official, a tax collector, to address the official glory of the Lord Jesus as rightful heir to David's throne.

The "Son of David" refers specifically to the office of king, but the Lord has not yet returned to the earth to establish His kingdom (Rev. 3:21). Matthew upholds the official glory of Christ as King; this is the prevalent theme of his testimony. Ten times he refers to Christ as the *"Son of David."* This is in contrast to Mark, Luke, and John, which contain only five references to this title (see Matt. 12:23 and Luke 11:14). Matthew is properly placed first among the Gospels: The Lord Jesus will fulfill God's covenants to David and Abraham by reigning on the throne of David in righteousness and over all nations forever (2 Sam. 7:13-16).

The reference to the "Son of Abraham" in Matthew 1:1 is of a much wider scope than the reference to the "Son of David." Through the son of Abraham *"shall all families of the earth be blessed"* (Gen. 12:3). Clearly, God's covenant with Abraham had not been completely fulfilled, for the Jews were under brutal Gentile rule and were clearly not the esteemed people of the earth. Second, they have never possessed, at any time during their entire history, more than about ten percent of the land promised to Abraham by God in Genesis 15. Through Christ, the Abrahamic covenant would be fulfilled (Luke 1:68-75).

Paul speaks of Abraham as the spiritual father of all spiritual seed and of the eternal blessings which God promised to Abraham that are likewise offered to all those who, like Abraham, would simply believe God's word (Rom. 4:13-16). This is God's means of saving souls throughout all human history, whether people lived during the Old Testament or the New Testament eras, or afterwards. There may be varying messages of repentance and obedience to heed, but justification only occurs by grace through faith in what God proclaims is our responsibility. As with Abraham, only by faith can the work of Christ be accredited to our personal account (Rom. 4:3-5).

If we want to work for our salvation, God is faithful to pay a fair wage; however, *"the wages of sin is death, but the gift of God is eternal life through Jesus Christ our Lord"* (Rom. 6:23). It may not seem logical, but God wants us to recognize that we cannot save ourselves and that we must accept His free gift of salvation as the only means to be reconciled with Him. Man's lingering guilt provokes him to do something to earn God's favor, but God is unimpressed with such attempts. The gospel message candidly proclaims, "You can't *do* anything to be accepted by God: It's all been accomplished in Christ – you must only believe." Faith is a living trust in God, which ascends beyond what our five senses or reasoning can verify. We become Abraham's children when we exercise his type of faith (Gal. 3:7)!

In Christ, we see the very best aspects of both Jewish patriarchs. As the Son of David, Christ was the righteous king and a man after God's own heart, and as the Son of Abraham, He was a friend of God and a great man of faith – He lived to do the Father's will (John 6:38).

The Genealogies of the Jewish King and Messiah (vv. 2-17)

In verses 2-16 we have the genealogies of Christ through the royal line of David and Solomon from the tribe of Judah to Joseph (the husband of Mary), the legal earthly father of the Lord Jesus. What is interesting about this listing is that Matthew does not include every descendant from Abraham to Joseph, but instead groups the descendants into three groups of fourteen to emphasize an important point about Jesus Christ. But to understand what Matthew is implying, we first need to understand what the number fourteen is used to symbolize in Scripture.

The number *fourteen* (including *fourteenth*) is found 49 times in the Bible; its first significant metaphoric use is found in Exodus 12 and 13. The Passover lambs were slaughtered, and their blood was applied on the door frames of each house where those within desired to be spared from God's judgment of the firstborn throughout Egypt. By faith, the applied blood of the lamb also brought *deliverance* from Egypt and slavery to that household. It is the same for those who apply, by faith, the blood of Christ's sacrifice to their own souls – they experience a deliverance from Egypt (worldliness) and from bondage (being enslaved to sin).

God's Passover Lamb for humanity is first introduced to us in the New Testament in this chapter. The apostle is proving to his Jewish audience that Christ is a descendant of Abraham through David and thus a legitimate heir to David's throne forever. Interestingly, Matthew purposely skips a generation here and there to provide a symbolic representation of the number *fourteen* in the order of Christ's genealogy:

> *So all the generations from Abraham to David are fourteen generations, from David until the captivity in Babylon are fourteen generations, and from the captivity in Babylon until the Christ are fourteen generations* (v. 17).

Why did Matthew carefully order Christ's genealogy around the number *fourteen*? Louis Barbieri explains the likely reason:

> Matthew obviously did not list every individual in the genealogy between Abraham and David (vv. 2-6), between David and the Exile (vv. 6-11), and between the Exile and Jesus (vv. 12-16). Instead, he listed only *fourteen* generations in each of these time periods (v. 17). Jewish reckoning did not require every name in order to satisfy a genealogy. But why did Matthew select *fourteen* names in each period? "David" in Hebrew numerology added up to *fourteen*.[10]

David is a lovely type of the Greater David who would eventually come to fulfill all of the Abrahamic covenant and be David's rightful heir to his throne forever. Hebrew numbers are composed of a series of letters and David's name (*dvd* in Hebrew) equates to the number *fourteen* (*dalet* = 4, *vav* = 6, and *dalet* = 4 for a total of *fourteen*). *Fourteen* is symbolic of salvation and deliverance in Scripture. The number *three* represents *resurrection* and *completeness*. By repeating the number *fourteen* thrice, the Holy Spirit is telling us Jesus Christ is the ultimate Deliverer of humanity – only in Him is there complete salvation of the human spirit, soul, and body (1 Cor. 6:20; 1 Thess. 5:23). The complete salvation requires resurrection and will therefore be complete at the believer's glorification when Christ comes back for His Church (1 Cor. 15:51-52; 1 Thess. 4:13-18).

Through Jesus Christ, we can rejoice that our souls are saved from the *penalty of sin*, and through the Holy Spirit we now have *power over sin*. Furthermore, we are to anticipate a future day when we will be saved from the *presence of sin*. At that moment, a believer's body will be transformed into holy humanity – like Christ's body (Phil. 3:20-21). In Christ, a believer has been saved (John 5:24; Eph. 2:8), is being saved (Phil. 2:12; Rom. 8:24), and will be saved (Rom. 13:11; 1 Thess. 5:9). Through trusting Jesus Christ alone for salvation, we experience a trifold-saving, which will completely deliver us from sin and this corrupt world.

The number *fourteen* is connected with God's complete *deliverance* and *salvation* offered through Christ in Scripture. The number *five*, symbolizing *divine grace and goodness* in the Bible, also appears in Matthew's genealogy to illustrate that God's grace to humanity is received through Jesus Christ. Women were seldom listed in Jewish genealogical records, so we may conclude that Matthew includes the names of five women (three Jews and two Gentiles) for a particular emphasis. Because of either their ethnicity, immoral behavior, or perceived depravity, each of these five women was unfavorably esteemed in Jewish society.

Rahab was a harlot from Jericho who sought mercy from the two Jewish spies and was not only spared from judgment, but was inducted into the tribe of Judah; she married Salmon. *Tamar*, through a one-time illicit relationship with her father-in-law Judah, conceived and gave birth to twin sons. *Ruth* was a despised Moabite, whom Boaz redeemed and married. *Bathsheba*, Uriah's wife, committed adultery with King David. Mary, the mother of Christ and a virgin, was said to be a fornicator by those Jews rejecting the angelic and prophetic declarations of Christ's incarnate birth. These *five* women are included in Christ's royal genealogy to show that anyone (Jew or Gentile, male or female) is never too lost to receive God's grace and have a life pleasing to God.

The genealogies of Christ presented in Matthew 1 and Luke 3 are different from each other and serve distinct purposes. The genealogy of Matthew 1 served as proof to the Jews that Jesus, through Joseph, was a direct descendant of David and, thus, the legal and rightful heir to David's throne. As to not distract from his theme of covenant fulfillment, Matthew begins with Abraham, not Adam, in rendering Christ's royal genealogy.

Luke's genealogy of Christ, however, is for a different purpose. Luke upholds Christ as the Son of Man, or more specifically, the Son of Adam. In so doing, Luke shows Christ to be the Last Adam, God's replacement representative of righteousness and the literal fulfillment of the prophesied Messiah being derived from the *"seed of a woman"* (Gen. 3:15-16). God thought it critical for mankind to understand that the Messiah would not be of the seed of fallen man, yet His royal lineage would be established through a man, Joseph, back to Solomon and finally David.

The two genealogies accomplish this: Luke focuses our attention upon the Lord's humanity derived from Mary through the power of the Holy Spirit, while Matthew demonstrates Christ's official authority, as a descendant of David, through Joseph.

Hence, Matthew's wording in verse 16 is precise to indicate the human lineage of Christ through Mary: *"Joseph the husband of Mary, of whom was born Jesus who is called Christ."* "Of whom" in the English is derived from *ek hos* in the Greek and the *hos* is a genitive, singular, feminine pronoun, meaning that the baby Jesus originated from Mary, but not Joseph.

The Unique Conception and Birth of Christ (vv. 18-25)

Matthew now affords us an account of Christ's conception and birth. In the previous verses, each generation was "begotten" by a human father, but not so with Jesus Christ; He did not have a human father, thus the fallen nature of Adam was not passed down to Christ. God chose a virtuous young woman named Mary, who was already betrothed to Joseph, to be the mother of the Lord Jesus. Although betrothed (i.e., they were under a formal marriage covenant), Mary and Joseph had not yet consummated their marriage by sexual relations. This time of purity normally lasted one year. Mary was a virgin and became pregnant through the power of the Holy Spirit (vv. 18, 22).

It must have been crushing news to Joseph to learn that his espoused wife was pregnant. He would have naturally thought that Mary had broken her marriage vow to him and been unfaithful. Under the Law, Joseph could have had Mary stoned for adultery, but being a just and kind man he rather thought to divorce her quietly and release her from the marital commitment (v. 19).

However, an angel appeared to Joseph in a dream and said to him, *"Do not be afraid to take to you Mary your wife, for that which is conceived in her is of the Holy Spirit"* (v. 20). The angel then confirmed that Mary would have a son, the prophesied Jewish Messiah, and that he should be named "Jesus" (v. 21). Jesus' name, like Joshua in the Old Testament, means "Jehovah's salvation." God's Son, the Messiah-King, had come to the earth by the power of the Holy Spirit to *"save His people from their sins."*

Matthew then pauses the narrative to acknowledge that God was now fulfilling Isaiah's prophecy concerning how Messiah would be born of a virgin and would be called *Immanuel*, meaning "God with us" (vv. 22-23; Isa. 7:14). Messiah would be the perfect God-man residing among His people to save them from their sins!

The prophet Isaiah further informs us that God the Father and the Holy Spirit sent the Son to earth to become the Redeemer, the Holy One of Israel (Isa. 48:16-17). "The Holy One" was a title the demons used to refer to Christ while speaking with Him during His earthly sojourn (Mark 1:24; Luke 4:34). Moreover, the Redeemer, the Person speaking in the Isaiah passage, clearly identifies Himself as the Lord, the God of Israel. Jesus Christ, the Holy One of Israel, is the second person of the Godhead – the Son of God.

New Testament Scripture further explains the meaning of what Isaiah declared: The Lord Jesus stated that He had come to the earth to do the Father's will (Luke 22:42; John 10:18, 14:31). The angel Gabriel announced to Mary that she would conceive and give birth to the Lord Jesus through the overshadowing power of the Holy Spirit (Luke 1:35). The Father sent the Son, and the Holy Spirit enabled the incarnation so the Son of God could come.

Joseph awoke and did as the angel had commanded him. He took Mary, his wife, into his care, but they remained sexually inactive until after Jesus was born (vv. 24-25). Not only was Jesus conceived in the womb of a virgin, but He was also born of a virgin, to remove any possibility of Joseph being alleged as his natural father. Just as the angel has proclaimed, Mary gave birth to her firstborn Son, and He was named "Jesus" by Joseph and Mary.

Matthew Chapter 2

Wise Men Come to Worship the King of the Jews (vv. 1-12)

Jesus was born in Bethlehem of Judea, while Herod the Great was king (v. 1). Sometime later (likely a year or more), Magi, wise men from the East came to Jerusalem inquiring, *"Where is He that is born King of the Jews? For we have seen His star in the East, and have come to worship Him"* (v. 2). How did these pagan Magi from the East know about the prophesied Jewish Messiah?

These Eastern mystics were knowledgeable men who observed and learned from nature and the heavens above. They realized that the sudden appearance of a star, or some type of unexpected astrodynamics phenomenon resembling a star, was a sign of immense importance. Perhaps they had access to ancient Jewish writings such as Balaam's vague prophecy predicting that a "star" would "come out of Jacob" or Israel (Num. 24:7) or Daniel's more specific prophecies (written in Babylon) concerning when the Jewish Messiah would appear (Dan. 9:24-26). Regardless, it seems more likely that the Spirit of God revealed to them news about the arrival of the Jewish Messiah, in the same way the Holy Spirit spoke through the pagan prophet Balaam to express His will in the days of Moses. It is clear from verse 12 that God was communicating with these magi as necessary by showing them His glory in some supernatural way.

The inquiry of the Magi, greatly disturbed Herod and those in Jerusalem with him (v. 3). The king called the chief priests and scribes together to examine the Scriptures to discern where the prophesied Jewish Messiah should be born (v. 4). This response indicates that the Jewish nation was not truly looking for their Messiah, otherwise they would have known Messiah's prophesied birthplace.

After some investigation by the scribes, the magi were informed that according to the prophet Micah, Bethlehem in the region of Ephrathah was to be the birthplace of the Messiah (vv. 5-6; Mic. 2:5-6). Herod then privately questioned the magi to determine when the star first appeared to them. This would indicate the approximate age of the young Jewish Messiah (v. 7). Herod then told the wise men to *"go and search carefully for the young Child, and when you have found Him, bring back word to me, that I may come and worship Him also"* (v. 8). Did Herod really want to worship Messiah? No, he later proved that his only reason for directing the magi as he did was so he could locate and murder any rival to his authority. The Jewish people had drifted so far from Jehovah that most had no desire for His Messiah, otherwise they would have accompanied the magi in their quest to find and worship Him.

The magi departed, and the star that they had witnessed before guided them to the house in Bethlehem that Joseph had apparently rented for his young family (v. 9). There have been many astrological suggestions as to what this star may have been (e.g., planetary alignments or orbital phenomena, a comet, or a supernova). However, the appearing and disappearing of the star over a period of many months (v. 7) and its near proximity to the earth to indicate the exact location of a house where the young Messiah was residing all indicate that this "star" was a miraculous navigational sign. Just as God daily guided the Israelites by a glorious cloud in the wilderness for forty years, God guided the Magi on a long journey to worship His Son.

The wise men were exceedingly joyful over the appearance of the star which led them to the house of the young child, Jesus, who was with his mother Mary (v. 10). The shepherds visited the newborn Christ in a stable, but the magi came to a house where He resided likely more than a year after His birth. The Gentile Magi fell before the Lord Jesus and worshipped Him and gave Him gifts of gold, frankincense, and myrrh (v. 11).

Gold was a valuable metal and spoke of purity and holiness. It was the only metal to be used in the Tabernacle furnishings of the Holy place and Most Holy place. Gold speaks of Christ's deity.

Frankincense was to be put on the meal offering when placed on the Bronze Altar and presented to the Lord as a burnt offering (Lev. 2:1, 15). The gum from the frankincense tree is an unusual spice which does not release its aroma until it is burned. This speaks of those superb, indescribable qualities that the Father appreciates about His Son, especially those exhibited in the agony of Calvary. The frankincense burning on the altar fully released its sweet aroma; likewise, the voluntary sufferings of Christ at Calvary produced a lovely fragrance which God the Father fully appreciated.

Myrrh was a burial spice and is associated with Christ's suffering and death (Mark 15:23; John 19:39). Interestingly, Isaiah foretold that Gentiles coming to worship Christ in Jerusalem (after His second advent) will bring him gold and incense (Isa. 60:1-7). These symbolize His divine glory and His fragrant character (Ex. 30:34), respectively, but no frankincense and myrrh, which are associated with his previous suffering and death, will be presented. As the writer of Hebrews tells us, *"Christ was offered once to bear the sins of many. To those who eagerly wait for Him He will appear a second time, apart from sin, for salvation"* (Heb. 9:28). In His kingdom, our righteous Lord will not be associated with sin or with suffering, but rather with blessing and joy.

These esteemed scholars from the East did not worship Joseph or Mary, but the young child Jesus – the King of the Jews. Having been warned in a dream that they should not return to Herod, they went back to their own country a different way (v. 12).

Joseph, Mary, and Jesus Flee to Egypt (vv. 13-15)

Matthew 1 reveals Joseph's viewpoint of the events surrounding Christ's birth, while Luke 1 presents Mary's perspective of the same. Being warned in a dream, Joseph removed his family to Egypt to protect young Jesus from Herod's murderous attempt on His life (v. 13). The gifts received from the magi would provide for their needs while in Egypt. Later, after learning of Herod the Great's death, Joseph returned his family to the land of Israel (v. 14). This activity fulfilled Hosea's prophecy that God would call His Son out of Egypt back to the land of Israel (v. 15; Hos. 11:1).

Herod Murders Bethlehem's Babies (vv. 16-18)

Herod was furious after learning that the wise men had disregarded his command and departed Judea without informing him whether or not they had found the Jewish Messiah (v. 16). Their change in demeanor towards Herod indicated that they had found the Messiah and chosen to protect his identity and location. Herod knew the approximate time of Messiah's birth and the general location, so he decreed that all the boys from two years old and under in Bethlehem and its surrounding districts should be killed.

Although a horrific deed, the early Church tended to exaggerate the number murdered by Herod. The Byzantine tradition sets the number at

14,000 and the Syrian at 64,000.[11] However, the overall population of Bethlehem and its surrounding districts was only about 1,000 persons at the time of Christ's birth. Given the high infant mortality rate of this era, the number of baby boys slaughtered by Herod would likely be between 20 to 30.[12]

Matthew states that this terrible deed had been forecasted by the prophet Jeremiah, for Rachel would weep again for her children and refuse to be comforted. The original reference pertained to the deadly aftermath of the Babylonian conquest of the region centuries earlier. Matthew affirms that this horrific event six centuries earlier foreshadowed Herod's murderous attempt to kill the Messiah by slaughtering all the baby boys in the region (v. 18). John Heading further notes why Rachel (the mother of the children in Bethlehem, so to speak) wept for her children, but received no comfort:

> Although Jeremiah largely deals with the captivity of Judah, yet in the opening part of chapter 31 the subject of the captivity of the northern kingdom of Israel (Ephraim) is under consideration. It appears in v. 15 (and Matt 2:18) that weeping at *both* captivities is being described, for Ramah was in the northern kingdom, and Bethlehem (near which Rachel died) was in the southern kingdom. But in v. 16 weeping is restrained, and eyes no longer shed tears, because there is the promise of restoration through the new covenant made with *both* the house of Israel *and* the house of Judah (v. 31). But Matthew quotes only the verse of weeping (v. 15) and not the verses of rejoicing, because as far as the mothers in Bethlehem were concerned, only tragedy had hit them. The later return of the Messiah from Egypt bypassed them, for He returned northwards to Nazareth.[13]

The parents of these murdered boys were weeping with Rachel at Messiah's first advent, but there was no comfort for them. Yet, in a coming day, all Israel would rejoice at Messiah's second coming, for the oppression and suffering for the Jewish people will end forever.

Joseph, Mary, and Jesus Settle in Nazareth (vv. 19-23)

Fearing Herod's son Archelaus and being warned by an angel in a dream, Joseph returned to Israel but journeyed north with his family to live in Nazareth within the region of Galilee (vv. 19-23). In a poetic sense, the Savior, in those early years, retraced the very steps of Israel's infant history (Canaan to Egypt in distress, and back to Canaan after the enemy had been vanquished).

Notice that earthly kings were responsible for the early movements of the Lord Jesus. His original pilgrimage to Bethlehem in the womb of Mary resulted from the registration decreed by Caesar Augustus. The Lord's hurried departure to Egypt resulted from the evil that Herod sought to do against Him, and the Lord traveled to Nazareth because Joseph feared Archelaus. To demonstrate the sovereign power of God, the highest human authorities on earth worked to accomplish the foreordained counsel of God. Through the presence and administrations of these three kings, the Old Testament prophecies pertaining to Christ's birth, foreign travels, and hometown were all fulfilled.

In the first two chapters of his gospel account, Matthew refers to Christ fulfilling five Old Testament prophecies relating to His birth and childhood. He is appealing to his Jewish audience – the Old Testament Scripture affirms that Jesus Christ is the long-awaited Messiah-King.

Behold, the virgin shall conceive and bear a Son, and shall call His name Immanuel (Isa. 7:14). **Jesus was born of a virgin** (1:23).

Bethlehem Ephrathah … out of you shall come forth to Me the one to be Ruler in Israel, whose goings forth are from of old, from everlasting (Mic. 5:2). **Jesus was born in Bethlehem** (vv. 5-7).

When Israel was a child, I loved him, and out of Egypt I called My son (Hos. 11:1). **Jesus lived in Egypt to escape Herod's wrath** (v. 15).

A voice was heard in Ramah, lamentation and bitter weeping, Rachel weeping for her children, refusing to be comforted for her children, because they are no more (Jer. 31:15). **In pattern, Herod murdered the baby boys of Ramah in an attempt to kill Jesus** (vv. 16-17).

There shall come forth a Rod from the stem [*netzer* – Nazarene] *of Jesse, and a Branch shall grow out of his roots* (Isa. 11:1). **He shall be called a Nazarene** (vv. 22-23).

On the latter prophecy of Isaiah, William MacDonald suggests that the connection of Hebrew *netzer* speaks more of disdain than of a location:

A more probable explanation is that "Nazarene" is used to describe anyone who lived in Nazareth, a town viewed with contempt by the rest of the people. Nathaniel expresses this by the proverbial question, "Can anything good come out of Nazareth?" (John 1:46). The scorn heaped upon this "unimportant" town fell upon its inhabitants as well. So when verse 23 says **He shall be called a Nazarene**, it means that He would be treated with contempt.[14]

A Nazarene was someone to be despised. Like Christ, those who inhabited Nazareth bore this reproach in association with the name of their town. In fact, if it were not for Jesus of Nazareth, we might not even know the town existed. It is not mentioned in the Old Testament or in the Talmud. The Jewish historian Josephus names 244 towns and cities in Galilee, but never mentions Nazareth even once.

Notice that Matthew does not specifically refer to Isaiah as the one stating Christ would be a Nazarene, but rather "the prophets." As L. A. Barbieri, Jr. explains, this is significant:

> Since Matthew used the plural prophets, perhaps his idea was not based on a specific prophecy but on the idea that appeared in a number of prophecies concerning Messiah's despised character. Nazareth was the town which housed the Roman garrison for the northern regions of Galilee. Therefore, most Jews would not have any associations with that city. In fact, those who lived in Nazareth were thought of as compromisers who consorted with the enemy, the Romans. Therefore, to call one "a Nazarene" was to use a term of contempt.[15]

Like Christ, the town of Nazareth was despised by the Jews.

Nazarene is the fourth name or title given to the Lord Jesus in the first two chapters of Matthew. He is "Jesus," "Emmanuel," "King," and "a Nazarene." God's Son came to the earth "to save," "to dwell," "to rule," but ultimately, He would be "despised and rejected of men" – *a Nazarene*.

Matthew Chapter 3

The authority theme of Matthew is obvious in Christ's preaching and parable telling. How did the Lord commence His public ministry? John the Baptist had been preaching to the Jews: *"Repent, for the kingdom of heaven is at hand!"* (Matt. 3:2). Although Herod silenced John by incarceration, he could not thwart the Messiah from taking up John's message. Matthew records the Lord's first words of public ministry: *"From that time Jesus began to preach, and to say, 'Repent, for the kingdom of heaven is at hand'"* (Matt. 4:17). The first word of both John and Christ's public ministry was "repent"!

The Lord Jesus was the literal fulfillment of the kingdom message John had been proclaiming. John *"was a burning and a shining light"* (John 5:35), but his brilliance was destined to be quenched as soon as the "Light of the World" (John 8:12) showed forth His illumination. With John in prison, the King of the Jews began to directly call His subjects to repentance, which meant they needed to acknowledge Him as the sinless Messiah and their rightful King.

In Matthew, God is still dealing with Israel as before at Mt. Sinai, on the ground of responsibility. Messiah had come. Would they accept or reject Him? The Kingdom Message itself was the culmination of a Jewish dispensational economy that began on Mt. Sinai – the giving of the Law to Moses – and would conclude at Mt. Moriah – the crucifixion of Christ. Fifty days later, the dispensation of the Church began, and both the message and the recipient of the message changed.

Matthew, more prominently than the other Gospel writers, shows the offering of Messiah, the Jewish rejection, and the consequential setting aside of Israel that the Gentiles might receive grace. *"Jesus Christ was a minister of the circumcision for the truth of God, to confirm the promises made unto the fathers; and that the Gentiles might glorify God for His mercy"* (Rom. 15:8-9). The Lord's ministry is mainly focused upon the *"lost sheep of the house of Israel,"* a term only found in Matthew (Matt. 10:6, 15:22-28). As long as Christ was on the earth preaching *"the kingdom of God has come,"* the disciples were instructed to only preach to the Jews – the kingdom Gospel was a specific message (a presentation of Messiah by words and signs) to the Jewish nation.

John the Baptizer – the Forerunner of Christ (vv. 1-12)

As prophesied by Isaiah, the Messiah was to be heralded by one who would go before Him to *prepare the way* (i.e., speaking of spiritually priming Israel to receive her Messiah; Isa. 40:1-5). John the baptizer, son of Zacharias, a priest, and his previously barren wife Elizabeth (Elizabeth was a relative of Mary), fulfilled Isaiah's prophecy (vv. 1-3).

John's ministry began perhaps a year or more before Christ began His own ministry after being anointed by the Holy Spirit at His baptism. John was a priest whom God called to be a prophet and a preacher to the lost sheep of Israel. John had a simple existence; he wore a cloak of camel's hair, which was fastened to his waist by a leather belt, and he ate locusts and wild honey while residing in the wilderness of Judea (v. 4).

John announced that "the kingdom of heaven" was at hand and called the people to repentance to enter it (v. 5). Many came to hear John's message, and many repented of their sins and were baptized by John in the Jordan River to publicly affirm their new commitment to follow the Lord (v. 6). John did not invent this baptism of repentance. Rather, it was assigned by God to lead those repenting of their sin to trust in the One who was coming to save them from their sin.

However, not everyone who came to hear John's message of repentance did so with an open ear. When John saw the Pharisees and Sadducees approaching him, he said to them, *"Brood of vipers! Who warned you to flee from the wrath to come? Therefore bear fruits worthy of repentance"* (vv. 7-8). The Pharisees and Sadducees, and indeed much of the Jewish nation, believed that being children of Abraham uniquely qualified them to receive God's blessing above any other people group (v. 9). But physical lineage did not mean that one was a spiritual child of Abraham and would receive God's blessing; rather, following Abraham's example of faith and obedience to God's Word is what pleases God (Rom. 4:16-17).

Consequently, John did not mince words with these self-righteous hypocrites, who in their own estimation did not need to repent of anything. They were immersed in the rabbinical traditions and therefore were in good standing with God. John warned them that there was only one way to avoid God's forthcoming wrath on the wicked: they must humble themselves before God and confess their sins to God (v. 10).

Ultimately, forgiveness for their sins would come through Christ, the One of whom John was foretelling.

John's message to these religious zealots was forthright: Your religiosity does not impress God; you need to experience a spiritual transformation, which begins with repentance. True repentance is more than lip service to God; it has tangible evidence of a changed heart. Repentance enables us to stand with God against ourselves and believes that God alone can make us right in His presence. The necessity of repentance is essential to gospel preaching and we do well to not neglect it (Luke 13:3).

Some in Christendom have equated the baptism of the Holy Spirit and of fire mentioned in verses 11-12 as being the same thing and a desirable blessing from God. But careful examination of four pertinent passages will reveal quite a different understanding. First, when used metaphorically in Scripture, "fire" speaks of various forms of divine judgment (Gen. 19:24; Num. 16:35; Matt. 13:39-40). This means that God's fire is not desirable, with the only exception being that the Lord permits His people to pass through refining trials to better them (Job 23:10; Mal. 3:2-3). But this is obviously not Matthew's meaning as he further clarifies that the baptism of fire is of an unquenchable nature that completely devours the chaff (unbelievers), in contrast to the wheat (true believers) which is gathered safely into God's barn (heaven).

Next, notice that in Matthew's account John is speaking to a mixed audience of believers and rebels, so he mentions both baptisms. In a future day, believers would be baptized by the Holy Spirit, while those rejecting Christ would be cast into the eternal Lake of Fire. Likewise, Luke records John speaking to a mixed group and also promises both baptisms will come upon those listening to him (Luke 3:16). Yet, Mark records a different scene in which John is only speaking to those who had repented and were baptized by him. To these he promises only the baptism of the Holy Spirit; there is no mention of fire (Mark 1:8).

Last, just before the Lord's ascension to heaven, He refers to John's promise: *"For John truly baptized with water, but you shall be baptized with the Holy Spirit not many days from now"* (Acts 1:5). The Lord is speaking to His disciples and there is no mention of fire. Dear believer, the Holy Spirit is not given in measure (John 3:34). If you have been born again, you have all of Him that you will ever get and all that you will ever need to achieve whatever God has for you to do.

The Baptism of Jesus Christ (vv. 13-17)

The Lord Jesus came to the Jordan River to be baptized by John (v. 13). At first, John refused, claiming that he needed to be baptized by the Lord (v. 14). Obviously, the Messiah had no sins of His own to confess, but what John did not understand was that the Lord had come to publicly identify with those He came to save (i.e., those who had publicly confessed their sins through baptism). Thus, the Lord told John to baptize Him, for *"it is fitting for us to fulfill righteousness"* (v. 15).

Notice, the Lord said to John that it was fitting for "us to fulfill righteousness" (both men were needed to perform His baptism). Baptism was not taught in the Law, so there could be no association of it with righteous Law-keeping. If the Lord had not been baptized by John, it would have hindered the people from listening to Christ's message, for by His action He would be saying to everyone that He was more righteous than them. Although this was true, it was necessary for Him to first be accepted as a teacher, so that He could both proclaim and demonstrate the righteousness of God to the people. In time, the Lord would show His fitness as God's righteous Savior and Messiah.

Directly after His baptism, the Spirit of God descended on Him in the form of a dove, and the voice of His Father was heard from Heaven praising His Son, *"This is My beloved Son, in whom I am well pleased"* (vv. 16-17). Luke tells us that the Lord Jesus was approximately 30 years of age at this time. His years of quiet obscurity were now over. Peter later confirms that the Holy Spirit anointed Christ to set Him apart for and to empower the ministry that His Father had sent Him to accomplish (Acts 10:38). This is the *kickoff*, so to speak, of the Lord's three-plus-year ministry to the lost sheep of Israel.

The Holy Spirit's anointing of Christ fulfilled the prophecy of Isaiah 61:1 which involves all three persons of the Godhead.

> *The Spirit of the Lord God is upon Me, because the Lord has anointed Me to preach good tidings to the poor; He has sent Me to heal the brokenhearted, to proclaim liberty to the captives, and the opening of the prison to those who are bound* (Isa. 61:1).

The person (identified as *"Me"*) in this passage is Messiah Himself. He was sent by the Father to preach tidings of good news to the lost sheep of Israel. The Father anointed the Lord Jesus with the Holy Spirit to enable His work to be effectual.

Matthew Chapter 4

The Devil Tests Jesus Christ (vv. 1-11)

Directly after his baptism, the Lord Jesus was led into the wilderness by the Holy Spirit, for the purpose of being *"tempted by the devil"* (v. 1). Israel's Messiah fasted for forty days, and Mark informs us that the devil solicited Him throughout that time, not just at the end of the forty-day stint when He was very hungry (v. 2). Matthew 4 and Luke 4 record Satan's final attempts to externally solicit the Lord to sin. In both accounts, the devil tested the Lord with appeals to hunger, to spiritual pride, and to commit a presumptuous action against God.

Scripturally speaking, the word "temptation" has different meanings depending upon the context of the related passage. The word *peirasmos,* normally translated as "temptation," may also be rendered as "trial" or "testing." *Peirasmos* means "to demonstrate the proof of something," either by suffering through a holy trial or enduring an evil solicitation. Holy trials are those tests that originate with God for our edification and perfection. Unholy temptations, as in the text before us, though allowed by God, do not originate with Him, but rather these solicitations to do sin come from Satan and his domain of influence in the world (Jas. 1:13).

Through the devil's attempts to stumble the Lord, He was proven to be holy and pure – God's acceptable Lamb for sacrifice. Satan proved that there were no "forbidden desires" within the Savior that had to be suppressed to exhibit God-honoring behavior. He was fully tested "sin apart" (Heb. 4:15), that is, there was no sin in Him to respond to Satan's solicitations. Lusting in the flesh comes from the fallen nature we inherited from Adam, and not from God (1 Jn. 2:16). The basis of lusting is dissatisfaction with what one presently has (i.e., God has wrongly limited us in some way). But unlike our first parents in Eden, the Lord Jesus, being God, was never prompted to act or think beyond the boundaries of contented holiness.

The number *forty* is used throughout Scripture to represent *probation* and *testing*. At times, God extended the nation of Israel's forty-year probationary periods to test or prove them: the Israelites were tested in the wilderness forty years (Deut. 8:2-5), then were delivered and had rest during the forty years that Othniel, Barak, and Gideon judged Israel (Judg. 3:11, 5:31, 8:28). They enjoyed dominion during the forty-year reigns of five kings: Saul, David, Solomon, Jehoash, and Joash (2 Sam. 5:4; 1 Kgs. 11:42; 2 Kgs. 12:1; 2 Chron. 24:1; Acts 13:21).

The Bible also records occasions when individuals went forty days without food or drink through the supernatural care of God: Elijah during his wilderness experience (1 Kgs. 19:8), Moses before Jehovah on Mount Horeb (Ex. 34:28), and Jesus Christ during His testing in the wilderness (vv. 1-11). Clearly, there are times when God supernaturally sustains an individual's body for the purpose of accomplishing His work. The application for the believer is that doing God's will should be the primary objective of one's life, and though the temporal elements of life such as food and drink are necessary, one should not be ruled by them.

This was the aspiration of the Lord Jesus, when He quoted from Deuteronomy 8:3 to counter Satan's test: *"Now when the tempter came to Him, he said, 'If You are the Son of God, command that these stones become bread'"* (v. 3). Though hungry after forty days of fasting, the Lord did not think so little of God's food, His Word, that He would turn stones into loaves of bread to satisfy His hunger. Instead, He quoted Scripture to demonstrate the power of God's Word to defeat Satan's attack: *"Man shall not live by bread alone, but by every word that proceeds from the mouth of God"* (v. 4). The outcome of this test was that the Lord Jesus was sustained in His hunger, God was glorified, and Satan was disgraced. We experience the same type of victory when we, by faith in God's Word, resist and ignore Satan's deception.

The Lord defeated the devil's second solicitation to cast Himself down from the pinnacle of the temple to prove that He was the Son of God (vv. 5-6) by quoting Deuteronomy 6:12: *"You shall not tempt the Lord your God"* (v. 7). Notice that in this solicitation the devil refers to Psalm 91:11-12. First, he does not quote from the Hebrew text, but from the Septuagint, as the translators had added *"at any time"* (in the KJV). Second, he left out *"to keep you in all your ways"* to change the context of the passage. The devil is never more dangerous than when he quotes (misquotes) God's Word, for he does so with the purpose to deceive. After observing this fact, F. B. Hole challenges all believers:

> The devil always sows doubts on the Divine Word. No sooner has God said, "This is My beloved Son," than the devil says twice over, *"If* Thou

be the Son of God" (Matt. 3:17, 4:3, 6). The little word "if" is a great favorite with the devil! Jesus appropriately met him with the Word of God. That Word is indispensable to Man's spiritual life just as bread is to his natural life. And man needs *every* word that God has spoken, and not just a few special passages only. Are we all finding our spiritual life in "every word that proceeds out of the mouth of God"?[16]

Satan's final attempt to get the Lord Jesus to bow down before him was by offering the Savior the kingdoms of the world (vv. 8-9). Since the fall of man by our first parents, the world has been under the devil's authority, and will continue to be until Christ reestablishes God's kingdom on earth and restores what was lost in Eden. The Lord again defeats the attack of the enemy by quoting Scripture: *"You shall worship the Lord your God, and Him only you shall serve"* (v. 10; Deut. 6:13). After the last attempt, the Lord commanded the Devil to depart, which he did (v. 11). This demonstrated that Jesus Christ is the Son of God and has authority over all angelic beings (e.g., Jude 9). After the testing was complete, angels came to minister to a hungry and victorious Messiah.

What was Satan's overall objective by tempting Christ? If Christ would have turned the stones to bread, He would have knelt before the devil to gather them off the ground. If Christ would have cast Himself down from the temple, He would have lowered Himself before the devil. If Christ would have bowed down to the devil to obtain those earthly kingdoms under his dominion, He would have exalted the devil and disdained His Father. The devil thought to gain the high ground over the Lord Jesus and cause Him to act outside of the Father's will, but because Christ accurately quoted and applied God's Word – Satan was defeated.

If we follow the Lord's example, we too will evade the lion's attack and trample the serpent under our feet (Ps. 91:13). Both metaphors are used in the New Testament in the context of a believer's victory in Christ over Satan (Rom. 16:19-20; 1 Pet. 5:7-9). As shown by Christ during His forty days of testing, it is God who supplies our sustenance, guides our service, and bestows to us honor and authority, not the devil.

There is an obvious difference in the order of satanic attacks on the Lord Jesus as recorded in Matthew 4 and Luke. The order maintained by each writer is for the purpose of upholding the prevalent theme of each Gospel. In Matthew, Satan first asks the Lord Jesus to turn the stones into bread, then bids Him to cast Himself down from the pinnacle of the temple, and thirdly offers to Christ all the kingdoms of this world, if

Christ will only worship him. Luke's order, however, is first the request to turn the stones into bread, then the offer of earthly kingdoms, and finally Satan adjures Christ to cast Himself down from the pinnacle of the temple to prove that the angels will protect Him. Why the different order? Arthur Pink explains:

> In Matthew, the order is arranged climactically, so as to make Rulership over all the kingdoms of the world the final bait which the Devil dangled before the Son of David. But in Luke we have the chronological order, the order in which they actually occurred, and these correspond with the order of temptation of the first man and his wife in Eden, where the appeal was made, as in Luke, to the lust of the flesh, the lust of the eyes, and the pride of life (1 Jn. 2:16; Gen. 3:6).[17]

Sovereign design accounts for the variation of the temptation accounts, which serves to further declare the wisdom of God and the distinct glories of His Son. Luke's order of temptations is chronological, while Matthew arranged it climactically unto kingship. It is worthy to note that John does not record the temptation of Christ, as that would be contrary to his theme. John presents Christ as God made flesh (John 1:14), and as James insists, *"God cannot be tempted"* (Jas. 1:13). This fact refutes any degrading doctrines that pertain to the Lord's ability to sin or to His members having the capacity to be enticed to sin. He was not only sinless, but His nature was impeccable; there was nothing in Him that could respond to sin (Heb. 4:15).

Christ's Galilean Ministry Begins (vv. 12-17)

There is about a one-year gap between verses 11 and 12. John chapters 1-4 provide information during this era of Matthew's silence. After hearing that John the baptizer was put into prison, the Lord departed from Nazareth and central Galilee to dwell in Capernaum. Capernaum would be the Lord's home base during His two-year ministry throughout Galilee. This included visits to the northern regions of Israel settled by the tribes of Zebulun and Naphtali, as prophesied by the prophet Isaiah. Matthew references and quotes Isaiah to again show that Jesus Christ is the foretold Jewish Messiah (vv. 14-16; Isa. 9:1-2).

Matthew identifies the message that Jesus Christ was now preaching throughout Galilee: *"Repent, for the kingdom of heaven is at hand"* (v. 17). As mentioned in the introduction, the phrase "kingdom of heaven" is found thirty-two times in Matthew but nowhere else in all of Scripture. This peculiarity must be associated with his Gospel's theme. The associated term "kingdom of God" is applied fifty-four times in the Gospel accounts, but only appears five times in Matthew and merely twice in John. What is the significance of these phrases, and how do the two terms relate to each other?

Centuries of debate on this subject prove insufficient to answer this question fully. The terms are used interchangeably by the Lord during the Sermon on the Mount and the Lord's discussion with His disciples concerning the rich young ruler who valued his wealth above following the Lord (Matt. 19:23-24). These instances seem to indicate that there is minimal difference in the meaning of the terms, or perhaps, an interrelated meaning (i.e., one term being a subset of the other).

Some Bible scholars note a distinction in that the kingdom of heaven is a subset of the kingdom of God. The "kingdom of heaven" in this case refers to the realm of human profession in which one acknowledges the sovereign rule of God or "the kingdom of God." C. I. Scofield writes:

> The kingdom of heaven is similar in many respects to the kingdom of God and is often used synonymously with it, though emphasizing certain features of divine government. When contrasted with the universal kingdom of God, the kingdom of heaven includes only men on earth, excluding angels and other creatures. The kingdom of heaven is the earthly sphere of profession as shown by the inclusion of these designated as wheat and tares, the latter of which are cast out of the kingdom (Matt. 13:41) and is compared to a net containing both the good and bad fish which are later separated (Matt. 13:47).[18]

Certainly, there is a realm of human profession within the kingdom of heaven, which is composed of true believers and mere professors, but there seems to be no tangible disagreement between the kingdom terms. Regardless, it is important to understand that the "kingdom of heaven" and the church are not synonymous terms, for the kingdom of heaven contains both the children of God and the children of the devil, while the universal church is only composed of true believers.

Christ Calls His First Disciples (vv. 18-22)

Matthew then recounts how the Lord called His first disciples into ministry. These and other disciples would continue their ministry between the initial offering of the kingdom and its realization later.

While walking along the shore of the Sea of Galilee, the Lord saw two brothers, who were fisherman, Simon called Peter, and Andrew (v. 18). They were fishing with nets at the time, but when the Lord called them to follow Him and He would make them fishers of men, they immediately left their nets and followed Him (vv. 19-20). Still walking along the shoreline, the Lord saw two more brothers, James and John, who were also fishermen (v. 21). They were in a boat with their father Zebedee when they were likewise called by the Lord and, immediately, they left their father in the boat and followed Christ (v. 22).

The Lord Jesus exhibited tremendous patience in calling His disciples. Initially, He invited two of John's disciples, including Andrew (Peter's brother), to His home to spend some time with Him, but at the end of the day they departed (John 1:39). Andrew then told Peter that he had found the Messiah, but Peter did not come to Christ on his own. The Lord had to repeatedly call Peter to follow Him, but after each time, Peter dedicated more of himself to Christ.

Initially, Peter forsook his fishing nets to follow Christ at His bidding (v. 20). Later, Peter forsook all to pursue the Savior (Luke 5:11). After Christ's resurrection, the Lord again called Peter to follow Him with the understanding that it would cost Peter his life (John 21:15-19). A few days earlier Peter had vehemently denied the Lord to protect himself from harm, but it is at this juncture that Peter settled "the death question" once and for all. He would learn that it was harder to live daily for the Lord than to die once for Him. In Acts 2 we do not see a shrinking, denying Peter, but a fully restored, Spirit-filled apostle preaching Christ to the saving of 3,000 souls. The Lord's patience with Peter is an encouragement to all those who are involved in training others. Those who mentor younger believers must be patient and tender.

Preaching the Kingdom Gospel and Healing Many (vv. 23-25)

The Lord, with His disciples, traveled through Galilee proclaiming the gospel of the kingdom and healing many people of their illnesses (v. 23). His "fame" (from *akoe*, which means "a hearing") spread into Syria, and many from that country also brought those afflicted with diseases and demons to be healed by Jesus Christ (v. 24). Matthew then notes that great multitudes from Galilee, Decapolis (literally, the region of "ten cities"), Jerusalem, Judea, and beyond the Jordan River to the east followed the Lord Jesus (v. 25).

It is important to understand that the "Gospel of the Kingdom" and the "Gospel of Grace" preached today in the Church Age are both founded in God's grace, and both require personal faith to appropriate God's blessing, but each has a distinct message, beneficiary, and dispensational focus. Arthur Pink notes the dispensational distinction of the gospel message:

> *"And Jesus went about all Galilee teaching in their synagogues, and preaching the Gospel* [not, be it noted, the "Gospel of the Grace of God" – Acts 20:24; nor "the Gospel of Peace" – Ephesians 6:15; but "the Gospel"] *of the Kingdom, and healing all manner of sickness and all manner of disease among the people"* (Matt. 4:23).[19]

Failure to draw a distinction between the gospel message of the Kingdom, preached by Christ to the "lost house of Israel," and the Gospel of Grace, preached presently during the Church Age, will result in doctrinal error. The gospel being preached now was not proclaimed during Christ's ministry, for if Satan had known what God was achieving through Christ, the princes of the world *"would have not crucified the Lord of glory"* (1 Cor. 2:8). Of course, the sufferings of Christ were predetermined by the counsel of God before the foundation of the world (1 Pet. 1:19-20) – thus God, not Satan, is responsible for Calvary.

Furthermore, the Lord Jesus visited Paul personally to convey to him exactly what the gospel message during the Church age would be: *"I declare to you the gospel which I preached to you ...that Christ died for our sins according to the Scriptures, and that He was buried, and that He rose again the third day according to the Scriptures"* (1 Cor. 15:1-4; also see Gal. 1:6-12). Spiritual application within the Sermon on the Mount for believers today will certainly be gleaned, but the literal intent of the message was for Israel. Today, those who are indwelt by the Holy Spirit can exhibit the behavior that honors the coming King. In this spiritual sense, the kingdom is present on earth, but in an invisible fashion. Hence, the Church will exhibit presently the true characteristics of Christ's future kingdom. The hope of the Jew is to see their Messiah reigning on earth and to be nationally restored with God as His covenant people. The hope of the Church will conclude prior to this when the Lord descends to the clouds and "catches up" the Church to be with Him in heaven (1 Thess. 4:13-18). The Church has a heavenly hope; the Jews have an earthly promise.

Matthew Chapter 5

The Beatitudes (vv. 1-12)

Matthew then describes one of the most famous scenes and messages in the ministry of the Lord Jesus – *The Sermon on the Mount* (chs. 5-7). Christ is on a mountain (symbolizing His kingly authority) with the subjects of His kingdom before Him (a great crowd of people including His disciples; v. 1).

The Sermon on the Mount is the manifesto of the King, literally the kingdom's constitution declaring how those who are in a right relationship with God should behave. Matthew documents the Lord's lengthy dissertation to His subjects, as Israel's yet-to-be-enthroned King. Luke records a portion of a similar message (approximately thirty verses) given on a different day, while Mark and John do not mention it at all. Thus, the Sermon on the Mount strongly fits with Matthew's perspective of the Lord Jesus Christ. Even the Jews that listened to the Lord Jesus understood the tone of His exhortation, in which He would say fourteen times, *"I say unto you."* At the conclusion of the sermon, we read *"that the people were astonished at His teaching, for He taught them **as one having authority**, and not as the scribes"* (7:28-29). The King spoke as the One in authority!

Within this lengthy discourse recorded in Matthew, the Lord addressed the ideal character and conduct of the subjects of His kingdom and what their circle of influence and testimony ought to be. Luke's focus pertains more to the lifestyle of the disciples in personal witnessing. For example: in Matthew, the Lord pronounced a blessing upon *"the poor in spirit"* (v. 3), but in Luke the blessing is to *"the poor"* (Luke 6:20).

Much of the Lord's declaration conveyed a flat rejection of the traditions and practices of the Pharisees (i.e., their religiosity) and the overall disposition of Gentile authority (i.e., their worldliness). In the closing, He told the people that they were now accountable for what they had heard: Would they follow Him and build their lives upon His teachings, or would they continue to follow empty religious traditions and human reasoning (i.e., building their house on a foundation of sand)? When the storms of life would come, the latter would prove to be a total "washout," while those who built upon His word (the rock) would stand fast and enjoy an abiding peace in life, despite difficulties.

The Sermon on the Mount will be the constitution of the millennial kingdom once Christ returns to earth to establish it. Although it is true that those in the Church Age who have the Holy Spirit indwelling them should be exhibiting behavior consistent with the Kingdom Constitution, the kingdom exists now in only that spiritual sense; the literal sense is future. The Kingdom Gospel message was delivered to Israel as an appeal to repent and receive Jesus as Messiah and King.

The Lord commences this discourse by pronouncing a blessing on those who are "poor in spirit." But what kind of disposition is the Lord speaking of? W. T. P. Wolston answers the question, "What does it mean to be poor in spirit?"

> Exactly the reverse of what you find in the world. In the world people stick up for themselves, stand for their rights. A person who does that is not in the kingdom of heaven at all, that is, is not in it in spirit. One who is poor in spirit is self-emptied. Self is out of sight. ... It is a blessed thing to be self-emptied (poor-spirited the world would call you); that is it, but the Lord reckons such "blessed." May the Lord give us to know in our hearts the meaning of it.[20]

"Poor in spirit" speaks of the humble inward quality, which is known by God, while meekness in verse 5 is the outward demonstration of that character towards others. The Lord wants all believers to learn what Paul learned: *"My grace is sufficient for you, for My strength is made perfect in weakness"* (2 Cor. 12:9). The Lord does not need our wealth, natural abilities, or religious feats; He simply wants our hearts soft, pliable, and beating for Him. To be poor implies a situation where there is a legitimate lack, but to be *poor in spirit* is a self-imposed disposition of helplessness – a willful discipline of emptiness. Paul warns, *"If anyone thinks himself to be something, when he is nothing, he deceives himself"* (Gal. 6:3). Those who talk about themselves and vaunt of their talents and accomplishments are not poor in spirit and therefore lose out on the Lord's blessing for being so inclined. Let us remember that the Lord is our all and all and without Him we are completely helpless!

Next the Lord said, *"Blessed are those who mourn, for they shall be comforted"* (v. 4). On one particular day, early in His ministry, the Lord Jesus ventured into a synagogue in His hometown of Nazareth. He was handed a scroll of Isaiah to read from. After announcing that the Spirit of the Lord was upon Him, He read Isaiah 61 verse 1 and half of verse 2 and then closed the book, returned it to the attendant and sat down. With every eye in the synagogue fixed on Him, the Lord then declared, *"Today this Scripture is fulfilled in your hearing"* (Luke 4:21).

The Jews understood that the Lord was claiming to be the One Isaiah was prophesying of, that is, the Messiah. They became so enraged by His claim that they sought to push Him over a cliff. The Lord did not read the remaining portion of verse 2 or verse 3, as that content pertained to His second advent, when He will return to judge the nations and restore Israel to a proper place of honor: *"And the day of vengeance of our God; to comfort all who mourn, to console those who mourn in Zion..."* (Isa. 61:2-3). For Israel, the Lord's promise to comfort those who mourn will be realized after the Tribulation Period. Obviously, believers in the Church Age can always approach the throne of grace for help when needed (Heb. 4:16), but this prophecy confirms the type of special comfort God provides for a particular group of mourners.

While there are many hardships in life that may cause us to mourn, the idea of Isaiah's prophecy is that Christ will be a special solace for all those who have suffered the contradiction of sinners, the sorrow of a God-hating world, or for upholding matters of righteousness or for identifying with Christ in His rejection. Our English word "comfort" is derived from two Latin roots, *con*, "to be with," and *fortis*, "strong." Literally "comfort" means "to strengthen by companionship."[21] God's infinitely strong arms fully embrace us with His tender mercies!

Like Israel, some of our sorrows may be caused by God's chastening hand over sin, but much suffering today results from those resisting God's rule for their lives. Godly comfort is the lasting remedy for life's sorrows. In a coming day, God Himself will wipe away every tear of those who mourn and they will be eternally comforted.

"Blessed are the meek, for they shall inherit the earth" (v. 5) is the next beatitude proclaimed. By nature none of us are meek, but rather we are temperamental, often volatile; if we have the means of getting our own way, we will do so. However, being spiritually bonded with Christ provides a different disposition towards what is important to God and what is self-seeking. A meek person is not self-willed, self-promoting

and does not force his or her way on others even when there is the ability to do so. Meekness is power in control and is not to be confused with weakness. Weakness means that one does not have the capacity to right a wrong, but in meekness, one chooses not to right the wrong even if there were an opportunity to do so. Meekness exercises restraint and self-control to do what is best for others and to honor the Lord.

The ultimate example of meekness is when the Lord laid aside His glory and position in heaven to become a man to be a humble substitute for us at Calvary (Phil. 2:6-8). At His crucifixion, He reminded His disciples that He could call twelve legions of angels to His rescue if He thought it was necessary, but He never summoned them (Matt. 26:53). The Lord Jesus was doing the will of His Father, in being His Lamb which would take away the sin of the world – He could not be rescued from doing the Father's will.

Meekness accepts a lowly position to extend mercy for the good of others. The Lord desires us to learn this aspect of His character: *"Take My yoke upon you and learn from Me, for I am gentle and lowly in heart, and you will find rest for your souls"* (Matt. 11:29). By being yoked with Him, believers learn of the Lord's gentle and humble spirit, enjoy fruitfulness, and gain His peace. Representing Christ to others in this way ensures that the meek will inherit disdain, injustice, and abuse presently. However, the Lord promises that when He returns to set up His kingdom, the meek will inherit the earth with Him!

Next the Lord declared, *"Blessed are those who hunger and thirst for righteousness, for they shall be filled"* (v. 6). Naturally speaking, we are born going our own way and seeking our own things, and good morality does not control our decision making. But after being confronted with the gospel message of grace in the Church Age and trusting in Christ alone for salvation, we receive a new nature from God that longs for righteousness. This is accomplished through an act of the Holy Spirit called regeneration (Tit. 3:4-5). The Holy Spirit washes us by bringing us to see the wrong in our sinful attitudes and desires. He makes us feel their uncleanness and leads us to repent of and repudiate them.

Regeneration is the implantation of a new life and a new order of living. Therefore, a regenerated person is referred to as a "new man" in Colossians 3:10; he or she received a new disposition which is to govern his or her thinking and behavior. This new disposition is God's own nature, which cannot sin (1 Jn. 3:9), though the believer may still sin by ignoring its moral reckoning (1 Jn. 1:9-2:1).

Having God's own nature within prompts every believer to pursue personal holiness and to yearn for God's righteousness to be evident everywhere. Only those who have a passion for holiness in their own lives will hunger and thirst for honesty, integrity, virtue, and justice in society also. When the Lord Jesus returns to establish His kingdom on earth, those yearning for righteousness will be completely satisfied, for Christ shall reign over the world with justice and in righteousness. Given God's great salvation to come, the prophet Isaiah exhorted his countrymen: *"Keep justice, and do righteousness, for My salvation is about to come, and My righteousness to be revealed"* (Isa. 56:1).

The next beatitude was *"Blessed are the merciful, for they shall obtain mercy"* (v. 7). Mercy and grace are complementary aspects of God's character (Ps. 103:12-13). It has been said that *mercy* is not getting what you do deserve, while *grace* is getting what you do not deserve. As sinners we deserved to spend eternity in the Lake of Fire, but God's mercy intervened on our behalf. As rebels opposing God, we certainly did not merit heaven, but by God's grace we gain entrance into God's marvelous abode.

In the Old Testament, God's prophets often threatened God's retribution for waywardness, but did not often speak of God's good character as a motivation for repentance. But Scripture reveals that God is gracious, merciful, slow to anger, and full of kindness and, consequently, longs to forgive those who confess their sin! God's holy character and attributes are perfectly and consistently demonstrated in all that He does; He can do nothing against His holy nature. Hence, God is completely satisfied with all that He does.

God's love does not overpower His holiness. His mercy does not ignore justice. His grace is not prompted by mere sympathy, but by what is best for those in need. God would be unjust if He did not prosecute that which opposes His nature, as a lack of action against sin endorses wickedness. Yet, His mercy tempers such judgments to permit every opportunity for the wayward to repent that they might be blessed. We also should mimic God's character by showing mercy to others for this same purpose. Mercy does not forget sin or ignore offenses, but rather it chooses not to act immediately so that grace might abound. Those who show mercy in this manner will have God's mercy also.

"Blessed are the pure in heart, for they shall see God" (v. 8) is the next beatitude. Those with pure hearts are assured of enjoying God's presence. For Israel this will be in the Kingdom Age, but for believers in

the Church Age, we continue to enjoy intimate communion with God by maintaining a pure heart. In Psalm 24, David affirms that the Lord, as Creator, reigns supreme over all His creation from His holy hill. He then asks the questions: *"Who may ascend into the hill of the Lord? Or who may stand in His holy place?"* (Ps. 24:3). The answer to both questions is the same: *"He who has clean hands and a pure heart, who has not lifted up his soul to an idol, nor sworn deceitfully"* (Ps. 24:4).

Although Satan wanted to *ascend to the hill of the Lord* and reign as God, his pride was judged, and he lost his privileged status as a covering cherub and was cast off God's holy mountain (Isa. 14:12-15; Ezek. 28:12-17). Only those within whom God has cleansed through the regeneration of His Spirit have the capacity to have clean hands and a pure heart; these alone are permitted to be with the Lord in His holy dwelling place. Because believers in the Church Age have a pure position in Christ forever, we should yearn to keep our hearts pure before the Lord by maintaining an untainted thought-life also (Phil. 4:8).

Believers today can know and enjoy God through His Word and by the illumination and communion of His Spirit. But this wonderful privilege requires maintaining short accounts with Him on the matter of sin. Sinful behavior, ungodly thoughts, and sins of omission must be confessed and forsaken immediately once we realize their true nature. The Lord promises that *"if we confess our sins, He is faithful and just to forgive us our sins and to cleanse us from all unrighteousness"* (1 Jn. 1:9). By the blood of Christ, God cleanses us to a condition of pureness so that we can again enjoy His intimate fellowship.

Continuing with the beatitudes, the Lord promised, *"Blessed are the peacemakers, for they shall be called sons of God"* (v. 9). The main Greek word rendered "peace" in the New Testament is *eirene,* which means to be "at one with." *Eirene* is used to describe the effort of Moses to bring two of his striving brethren into peace; he sought *"to set them at one again"* (Acts 7:26; KJV) or *"to reconcile them"* (NKJV). This is what Christ accomplished for us. We were once enemies of God, but through His finished work at Calvary, Christ has reconciled us with a holy God to become His children with the privilege of a full inheritance. Positionally speaking, we have *peace with God* through Christ (Phil. 1:2). Practically speaking, we have the *peace of God* when we adopt the mind of Christ in our thinking (Phil. 4:7-8). When believers have God's perspective on their circumstances, they will cease to be anxious over what is beyond their control.

We learn from Paul's opening salutations in many of his epistles that grace is the forerunner of peace: *"Grace to you and peace from God"* (Eph. 1:2). We cannot enjoy God's peace without the work of His grace in our lives. Peace in our hearts is positive proof that God's grace has been at work in our lives. He cannot give peace unto those who have not given over their lives to Him (John 14:27). This means there are two components to being a God-honoring *peacemaker*:

First, we must be faithful to share the good news message of Jesus Christ, so that those who are dead in their trespasses and sins can be forgiven and thereby reconciled with God. These receive the peace of God and become one with Him. This mimics the ministry of God's own Son, thus, such peacemakers *shall be called sons of God.*

Second, we must be faithful to uphold the mind of Christ in all conversations to pursue peace. Paul writes: *"If it is possible, as much as depends on you, live peaceably with all men"* (Rom. 12:18). Because the fountainhead of strife is pride, it is not always possible to come into oneness if the flesh has any part in the reconciliation effort. At such times it is good to remember that the promised blessing is for those who humble themselves and genuinely labor for peace; it is not contingent on bringing one or more antagonists into peace, as only the Spirit of God can accomplish true and lasting peace.

The next beatitude spoken was *"Blessed are those who are persecuted for righteousness' sake, for theirs is the kingdom of heaven"* (v. 10). Previously, the Lord promised a blessing for those who hungered and thirsted after righteousness. These individuals desire to know what God determines is right and proper. Furthermore, they yearn to see such a standard of morality upheld by everyone, everywhere. The blessing of this beatitude is for those who not only yearn for righteousness but are determined to live righteously despite the personal repercussion of doing so. This blessing is afforded to those who suffer, not for their own wrongdoings, but because others condemned their right conduct.

The kingdom of God is pledged to those who suffer for doing what is right. William MacDonald explains the hostility: "Their integrity condemns the ungodly world and brings out its hostility. People hate a righteous life because it exposes their own unrighteousness."[22] The Lord later reminded His disciples to expect this type of hatred from those who do not appreciate having their sin exposed (John 15:21-25).

The unregenerate do not appreciate having their sin exposed by the validity of a righteous life. Yet, we may be encouraged that their displayed anger is proof that the Lord is speaking to the conscience of the oppressors. Expressed anger of this fashion reveals insecurity in their flawed belief-system and worldview (Phil. 1:27-28). Suffering for righteousness is a powerful testimony to the lost of what is real.

The Lord Jesus concludes his list of kingdom-tied blessings by speaking directly to His disciples:

> *Blessed are you when they revile and persecute you, and say all kinds of evil against you falsely for My sake. Rejoice and be exceedingly glad, for great is your reward in heaven, for so they persecuted the prophets who were before you* (vv. 11-12).

First, notice that the Lord switches from announcing general beatitudes to addressing the disciples personally: *"blessed are you"* instead of "blessed are those." In the original language the "you" is plural, so no doubt the disciples perked up a bit to hear what the Lord was directly promising them, and by implication to succeeding generations of disciples in the Church Age.

Second, at first glance this beatitude may seem redundant to the one in verse 10, *"blessed are those who are persecuted for righteousness' sake."* While the outcome of suffering persecution is consistent, the reason for it is different. Verse 10 speaks of those who suffer for doing what is right and just. Their integrity rebuffs the wicked and condemns ungodliness. However, verse 11 addresses believers who are persecuted for Christ's sake. Because the world hates Christ, it also will hate those who identify with His name and live for Him (John 15:19-20).

Where the former group was persecuted for their righteous living, the latter group is simply hated for associating with Christ's name. Clearly then, believers should expect worldlings to isolate from them, revile them, and speak evil of them, even when nothing was done to deserve such disdain. Yet, the Lord told His disciples to rejoice greatly in their afflictions at such times, for their reward was waiting for them at the Judgment Seat of Christ (in heaven). It is waiting there for us too.

The Similitudes (vv. 13-16)

Still speaking to His disciples, the Lord likened their ministry for him to that of salt and of light: *"You are the salt of the earth"* (v. 13) and *"You are the light of the world"* (v. 14). A brief review of how salt was used in the Old Testament sacrifices will increase our appreciation of what the Lord was implying by this similitude. Salt is a symbol of purification in Scripture (Num. 18:19) and was thus required to be added to the various burnt offerings on the Bronze Altar. Salt stands in sharp contrast with leaven, which corrupts and, accordingly, was never permitted on the Bronze Altar. When the salt put on the Levitical offerings was burned, it created billowing white smoke. It was unnoticed until tested by fire and then the evidence of its presence was unmistakable. In this sense, salt speaks of pure, uncompromised truth (e.g., Col. 4:6).

Salt also enhances the flavor of what we eat and serves as a food preservative. Combining all these useful facets of salt we can understand why the Lord Jesus exhorted His disciples to have a "salty" testimony – declaring preserved truth enhances our testimony. Like salt, light also portrays a meaning of undefiled truth in Scripture: *"God is light and in Him is no darkness at all"* (1 Jn. 1:5).

Salt that is no longer salty and a lamp that is hidden under a basket have no value (v. 15). A believer who no longer lives to declare the goodness of Christ in word and by deed is become "good for nothing" and his or her testimony will be trampled for being meaningless by the children of the devil. The disciples were thus encouraged to let their lights shine in a world that desperately needs to see Christ in their good works – such behavior would glorify their Father in heaven (v. 16).

Relationship to Christ and the Law (vv. 17-20)

Many of Israel's religious leaders believed that Jesus of Nazareth was preaching a message that opposed the Law and the teachings of the prophets (v. 17). However, the Lord had come to fulfill Old Testament Scripture, not make it void. As prophesied by Isaiah, Jeremiah, and Ezekiel (Isa. 61:8; Jer. 31:31-34; Ezek. 36:24-28), He was going to establish a New Covenant with Israel and seal it with His own blood (Heb. 8:7-12; Luke 22:20). The New Covenant would permit God to righteously save those who realized that they were condemned by the Law (Rom. 3:20) and needed a Savior – Christ (Gal. 3:24). The Lord did not say that the Law would never pass away, but rather that God would put the Law away when it had fully served its purpose (2 Cor. 3:7-11).

In the heart of Christ alone could God's Word be found intact and unbroken. Hence, Jesus Christ is the fulfillment of the Law and could say, *"Do not think that I came to destroy the Law or the Prophets, I did not come to destroy but to fulfill"* (v. 17). John Phillips explains the important truth that the Lord was declaring:

> God's Law had two parts: the moral law and the ceremonial law. In His amazing life the Lord Jesus fulfilled the demands of the moral law. In His death [and resurrection] He fulfilled the details of the ceremonial law, which was chiefly concerned with sacrifices and offerings.
>
> He fulfilled the rich symbolism of the sin offering and the trespass offering. Jesus was the goat that was slain on the day of atonement, whose blood was taken into the holy of holies; and He was the scapegoat upon which were laid the sins of the people before it was led away into "a land not inhabited" (Lev. 16:22). He was the bird that the cleansed leper brought to be slain in his stead and He was the other bird that the cleansed leper brought to be dipped in the blood of the first bird before being set free to fly heavenward and home. Jesus was the unleavened bread of the Passover, and He was the paschal lamb. His were the ashes of the red heifer, and His was the blood that was shed for sin. The red rivers that poured from ten thousand times ten thousand sacrifices were but a feeble type of His precious blood.[23]

Therefore, the Lord said that heaven and earth would not pass away until every "jot" (the smallest Hebrew letter) and "tittle" (the smallest stroke in creating a Hebrew letter) of the Law was fulfilled. Heaven and earth pass away only after all evil has been dealt with and the redeemed are in glorified bodies before the Lord forever (Rev. 21). Then it will be shown that the Lord Jesus Christ has restored creation back to a state of perfection because it will be subject to Him and not sin; then God will be all in all (1 Cor. 15:27-28).

Man's tendency is to compromise or to rationalize away God's commandments because they seem, naturally speaking, unattainable. But the point of the Law was to show man his sin and cause him to seek God for a solution beyond the Law and humanized religion to be made acceptable to Him. Hence, the Lord warned against this type of behavior: anyone breaking any part of God's Law and then teaching others to do the same will be the least in the kingdom of heaven (v. 19). Recall that the kingdom of heaven includes the realm of false profession and evil influences (Matt. 13:19, 25), the point being that entrance and honor in Christ's kingdom (the real part of the kingdom of heaven) are gained through faith and obedience in what He says.

In His sermon, the Lord declared His authority over His audience by using the expression *"I say to you"* fourteen times (e.g., vv. 18, 20, 22). Consequently, in verse 20, the Lord posed a hyperbole (an exaggeration) to warn His audience that they would need more righteousness than the self-righteous Pharisees, who loved ceremonial tradition, to enter His kingdom. Outward doings without inward spiritual renovation counts for nothing with God (John 3:3; Tit. 3:5). The only righteousness that God will accept is the positional righteousness of His Son that is imputed to repentant sinners at their regeneration (Tit. 3:5). Afterwards, practical righteousness will give evidence of the inward reality of Christ's life (Jas. 2:17).

Murder and Hatred (vv. 21-26)

The Lord now provided several illustrations of how the righteousness of the Pharisees was deficient; thus, they could not enter Christ's kingdom. First, the Lord upheld the sixth of the Ten Commandments: *"You shall not murder"* (v. 21). The Pharisees taught that murder was the wrongful taking of another's life, but the Lord taught that the unrighteous anger in the heart that prompted murder was wrong also (v. 22). When the flesh controls our anger, we will be prompted to assume a superior position over others and then degrade them by our speech or punish them by venting unrighteous anger. Calling another "Raca!" meaning "You fool!" is an example of this derogatory behavior. Such sinful speech spews out of a sinful heart (i.e., from someone that has not been made right with God). Hence, without Christ, such a person is heading to the eternal judgment of hellfire.

Anger is a powerful emotion that heightens the body's physical capability to respond in a way it would not normally be able. However, righteous anger must serve God and others and be quickly extinguished after accomplishing its work or it will lead us into sin. Hence, the Lord warns us against harboring congealed anger in our hearts towards others; such resentment will ultimately result in bitterness. Bitterness negatively affects all relationships of a person who willfully swallows such poison.

Therefore, we are to keep short accounts with God and with others. If we know that someone has been offended by us, we are to attempt to resolve the issue through reconciliation before we try to worship the Lord. In the Jewish economy, this is what is meant by leaving "one's gift at the altar" (vv. 23-24). Without attempting personal reconciliation, the gift to God would not be accepted. Even in the extreme situation of an approaching civil trial, the defendant should attempt to resolve the problem with the plaintiff (v. 25). Otherwise, the judge may rule against you and put you in prison until justice is rendered and every penny of restitution, as determined by the court, is paid (v. 26).

Adultery and Divorce (vv. 27-32)

Next, the Lord validated the seventh of the Ten Commandments: *"You shall not commit adultery"* (Ex. 20:14). While the word *fornication* encompasses a broader range of sexual sins, including those outside of marriage (e.g., Mark 7:21; 1 Cor. 6:13), *adultery* occurs when the sexual sanctity of a marriage covenant has been violated. When a married person has intercourse with someone other than his or her spouse, this is the sin of adultery (Rom. 7:3).

While all immorality is an abomination to God, the willful desecration of one's marriage vows is particularly grievous. Adultery is rebellion against God's original design for marriage (Gen. 2:22-24). This commandment secures and protects the sexual union of a husband (a biological male) with his own wife (a biological female; Matt. 19:4-6). God created male and female and thereby He designed the sexual union to be an enjoyable experience within the bounds of marriage and for the purpose of procreation. Later, the Lord affirmed that divorce only became permissible under the Mosaic law because of the hardness of man's heart, that is, the Jews would not adhere to God's original design for marriage (19:8). As a result, the Law put constraints on God's covenant people concerning divorce and remarriage.

For example, a man could not divorce his wife if he had erroneously charged her with sexual promiscuity before marriage (Deut. 22:19) or if he had a sexual relationship with her before marriage (Deut. 22:28-29). On the other hand, God expected Jewish men to divorce their foreign wives whom they had married in defiance of the Law (Ezra 10). If a man divorced his wife, he was to write her a bill of divorce, and if she remarried another man, then she could not go back to her previous husband, even if her subsequent husband died (Deut. 24:1-4). Such regulations were to prevent frivolous divorces. All the above stipulations and more resulted because of man's unwillingness to obey God's original design for marriage. Sin ruins God's best for us and results in all sorts of complications and consequences.

Regrettably, divorce had become rampant in the Jewish society and God hated that reality (Mal. 2:14-16). So, when the Lord affirmed God's original design for marriage to His audience, that would have been received as a stern rebuke to what had become common behavior, divorce for other reasons than adultery. If someone remarries a divorced person who was unscripturally divorced, then both parties are guilty of adultery in God's estimation. Under the Law, those guilty of adultery were to be put to death, so divorce was not necessary. A married spouse would be free to remarry again after his or her guilty spouse was stoned for unfaithfulness to his or her marriage covenant.

But the Lord did not stop there; He went beyond the actual act of sin to the source of the sin – unchecked lusting in the heart (v. 28). While some might be guiltless of adultery, they were not free of adulterous thoughts. Peter states that one of the marks of a false teacher is to have "eyes full of adultery" (2 Pet. 2:14). These carnal men were so destitute of the truth that their first inclination when they saw a woman was to lust after her, rather than desiring to assist her.

Subjects of the kingdom must be committed to holiness, and it is impossible to control one's behavior until one's thoughts and desires are brought under God's control. To look at a woman for the purpose of lusting after her is to commit adultery in the heart. To admire a woman's qualities and beauty is one thing, but it is quite another to imagine satisfying lustful desires with her. A sanctified sex-life begins when our inner desires have been yielded to God's will for marriage. If not, then seeing will lead to touching, and touching to immorality. We must realize that lusting in our hearts for what God hates is no less offensive to Him than engaging in it.

Although the Lord is not advocating marring the body, He said that it would be better to remove a hand or an eye than to be carried away by unchecked lusting, for the end of that journey is destruction (vv. 29-30).

Oaths (vv. 33-37)

Referring to the ninth of the Ten Commandments, the Lord reminds His audience that it was a sin against God to swear falsely (e.g., as a witness of the truth) or to fail to do what had been vowed to the Lord (v. 33). The Lord warned His listeners not to further validate what was being said by swearing on other things, like heaven, or God's throne, or the Earth, or Jerusalem, etc. (v. 34). No one was to even swear by his or her head, as no one can change the color of one hair on their head by what they said (v. 35). The point was to let the truth stand for itself. What was true did not need any verbal fanfare to make it more valid; the truth is the truth. Truth can never contradict itself; rather, it validates itself.

In the Old Testament, swearing (i.e., the taking of an oath) to validate a promise was quite common among the Jews. It was done to strongly affirm a promise or statement by using the Lord's name. In the New Testament, however, the Lord Jesus traversed the high moral ground on the subject of swearing. The Lord reminded His audience that what they said should always be accurate. If they promised to do something, their words should stand alone without trying to reinforce their validity by swearing.

Believers today should not swear to increase the credence of what they say; the merit of everything said should be consistently wholesome and truthful without adding God's name to it. We should never think that somehow by starting a statement with the words "To be honest..." somehow strengthens the worth of what we are about to say.

Swearing involves tying God's name to our statements to better validate what we say – to heighten the credibility of our words. The believer should not engage in such practices, for to do so would certainly bring low the name of God. James reiterated what the Lord directed in verse 37: *"But above all, my brethren, do not swear, either by heaven or by earth or with any other oath. But let your 'Yes' be 'Yes,' and your 'No,' 'No,' lest you fall into judgment"* (Jas. 5:12). Demeaning the name of the Lord by swearing falsely is a terrible thing. As we are forgetful creatures and are rarely perfect in our speech, it behooves us to refrain from doing so.

Retaliation and Vengeance (vv. 38-42)

In this portion of the Sermon on the Mount we find the Lord declaring the true nature of the Law, where grace is all but absent: *"An eye for an eye and a tooth for a tooth"* (v. 38). If someone intentionally or unintentionally caused you harm, the exact equivalent retribution was demanded by the Law – no more, and no less. But the Lord was introducing His Jewish audience to the concept of extending unmerited favor; He wanted them to realize that grace had the power to remit every claim of retribution. But such thinking is difficult to receive unless one has first experienced God's abounding grace, has received a full pardon, and has been forgiven all debt.

The Law taught stringent justice for crimes and offenses, even if they were unintentionally committed. Its tit-for-tat restitution would satisfy the injured party's desire for vengeance, but it did not teach man how the divine qualities of love, grace, and mercy should govern one's behavior. Certainly, the lack of these in resolving life's offenses would cause man to be more appreciative of God's ultimate means of making restitution for our intentional and unintentional offenses against Him – the giving and judging of His Son in our place.

The Lord Jesus Christ would be, and indeed was, the sin-sacrifice for all humanity. Through Christ we don't get what we do deserve (all the horrors of hell) and we do receive what we don't deserve (all the blessings of heaven); the former is God's mercy to us and the latter is His grace. Consequently, every aspect of our salvation is permeated by the sweet aroma of Christ's love. May we never get over the love of Christ and may we long for others to know it too!

This is the motivation for enduring social injustice and persecutions related to the cause of Christ. When viciously struck in the face by an ignorant, self-righteous worldling, the only motivation for turning the other cheek and enduring more hardship is to declare the power of Christ's grace (v. 39). Love for Christ will cause us to give to someone above what he or she is threatening to take from us through litigation (v. 40). Likewise, in Christ we receive the patience to go the extra distance with someone undeserving of a second chance and to provide to others more than what they expect when they ask us for help (vv. 41-42).

Love Your Enemies (vv. 43-48)

Following the "Turn the Other Cheek" challenge, the Lord offered a second contrast between the lifestyles of rigid Law-keeping and of yearning to extend grace. The Law commanded the Jews not to hate each other, or take vengeance on each other, and to love their neighbor (Lev. 19:17-18). However, it was socially acceptable for the Jews to hate their enemies because the Law did not expressly forbid it (v. 43). The Law did teach that they should love those near and dear to them (Lev. 19:18), so the Pharisees believed that hatred for one's enemies was acceptable and even prompted God's means of punishing them.

But the Lord said that God's love was much deeper than just doing good to those who do good to you or greeting those who greet you (vv. 46-48). The unregenerate behave that way, so there is nothing gained for the kingdom in acting as they do (v. 46). But just as God is impartial in showing goodness (e.g., by providing rain and sunshine to both the wicked and the just), we should have no partiality in being kind to others (v. 45).

Divine love looks past righting the offense to righting the offender. Accordingly, those of Christ's kingdom should love those who oppress them, as shown by acts of kindness and by praying for them (v. 44). This latter ideology would not only be possible but expected conduct during the Church Age.

The "eye for an eye" doctrine of the Law taught the Jews that disobedience must be punished, whereas the "love your enemies" exhortation reflected a much deeper truth pertaining to the New Testament: Believers in the Church Age would come to realize that no one could earn heaven by Law-keeping and therefore must trust in Christ alone for salvation. After Christ's resurrection, believers would receive the Holy Spirit and then have the wherewithal to *keep* the Law (i.e., sin is a conscious choice for a true Christian) and *fulfill* the Law (which would actively demonstrate both God's character and the outworking of His grace).

We do not naturally want to bless our enemies, so the Lord offers us the means of transforming our selfish thinking into wanting to do what He asks – we are to pray for our enemies. Have you ever tried to pray to God while you were angry with someone? It doesn't work. As we pour out the sorrows of our hearts to the infinite Creator, our hearts become humbled and softened. Prayer is transforming! We may start by asking the Lord to "smash 'em," but as we continue to pray, we are overtaken by the hurt and pain that the offending party is inflicting on themselves, their family, the Church, and Christ. Suddenly, our pain does not seem so great when looking at the big picture.

How much less contention would there be in the Church today if believers permitted the Lord to judge all the injustices, false gossip, and slander among us? How much more powerfully would Christ be displayed to the lost through genuine acts of self-sacrifice? The love of Christ can soften the hardest of hearts to consider the truth.

Matthew Chapter 6

Sincere Charity (vv. 1-4)

In contrast with showing love and doing acts of kindness to those who are lovable and then expecting the same in return (5:46-48), the Lord challenged His audience to selflessly love those who were undeserving and to do so without any expectations of thanks or a return favor. Such conduct was beyond anything the Law demanded but would mark those who had truly experienced grace in Christ (Rom. 13:8).

The Lord then reminded everyone that when people do good deeds to be seen and to be praised by others, they have their reward, but regrettably they do not have God's approval (v. 2). Therefore, He stresses three times with different wording the "secret" nature that true giving must have to receive God's appreciation: First, Christ spoke of doing deeds without wanting to be seen by others (v. 1). Second, He addressed those doing good deeds and then wanting others to appreciate what they had done (v. 2). Third, the Savior reproved those doing good deeds without keeping the matter secret (v. 3). *"Do not let your left hand know what your right hand is doing"* was an idiom expressing personal privacy. His main point being that if we want an eternal reward for our service, we must seek God's approval alone (v. 4). Wanting to be seen by others for the purpose of recognition and praise when we do something is a warning to us that our hearts are not right before the Lord.

The Lord is still on the mount, and still declaring the manifesto of His coming Kingdom. During the Church Age, the outworking of this constitution would be evident in only a hidden, spiritual sense (the fruit of the Spirit in Christians). Regardless, the kingdom reality is not measured by external doings, but rather by the hidden power that brings them about. Hence, doing things to be seen by men is evidence of poor spirituality in any age.

Sincere Prayer (vv. 5-15)

The Lord Jesus carried the "in secret" motivation into the matter of prayer. Obviously, there are times believers should meet corporately to pray together (Acts 4:24-31, 12:12), but here the Lord is addressing our personal prayer life. The Lord wanted the subjects of His kingdom to follow His example of spending much time in seeking the face of His Father in prayer. The Lord would often rise early in the morning to be able to pray without distraction or without observation.

In contrast, many religious leaders at that time sought to impress others by their long and ostentatious public prayers uttered in places such as the temple and in synagogues. Those prayers uttered to be heard by men never reach heaven. These men clearly esteemed the praise of men more valuable than receiving God's blessing and appreciation. The Lord said of these religious facades, *"they have their reward"* (v. 5).

The Lord employed the expression "when you pray" three times to uphold the type of attitude God appreciates when we pray: First, do not seek to be noticed by men (v. 5). Second, go to a private place free of distractions and the temptation of showing off (v. 6). Third, pray from the heart, not by rote (v. 7). It is not our many words that God appreciates, but rather our meaningful communication which shows Him that we value who He is, not just what He can do (v. 8).

Lawrence Richards summarizes Christ's "in secret" message:

> In this age, before Jesus comes in power, the kingdom and the Father exist "in secret." But the God who sees us in secret does reward us. The God who sees us *is* and He does act in the world of here and now. If we seek the kingdom, we dare not let the traditions of the men of our age draw us away from the God who *is*. It is our secret life with Him which is the key to our experience of the kingdom.[24]

The Lord Jesus taught His disciples to pray through His personal example and by providing them with a model prayer, but not one to be repetitiously prayed. The Lord began, *"Our Father in heaven, Hallowed be Your name"* (v. 9). God, His name, and His dwelling place transcend all that is common and earthly. God is Holy; He is separate from all else! All that is associated with Him, including His name, should be revered.

The Lord Jesus compels us to first ponder the character and attributes of God when approaching Him in prayer. Why? The more we understand of our God's awesome nature, the faster the enormity of our problems diminish by comparison. C. H. Spurgeon, commenting on verse 9, wrote:

> The proper study of a Christian is the Godhead. The highest science, the loftiest speculation, the mightiest philosophy which can ever

engage the attention of a child of God is the name, the person, the work, the doings, and the existence of the great God whom he calls his Father.[25]

Next, we are to pray for the advancement of all that God desires, which means that we must know His will, as expressed in His word to pray in this way: *"Your kingdom come. Your will be done"* (v. 10). To pray "on earth as it is in heaven" is to ask God to powerfully declare His holiness, His kingdom, and His sovereign rulership in such a way to make it permanent on the Earth.

After putting what is important to God first, we are to acknowledge our own needs, including spiritual and physical food to nurture our souls and bodies (v. 11). Next, we must have hearts free of bitterness and hatred if we want to enjoy fellowship with God (v. 12). We understand from the parallel passage in Luke – *"Forgive us our sins, for we also forgive everyone who is indebted to us"* (Luke 11:4) – what the debt in verse 12 is to be forgiven – our sins. To pray, *"forgive us our debts, as we forgive our debtors,"* means that we understand that because of our sin, we owe God a debt that cannot be repaid.

The Lord is speaking to a large Jewish audience, which included His disciples and many who had not believed His message. He speaks of their heavenly Father from a Jewish perspective. So, there was an application for both believers and non-believers. Because the Lord instructed us to plead with God to show mercy by granting the forgiveness of what we could not repay, we also should be willing to show the mercy to others who have sinned against us. We would only reject this behavior if we had an erroneous appreciation of God's forgiveness to us through Christ. Thus, an unforgiving heart in the non-believer would show that he or she was still in their sins (i.e., had not received God's judicial forgiveness), while the unforgiving believer would forfeit God's parental forgiveness and invite His chastening hand.

God is a merciful God, who wants us to experience His forgiveness and liberation from sin. This means that those who are truly His children must release, to God's judicial care, those offenses committed against us, so that we may enjoy unhindered communion with Him (vv. 14-15). Matthew is not saying that God's judicial forgiveness for sin can be received by forgiving others, or for any other reason, for that matter. But a forgiving heart is a testimony that someone has received His forgiveness and experienced His mercy.

To petition God not to "lead us into temptation" does not mean that He may choose to entice us to sin; it is our flesh, the world, and the devil who do that, not God (Jas. 1:13). Rather, we are admitting to God that our flesh is weak and that our full confidence is in Him to preserve us when we are solicited to sin. To be divinely delivered from evil's grasp means that we were not led into temptation. However, the Greek word rendered "temptation" carries the connotation of "proving the validity" of something, that is, a testing that proves the reality of something. James tells his audience, "The testing of your faith produces patience" (Jas. 1:3). Hence, we should not expect God to remove us from those difficulties which He has predetermined to use to refine us and cause us to act more like His Son (Rom. 8:29).

The Lord concludes His example prayer with a doxology, *"For Yours is the kingdom and the power and the glory forever. Amen"* (v. 13). This portion of verse 13 is not in the critical text, but is a most appropriate praise to God, as confirmed in verse 10 and 1 Peter 5:11. Interestingly, the Lord taught them again this same model prayer about a year and a half later at a different location (Luke 11:1-4). Apparently, after observing the Lord's passionate prayer-life, they still felt deficient in how they were conversing with God.

Sincere Fasting (vv. 16-18)

The Pharisees projected self-righteousness through insincere charitable deeds (vv. 1-4), insincere prayers (vv. 5-15), and insincere fasting (vv. 16-18). Thus, the Lord refers to them as "hypocrites" (vv. 2, 5, 16). Then He warns His audience not to be like them. We may glean several important points concerning the type of fasting that pleases God from the Lord's directions about fasting.

First, notice that the Lord said, *"when you fast"* (v. 17). This affirms that fasting should be a normal part of the believer's life. Second, fasting is not simply debasing oneself or appearing sad to appear spiritual to others, but rather a time of intense inner reflection and focused listening (v. 16). Fasting for public display is contrary to its purpose and therefore negates its benefit. Hunger pangs remind us of our dependence on the Lord and lengthy times of introspection result in mental clarity to see things as God does.

Additionally, Isaiah reminds us that heartfelt affliction of the soul would result in just and good conduct: the oppressed would be freed, those who were hungry would be fed, and the poor would be clothed. So then, Isaiah asked his countrymen, *"Is your fasting what God has chosen?"* (Isa. 58:6). Isaiah's response in the next verse indicated that the answer to his question was "no," as he suggested that the type of fasting that would be acceptable to God would emphasize moral transformation rather than ceremonial fanfare.

The Lord Jesus declared a similar message to hypocritical and ceremonial Israel during His first advent when He quoted Hosea 6:6 (on two different occasions): *"I desire mercy and not sacrifice"* (9:13, 12:7). Fasting should result in a greater awareness of God's will and in a moral transformation. If our fasting does not lead to changed attitudes and behavior, then it did not achieve God's intended outcome.

Let us remember that vain, especially non-commanded, religious activities do not prompt God's blessing, but humble acts of righteousness done in the name of Christ do, because these reflect His gracious and lovely character to others.

The Church would be wise to consider the Lord's rebuke of Israel's futile practices. God is not impressed by religious ritual, developed church tradition, sanctimonious form, and denominational smugness, but rather with personal living fostered in divine truth (Col. 2:20-23). May we not get sucked into meaningless modern-day legalism, but rather engage in *"pure and undefiled religion before God"* (Jas. 1:27). Only having a love relationship with Jesus Christ can produce that kind of religion!

The Lord Jesus affirms again that believers have the wonderful privilege of entering their own secret place to speak to their heavenly Father in His secret place (v. 18). The Lord had already spoken against vain prayers; now He addresses another self-exalting behavior – vain fasting. Fasting to appear humble or spiritual was putrid to God.

Treasure for Heaven (vv. 19-24)

Worldliness and materialism walk hand in hand with spiritual complacency. Materialism is a carnal attitude that has plagued God's people through the ages. Love for the Lord and His Word are supplanted by materialism and other worldly ambitions, which have no eternal value (vv. 19-20). Little in one's life has value to God after a man or a woman has become mesmerized by earthly things!

What or who we love is demonstrated by what we spend our time thinking about, talking about, and how we spend our money. This is what the Lord meant by, *"For where your treasure is, there your heart will be also"* (v. 21). The world offers many tantalizing thrills to sequester the believer's affection – you can have whatever you see (vv. 22-23). Participating in or watching sporting events, acquiring wealth, educational pursuits, seeking fame, political ambitions, professional growth, and talent competitions are only a few of the entrapments that cause us to treasure what we ought not.

The Lord Jesus said, *"No one can serve two masters. ...You cannot serve God and mammon"* (money; v. 24). If Christ is truly the Lord of our lives, then He must have first place in our thinking; every activity, every relationship, and every conversation must have His approval. He must be Lord of all we are and have or He is not really Lord at all.

Other than our children, everything else that the Lord bestows to us in grace is going to eventually rot, disintegrate, corrode, or burn. The Lord was asserting that it did not make much sense to stockpile earthly things which one could not take to the grave; rather, it would be better to invest what one has for eternity and be rewarded by God for doing so. Only what is invested for eternity has value to the Lord. On judgment day all else will be shown to be worthless and will be incinerated by the brilliance of God's holy presence (1 Cor. 3:11-15). May we all live for eternity and not passing things. As Jim Elliot proclaimed: "He is no fool who gives what he cannot keep, to gain what he cannot lose."

Why Worry? (vv. 25-34)

In teaching His disciples how to pray, the Lord had emphasized their needed daily dependency on God: *"Give us this day our daily bread"* (6:11). If they were truly trusting God to provide their daily necessities (food, water, clothing, etc.), then there would be no room for worry in their hearts (v. 25). If they were anxious, that meant that their faith was deficient. Furthermore, who can add anything to what is lacking through the act of worrying about it? Worry cannot change the reality of things, but God can, so commit your needs to Him in prayer! We cannot serve the Lord faithfully if we are given over to anxiety; we waste time fretting about things we cannot change anyway. For example, can anyone increase his or her stature by worrying about his or her height (v. 27)? Worrying robs us of our peace and is a poor testimony of Christ to the world.

To illustrate the point, the Lord reminded them that His Father took wonderful care of the birds of the air (v. 26). Yet, the birds did not spend time sowing seed or reaping a harvest for later use – they were dependent on their Creator every day for their food. Are not we who are created in God's image (mankind) of higher importance in creation order than birds? Therefore, we can especially trust God to care for those who are His own children. Worrying about the future is futile and shows God that we do not trust His sovereign abilities and purposes. William MacDonald explains the next example of this principle given in verses 28-30:

> Next the Lord deals with the unreasonableness of worrying that we will not have enough clothing in the future. The lilies of the field (probably wild anemones) neither toil nor spin, yet their beauty surpasses that of Solomon's royal garments. If God can provide such elegant apparel for wildflowers, which have a brief existence and are then used as fuel in the baking oven, He will certainly care for His people who worship and serve Him.[26]

Believers are not to be in anxious pursuit of life's necessities, as if one's life depended on our very next meal or having a piece of cloth in hand (v. 31). The Gentiles (referring to the unregenerate) think this way because they do not know how good the one true God is (v. 32). But for those who truly know Him, there is nothing to be concerned about, as He already knows what our legitimate needs are, and He is the only one that can unquestionably supply them.

Hence, believers are to give first place in their thinking to what is important to God and what will please Him (v. 33). When we pursue what is significant to God, He supplies what is most needful for us so that we can do what is important to Him. Therefore, we do not need to worry about tomorrow; rather, we need to live for Him today (v. 34).

For those of us who live within the affluent Western culture, the idea of trusting the Lord for our daily bread is mostly an untested theoretical concept. Little of our abundance is needed to supply our actual daily necessities and even less of it is used to feed and clothe the poor. Rather, our vast wealth is used to insulate ourselves against any conceivable mishap, to collect stuff we really don't need, and to indulge or pamper our flesh with thrills and creature comforts that last only a moment and waste valuable time. There is certainly nothing wrong with planning ahead; the point is this: few Christians in our post-modern society rely on God for their necessities, let alone everything. No wonder the Western world is becoming a God-denying and self-centered culture. The cosmopolitan man does not need God because he is self-sufficient in himself.

Matthew Chapter 7

Do Not Judge Others (vv. 1-6)

This section on judging others immediately follows the Lord's warning of pursuing earthly riches and worrying about temporal needs. What God has entrusted to us should never keep us from fulfilling our divine calling but is to be used to supply legitimate needs and to support His work. We are to care for loved ones, our neighbors, and to show love to the unregenerate. Saints will have differing views on what it means to forsake all to follow Christ and still maintain the means to care for loved ones. As no one lives completely by faith, the Lord begins with a warning about judging others in areas of life that we should not.

"Judge not, that you be not judged" (v. 1). It is often the wayward that quote this verse to avoid personal accountability for their sin. There are at least two important applications of this verse. First, as the verses that follow explain, the context of what the Lord is saying is not that God's people should not judge each other in matters of sin, but rather we should not do so with un-Christ-like attitudes, and we should not judge in areas that we have no authority to (v. 2). Second, the Greek verb tense for the English word rendered "judged" in verse 1 is aorist. This indicates that all believers will stand before the Lord in a coming day for a once-for-all time judgment; knowing of this accountability, we should be actively judging ourselves now (1 Cor. 3:11-15; 2 Cor. 5:8).

The fact that the Lord goes on to say that believers should "beware of false prophets [teachers]" (v. 15) clearly shows that there are things that must be judged (evaluated), namely, sinful behavior and doctrine. On this point, C. H. Mackintosh writes:

God's assembly is responsible to judge the doctrine and morals of all who claim entrance at the door. ...We do not judge and put away bad doctrine in order to maintain *our* orthodoxy; neither do we judge and put away moral evil in order to maintain our reputation and respectability. The only ground of judgment and putting away is this, *"Holiness becomes Thine house, O Lord, forever."*[27]

73

Scripture commands Christians to judge each other in the areas of life and doctrine. Paul instructed the assembly at Corinth to put out a man from the assembly fellowship who was committing blatant acts of immorality and then bragging about it (1 Cor. 5). When someone is in unrepentant sin, he or she cannot be in fellowship with God, nor His people. Believers can only enjoy Christ's fellowship with each other while being in unbroken communion with Him. Paul instructed the believers at Thessalonica not to have close association with those claiming to be Christians, but that were not holding to the apostles' teaching (2 Thess. 3:6, 14). Believers are required to judge others identifying with Christ in doctrine and life to determine whether association is permitted.

While believers are to judge each other to confirm soundness of doctrine and life, the Lord issued a warning in how this was to be accomplished (vv. 3-5). For example, we cannot properly see to pull a speck from our brother's eye if we have a plank in our own eye. The plank may be unconfessed sin, but more often it is simply un-Christ-like attitudes that keep us from responding as Christ would in the situation.

It is often those initial thoughts that come to mind, when someone abruptly intrudes into our day with their problems, that give evidence of the plank: "Why is she calling me again with the same old issue?" "I wish he would get his act together and quit bothering me." "I hope that he will tell others how I helped him." If we are not motivated by selfless love for the good of others, we are not going to skillfully remove the speck as Christ would. We need to first confess our own failures, wrong motives, and bad attitudes before we can help others.

It is also good for us to remember that, though we are to judge the behavior and doctrine of others, we are not to judge fellow believers in the following areas: their personal liberty (Rom. 14:1-3), their motivation for service (7:1-5), their ministry's profitability (1 Cor. 4:1-4) or their salvation in Christ (John 5:21-24). Concerning the matters of Christian liberty, someone's motives, the value of someone's ministry, and the validity of their salvation – only the Lord knows what is in our hearts and why we do what we do, so let us be careful judging such things.

For this reason, Paul warns fellow servants of Christ not to judge each other, for only the master will judge his own servants: *"Who are you to judge another's servant? To his own master he stands or falls"* (Rom. 14:4). If we can help others, let us behave as Christ would and let us not intrude in matters that only He can judge properly.

The fact that Christ warned His disciples not to give holy things to dogs or to cast pearls before swine proves He was not prohibiting all forms of personal judgment (v. 6). Dogs and swine were unclean animals under the Law and are used here by the Lord to depict wicked people. When people become malicious towards spiritual truth, continuing to share the gospel with them only makes them more indignant towards the truth. This has the effect of further hardening their hearts to the truth and increasing their divine accountability before God on judgment day. It is better to pray and wait for the Lord to soften such a heart. Once He breaks up the fallow ground, then the gospel seed can be sown more beneficially.

Ask, Seek, and Knock (vv. 7-12)

The Lord has spent two chapters identifying the high character and virtuous behavior of individuals enjoying His future kingdom on earth. Those receiving the Holy Spirit during the Church Age would be equipped to exemplify such traits before the Kingdom Age but not without receiving wisdom and power from above. For this reason, the Lord next spoke of the type of praying that believers were to be engaged in – *ASK*: keep *asking*, keep *seeking*, and keep *knocking* (vv. 7-8). The idea is that persistent praying in the Spirit prepares us to gratefully receive God's answer. What may seem like unanswered prayers are just inopportune timing for God to bring about the best outcome of our prayers for everyone involved.

The Lord Jesus desires us to obtain all that is necessary to serve and honor Him. To properly judge ourselves and others, as just discussed, we need wisdom and grace from above. Hence, the disciples were to petition His Father in His name for that which was lacking or needful: *"Most assuredly, I say to you, whatever you ask the Father in My name He will give you. Until now you have asked nothing in My name. Ask, and you will receive, that your joy may be full"* (John 16:23-24). James puts the matter of receiving what is needed this way: *"The effective, fervent prayer of a righteous man avails much"* (Jas. 5:16). When believers walk in integrity with God and are burdened over what concerns Him, God is inclined to honor their prayers for the honor of His own name: *"Now this is the confidence that we have in Him, that if we ask anything according to His will, He hears us"* (1 Jn. 5:14).

Our heavenly Father knows what we need to serve Him, and He desires to supply us with all that is necessary to do so. If it would be inappropriate for a father to give his son a stone, when bread was requested, or to give him a serpent when he asked for a fish, how much more unfitting would it be for our heavenly Father not to bestow good things to us when we ask Him (vv. 9-11)? The implication of this statement is that our Father in heaven will not withhold from us what is asked for in faith and according to His will but will freely give it.

If desiring such an effectual prayer life, James tells us how we must approach God: *"If any of you lacks wisdom, let him ask of God, who gives to all liberally and without reproach, and it will be given to him. But let him ask in faith, with no doubting"* (Jas. 1:5-6). In faith, let us keep asking, seeking, and knocking at the throne of grace!

"Therefore, whatever you want men to do to you, do also to them, for this is the Law and the Prophets" (v. 12). This axiom is often referred to as the "Golden Rule." Here, it directly follows the Lord's teaching on prayer and the opportunity to receive all good things from our heavenly Father. He desires to bountifully provide all our legitimate needs. Some have put a negative spin on the Golden Rule to infer that if someone treats you poorly, then that is how he or she desires you to treat them in return. But that type of thinking reflects the Law's "eye for an eye" mentality, not the grace that God wants His people to both experience and to exercise towards others (Jas. 1:17-28).

What should the proper conduct of believers be when treated poorly by others: *"Repay no one evil for evil"* (Rom. 12:17) and *"Do not be overcome by evil, but overcome evil with good"* (Rom. 12:21). Those infused with God's grace can rise above temporal offenses knowing that God will accomplish eternal good in every situation.

What did the Lord mean by the expression, *"for this is the Law and the Prophets?"* To do good to others even when it is not deserved fulfills the moral teaching of the Law of Moses (the Pentateuch) and the writings of the prophets (speaking of the prophetic books of the Old Testament). William MacDonald explains that this is a summary statement of God's great intention of Old Testament Scripture:

> The righteousness demanded by the OT is fulfilled in converted believers who thus walk according to the Spirit (Rom. 8:4). If this verse were universally obeyed, it would transform all areas of international relationships, national politics, family life, and church life.[28]

Souls transformed by grace desire others to be changed also. True Christianity is more than refraining from sin; it is engaging in selfless acts that demonstrate the love of God to others. Divine love has a cause-and-effect relationship; thus, what has been received is to be shared with others (John 3:16; 1 Jn. 4:19).

Two Ways and Two Destinies (vv. 13-14)

The Lord warned that the gate leading to experiencing the abundant life in Him was narrow and the way (the lifestyle) was difficult (v. 13). In contrast, the gate of living for selfish ambitions and pleasure was wide, and posed an effortless pathway leading to destruction (v. 14). The wide way is the natural course of life for all that are born with Adam's nature: *"There is a way that seems right to a man, but its end is the way of death"* (Prov. 16:25). Living for self, instead of God, results in separation of some sort – which is the meaning of death in Scripture (Rom. 3:23).

Only by being born again (entering the narrow gate) and submitting to Christ's Lordship (the difficult way) can one enjoy Christ's life and please God. While entering the narrow gate may be a metaphor tied with believing the gospel message, the main idea here is that we can only have a life pleasing to our Creator by being in and following Christ.

Fruit Reveals What Is Good and Bad (vv. 15-20)

As in the Old Testament, false prophets and teachers were a constant, ongoing threat to Israel's spiritual vitality. The Lord did not want His disciples fooled by high-sounding speech or humanized religion. Often false teachers appear in sheep's clothing (feigning to be true believers), but inwardly are ravenous wolves, desiring to devour God's people. Naive, immature, and unstable believers become easy prey for these disguised evil predators (v. 15).

The Lord's point is that the virtue of one's character validates what we believe to be true (v. 16). Like a bad tree, an unregenerate person cannot produce spiritual fruit pleasing to God; only someone that has been born again (a good tree) can bear such good fruit (vv. 17-18). As we do not know an individual's heart, we cannot judge his or her salvation, but we can be fruit inspectors. If a person's life is not consistent with sound doctrine, we are to ignore that individual's influences; he or she is not going to bring us closer to God.

With that said, it is also possible to be fooled by someone that carefully conveys themselves as a Christian in outward appearance and through service who is not, but time and hardship always reveal the truth of the matter eventually (v. 20). Continual fruit-bearing is evidence of Christ's life within a believer. If someone claims to be saved, but the life of Christ is not witnessed in his or her behavior, that individual is merely a professor of the truth, not a possessor of it and will receive God's eternal judgment (v. 19). A good tree consistently bears good fruit!

I Never Knew You (vv. 21-23)

The Lord said many will know who He is without trusting Him for salvation and making Him Lord of their lives. Many who identify with Him and do things in His name are not saved (v. 22). Clearly, it is possible for people to know a lot about the Lord and serve Him without ever being born again (v. 23). The Lord knows who are really His and who the counterfeits are. Having information about the Lord and doing ministry in His name does not necessarily equate to loving Him. Many identifying with Christ, even calling Him Lord, are not actually saved. The true test of knowing and serving the Lord is found in our desire to do God's will (v. 21).

Believing that some *higher power* exists, or even in the one true God, does not save anyone. James warns, *"You believe that there is one God. You do well. Even the demons believe – and tremble!"* (Jas. 2:19). Clearly the demons believe in God but are still condemned to the Lake of Fire because of their past rebellion against God (25:41). We must acknowledge and repent of sin and receive Christ alone as our Savior to be born again and receive eternal life in Christ. Only when we have the Holy Spirit with us will we both want to know God's will and be able to do it.

The Two Houses and Two Foundations (vv. 24-27)

This parable concluded the Lord's *Sermon on the Mount* address which occurred early in His Galilean ministry, not long after the *New Cloth and New Wineskin* parable was spoken. The purpose of this parable was to verify that true disciples obey and live by God's Word, rather than following their emotions and secular philosophies.

The Lord had just informed His audience that the way leading to destruction was wide and the way leading to life was narrow, which meant few would find it. He also had just taught them that there were true and false teachers and true and false professors. Hence, the parable of the two houses posed two types of builders, one that chose a good foundation to build a house on and the other a poor foundation.

What is the rock in the parable? True disciples must base their faith on Christ's teachings and live accordingly (v. 24). This is the stable bedrock to build one's house, or life, upon. The house (a life) built on this foundation of Scripture can weather the storms of adversity, and the battering winds of humanism (v. 25). A house built on a rock foundation is a permanent structure. The life built on Christ's teachings is an eternal abode for God to dwell in.

However, the house with a foundation on the sand will not survive such testing. The house that is built on a foundation of sand represents a life lived according to secular philosophies and the world's religion of thinking apart from Christ (v. 26). Such a structure is temporary, and the shallow footings of humanism provide no lasting stability when life's storms (hardships) pound its walls (v. 27). This represents someone living for the present, for self, by sight and is easily swayed by emotional appeals and relative thinking.

True believers must build a *fact – faith – feelings* style of belief-system to interpret the issues of life accurately and safeguard their souls against satanic attack. The *fact* of God's Word is accepted as the only foundation to build on. We then develop our *faith*, what we believe God's Word means. From our established *faith*, we are then able to judge our *feelings* properly. If we flip the building program upside down, then we will allow our feelings to determine our faith, which then will cause us to interpret God's Word erroneously. May we choose to build our lives on the solid Rock – Christ and His Word!

Response to the Sermon on the Mount (vv. 28-29)

The Sermon on the Mount was the manifesto of the King, literally the kingdom's constitution. The Lord's sermon to His Jewish countrymen conveyed an admonishing tone. Fourteen times He had said to them, *"I say unto you."* After the Lord concluded His message to the lost sheep of Israel, we read *"that the people were astonished at His teaching, for He taught them as one having authority, and not as the scribes"* (7:28-29). The Lord Jesus was the Messiah-King and He had spoken with authority because He was the One in authority!

Matthew Chapter 8

Power to Heal Leprosy (vv. 1-4)

The prophet Isaiah predicted that when the Messiah arrived in Israel, He would heal blindness, deafness, lameness, dumbness, and various diseases (Isa. 35:5-6, 53:4). Matthew continues to use fulfilled Old Testament prophecies to prove to his Jewish audience that Jesus Christ is the promised Messiah and legitimate heir to David's throne. In chapters 8-12, Matthew shows that Jesus Christ did indeed heal all types of disabilities and infirmities and had power over demonic spirits; therefore, He must be Israel's Messiah.

Despite this overwhelming evidence, Israel's religious leaders have rising animosity towards the Lord Jesus and are leading their countrymen away from their Messiah. On the other hand, there is increasing interest among Gentiles to believe in the Jewish Messiah.

Having concluded His lengthy sermon, the Lord descends the mount and is followed by a large crowd (v. 1). A leper saw Jesus Christ and came to worship Him, saying, *"Lord, if You are willing, You can make me clean"* (v. 2). The Lord then put out His hand and touched the leper and said, *"I am willing; be cleansed,"* and immediately his leprosy was gone (v. 3). The Lord then told the cleansed leper not to tell others of what had happened, but to immediately go to the temple and be inspected by the priests and offer what was required by the Law (Lev. 14). This would serve as a testimony of Himself before all the priests.

Whether the Lord did not want the cleansed leper to speak of the miracles to others, or just not to be delayed in going to the temple by doing so is unclear. However, after this instance, the Lord often instructed those He had healed or had observed a healing to keep quiet about the miracle. This was likely to avoid His premature enthronement by the Jewish populace who wanted relief from Roman rule but were yet unwilling to repent and accept the spiritual aspects of His kingdom. Miracles drew sign-seekers and the curious. The Lord was not seeking fame; rather He wanted His words to penetrate deep within the hearts of those listening to Him.

As used in reference to people, the generic term for *leprosy* in the Old Testament not only described Hansen's disease (the chronic infection), but many other skin diseases as well. This is why Leviticus 13 supplied the priests with detailed procedures for properly inspecting various infections and correctly diagnosing the disease. As there was no cure for leprosy, the priests were not acting as physicians, but rather as public health officials protecting their brethren from an epidemic crisis. Those who were diagnosed with such were forced into isolation. The provision for ceremonial cleansing in Leviticus 14 seems to indicate that natural healing did occur for some types of skin diseases, but not for the dreaded Hansen's disease.

Hansen's disease is primarily a granulomatous disease of the peripheral nerves, skin, and mucosa of the upper respiratory tract; skin lesions are the primary external sign. Left untreated, leprosy is usually a progressive disease that caused permanent damage to the skin, nerves, and eyes. The resulting numbness from nerve damage allowed dangerous secondary injuries and infections to develop. Even apart from secondary infections, left untreated the disease readily advances and causes fingers and toes to become shortened and deformed, and in some cases leads to blindness and even death.

While today there is effective treatment for Hansen's disease, there was none in biblical days, meaning that if someone contracted the disease, he or she was isolated from the Jewish society to suffer a slowly deteriorating and miserable existence. To prevent the spread of the disease, lepers normally communed together in remote colonies and were dependent on loved ones to supply their necessities. For this reason, leprosy was intensely feared and led to an understandable social paranoia. As there are twelve cases of leprosy mentioned in the New Testament, the disease was still common during Christ's earthly ministry.

The Lord Jesus showed compassion in two ways by performing this miracle. First, He was not afraid to convey love to the leper by touching him who was unclean under the Law. Not only did He have power to heal the disease, but He also showed that He could not be brought under its power. He thus remained a fit and clean sacrificial Lamb for God. Second, by sending the healed leper immediately to the priests, He was able to declare the gospel message to hard-to-reach religious leaders sequestered in the temple. Healing a blind or lame person would not accomplish this, as there was no requirement in the Law for them to be inspected and ceremonially cleansed.

There is no Old Testament record of a healed leper ever going through the ceremonial purification process as supervised by Levitical priests (Lev. 14). This meant that there was something new in Israel. Did this mean that Isaiah's prophecy had been fulfilled? Was Messiah in Israel? The Lord Jesus sent a steady stream of healed lepers to the temple over the next three years. Throughout Israel's history nothing like this had ever happened before, which meant that something better than the Law was now in Israel – the Messiah. As a result, a multitude of Jewish priests believed on Jesus Christ and were saved (Acts 6:7).

Power to Heal Paralysis (vv. 5-13)

Luke's account of this story provides a few more details than what Matthew wrote. Apparently, after hearing of the Lord Jesus' arrival at Capernaum, a Roman centurion sent Jewish elders to ask Him for assistance. The centurion had a faithful servant that was suffering from severe paralysis and was near death (vv. 5-6; Luke 7:2). This scene is ironic, as we have Jewish leaders that did not believe that Jesus was the Christ being constrained to beseech Him for Messianic power on behalf of a Gentile that they esteemed more important than Himself. The elders told the Lord that the centurion loved the Jewish people and was kind to them; he had even built them a synagogue. This was to convince the Lord that the centurion was worthy of His help.

The Lord agreed to go, but before arriving at the centurion's home the officer sent messengers to tell the Lord not to trouble Himself any further, but just say the word and his servant would be healed (vv. 7-8). The messengers then explained that as an officer in authority, the centurion commanded the affairs of his soldiers; he understood that one must be under authority to have authority (v. 9). Since the Lord Jesus had authority over diseases, the centurion knew that He was under authority and could therefore heal his servant. Furthermore, the honorable centurion did not feel that he was worthy enough for the Lord to come under his roof.

The Lord was astonished by the officer's response. The centurion possessed little truth, but enough to exercise tremendous faith, which the Lord praised (v. 10). There are only two authority structures today: God-ordained and Satanic-controlled. Remaining under God's authority enables us to exercise His authority and bless others. But those who reject His authority do not escape authority, but rather find themselves under Satan's authority, and there is only misery to be found there.

The centurion's confession caused the Lord to point out that in His kingdom, believing Gentiles would enjoy fellowship with the Jewish patriarchs. However, "the sons of the kingdom" (i.e., those who were privileged to have a Jewish heritage, but did not believe the truth revealed to them about Jesus Christ) will be cast into outer darkness (i.e., eternal judgment in Hell; vv. 13-14). The benefit of more revelation also results in more accountability if rejected (Luke 10:13-16; 12:48). The Lord honored the centurion's faith by healing his servant (v. 13).

At this point in His ministry, the Lord Jesus was seeking the lost sheep of Israel to receive Him as their Messiah; His efforts were not directed to the Gentiles. This explains why He performed only two miracles in association with Gentiles. Both healings were performed at a distance on behalf of a Gentile who had great compassion for someone else who was suffering and great faith in the Lord to resolve the issue. The Canaanite woman seeking help for her demon-possessed daughter is the other occurrence (15:21-28). The Lord was thrilled by their sincere faith and granted both their requests. A. C. Gaebelein summarizes how these Gentile healings point to dispensational truth:

> Whenever the Lord heals by touch it has reference, dispensationally, to His personal presence on the earth and His merciful dealing with Israel. When He heals by His Word, absent in person, … or if He is touched in faith, it refers to the time when He is absent from the earth, and Gentiles approaching Him in faith are healed by Him.[29]

This explains why the prophet Elisha, who prefigured Christ's ministry, also healed Naaman, the Gentile captain, of his leprosy from a distance, but healed his Jewish countrymen in person. Elijah, who called the nation of Israel to repentance, typified the ministry of John the baptizer, but Elisha was a champion of the people and engaged in personalized ministry to heal and assist his countrymen.

Power to Heal Fever (vv. 14-15)

After leaving a synagogue service, the Lord and His disciples came to Peter's home (Mark 1:21). The Savior found Peter's mother-in-law sick with fever and lying on a bed (v. 14). He touched her hand without saying a word, and her fever was immediately gone (v. 15). Not only was she no longer sick, but she was fully restored from her weakened state such that she got up from her sickbed and promptly "served them" (their houseguests). The critical text states that Peter's mother-in-law "served Him" (the Lord). When the Lord heals, He not only fixes the problem, but restores what was lost so that we can effectively serve Him. When we serve Him, others will benefit from our ministry also.

Power Over Various Diseases (vv. 16-17)

It did not take long for the word to get out where the Lord Jesus was residing. That very evening, many sick and suffering people were brought to Peter's home. Mark uses a hyperbole to describe the chaotic situation, *"the whole city was gathered together at the door"* (Mark 1:33). The Lord Jesus cast out demons and *"healed all who were sick"* (v. 16). Matthew again refers to one of Isaiah's predictions: when Messiah comes, He would take away the infirmities and sicknesses of others and would bear them Himself (v. 17). This Isaiah 53 prophecy would be completely fulfilled at Calvary, when the Savior would suffer God's chastisement for our sins and iniquities.

Resistance to Christ's Authority (vv. 18-22)

Because there was a great crowd following Him, the Lord instructed His disciples that they should leave Capernaum and cross over to the opposite shore of the Sea of Galilee (v. 18). Apparently, many wanted to follow the Lord at this time, which provided Him an opportunity to speak about what it meant to be a true disciple of His. Matthew records the Lord's dialog with two men (a scribe and another man who wanted to follow Him), while Luke identifies three men in the story (Luke 9).

The first man is enthusiastic and volunteered to follow the Lord anywhere, no matter what the cost might be (v. 19). But the Lord reminded him that He was a homeless wanderer; He did not even have a pillow to lay His head on at night (v. 20). The implication was, "Are you really ready to give up all the material comforts of life to follow me?" Apparently not, as we hear no more from him.

The second man did not volunteer (Luke 9:59), as the first man did, but rather the Lord called him to be His follower. This man was interested, but he had something he wanted to do first. Burying one's father is an important task, but certainly the Lord would have known all about it, yet He still called the man. Under the Law, anyone touching a dead person was unclean for seven days (Num. 19:11), which meant that the man was putting the Lord off for a week to bury His father. Anytime we say, "Lord, let me first," we have sinned against Him. He is never to have second place in anything.

The Lord told this man to *"Let the dead* [the spiritually lost] *bury their own dead* [their deceased], *but you go and preach the kingdom of God"* (v. 22; Luke 9:60). It was far more important to preach the gospel to the living that they might inherit eternal life, than to bury the corpse of someone whose eternal state had already been determined (Heb. 9:27).

The third man resembled the first in that he volunteered to follow the Lord (v. 21). Yet, he is like the second in that he used those same contradictory words, "Lord, let me first...." There is certainly nothing wrong with showing love to one's family by bidding them farewell, but the man permitted his family ties to supersede Christ's proper place. The Lord responded to him, *"No one, having put his hand to the plow, and looking back, is fit for the kingdom of God"* (Luke 9:62).

The Lord's illustrative response concerning the hard and focused work of plowing indicated that His disciples could not be self-centered in following Him; rather, they must remain fully focused on the tasks He gives them. Earthly comforts, jobs and important doings, and tender relationships still hinder people from following the Lord today. This is a remarkable illustration of three would-be disciples who allowed something to hinder their dedication to Christ.

Power Over the Elements (vv. 23-27)

After leaving Peter's home and having a dialogue with three men concerning the cost of discipleship, the Lord enters a boat with His disciples; they are heading southeastward across the sea to the Gergesenes (v. 23). Mark informs us that it was evening when they departed Capernaum (Mark 4:35). The Lord went to the stern of the boat and laid down on a pillow and went to sleep (v. 24; Mark 4:38). As the disciples were rowing, a violent tempest suddenly arose, which caused huge waves to beat against the boat and fill it with water.

Can you imagine the life of the Lord Jesus? Day in and day out, at any time of day or night, people were coming to him with their problems and ailments, while others were continually rejecting His message. No wonder He fell asleep in the stern of a boat and did not wake up when the boat was being tossed to and fro in a violent storm.

The frantic disciples woke the Lord and pleaded with Him to save them, for they were perishing (v. 25). The Lord rebuked His disciples, *"Why are you fearful, O you of little faith?"* (v. 26). He then stood up and rebuked the wind and the sea and there was a sudden great calm. Seeing this powerful feat, the disciples said to themselves, *"Who can this be, that even the winds and the sea obey Him?"* (v. 27). Obviously, they were still growing in their understanding of who Jesus Christ is. He is the Son of God who created all things and by Him all things consist (John 1:3; Col. 1:17).

Power Over the Demons (vv. 28-34)

The Lord Jesus often cast out demons to heal the populace of their physical and mental infirmities, and spiritual oppression. In this story, our Lord was willing to sail to the southeast shore of the Sea of Galilee with His disciples to meet one demon-possessed man in much turmoil. This was the region of the Gadarenes (or Gerasenes, or Gergesenes). The town of Gadara was about seven miles southeast of the seashore. The Lord teaches us to go the extra mile to assist those suffering affliction.

Matthew records that there were two "exceedingly fierce" demon-possessed men residing in the tombs near the shoreline (v. 28). These men were so violent that no one could safely travel through the area. Though there were two possessed men, the story centers around the one called Legion. We are not told if the other man was healed or not.

One of the possessed men immediately came out of the tombs to meet the Lord (v. 29). Luke tells us that he was naked and had been demon-possessed for a long time (Luke 8:27). He had often been shackled and chained but broke his bonds (Luke 8:29). Day and night the demoniac was screaming and cutting himself with stones (Mark 5:5). His condition was one of utter misery. After seeing the Lord, he fell down before Him and acknowledged His authority as the Son of God (v. 29). The demons speaking through the man were afraid that Christ had come early to render final judgment on them, but that was not the case. They sensed that the Lord was about to cast them out of the man, so they begged Him for permission to enter a herd of swine (about 2,000 pigs).

Notice that it is the demons that ramble on in the dialogue; the Lord spoke few words: "What is your name?" "Come out of the man." "Go."

(v. 32; Mark 5:8-9). The demons answered the Lord and yielded to His authority by coming out of the man. They then entered a large herd of swine, which ran violently off a cliff and perished in the sea (vv. 31-32). The enemy often will use the tactic of verbal fogging to avoid accountability, but it does not work with the Lord. An entire legion of demons was cast out of the man.

But why would the Lord grant the demon's request to enter the swine? Scripture is silent on this matter, but William MacDonald offers two possible reasons:

> Why should the Sovereign Lord accede to the request of demons? To understand His action, we must remember two facts. First, demons shun the disembodied state; they want to indwell human beings, or, if that is not possible, animals or other creatures. Second, the purpose of demons is without exception to destroy. If Jesus had simply cast them out of the maniacs, the demons would have been a menace to the other people of the area. By allowing them to go into the swine, He prevented their entering men and women and confined their destructive power to animals. It was not yet time for their final destruction by the Lord.[30]

Additionally, it is observed that the Law deemed swine as unclean animals. The Jews were not to touch or eat, nor offer to the Lord what was unclean (Deut. 14:8). By permitting the demons to go into the swine, which brought about their destruction, the Lord was reproving His countrymen for their disobedience of the Law. The Lord demonstrates His authority over rebel spirits and disobedient men to the glory of God.

When the townsfolk heard of what happened, they traveled to the location of the miracle and found the previously possessed man sitting, clothed, and in his right mind. This meant that the one who had accomplished this miracle was more powerful than a multitude of demons and they were afraid; they even asked the Lord to leave the region (vv. 33-34). They did not want to receive the One who had shown Himself more powerful than an entire legion of demons!

Notice that the healed man was clothed. Perhaps a disciple donated clothing, but it seems more likely that Christ crossed the sea with every provision to resolve this man's pain and shame. If we decide to help someone, let us do our best to do so and in a way that restores dignity.

Matthew Chapter 9

A Paralytic Is Healed and Forgiven (vv. 1-8)

After being rejected by those at Gergesa, the Lord returned with His disciples across the Sea of Galilee to Capernaum. This city became His home after those in His hometown of Nazareth attempted to push Him off a cliff (v. 1; Luke 4:29-31).

Mark informs us that the Lord was in a house teaching a large gathering of people when this story takes place (Mark 2:1-2). Four men brought a paralyzed man on a stretcher to the Lord to be healed but could not gain entrance to the house because of the crowd. Therefore, they carried the paralytic to the roof top, broke through the roof (perhaps removing tiles) and then lowered the man down to Christ (Mark 2:3-4). When the Lord saw the faith of the four men and that of the paralytic who desired to be lowered down to Him, despite the possibility of bodily injury, He said to the paralytic, *"Son, be of good cheer, your sins are forgiven"* (v. 2).

When the scribes heard this statement, they said within themselves, *"This Man blasphemes!"* (v. 3). Obviously, only God can forgive sins, so the Lord Jesus was claiming to be God, which infuriated these religious leaders. The Lord, overhearing their thoughts, asked them two questions. First, He asked them why they thought evil of Him for this declaration; if they truly understood who He was, then they would not think that He was blaspheming God (v. 4). Second, He asked them *"Which is easier, to say, 'Your sins are forgiven?' or to say, 'Arise and walk'?"* (v. 5). The Lord was implying that it was much easier for man to engage in religious jargon than to cause spiritual change in one's life.

As the forgiveness of sins was a spiritual matter, it could not be visually confirmed and thus was easy to say, the outcome of which could not be humanly verified. Therefore, to prove that He did have the authority to forgive sins, the Lord commanded the paralytic to *"arise, take up your bed, and go to your house"* (v. 6). If the Lord's command was obeyed, the evidence of the miracle would be evident to everyone. The paralytic was instantly healed and gained the ability to use his muscles in such a way to walk home – he did not have to struggle to do what the Lord commanded him to do (i.e., he did not have to learn to walk). Again, we see the Lord not just healing someone, but also fully equipping them to be a testimony for Him. When the multitudes saw the miracle, they marveled and glorified God, that He could work through a mere human to accomplish the spectacular (v. 8). Yet, the people were blind to the true crux of the matter: Christ was the source of the miracle. He did not pray for heaven's assistance; He was heaven's authority on earth. He thus confronted Israel's corrupt authority and then commanded the healing to occur.

This scene conveys a wonderful truth about repentance and faith. The Lord Jesus said that unless someone repents of their sins, they cannot be saved (Luke 13:3, 5). Therefore, there is the necessity of confessing sin before forgiveness is to be granted (e.g., Luke 17:3). We also know that unless someone believes on Christ as Savior, he or she cannot be saved (John 3:16-18, 5:24, 8:24). Repentance and faith swing on the same hinge of gospel truth. Repentance agrees with God on the matter of sin and turns away from what displeased God and could never earn His favor. But one must turn from sin to embrace in faith God's solution for sin, Christ. So, although the paralytic did not confess his sin before receiving forgiveness, the Lord granted him mercy on the basis of his demonstrated faith in Him.

The physical condition of the disabled man prophetically represents the spiritual condition of Israel at that time. God's covenant people were paralyzed by legalism and religiosity and needed liberation from sin through Christ to be healed. Only twice in the Gospels does the Lord explicitly say to someone, "your sins are forgiven." Here the Lord's declaration was in response to exhibited faith in Him, and in Luke 7:48 forgiveness was granted because of a woman's repentance and love for Him. Repentance of sin to the Savior, profession of faith in the Savior, and confession of love for the Savior all walk together. These provide evidence of spiritual renewal and the receipt of salvation in Christ.

The Call of Matthew (v. 9)

Matthew briefly pauses the narrative to explain how he became a disciple of Christ. One day, while he was sitting in his tax office in Capernaum, the Lord walked by and seeing Matthew said, *"Follow Me"* (v. 9). Matthew instantly obeyed the invitation and was a tax collector no more. Because tax collectors were notoriously crooked and collected more from the people than Rome required, they were hated by the Jews. Matthew (also called Levi) left a lucrative and hated occupation to become a poor but loved disciple of Christ, who wrote this Gospel for us to appreciate.

Eating With Tax Collectors and Sinners (vv. 10-13)

After being called to be a disciple, Matthew (Levi) hosted a large gathering in his own home in or near Capernaum so that others, including tax collectors, could hear Christ's teachings (v. 10; Luke 5:29). The sight of Christ eating a meal with tax collectors and sinners infuriated the Pharisees who asked His disciples why He did so (v. 11). When the Lord heard their indictment, He said, *"Those who are well have no need of a physician, but those who are sick"* (v. 12). The Lord had come to help spiritually sick people find healing (salvation in Himself). He was not rubbing shoulders with sinners for social camaraderie. Although the Pharisees did not have the courage to address Jesus directly, it did not stop Him from admonishing them. Brown, Fausset, and Jamieson write:

> They that be whole need not a physician, but they that are sick. "You deem yourselves whole; My mission, therefore, is not to you: The physician's business is with the sick; therefore, eat I with publicans and sinners." ... But go ye and learn what that means (Hos. 6:6), I will have mercy, and not sacrifice – that is, the one rather than the other. "Sacrifice," the chief part of the ceremonial law, is here put for a religion of literal adherence to mere rules; while "Mercy" expresses such compassion for the fallen as seeks to lift them up. The duty of keeping aloof from the polluted, in the sense of "having no fellowship with the unfruitful works of darkness," is obvious enough; but to understand this as prohibiting such interaction with them as is necessary to their recovery is to abuse it. This was what these Pharisaical religionists did, and this is what our Lord here exposes, "For I am not come to call the righteous, but sinners to repentance."[31]

Self-righteous sinners like the Pharisees did not want what the Lord was offering them, so He did not waste time with those who were not interested in receiving His offer of salvation. This is why the Lord told the Pharisees, *"But go and learn what this means: 'I desire mercy and not sacrifice.' For I did not come to call the righteous, but sinners, to repentance"* (v. 13). This quotation from Hosea 6:6 was to declare that

God did not want heartless, ritualistic worship from those who called upon Him, but rather inward humility, righteousness, and holiness. The Pharisees looked good outwardly, but inwardly, they were as lost as the tax collectors, yet they were in a more dangerous condition, for they were oblivious to their condemnation.

The Pharisees believed that they were spiritually well and righteous before God, therefore, they did not need to repent and be saved by Jesus Christ. However, the outcasts of society, like the tax collectors, were not self-righteous and more willing to acknowledge the true condition of their souls and seek God's forgiveness through Christ. The fact is, wherever the Lord went, He associated with sinners, for He came to seek and save the lost.

The Disciples Do Not Fast (vv. 14-17)

John the baptizer was likely in prison when John's disciples came to the Lord Jesus with a question about fasting (v. 14). Apparently, they were fasting often, as were the Pharisees, but they had noticed that the Lord's disciples were not fasting. The Lord affirmed that His disciples were not given to fasting because the bridegroom (Himself) was still with them, but soon He would not be – then they would regularly fast (v. 15). His answer indicated that a new dispensation was coming.

A dispensation in Scripture is not an era of time, per se, but rather an economy of truth that God reveals to man and holds him accountable to obey. Dispensations do have their outworking in time and may overlap to some extent. For example, the dispensation of human government established in Genesis 9 was concurrent with the dispensation of the Law instituted with Israel at Mount Sinai and is still in effect during the present dispensation of grace (i.e., the Church Age).

The Lord cited two examples (these were likely His first spoken parables), a new cloth on an old garment and new wine in an old wineskin, to show that the purposes of the dispensations of the Law and of Grace were quite different (vv. 16-17). The Law of Moses was rigid in that, if broken, it did not offer mercy, only condemnation. Accordingly, Paul explains that the purpose of the Law was to show sin (Rom. 3:20) and point guilty sinners to the solution – Christ (Gal. 3:24). The Law only brought condemnation, as no one could keep all of its precepts. But grace through Christ was offered to those who realized that they had fallen short of God's righteousness and needed to be justified by Him to be acceptable before Him (1 Tim. 2:3-6). Grace is receiving the unmerited favor of God.

In summary, lost souls may approach God through law-keeping (i.e., by self-justification) and be found wanting, or by humbly acknowledging their sinful state and receiving redemption and justification through Christ by grace. Consequently, the purpose of both parables was to show that one can choose to live by the Law or by grace, but not both; the two systems cannot be mixed. The purpose of the first was to show the necessity of the second for salvation.

Both parables illustrate this point. A piece of new cloth (unshrunk material) is a poor patch for an old garment, for after it becomes wet and dries, it will shrink and pull away from the old cloth. The latter situation creates a worse outcome than the original problem. Likewise, those trying to mix efforts of self-reformation with God's work of grace will become more resistant to the truth of the gospel message, which has its basis in grace alone.

For the same reason, putting new wine in an old wineskin (which has no elasticity) will result in a bad outcome. As the new wine ferments, it will expand and burst the old wineskin, making it unusable. It would have been better to hold to the law alone than to try to mix Law-keeping with God's grace for salvation. Grace plus a nickel is not grace!

The Law was stringent and rigid; its purpose was to condemn, not to save. The Law was designed to highlight man's lost state before God and show his need for God's Savior. Because Christ was born under the Law and completely kept the Law, He was proven to be an acceptable sacrifice on the account of the guilty (i.e., everyone). By the process of substitution, then, God was able to righteously judge human sin and offer forgiveness and acceptance through Christ. This means that those who resort to Law-keeping to earn God's favor instead of believing in Christ's redemptive work alone are telling God, "Your Son did not do enough to save me; you need my help too." This is an offensive notion to God.

Besides the clear meaning of the parables, there is an application that Christians today do well to heed. It is our tendency to want to surround ourselves with pious ornaments to feel like we have had a religious experience. Christendom often pulls in elements and terminology from the Old Testament economy (the Mosaic Law) to create a religious ambiance during church gatherings. Speaking of the church building as "the house of God," for example, is incorrect. The Christian's sanctuary is in heaven now, not the auditorium of an earthly building. In the Old

Testament, the temple was the house of God, but in the New Testament the house of God is a spiritual building called the Church – God dwells in His people, not just with them, as in the Old Testament (1 Tim. 3:5). This means that all believers are able priests now to worship God at any time (1 Pet. 2:5), whereas the Levitical economy permitted only the sons of Aaron before the Lord at certain times.

Accordingly, the use of special robes, lamps/candles, incense, and altars do not belong in the *Dispensation of Grace*. These former religious relics tend to distort our focus of Christ's centrality in our gatherings. This is why the Lord instituted something new, the Lord's Supper, with the emblems of bread and wine, to remind us of Him and His sacrifice for us. Let us be careful of mixing any elements of the Law with all that God wants us to appreciate in grace!

Christ Has Power Over Hemorrhaging and Death (vv. 18-26)

Matthew records that a certain ruler fell down before the Lord and worshipped Him, saying, *"My daughter has just died, but come and lay Your hand on her and she will live"* (v. 18). Mark and Luke tell us his name, Jairus, and that he was a ruler of the synagogue (Mark 5:22; Luke 8:41). Apparently, his daughter was in a coma and near death when Jairus departed to petition Jesus Christ for help (Luke 8:42). In his initial conversation with the Lord, Jairus may have presumed that his daughter was likely deceased by that time. Regardless, the Lord agreed to help, but both navigating through the crowd and the healing of the woman with the issue of blood caused a delay. After the woman was healed, a servant of Jairus arrived to inform him that his daughter had died and that there was no need to trouble "the Teacher" (Luke 8:49). Apparently, all attempts to revive her had failed and she was now past any hope of resuscitation.

Matthew condenses the dialogue between the Lord and Jairus, while Luke provides more information. The Lord consoled the grieving father, *"Do not be afraid; only believe, and she will be made well"* (Luke 8:50). Matthew records Jairus' declaration of faith in verse 18. This was an incredible statement, as the last resurrection of the dead had not occurred since the days of the prophet Elisha, more than eight centuries previous. The Lord and His disciples then accompanied Jairus to his home (v. 19).

While en route, a woman who had an ongoing flow of blood for twelve years touched the hem of the Lord's garment to be made well and she was (vv. 20-21). Mark and Luke record more dialogue pertaining to this situation than Matthew. Luke, the physician, mentions that this woman had spent all her livelihood on physicians, but no one could cure her hemorrhaging, which Mark states was worsening (Mark 5:26; Luke 8:43). That is, until she came to the Great Physician.

The Lord, knowing that power had come out of Him to accomplish the miracle, did not want the matter of the woman's faith and healing to be a secret, so He asked, *"Who touched Me?"* (Luke 8:45-46). Of course, the disciples did not understand the Lord's question as they were trying to pass through a large crowd of people as they followed Jairus. But the woman did, and she came trembling and fell down at the Lord's feet and publicly confessed to what she had done and why (Luke 8:47). The Lord responded, *"Be of good cheer, daughter, your faith has made you well"* (v. 22). Interestingly, "has made" and "well" in this statement are derived from the same Greek verb *sozo* in the perfect tense. *Sozo* is usually rendered "save" in the New Testament. Literally, then, the woman's faith "saved her safe" forever. When Christ heals or saves, a permanent state of physical or spiritual wellness is always received.

True faith is always appreciated by the Lord. Because He chose to handle the situation in this manner, the woman who had been perpetually deemed *unclean* by the Law for years would now be able to resume normal life in Jewish society, for she had been healed and declared "well" by Jesus Christ. This is what Christ came to do – make those declared unclean by Law clean before God by grace through faith.

Sometime later, the Lord arrived at Jairus' home, which was crowded with wailing people and hired flute players (v. 23). The Lord said to them, *"Why make this commotion and weep? The child is not dead, but sleeping"* (v. 24; Mark 5:39). It seems likely that the Lord knew the outcome of what He was about to do and did not want the fame of it to be publicized, so He poetically describes her as merely "sleeping" rather than being permanently or irrevocably dead. Paul also speaks of those who have died in Christ and are awaiting resurrection as being poetically "asleep" (e.g., 1 Thess. 4:13). Luke, the beloved physician, states the clinical facts of the situation, *"They ridiculed Him, knowing that she was dead"* (Luke 8:53).

The Lord responded to their mockery by putting them all out of the house, especially the noisy professional mourners (v. 25; Mark 5:40). The Lord only permitted the girl's parents, and Peter, James, and John to accompany Him to where the dead girl was lying (Luke 8:51). The Lord took the child's hand and said, *"Little girl, I say to you, arise"* (Mark 5:41).

To everyone's amazement, the girl (being about twelve years of age) immediately arose and walked (v. 25; Mark 5:42). The Lord not only resolved the problem (death) but He did so in such a way that the girl was not living in a reduced condition, for she could walk about and digest food normally. This is the first recorded resurrection in the New Testament and the fourth in the whole of Scripture. The Lord charged those who had observed the miracle to keep it secret and that her parents should give their daughter something to eat. However, Matthew notes that the report of the miracle spread throughout the region (v. 26).

Christ Has Power to Heal Blindness (vv. 27-31)

As the Lord departed Jairus' home, two blind men followed him pleading for their sight (v. 27). They addressed Him as the "Son of David," which was to say that they believed He was the long-awaited Messiah and heir to David's throne. This being the case, they also knew that Isaiah prophesied that the coming Messiah would heal the blind (Isa. 35:5). Therefore, desiring to be healed, they were coming to Israel's Messiah and claiming God's Word in faith.

Before performing the miracle, the Lord tested their faith. He asked them if they believed that He could cure their blindness, and they both answered, "Yes, Lord" (v. 28). By saying *Lord*, instead of *Jesus* or *Teacher*, the blind men were recognizing Christ's authority over them.

The Lord responded to their faith by touching their eyes and healing their blindness (v. 29). Immediately, their sight was normal (v. 30). He charged them to keep the matter quiet, but after they departed *"they spread the news about Him in all that country"* (v. 31). The Lord often instructed those He had healed or had observed a healing to keep quiet about the miracle. It seems likely that this was to avoid being prematurely enthroned by the Jewish populace wanting relief from Roman rule, rather than accepting in faith the spiritual aspects of His kingdom, such as repentance.

This miracle of restoring a blind man's sight at Capernaum should not be confused with similar miracles in which the Lord healed blind men. A blind man was healed in Bethsaida shortly after the feeding of the 4,000, but before the Lord's transfiguration on a mountain in Galilee (Mark 8:22-26). Luke states that a blind man was healed near Jericho in the final days of the Lord's earthly ministry (Luke 18:35-43). This may be the same miracle that Mark describes (the healing of Bartimaeus; Mark 10:46-53). Then, as the Lord was departing Jericho, He restored the sight of two blind men (it is possible that Bartimaeus was one of these men; 20:30-34).

Christ Has Power to Heal Muteness (vv. 32-34)

Someone was concerned enough about a demon-possessed man who had been stricken with dumbness to bring him to the Lord Jesus (v. 32). The demon was cast out and the mute man spoke (v. 33). The multitude who had witnessed the miracle marveled, and said, *"It was never seen like this in Israel"* (v. 33). But the Pharisees accused the Lord of casting *"out demons, by the ruler of demons"* (v. 34).

William MacDonald suggests the following application after observing the order of the last three miracles performed by Christ:

> First Jesus gave life to the dead; then sight to the blind; now speech to the dumb. There seems to be a spiritual sequence in the miracles here – life first, then understanding, and then testimony.[32]

The Need for Laborers for the Harvest (vv. 35-38)

The Lord spent about two years with His disciples preaching the kingdom message to the lost sheep of Israel in Galilee. Capernaum became His central base of operation during this time. During this era, the Lord demonstrated His compassion for His fellow countrymen by not only sharing His message but healing them of their infirmities and disabilities (v. 35). The Lord could not casually stroll by those in need and not be prompted to act. Oh, that all believers would have such a burden for the spiritual welfare of those lost in trespasses and sins.

While looking over the masses that were wandering aimlessly without a shepherd, the Lord told His disciples that there was a great harvest of souls that needed to be reaped and gathered into God's barn, but there were few willing to labor with God to do it (vv. 36-37). With this incredible need identified, He instructed His disciples to pray that *"the Lord of the harvest would send out laborers into His Harvest"* (v. 38). We will learn in the next chapter how the Lord answered His disciples' prayers for more harvesters.

Matthew Chapter 10

The Twelve Are Sent Into the Fields of Galilee (vv. 1-4)

In the previous chapter, we read of the Lord's compassion over the multitudes, *"because they were weary and scattered, like sheep having no shepherd"* (9:36). J. G. Bellett describes the anguish of our Lord at this juncture over the spiritual plight of His countrymen:

> This was the assessment of the Great Shepherd although there was much *religion*. Sects were numerous; feast-days were kept; and there was a great stir in all that which might have marked a day of public religious decency and devotion. That generation were soon to bear witness to themselves that they would not go into the judgment-hall of the Gentiles, lest they should be defiled, and be thereby hindered from keeping the Passover. The money that was soon to purchase the blood of a guiltless Man they would not put into the treasury. Excision from the synagogue was dreaded, and Moses was boasted in; the Gentile was despised likewise, and the Samaritan was shunned. Ceremonial cleanness would be preserved. Teachers abounded, and zeal. And yet, under the eye of Him who saw them as God saw them, Israel was without a shepherd, an unkept, unfed flock. The land was as a field which needed the tillage of spring. It was no *reaping* time then, as it ought to have been, where all this religiousness was, and when the Heir of the vineyard had come. In the thoughts of the Lord of the harvest it was rather a time for "the first works" to be done over again, a *sowing* time; and the servants had to be sent into the field with the plough and the seed, and not with the sickle.[33]

Moved with compassion over the field of Israel that must be plowed and seeded to restore fruitfulness to God, the Lord instructed His disciples to pray that *"the Lord of the harvest would send out laborers into His Harvest"* (9:38). Now we read of how the Lord answered His disciples' prayers for more laborers in the fields of harvest: *"And when He had called His twelve disciples to Him, He gave them power over unclean spirits, to cast them out, and to heal all kinds of sickness and all kinds of disease"* (v. 1).

This verse reveals two important truths for us to consider: First, the Lord Jesus is the Lord of the harvest, for He is the one sending and equipping laborers for the work of harvesting souls.

Second, that prayer was used to both burden and prepare the disciples to answer the call for needed laborers. They, themselves, were the answer to their own prayers concerning the need for laborers. This shows the transforming power of prayer and that we should be willing to pray for the needs we are aware of without presupposing what God's solution might be. We just might be God's answer to our own prayers.

The Lord not only commissioned His disciples to preach the Kingdom message in Galilee, but also gave them authority over unclean spirits and all kinds of ailments also. Whenever the Lord places responsibility, He also fully equips His servants to accomplish all that He desires them to do. Warren Wiersbe describes what was to be accomplished by the authority the disciples had received from the Lord:

> These Apostles were given special power and authority from Christ to perform miracles. These miracles were a part of their "official credentials" (Acts 2:43; 5:12; Heb. 2:1–4). They healed the sick (and note that this included *all* kinds of diseases), cleansed the lepers, cast out demons, and even raised the dead. These four ministries paralleled the miracles that Jesus performed in Matthew 8 and 9. In a definite way, the Apostles represented the King and extended His work.[34]

Although the Lord has not given His servants today the same specialized ministry and authority of the twelve, He has given each believer a calling and spiritual gift(s) to accomplish it (Eph. 4:11-12). All believers are to be Christ's witnesses in the world (Acts 1:8).

Matthew lists the names of the twelve that were sent out (vv. 2-4). Although it was Andrew who first introduced his brother Peter to the Lord, the inner circle of disciples closest to the Lord later became Peter, James, and John (the latter two were also brothers). James was the first of the twelve to be martyred in the Church Age (killed by Herod Aggripa I; Acts 12:2). John was the "beloved" disciple and the one to whom the Lord entrusted the care of His mother (John 19:26). All four men were fishermen by trade before following Christ.

Philip was from Bethsaida and introduced Nathanael (or Bartholomew), the man without guile, to the Lord (John 1:47). Thomas had doubts about Christ's resurrection later, but also declared Christ as "Lord and God" (John 20:28). Matthew, the author of this book, was a former tax collector and likely the wealthiest of the disciples initially. Not much is known about James, the less, the son of Alphaeus, or Lebbaeus, whose surname was Thaddaeus (also called Judas), the son of James (Luke 6:16). Simon, the Canaanite, had been a Jewish Zealot that opposed Roman rule (Luke 6:15). Judas Iscariot betrayed the Lord.

The Commissioned Disciples Receive Instruction (vv. 5-42)

The disciples had been uniquely equipped by the Lord to be His workers in the harvest. Believers today should not think that they have been given the same credentials or calling that were bestowed on the twelve at this juncture. Their equipping for the work was unique, their task was to preach the kingdom gospel, and to a specific audience, the lost sheep of Israel in Galilee (vv. 5-7). To accomplish this task, Christ gave His disciples power to heal diseases and cast out demons (v. 8).

The Lord told His disciples that their ministry was to be free of charge and that they were to depend on the Lord for their support (v. 9-10). This would demonstrate that the nature of the kingdom message itself was founded in grace and not the Law. Isaiah foretold the nature of Messiah's message centuries earlier: *"Everyone who thirsts, come to the waters; and you who have no money, come, buy and eat. Yes, come, buy wine and milk without money and without price"* (Isa. 55:1). While it is true that God does supply the physical needs of those who trust in Him, the primary focus of this invitation is the spiritual satisfaction of individuals in the Jewish nation. Why spend money on bread which cannot satisfy one's true need? It would be wise to receive from God that which abundantly delights the soul forever.

God promises to satisfy our spirit's deepest need without any human compensation (i.e., no one can buy or earn His forgiveness through payment or doing "good works"). For this reason, the disciples were to freely receive from those responding to their no-cost message (vv. 11-13). They were not to worry about where their next meal would come from. Neither were they to hoard funds and store up provisions for their journey; these would only encumber them in performing the task that they had been assigned. Storing up what might be needed would also hinder them from seeing God's hand in providing for their daily needs.

The disciples were to go forth into the harvest being completely dependent on the Lord to direct their way, to empower their ministry, and to provide whatever they needed in shelter, clothing, and food. If a town or city rejected their message, they were to depart that place, shake off the dust from their sandals, and go to the next town. The act of shaking off the dust from one's sandal was to visibly indicate that the recipients of the gospel had rejected Christ and therefore would not receive His peace, but rather His wrath in the day of judgment (vv. 14-15). Thus, the apostles were leaving the house remaining under judgment (including its dust), as it had been when they entered it (e.g., Acts 13:51).

The Lord understood the dangers of the mission field and warned His disciples that He was sending them like sheep into a pack of wolves (v. 16). Therefore, they were to *"be wise as serpents and harmless as doves"* in the ministry and expect to suffer hardship, including being arrested and beaten by Jewish leaders (v. 17). While the disciples apparently did not suffer during their first apostolic ministry, the Lord's words would come true during the Church Age. Regardless of their reception, the disciples would learn of Christ's sufficiency in all matters of life as they shared His message of life with others. We too learn of Christ as we go!

The Lord told His disciples they would have the opportunity to testify of His name before kings (v. 18). When a believer chooses to obey God's calling for his or her life, God will equip and enable that individual to successfully answer every difficulty associated with fulfilling that call. The disciples did not need to worry about what to say or how to say it; the Holy Spirit would enable them to speak the truth that God wanted them to convey (v. 19-20).

The Lord told His disciples that their message would cause great social division, such that even family members would betray each other because of it (v. 21, 34-36). He warned them that they would be hated for identifying with Him (v. 22). If suffering rejection and persecution in one city, they were to flee to the next, but to keep preaching. All cities must hear the good news message, and evidence of possessing the truth is faithfulness to the Lord until He calls His servants home (v. 23). The Lord's command will be ultimately fulfilled during the Tribulation Period, when 144,000 Jewish evangelists will be preaching the Kingdom message again throughout the world (24:14; Rev. 7:1-8).

Hudson Taylor, a pioneer missionary into China in the mid-nineteenth century, had two important sayings on the matter of spiritual resources in God's work. First, "God always gives his very best to those who leave the choice with him."[35] Second, quoting the missionary Anthony Norris Groves, Taylor said, "When God's work is done in

God's way for God's glory, it will not lack for God's supply."[36] This is especially true in times of ministry crisis.

Later in his ministry, Taylor noted that every time there had been a wonderful expansion of the missionary work in China, it had been preceded by a time of deep trial. This had required the missionaries to cast themselves on the Lord afresh and to look to Him alone for the Lord's help. The Lord enables His people both to suffer for Him and to serve Him, that is, if they will remain faithful to Him. Faith forged in fiery trials is made stronger than it was before.

When a ministry is a true work of God and its minister is truly doing the work of God, there will be no lack of God's enablement for both (vv. 27-33). The believer must be faithful to his or her calling and must learn to trust the Lord for wisdom and grace in every situation. Faith that is not tested will not be trusted; trials, therefore, become a necessary part of any ministry. The good news is that because believers are one in Christ, everything that comes into our lives also comes into His, and He is able to rise above every perceived obstacle and hardship. Accordingly, believers are only to fear the Lord and not those opposing His message, nor are they to fret about the necessities of life while doing God's will – He will not neglect His servants.

Thus, the Lord challenged His disciples, *"Do not fear those who kill the body but cannot kill the soul. But rather fear Him who is able to destroy both soul and body in hell"* (v. 28). The worst thing the enemy can do to a believer, if permitted by God, is to kill the body and release his or her soul to be with the Lord in heaven (2 Cor. 5:8). So physical death should not be feared, unless the individual dies without Christ. Then God will raise that person up in judgment and he or she will experience utter ruin and uselessness of the body and soul in hell forever. The meaning of the Greek word *apollymi* rendered "destroy" means to perish with complete ruin and uselessness. F. B. Hole further notes that verse 28 affirms the immortality of the human soul:

> Verse 28 ... teaches that the soul is not subject to death, as is the body. God can destroy both soul and body in hell; but the word for "destroy" is different from the word for "kill," and is one meaning to cause to perish, or to ruin, and has in it no thought of annihilation. The exact words, "the immortality of the soul," do not occur in Scripture, but here are words of our Lord which assert that fact.[37]

In the next chapter, the Lord invited all those who wanted to follow Him to take His yoke to learn of Him (11:28-30). The main objective of discipleship is to learn Christ, completely identify with Him, and to become like Him (vv. 24-25). This is accomplished by yielding to His yoke (His Lordship). True disciples of Christ never gain disciples to themselves – they point others to Christ. As Amos Alcott has said, "The true teacher defends his pupils against his own personal influence."[38]

Mentoring those younger in the faith is not a process of making clones of oneself; rather, it is a ministry that selflessly encourages others to forsake all and follow after the Lord Jesus Christ. The Greek word for "disciple" is *mathetes*, which literally means "a learner." The pursuit of the disciple is to learn Christ and to be like Him. Guilt trips and accountability may work for a short time, but only love for Christ will propel the new believer onward in growth and service.

The Lord Jesus tells His disciples the type of devotion He expects from those who follow Him: *"He who loves father or mother more than Me is not worthy of Me. And he who loves son or daughter more than Me is not worthy of Me"* (v. 37). The Lord must have the first place in a believer's heart for him or her to gain a life worth living (v. 39). This was not a new concept to the Jewish mind, for Moses had declared the same truth long ago to his countrymen (Deut. 13:6-8).

Luke records the parallel account of the Lord's statement in a slightly different way: *"If anyone comes to Me and does not hate his father and mother, wife and children, brothers and sisters, yes, and his own life also, he cannot be My disciple"* (Luke 14:26). By comparing the narratives of Matthew and Luke, we understand that the word for "hate" expresses a comparison: our love for the Lord should be so great that any natural affection would, comparatively, seem like hate.

The Lord was wary of shallow followers; He wanted true disciples. He desired quality in consecration, not a large quantity of half-hearted patriots. Those who identified with Him and would not turn away from Him would be confessed by Him before His Father in heaven – faithfulness proves loyalty and will be rewarded (vv. 32-33).

When it comes to misplaced affection and devotion, there is no middle ground with the Lord. The Lord expects our love for Him to be so astounding that by comparison our affections for anyone else would seem like hate! To love anyone or anything more than the Lord is a form of idolatry and proves we are not worthy of Him. God desires His people to be totally committed to Him and to love Him above all else.

Commitment is being given over to a cause without reservation, even if death is required. This means that we are willing to set aside our personal agendas and our own expectations to live for Christ and gain a life that has value to God. It is only by losing ourselves for the cause of Christ that we find a life worth living. The subject matter of this chapter is discipleship, not sonship! The believer's sonship is guaranteed in Christ, but discipleship is achieved by learning and yielding to Christ.

True discipleship requires each believer to settle the death question, as the Lord forced Peter to do in John 21: "Do I love the Lord enough to be willing to live for Him no matter the personal cost?" Only by answering "yes" to this question will a believer have the unwavering obedience and devotion that the Lord demands of us. The cross is a symbol of shame and of death, but we gladly take up our cross for the Lord, because He bore His cross to save our souls from hell (v. 38).

If a commission by an earthly king is considered an honor, how can a commission by a Heavenly King be considered a sacrifice?

– David Livingstone

As the disciples went from town to town with the Kingdom message, some would graciously receive them because they recognized that the disciples were representing the Messiah (v. 40). Because they were relying on the Lord to supply their needs, the disciples would have limited ability to return such kindness, but they were not to fret; the Lord would reward those who showed them hospitality.

By receiving them, their hosts were receiving Him and He would reward them for doing so: *"He who receives a prophet in the name of a prophet shall receive a prophet's reward"* (v. 41). Israel's kings and priests were esteemed for their distinct roles, but as prophets were divinely sent to instruct both kings and priests, and often perished for doing so, the people viewed their heavenly reward as being greater.

Those recognizing that the disciples were righteous men representing the Lord, would be rewarded for receiving them as such (v. 42). Therefore, those showing kindness to the Lord's servants were demonstrating kindness to the Lord and He would remember such deeds. This is a good reminder that the way we treat the lowliest believer in the Body of Christ shows our overall esteem for the Lord Jesus (25:40). May we not be respecters of persons but receive everyone justified in Christ as "a righteous man."

Matthew Chapter 11

John the Baptizer Is Imprisoned (vv. 1-15)

After commissioning and sending out the twelve disciples to preach the Kingdom Gospel message throughout Galilee, the Lord Jesus returned to teach and preach in the cities of that region where the disciples had previously lived (v. 1).

Herod had put John the baptizer in prison. Being somewhat discouraged in this harsh and lonely situation, John sent two of his disciples to ask Jesus if he was the One (i.e., the Jewish Messiah) that the prophets had foretold of or if they should be looking for another (vv. 2-3). Matthew frequently mentions the number two in his record to align with the Law's requirement of at least two witnesses to validate the truth.

The Lord affirms to these witnesses that He is the prophesied Messiah, by noting that he was performing the types of miracles that Isaiah had previously foretold (vv. 4-5): the blind see, the deaf hear, and the lame walk (Isa. 35:5-6), and lepers had been cleansed (Isa. 53:4). Having performed these predicted miracles, the Lord Jesus had proved that He was Messiah. He had even gone beyond these prophesied feats to raise the dead. The Lord told John's disciples to inform John that the gospel message was being preached throughout the land; even the poor (Isa. 61:1), who were often neglected, were hearing and receiving the good news message.

The Lord's preaching and signs composed the kingdom message to the Jews; Arthur Pink explains:

> Our Lord's miracles of healing were not simply exhibitions of power, or manifestations of mercy, but they were also a supplement to His preaching and teaching, and their prime value was *evidential*. These miracles, which are frequently termed "signs," formed an essential part of Messiah's credentials. This is established, unequivocally, by what we read of in Matthew 11. When John the Baptist was cast into prison, his faith as to the Messiahship of Jesus wavered, and so he sent two of His disciples unto Him, asking, *"Art thou He that should come or do we look for another?"* (Matt. 11:3). Notice, carefully, the Lord's reply,

"Go and show John again those things which ye do <u>hear and see</u>: The blind receive their sight, and the lame walk, the lepers are cleansed, and the deaf hear, the dead are raised up, and the poor have the Gospel preached to them" (Matt. 11:4-5). Appeal was made to two things: His teaching and His miracles of healing. ... Miracles of healing, then, were integrally connected with the kingdom testimony. They are among the most important of "The *Signs* of the times" concerning which the Messiah reproached the Pharisees and Sadducees for their failure to discern (e.g., Matt. 16:1-3). Similar miracles of healing shall be repeated when the Messiah returns to the earth (Isa. 35:4-6).[39]

Lastly, the Lord told John's disciples, *"And blessed is he who is not offended because of Me"* (v. 6). The Lord's lowly, servant style of leadership was out of step with the self-exalting character of civil rulers and the self-promoting disposition of the religious leaders. The Lord's methods and demeanor would stand in sharp contrast to any kind of leadership that the people were accustomed to at that time. He was not operating in the flesh, but in the power and the character of God. Christ served others; He did not come to be served. No doubt John and other Jews were looking forward to being liberated from all Gentile oppression by the promised Messiah as prophesied, but that would not be accomplished until Christ's second advent to the earth.

After John's disciples departed to deliver Christ's message to John, the Lord turned to the multitude and affirmed glowing praise for John. He reminded the crowd that when they had previously ventured out to the wilderness to hear John's message, they observed a man fully controlled by the power of God. He was not some bent papyrus reed that had no strength to stand firm against the winds of adversity, speaking of religious opposition and vacillating human opinions (v. 7). Even John's simple diet and modest attire were a rebuke against the luxurious and materialistic disposition of the Jewish leaders. John lived the message that He preached while those who were to lead and to serve God's covenant people served themselves (v. 8).

Had the Jews gone to the wilderness to see a prophet (v. 9)? Indeed, John was a prophet, and in fact the greatest of the prophets because He was Christ's chosen forerunner as prophesied in Isaiah 40. It was not that John was greater in character or eloquence than those preaching before him, but his task of being the Messiah-King's herald was greater in grandeur than the assigned duties of previous prophets (v. 10).

The Lord's next statement proves that He was speaking of John's honor to a specific service rather than his personal character, *"He who is least in the kingdom of heaven is greater than he* [John]*"* (v. 11). To be a citizen of Christ's kingdom, positionally speaking, is a greater privilege than just being the one who announced that the kingdom was coming.

Yet, the Lord acknowledged that since the announcement of the coming kingdom by John, there had been intense opposition against it – *"the kingdom of heaven suffers violence"* (v. 12). Additionally, the Lord said that "the violent" want to seize the kingdom by force. This likens the kingdom to a besieged city in which outsiders are trying to force their way into it, by personal effort based on incorrect ideologies, instead of through repentance and experiencing spiritual revival. But no one can enter Christ's kingdom through personal effort – the truth must be known and believed. Consequently, because Israel was expecting a different kind of kingdom, the Jews had largely rejected their Messiah-King.

The Lord Jesus confirmed that "all the prophets and the Law" foretold of the coming kingdom, but when John arrived to announce that Christ had arrived, Israel rejected Him and His literal offer of an earthly, political kingdom (v. 13). The prophet Elijah labored to call the hearts of his idolatrous countrymen back to Jehovah, but the people rejected his ministry. If Israel would have received John's message, who was preaching in the spirit and power of Elijah (Mal. 4:5-6), then Elijah's ministry would have finally been fulfilled, but it was not to be (v. 14).

The Lord then said, *"He who has ears to hear, let him hear!"* (v. 15), the idea being "you should receive this as true." The Lord Jesus uses this expression fifteen times, seven times during His earthly ministry and eight more times after His glorification and exaltation. The expression was never used by a mere mortal man, but by Him who speaks with divine authority and power. The expression is used in verse 15 to warn His audience not to repeat the sin of disbelief that had plagued Israel in Elijah's day. If John fulfilled Malachi's prophecy of being Christ's forerunner, then Jesus must be the foretold Messiah. Accepting John's ministry meant that Jesus was Christ, the Son of God, and accepting Him also meant that one believed that John was His forerunner.

The Rejection of This Generation (vv. 16-19)

While the Pharisees held the respect of the people, they did not have God's favor. They were self-exalting and self-focused; they measured the spirituality of others by their own standards of religiosity. The Lord told this parable to rebuke those of "this generation" who were of this spiritual disposition. Hence, He is mainly speaking to the Pharisees and scribes, who were supposed to be the spiritual leaders of the people (Luke 7:30).

The Lord likened the Pharisees to children in the street dancing to their own piped songs (vv. 16-17). William MacDonald writes:

> They didn't want to play either wedding or funeral. They were perverse, wayward, unpredictable, and refractory. No matter what ministry God used among them, they took exception to it.[40]

Anyone who did not join their religious escapades was rejected by them. For example, John the baptizer lived a simple existence in the wilderness while he fulfilled his ministry (v. 18). Additionally, the Pharisees accused the Lord of extravagant living because He ate and drank with those He came to save (v. 19). Neither John's near impoverished lifestyle in the wilderness while calling sinners to repentance nor the Lord's compassionate efforts to awaken the wealthy of their spiritual need had their approval.

Religious moralizers will attack those faithfully declaring God's Word in whatever way they can to avoid considering what God wants them to hear. The Old Testament prophets repeatedly suffered this type of abuse and at times were imprisoned or put to death to suppress their preaching. Clearly, those who live for the Lord will never be able to please the Pharisaical mentality. Whether today or in Christ's day, Pharisees only dance to their own music! Israel's leaders had lulled themselves into a self-absorbed sway and willful complacency of the things important to God, especially the care of His people.

Thankfully, the Lord Jesus was not distracted by their criticism or by their rejection of His message. Rather, He ignored their opposition and kept to the work that God gave Him to do. When faced with pharisaical pride, this is a good example for us to follow also. If you are faithfully serving the Lord in your divine calling, you will be criticized; so, expect it. Benefit from what is profitable, and forget what is not, but keep serving the Lord regardless. If the devil can get us defending ourselves against unjust criticism – he gains the victory over us. Satan gains a victory when he pulls us out of God's work into his own wicked agenda!

Woe to the Unrepentant (vv. 20-24)

How is it possible for the Lord to be more tolerant of wicked cities such as Tyre, Sidon, and Sodom in the day of judgment than the Jewish cities such as Chorazin, Bethsaida, and Capernaum (vv. 20-24)? Because where God extends greater responsibility there will always be greater accountability. The former cities had little revelation of truth to reject (Sodom only had the half-hearted testimony of one carnal believer named Lot), but the latter cities had the Son of God standing in their midst and they rejected His message.

Just as there are different rewards in heaven for faithfulness, there are differing degrees of eternal judgment depending on how much truth was rejected (Luke 10:11-16, 12:41-48, 20:47). Everyone is given some divine truth to consider. For example, Paul explains that sophistication of creation demands a Creator, and that the human conscience contains moral reckoning of God's Law (Rom. 1:19-20; 2:11-15). Some individuals do receive more truth to consider, but these also have more accountability with God, if they reject what is revealed.

The prophet Ezekiel foretold that many of the Jewish cities destroyed by Gentile rulers would be rebuilt and resettled in exactly the same locations after God gathers His covenant people back to their homeland in the Kingdom Age (Ezek. 36:11, 24). Today, there are many cities in Israel that bear the ancient names of previous biblical cities: Cana, Jericho, Nain, Bethany, Bethlehem, Hebron, Gaza, etc. However, only a few ruins remain of those cities which the Lord Jesus cursed, Chorazin, Bethsaida, and Capernaum, for their rejection of His message. No one can escape His righteous judgments.

The Savior's Rejection and Invitation (vv. 25-30)

The Lord Jesus knew that the rejection of Chorazin, Bethsaida, and Capernaum was merely a foretaste of the wider rejection of the Jewish nation to His offer of the kingdom. The Lord thanked His Father, the Lord of Heaven and Earth, for hiding certain things from the wise and the self-prudent but revealing them to babes (v. 25). This is not to say that God had withheld light from those residing in these three cities. Rather, enough truth had been declared to draw them to their Savior, but having rejected it, God gave them no more revelation to consider, for their stubborn hearts would have just rejected that also, thus earning themselves more condemnation on Judgment Day (v. 26).

It is at this time that the Lord's public ministry to the lost sheep of Israel (especially in Galilee) diminishes, and the Lord widens His invitation to include the Gentiles also:

Come to Me, all you who labor and are heavy laden, and I will give you rest. Take My yoke upon you and learn from Me, for I am gentle and lowly in heart, and you will find rest for your souls. For My yoke is easy and My burden is light (vv. 28-30).

The Lord conveys a two-part message in these verses. First, there is an invitation in verse 28 for all those who are burdened by the weight of their own sin. Anyone desiring to be liberated from their ongoing guilt must come to Christ; hence, He implores His audience, "Come to Me." Christ is the object of our faith and God's only solution for our sin. Once forgiven by Him, we experience God's peace and enter into His rest. The blood of Christ cleanses the guilty conscience, and we have a new beginning with God (Heb. 9:14).

The remainder of the Lord's message pertains to discipleship. The main objective of discipleship is to learn of Christ and to become like Him (10:25). His means of achieving rest in our souls is quite unusual – we must be willing to take His yoke about our necks and then go on with Him. A yoke was used to harness two or more animals together for the purpose of getting more pulling power for transportation or agricultural purposes.

A yoke is normally connected with slavery or laboring in Scripture, but the Lord promises that His yoke is easy. Those who choose to walk in step with Him will not be burdened, because He would be the One pulling the load that He has assigned us to bear (Gal. 6:5). However, if we attempt to walk ahead or behind the Lord while being yoked with Him, we create work and stress in our lives. He is not the source of it – we are, because we are attempting to walk outside of His will for us. This is why learning the Lord's character, His mind, and His desire for our lives is an essential part of being one with Him in service.

This is the only passage in the New Testament where the Lord Jesus informs His disciples of what He is like and tells them that they should learn of Him. May we learn of Him and be like Him, for He is meek and lowly in heart. Believers learn of the Lord's gentle and humble spirit by being yoked with Him in service and they enjoy the peace of His presence by resting in Him.

Matthew Chapter 12

This chapter marks a transition from Christ's public teaching ministry (as accompanied by signs) to one of parable telling with more personalized ministry. Because of Jewish unbelief, the Lord not only invited the lost sheep of Israel to come to Him, but anyone who had a burdened soul could receive His peace (11:28). Concerning this chapter, John Heading observes:

> This chapter terminates the major section in which the Lord's teaching is mingled with miracles, those mighty works, and signs that the cities of Galilee and the Pharisees so lightly disregarded. We subdivide the chapter into four paragraphs:
>
> 1. The Pharisees and the Sabbath (vv. 1–13).
> 2. The Pharisees and Their Council (vv. 14–21).
> 3. The Pharisees and Their Blasphemy (vv. 22–37).
> 4. The Pharisees and Their Demand of a Sign (vv. 38–50).
>
> No signs are promised, and the character of the Lord's ministry changes by the introduction of parables so as to hide the truth from unbelievers.[41]

Laboring on the Sabbath Controversy (vv. 1-8)

While venturing through ripened grainfields near Capernaum on the Sabbath Day (Mark 2:1), the Lord's hungry disciples plucked and ate a few heads of grain (v. 1). Their actions were abruptly challenged by the Pharisees who said, *"Look, Your disciples are doing what is not lawful to do on the Sabbath!"* (v. 2). The Pharisees' accusation afforded the Lord Jesus with an opportunity to rebuke their religious pride, which had blinded them from comprehending who He really was. He was not the son of a fornicator, nor a Samaritan, nor a man possessed by demons, as they claimed. Rather, He was their Messiah – the Son of God. The Lord's rebuttal contained one historical illustration and a reference to priestly temple service.

First, the Lord Jesus reminded them of what David and his men had done to alleviate their hunger; they entered the House of God and ate the showbread (vv. 3-4). Only the priests were allowed into the house of God and only the priests could eat the twelve unleavened cakes, and then only on the Sabbath Day. Yet, David and his men were not punished by God for their actions. Why? It was because David was a righteous man, God's chosen man, who had been rejected by the nation under King Saul's reign. Given their dire and unjust situation, their necessary action was permitted – it would never have occurred if David had been treated properly by Saul.

This historical example was chosen for its direct correlation between David and his men and the Lord and His disciples. Just as David's leadership had been rejected by the nation under Saul's reign, the Pharisees had prompted the people to reject Jesus Christ as their Messiah. If the Pharisees had received Jesus as their Messiah, His disciples would not have been scavenging for food.

Next, the Lord asked the Pharisees to consider the priests who labored every day, including the Sabbath Day, in the temple (v. 5). Even though they profane the Sabbath by killing animals and preparing sacrifices, they were blameless before God. Why? God expected them to work on the Sabbath to offer Him worship on behalf of the nation. Their Sabbath service did not desecrate the temple. Why then should the Pharisees criticize the disciples, who were laboring on the Sabbath while in the presence of *"one greater than the temple"* (v. 6)?

What did the Lord mean by this statement? The tabernacle and the temple were merely a heavenly pattern of good things to come: *"But Christ being come an high priest of good things to come, by a greater and more perfect tabernacle, not made with hands, that is to say, not of this building"* (Heb. 9:11). The kingdom of God had come to the Jews in the person of the Lord Jesus Christ, and they were rejecting it (i.e., its spiritual aspects and its King).

The Lord then addressed the key matter: *"But if you had known what this means, 'I desire mercy and not sacrifice,' you would not have condemned the guiltless"* (v. 7). God is not heartless; He values mercy, compassion, and kindness much more than mechanical rituals and pious traditions. The Pharisees had become uncaring; they valued cold religious forms more than pursuing the heart of God and making Him rightly known among the people as a good and generous God. The Lord punctuated this point by declaring Himself as the Lord of the Sabbath (v.

8). Since He was the one who had instituted the Sabbath, He was the best one to declare its meaning. In both an authoritative and a practical sense, He was doing what the Pharisees had failed to do – display the full merciful and gracious character of God. Yes, there was One standing before them who was greater than the temple – He was the Lord of the Sabbath and the rightful heir to the throne of David.

Is it possible for believers today to fall into the same religious snare which hindered the Pharisees from more fully knowing God? Though Christians understand that the Lord Jesus is their Savior, they may still suffer from pharisaical pride and misrepresent His character to others. Regrettably, some Christians value symbolic truth and Church order to the extent that commonsense would not rule their actions in unusual situations. In the normative sense, symbolic truth, scriptural principles, and God-ordained order are to be demonstrated in meetings of the Church. But in some circumstances, there may be weightier matters to consider than form. For example, if a sister noticed that one end of the Church building was ablaze, there would be nothing wrong with her blurting out a public alarm during a church meeting, although normally she would have refrained from speaking publicly (1 Cor. 14:34). Is not religious form less important than saving lives? A Pharisee, however, would value sacred form over all else – no exceptions. We should follow what Scripture teaches, but let us not neglect to display God's gracious character to others when unusual circumstances do arise – in so doing we demonstrate to others that we know more about the Lord than just His name and His teachings.

The Lord Jesus had proclaimed to the Pharisees that He was greater than the temple and by implication the priests serving in the temple (v. 6). But Israel's religious leaders flatly rejected Christ's priesthood. In verse 41, they will reject Him as God's unique prophet, and in verse 42, as Israel's King-Messiah.

Healing on the Sabbath Controversy (vv. 9-13)

The Lord ceased His dialogue with the Pharisees, but then ventured into "their" synagogue on the following Sabbath day (v. 9; Luke 6:1). A week earlier, He had proclaimed that "the Son of Man was the Lord even of the Sabbath" (v. 8). He, as God, had created the Sabbath for man, and therefore, He was the One who could best explain its meaning and purpose. The Lord Jesus would validate His claim by performing a miracle on the Sabbath, which would also illustrate the purpose the Lord of the Sabbath had for His Sabbath.

There was a man with a withered hand present in the synagogue. Looking for an opportunity to accuse the Lord of wrongdoing, the Pharisees asked Him, *"Is it lawful to heal on the Sabbath"* (v. 10). The Lord Jesus responded by pointing out the fact that any one of them would rescue one of his sheep if it had fallen into a pit on the Sabbath day (v. 11). Yet, to God, a man is much more valuable than a sheep; so, it would be "lawful to do good on the Sabbath" (v. 12). Showing compassion and selfless love to others always honors God regardless of what day it is. Then the Lord demonstrated this truth by commanding the man with the withered hand to stretch his hand out. The man obeyed the Lord, and the Lord immediately and fully restored the disabled man's hand (v. 13). There was now no functional difference between either of his hands.

Christ Performed Many More Miracles (vv. 14-23)

Rather than praising God for the miracle performed, the Pharisees were enraged that Christ had healed the man on the Sabbath day. The Lord could have healed the man the next day but chose not to. Why should the man suffer his disability even one more day when the Lord had the power to heal the man? Additionally, the situation provided a perfect opportunity for the Lord to confront the coldhearted attitudes of the Pharisees. Matthew informs us that the Pharisees began plotting against Him, desiring to destroy Him (v. 14). Mark adds that the Pharisees sought counsel from the Herodians as to *"how they might destroy him"* (Mark 3:6). Rather than being amazed by the miracle or rejoicing with the healed man, the Pharisees wanted to kill the One that performed the good deed.

The Lord knew all about their plans, so He withdrew from the area and continued preaching to the multitudes (v. 15). Mark records that the Lord withdrew to the Sea of Galilee and that a great multitude from Galilee, Jerusalem, Idumea, and even some from as far as Tyre and Sidon followed Him (Mark 3:7-8).

Christ healed all those coming to Him with their infirmities, yet He requested that those healed not publicize what He had done for them (v. 16). Matthew explains why the Lord requested this in verse 17 by quoting Isaiah (Isa. 41:9, 42:1-4). Jesus Christ was God's Servant and their Messiah, and therefore, a Conqueror, but as they had witnessed by

His ministry, He was gentle and tenderhearted towards them. He was not seeking fame and honor for Himself, but rather expending Himself to selflessly serve others:

> *Behold! My Servant whom I have chosen, My Beloved in whom My soul is well pleased! I will put My Spirit upon Him, and He will declare justice to the Gentiles. He will not quarrel nor cry out, nor will anyone hear His voice in the streets. A bruised reed He will not break, and smoking flax He will not quench, till He sends forth justice to victory; and in His name Gentiles will trust* (vv. 18-21).

A reed is stiff until it is bent, then it has no strength to remain upright in the wind. When a lamp's wick is merely smoking, there is no flame to produce light. A smoking wick (flax) is nearly extinguished altogether. Given the spiritually weak state of the Jewish people, the Lord had patiently declared the Kingdom Gospel message to them. In a coming day, He would aggressively deal with their spiritual blindness and refine and restore the nation of Israel to Himself. At that time, the Gentiles would honor Him in faith also. Both realities will occur during the Day of the Lord, which culminates with Christ's return to the earth to establish His kingdom. But during His first advent, the Lord was determined not to bend over the bruised reed or to quench the last glowing ember of a lamp's wick.

Directly after this declaration, Matthew records a miracle that Christ performed: *"Then one was brought to Him who was demon-possessed, blind and mute; and He healed him, so that the blind and mute man both spoke and saw"* (v. 22). Given the context of Isaiah's prophecy, it may have been the Pharisees who brought Christ what they felt was a hopeless case, as the blind man could not communicate his distress. The miracle itself became an extension of the same text that the Lord had already quoted. After concluding the Messianic portion of the prophecy, Isaiah then describes Israel's demeanor towards Him: They would act like a blind and deaf servant (Isa. 42:18-19). God's indictment against His people is candid: *"Seeing many things, but you do not observe; opening the ears, but he does not hear"* (Isa. 42:20). The Jewish crowds were amazed by the Lord's miracles, but rather than accepting Him as their Messiah, they merely pondered the question, *"Could this be the Son of David"* (v. 23)? Given the evidence supplied by Christ, such a quandary is to reject the truth that faith must embrace.

Matthew's placement of Isaiah's prophecy accomplished two things: First, Jesus Christ is identified as God's Beloved Servant who had been anointed by the Holy Spirit. Second, the healing of the blind and mute man provided hope to Israel. In a coming day, God's Servant will heal His unfaithful servant, the Jewish nation, of their spiritual blindness and then Isaiah predicts that all they will want to do is talk about the Son of David. All their questions will be answered, and they will praise their Messiah – the Lord Jesus Christ.

Blasphemy of the Holy Spirit (vv. 24-32)

Not only did the Pharisees reject Christ's message, but they also accused Him of performing a counterfeit miracle because He was in league with Beelzebub, the ruler of the demons (v. 24). First, the Lord pointed out that such a conclusion was not logical because a kingdom divided against itself cannot stand (v. 25). If Satan casts out Satan, how can his kingdom stand (v. 26)?

Second, the Lord pointed out that Jewish exorcists (the Pharisees' sons, so to speak) claimed to cast out demons. Although the Lord did not affirm or deny their assertion, His point was that they too must be in league with Satan, for if the power to cast out demons came from Satan, then whoever exercised that power was under Satan's authority. But the Jewish exorcists would strongly reject such a notion; they believed that God was enabling them to perform exorcisms. This meant that the Jewish exorcists would judge the Pharisees as being inconsistent in their reasoning by concluding that Jesus Christ had cast out demons by Satan's authority.

The Lord then states a more logical conclusion: If He was casting out demons by the Spirit of God, then certainly the kingdom of God had come (v. 28). For the kingdom of God to be powerfully proclaimed by Christ meant that the "strong man" of the house (Satan's authority on earth) must first be constrained (v. 29). There could be no middle ground in this matter; one must believe who the Lord Jesus proclaimed Himself to be – God's sent Messiah – or reject His claim and remain under Satan's control. There are only two authorities in the world today – God's authority and Satan's rebellious authority, which our Sovereign Creator limits to accomplish His own purposes. Thus, the Lord concluded, *"He who is not with Me is against Me, and he who does not gather with Me scatters abroad"* (v. 30).

Third, the Lord had a stern message for the Pharisees; they had committed the unpardonable sin: *"I say to you, **every sin and blasphemy will be forgiven men, but the blasphemy against the Spirit will not be forgiven men**. Anyone who speaks a word against the Son of Man, it will be forgiven him; but whoever speaks against the Holy Spirit, it will not be forgiven him, **either in this age or in the age to come"** (vv. 31-32).

First, notice that different forms of sin and blasphemy exist and that forgiveness for these is possible. Second, a specific sin entitled *"blasphemy against the Holy Spirit"* is unforgivable, and this specific sin relates to a particular age. "In this age" relates to the public ministry in which Christ was presently engaged. "The age to come" relates to His Second Advent to restore Israel and establish His kingdom on earth. In between these ages of Messiah's initial offer and rejection, and second offer and reception, is the Church Age. During the Church Age, Christ is not personally on the earth declaring the "Kingdom Gospel" message to the lost house of Israel and working miracles to authenticate His message. During the Tribulation Period, the kingdom message will be again preached (24:14), and Israel shall be converted (24:30; Zech. 10:12).

The specific sin that the Pharisees had committed was to ascribe a miracle which Christ had done through the power of the Holy Spirit to Beelzebub, the prince of the demons (v. 24). William MacDonald surmises that this specific sin cannot be repeated today:

> There is reasonable doubt whether the unpardonable sin can be committed today because He [Christ] is not bodily present performing miracles. The unpardonable sin is not the same as rejecting the gospel; a man may spurn the Savior for years, then repent, believe, and be saved. (Of course, if he dies in unbelief, he remains unforgiven.) Nor is the unforgivable sin the same as backsliding; a believer may wander far from the Lord, yet be restored to fellowship in God's family.[42]

These hardhearted, stiffed-necked religious leaders had not only rejected Him, His message, and His miracles, but they likened the Holy Spirit in Him to Satan; this insult, blasphemy, would not be forgiven. Their sin had gone too far, and the Holy Spirit would no longer strive with them to bring them to repentance; thus, they were eternally condemned. Without His help, it is impossible for anyone to believe the gospel message (1 Cor. 2:9-13). They were already dead in their sins and condemned. (Everyone is born "condemned already" in Adam; John 3:18.) Though the sin of disbelief still occurs today and keeps people from being saved, this specific unpardonable sin cannot be committed today, for the Lord is in Glory and not before us, pleading, preaching, and doing miracles.

The fact that some still worry about committing the "unpardonable sin" is a good indication that the Spirit of God is still working to bring them to Christ, otherwise there would be no concern about the matter. Thus, the only sin which can be called unforgivable and that is still possible to commit today is the sin of disbelief – rejection of Jesus Christ ensures one's eternal condemnation (John 3:18, 36).

Words Justify or Condemn (vv. 33-37)

The virtue of one's character validates the source of the message. Like a bad tree, an unregenerate person cannot produce spiritual fruit pleasing to God; only someone that has been born again (a good tree) can bear such good fruit (v. 33). The Lord then called the Pharisees that He was speaking to a brood of vipers (v. 34). Because evil resided in their hearts, nothing out of their mouths would be found acceptable to God (v. 35). The tongue is the tail of the heart that wags out of the mouth – our words are the windows of our heart! What our minds muse on will be evident by our speech. The spiritual reality of the root and of the tree is observed in the fruit that appears on the branches. A good tree consistently bears good fruit, while a bad tree cannot produce what is good. The Lord Jesus then issued a stern warning concerning our speech:

> But I say to you that for every idle word men may speak, they will give account of it in the day of judgment. For by your words you will be justified, and by your words you will be condemned (vv. 36-37).

Not only will our ungodly speech be judged in a coming day, but we will have to give account of all our idle chit-chat also (i.e., words having no value for eternity). This would include making empty promises after invoking the Lord's name. Swearing involves tying God's name to our statements to better validate what we say – to heighten the credibility of our words. The believer should not engage in such practices, for to do so would certainly bring low the name of God. James warns: *"But above all, my brethren, do not swear, either by heaven or by earth or with any other oath. But let your 'Yes' be 'Yes,' and your 'No,' 'No,' lest you fall into judgment"* (Jas. 5:12). Demeaning the name of the Lord by swearing falsely is a terrible offense and speaking frivolous words is a waste of time and depreciates our eternal calling in Christ.

The Sign of the Prophet Jonah (vv. 38-41)

The word "miracle" is not found in Matthew's Gospel; rather, the miracles that the Lord performed are referred to as "signs." Signs of what? The signs witnessed by Israel were irrefutable evidence proving that Christ was who He claimed to be – the Messiah. The Lord's preaching and signs composed the kingdom message to the Jews. Though the signs provided proof that Jesus was the Christ, they would prove insufficient to cause the people to trust the Messiah for salvation. *"Without faith it is impossible to please Him* [God]*"* (Heb. 11:6), and faith requires the soul to venture beyond what the senses can verify.

The Lord Jesus stated that it was the unrighteous who wanted to see a "sign or a wonder" to believe in Him. He called these "sign seekers" an evil generation (vv. 38-39). Even those people who had witnessed the miracle of the feeding of the 5,000 were pestering the Lord the very next day: *"What sign will You perform then, that we **may see it and believe** You?"* (John 6:30). Did they not recall the miracle the day before? Did they not fill their bellies with a boy's multiplied sack lunch? The Israelites saw miracles every day in the wilderness for forty years, yet it did not increase their spirituality – for they constantly murmured against God and His leadership. This shallow spiritual mentality was clearly evident while the Lord Jesus was hanging on the cross: *"Let the Christ, the King of Israel, descend now from the cross, that we **may see and believe**"* (Mark 15:32).

Jonah is a type of Christ in many respects. First, like Christ, Jonah was from Galilee (Gath-Hepher was only three to four miles from Nazareth). Second, the Jewish leaders were in error when they said to Nicodemus: *"Search and look, for no prophet has arisen out of Galilee"* (John 7:52). In their proud religiosity, the Pharisees probably ignored Jonah because he preached to Gentiles; they simply could not bear the thought that God's grace should benefit publicans and sinners. Likewise, the Sanhedrin despised Jesus from Galilee and His mission. Third, the Lord referred to the "three days" Jonah was in the belly of the great fish to foretell His death, burial, and resurrection. However, our Lord tasted death in all its appalling reality as the righteous judgment of God against sin, your sin and mine (Heb. 2:9), whereas Jonah suffered for his own disobedience.

Hence, the Lord Jesus offered a prophetic sign to the Pharisees: *"For as Jonah was three days and three nights in the belly of the great fish, so will the Son of Man be three days and three nights in the heart of the earth"* (v. 40). Later, the Lord clarified the exact meaning of His earlier statement about His own resurrection: He would be *"killed, and be raised up **on the third day**"* (17:23; NASB), but also be *"killed, and **after three days** rise again"* (Mark 8:31). The Lord Jesus implies that these are interchangeable expressions though appearing contradictory to us. In fact, most references speaking of the resurrection declare that it would occur **on** the third day (17:23, 20:19; Luke 9:22, 18:33) or **in** the third day (John 2:19-22). The Lord Jesus used Jonah as a type to signify to the Pharisees what was going to happen to Him: three days and three nights Jonah was in the belly of a great fish; likewise, for three days the Son of Man shall be in the earth (the grave).

Jonah told the Ninevites that their sins had reached up to heaven and that God was going to destroy their city in forty days. The Ninevites humbled themselves and repented after hearing Jonah's message. Now, One greater than the prophet Jonah was in Israel, but His divine message and personage were being blatantly rejected by God's covenant people. Therefore, on judgment day those rejecting a greater message and Messenger will stand guilty before the pagan Ninevites who repented after heeding Jonah's warning (v. 41). As Gentiles, the Ninevites had less privilege and less light, but were spared judgment because they believed Jonah's message and humbled themselves before God. The Pharisees had already rejected Christ's priesthood in verse 6 and now they rejected His prophetic ministry also. In verse 32, they will reject the Lord's kingship, that He is the rightful heir to David's throne.

The Sign of the Queen of the South (v. 42)

The queen of the South is the queen of Sheba mentioned in 1 Kings 10:1-13 and 2 Chronicles 9:1-12. After hearing of Solomon's fame, the queen of Sheba (Yemen in Arabia) traveled nearly 1,200 miles to test his wisdom with hard questions. Solomon's mercantile navy operated along the Arabian coast and would have had contact with this influential Arabian kingdom.

The queen's large caravan brought exceptional spices, gold in abundance, and precious stones as gifts for Solomon. Such spectacular presents corroborated her prestige and wealth. The queen spoke with Solomon about all that was in her heart, and he explicitly answered all of her questions expertly. Her interaction with Solomon was beyond anything she could have imagined. The king's incredible wisdom, immense wealth, enormous table provisions, and the incredible accomplishments were all true. In fact, she concluded that the half had not been told to her.

The queen gave Solomon all the gifts that she had transported from her homeland: 120 talents of gold (about 4.5 tons), and an abundance of rare spices and precious stones (2 Chron. 9:9). In return, King Solomon gave to her *"all she desired, whatever she asked, much more than she had brought to the king,"* and then she returned to her own country.

By referring to the queen of Sheba's thorough investigation of Solomon, the Lord was reprimanding the careless attitude of the Jewish nation towards Him. Despite the incredible expense and great distance, she wanted to know for herself if the stories concerning Solomon were true. In contrast, God had sent His own Son directly to Israel; the Jews did not have to travel to a faraway land to hear God's message to them. Yet, they had no room in their hearts for their Messiah, even though He was far greater than Solomon. The queen of Sheba's testimony was a rebuke of the callous attitude that the Jewish nation had towards Christ.

Humanized Religion Is Worthless (vv. 43-45)

The Lord offers an allegory to summarize unbelieving Israel's past, present, and future. The man in the story represents the Jewish nation, while the unclean spirit typifies Israel's stubborn idolatrous tendency throughout their history. From the Egyptian exodus in fifteenth century B.C. to the Babylonian dispersion in sixth century B.C., God repeatedly judged His covenant people for their blatant idolatry.

The destruction of Jerusalem and the Babylonian exile did largely purge idolatry from the surviving Jewish population. This is what is referred to in the story when the unclean spirit departs from the man (i.e., the house was swept clean of the idolatrous spirit by divine judgment; v. 43). However, as William MacDonald suggests, "the empty house speaks of a spiritual vacuum – a dangerous condition, as the sequel shows. Reformation is not enough. There must be the positive

120

acceptance of the Savior."[43] After the Jews returned to Israel from their Babylonian captivity, a system of religious doings developed in Israel that circumvented the necessity of substitutional sacrifices for sin.

Modern-day Judaism continues to blind the Jewish people from recognizing their need for God's solution for sin, His provided Savior. The purpose of the Law is to show sin (Rom. 3:20) and point the Jews to the only One who could redeem and cleanse them – Jesus Christ (Gal. 3:24). So, though Israel was swept clean of idolatry by God's Babylonian chastisement, Israel's humanized religion of doings to earn God's favor was a worse travesty than their previous idolatry. This is pictured in the disposed unclean spirit returning with seven evil spirits more wicked than himself to indwell the previously possessed and cleansed man (vv. 44-45). The latter situation is much worse than Israel's previous idolatry, for, having rejected Christ, the Jewish people must work to save themselves. The full outcome of the seven spirits will be realized during the Tribulation Period when the apostate Jewish nation will worship the Antichrist.

Modern Judaism is not idolatry in the sense that the Jews are worshipping false gods instead of Jehovah, but rather, the Jews do not need God's provided Savior. They can atone for their own sins and earn God's favor by doing good works. Jewish Rabbis no longer teach that blood sacrifices are necessary to atone for sin, but that repentance, good deeds, or prayer have atoning value and thus replace the animal sacrifices demanded by Scripture. Yet, these all pictured the future once-for-all blood sacrifice of Christ providing propitiation for human sin. Judaism teaches that individuals can make atonement for their personal sins against God without shedding blood (quotes from *Everyman's Talmud* by Abraham Cohen):

What can be a substitute for the bulls which we used to offer before thee? Our lips, with the prayer which we pray unto thee (Pesikta 165*b*; p. 158).

If one has been utterly wicked throughout his life and repents in the end, his wickedness is never again remembered (by God) against him (Kid. 40*b*; p. 109).

Whence is it derived that if one repents, it is imputed to him as if he had gone up to Jerusalem, built the Temple, erected an altar and offered upon it all the sacrifices enumerated in the Torah? (Lev. R. VII. 2; p. 105).

This idea of alternative atonement (doing good works to atone for one's sins) is utterly contrary to Scripture: *"For the life of the flesh is in the blood, and I have given it to you upon the altar to make atonement for your souls; for it is the blood that makes atonement for the soul"* (Lev. 17:11). God's justice concerning a guilty sinner is satisfied through the judging of an innocent substitute – God's own Son paid the price for our sin by giving up His own life. So, the idea that the Jews could save themselves through self-reform and self-effort is deeply offensive to God, for it devalues the sacrifice of His Son.

A New Relationship (vv. 46-50)

While the Lord Jesus was still speaking, He was informed by someone in the audience that His mother and brothers had arrived and desired to speak to Him (vv. 46-47). The Lord used this interruption and information to speak of a spiritual union that was more intimate than natural relationships. He asked, *"Who is My mother and who are My brothers?"* (v. 48). Then, while pointing to His disciples, He answered His own question: *"Here are My mother and My brothers"* (v. 49)!

He then clarifies that those who do the will of His Father in heaven are His family (v. 50). Mary and His half-siblings represented the nation of Israel, which had largely rejected Him and His message (even Christ's half-siblings did not believe that He was the Messiah; John 7:5). As in the last chapter (11:28-30), the Lord was giving an open invitation to anyone who wanted to receive Him to do the will of His Father.

The Lord was not belittling His earthly family or denying His love for them, but rather He was highlighting that having a spiritual relationship with Him was much more important. Our natural relationships all end with death, but our spiritual union with Christ lasts forever. In Him is life and in His presence is unspeakable joy and complete satisfaction.

We may not say that we have the answers. Questions of how to conduct oneself as a Christian, or how to serve as a Christian, must be answered by life itself – the life of the individual in his direct responsible relationship to God.

– Elisabeth Elliot

Matthew Chapter 13

The Mystery of the Kingdom (vv. 1-2)

In the *Mystery of the Kingdom* parables of Matthew 13, the Lord reveals a chronology of events that would characterize the "kingdom of heaven" from His first advent (a seed-sowing mission) until His return to rule the world in peace. It must be observed that the Lord did not speak of any "mysteries" pertaining to the kingdom of heaven until after the Lord's withdrawal from public ministry because of Jewish rejection.

Satan is busy in the first four parables undermining the kingdom of heaven (the realm of human profession of God's sovereignty). In these parables, Satan is seen attacking the gospel message, trying to neutralize the influence of believers on earth, corrupting church leadership, order, and structure, and finally, promoting the corruption of God's Word and spreading false doctrine within the Church. However, in the last three parables, Satan is absent, and God demonstrates His fathomless grace in saving sinners. Christ paid the great price to redeem the hidden treasure (yet unrestored Israel), the pearl (the Church), and those Gentiles who would not bow to the Antichrist (the good catch found in the net).

The Sower and the Soils (vv. 3-9, 18-23)

The Jews were a nation composed of shepherds and farmers. So, when the prophets Hosea (Hos. 10:12-13) and Jeremiah (Jer. 4:3) had sternly warned them centuries earlier to plow up their fallow ground, they understood the analogy. Fallow ground is soil that was once cultivated, but now lies waste and is completely fruitless. The longer it remains uncultivated, the harder it becomes; such is the nature of the human heart that rejects God's Word. For fallow ground to be made profitable again, it must be broken up with a plow; only then can it be planted and made fruitful. The purpose of this Old Testament soil analogy was to call Israel to repentance. The Lord continues that message in the parable of *The Sower and the Soils*.

The ground in which the seed (God's Word) is sown is likened to the various dispositions of the human heart. Four types of "soils" or hearts are identified: the wayside, stony, thorny, and fruitful ground.

The key components of this parable must be properly identified if we are to understand its meaning:

The seed = the Word of God (specifically the Kingdom message).

The sower = Christ primarily.

The soils = various human hearts (i.e., as God knows them).

The birds = Satan's opposition to God's Word being shared.

The sun = persecution and suffering.

The thorns = the influence of humanism and worldly affairs.

The plant = the visible evidence of God's Word at work.

The fruit = the visible evidence of true salvation.

The wayside = someone with no time for or interest in God's Word.

The stony ground = someone emotionally affected by God's Word.

The thorny ground = those who allowed worldliness to negate the Word.

This parable represents the proclamation and offering of the kingdom to Israel by a sower, who primarily represents Christ, but may include John the baptizer also (3:2, 4:17). The seed in the parable is God's Word, which is "living and powerful" (Heb. 4:12). A seed contains life and God's Word offers life to those who will receive it in faith. Specifically, the seed in this parable represents the kingdom message offered by Christ to the Jewish nation; this invitation could not be received without genuine repentance. The various soils represent the spiritual disposition of human hearts that God's message would confront. Only those having a softened and prepared heart received God's message and became fruitful to Him.

The birds depict Satan's adverse efforts to oppose the receipt of God's Word once sown among the populace. Birds are often used in Scripture to metaphorically convey satanic opposition. For example, even after Abram had obeyed God's word and prepared animals and birds for an offering, he still had to drive the unclean birds from devouring his sacrifice until later in the day when God confirmed His covenant with Abram (Gen. 15). Satan was opposing God's covenant with Abram and thus the forthcoming Messiah that would come through it – the One who would bless all families of the earth (Gen. 12:3). Likewise, in this parable, the birds symbolize Satan's evil influence and operations to oppose God's kingdom and the efforts of Messiah to establish His kingdom.

Many have interpreted the visible plant in the parable as a sign of conversion and regeneration, but the Lord clarifies in the explanation that that is not the case. What is seen above the ground is a counterfeit life because the plant does not have a root of faith below the ground (i.e., in the heart). Only God sees what is in each of our hearts, that is, what is below the ground in the parable. We can only see the outward manifestation of the heart in visible behavior. The plants in this parable represent the visible evidence that the Word of God has had an impact on a person's heart, but it is not necessarily conversion.

Some people feel conviction and guilt after being confronted with the gospel message and respond by self-reformation, rather than by true repentance and acceptance of Christ. In time, trials (intense sunlight) and the cares of the world (the thorns) reveal the true reality of things – no true conversion (no root below ground). In this parable, the plants associated with the stony and thorny ground do not represent true life, but merely an emotional response to God's Word. Only the ground that produced fruit represents a true conversion – there can be no fruitfulness to God unless His seed has produced a root of faith in the human heart.

The Lord Jesus said that you will know a tree (a true believer) by whether he or she bears good fruit (behavior and deeds which honor God) or not (7:17-18): *"Therefore by their fruits you will know them"* (7:20). This means that at times we may be conned by well-meaning, moral, and Christ-identifying people, but the Lord is not fooled by the facade of an unregenerate person. In fact, the Lord said there are many who know things about Him, but have not trusted Him for salvation; hence, they have not shown Christ to be their Lord (7:21-23). Clearly, it is possible to know a lot about the Lord and do things in His name without ever being born again. The Lord knows who are truly His and who the counterfeits are. Many identifying with Christ, even calling Him Lord, are not actually saved. The true test of knowing and serving the Lord is found in our desire to do God's will – this is true fruit-bearing. Only those who do the will of God are really His people (Mark 3:35).

The following summarizes the four kinds of soils identified in this parable.

The wayside: The heart that has no interest in the things of God and blatantly rejects the gospel message. The Word had no visible influence on the hearer.

The stony ground: The heart in which the Word of God did not penetrate deep enough to cause the reality of new birth. These people are mere professors in religious camouflage; they had an emotional response to the gospel message instead of brokenness and repentance before God. A little suffering shows them for who they really are.

The thorny ground: The heart in which the Word of God causes the individual to feel guilt and to change his or her conduct through self-effort, but because there is no true conversion, the cares of the world quickly choke out the effect of God's Word in this life.

The good ground: The heart that is well-prepared and receives the Word of God by faith alone unto salvation. True salvation is evidenced by fruit-bearing.

Why Speak in Parables? (vv. 10-17)

The disciples asked the Lord, *"Why do You speak to them in parables?"* (v. 10). The Lord Jesus then explained that He intentionally spoke in parables to reveal truth, but in a partially-veiled manner that would test His audience (vv. 11-12). The parables were not just enjoyable stories but served as a test to the hearers. The casual onlooker, the "window shopper," would hear and not understand, nor would he or she desire any more insight concerning the parable – "thanks for the good story." This fulfilled Isaiah's prophecy that at Messiah's first advent, Israel would hear but not understand, and see but not perceive the truth being proclaimed (vv. 13-15; Isa. 6:9-10). The Jewish nation, being spiritually despondent, would not regard the Messiah's message of life.

But those individuals longing to understand the spiritual significance of the parable would seek the Lord for further instruction (vv. 16-17; Mark 4:10-12); those who merely enjoyed the story would go their own way. Often it was only the Lord's disciples who sought to learn the deeper meaning of His stories. By design, then, a parable is concealed truth that tests the heart of each one who hears the story.

As the Lord approached the cross, the parable veil thinned, and the meanings became more obvious, even to the dissident. While speaking parables in Jerusalem on the Tuesday before His death, even the Pharisees understood that He was speaking of them.

The Wheat and the Tares (vv. 24-30, 36-43)

In this parable the Lord tells of an enemy sneaking in at night and planting tares alongside the wheat the master of the field had sown previously. The tares, or darnel (*Lolium temulentum*), is a prolific weed that looks much like wheat until harvesttime. When wheat matures, it develops a fruit-laden head of grain that bows down before its Creator as it ripens. The darnel has no such fruit-laden head of grain and thereby maintains an upright and haughty disposition before God.

After the tares were discovered, the master told his servants not to uproot the darnel, as that would also damage the wheat. Rather, the matter would be settled at harvesttime. The wheat (i.e., God's children) would be gathered into God's heavenly barn, while the darnel, the children of the devil, would be gathered up by holy angels and cast into eternal fire.

The key components of this parable are:

The laborers = servants of God.

The wheat = true believers – children of God.

The tares = children of the devil.

The field ▬ the world.

The barn = heaven.

The fire = judgment in hell.

If you are doing anything for the Lord, expect the devil to notice and sow his workers right next to you to attempt to neutralize your testimony for Christ or to negate your ministry for Him. God has you right where He wants you in the world (His field), so expect opposition from the enemy until such time that the Lord takes you home (2 Tim. 3:12).

The Mustard Seed (vv. 31-32)

In this parable the kingdom of heaven is compared to a mustard seed that quickly grew into an herb and then into a tree that birds could build their nests in. The mustard seed would be the smallest seed familiar to the Lord's audience, and represents the humble beginning of the kingdom, when it was relatively small, pure, and fruitful – becoming a fruitful herb as intended. This demonstrated the power of the Holy Spirit to develop and prosper the kingdom through the preaching of the gospel message. This analogy compares well with the first three centuries of the

Church Age. Roman oppression during this time had a purifying effect on the Church and resulted in believers taking the message of salvation in Christ alone throughout the empire.

However, the mustard herb continued to grow at a supernatural rate beyond this healthy and fruitful state into a sizable tree which became home to many birds. As the Lord did not explain the meaning of this parable, we must use Scripture to interpret its metaphoric language. Both Ezekiel and Daniel use a tree to depict a world power (Ezek. 17:23; Dan. 4:12). The evil birds that stole the seed (the Word of God; 13:19) in the first parable find a haven in the branches of the tree in this parable. Given these components, Warren Wiersbe discusses the parable's meaning:

> These facts suggest that the parable teaches an abnormal growth of the kingdom of heaven, one that makes it possible for Satan to work in it. Certainly "Christendom" has become a worldwide power with a complex organization of many branches. What started in a humble manner today boasts of material possessions and political influences.[44]

Thus, the parable depicts Satan's evil influences in undermining the message, order, and mission given to the Church originally by Christ. The birds picture the many erroneous religious systems that are associated with Christ's name, but not founded in biblical truth. Some have suggested that the birds in the branches speak of the kingdom's prosperity, but that is not how the Lord invokes the bird imagery in this parable series. An enemy is present in the first four parables and is opposing God's kingdom. It is not until the crowd disperses and Christ is speaking privately with His disciples that the enemy of the kingdom disappears and God's ability to establish it is declared.

The tree with its many birds represents the condition of the kingdom of heaven in the later days of the Church Age; this reality likely refers to Christendom. Christendom has many branches and would include the true Church, but also the cults and various humanized movements that promote what is false and corrupt. In the last days, many will identify with Christ, but deny His deity, His headship (including His order for the Church), and His message of salvation. These religious establishments will deny such scriptural teachings as the Godhead (the Trinity), the eternality of the human soul, and the eternal punishment of the wicked.

Today, much of Christendom embraces false doctrine, and ignores God's expressed requirements for church leaders, roles among genders, and the Great Commission. In summary, Christendom, as pictured in the mustard tree, includes the true Church, but also many religious venues and people who are associated with Christ in name only. Christ has no fellowship with what opposes His authority and rule.

The key components of this parable are:

The mustard seed = the simple but powerful gospel message.

The mustard tree = Christendom.

The birds = Satan's corrupting influence on Christendom.

In Revelation 18:2, unclean birds are confined to a cage before being destroyed. During the Tribulation Period, Satan will work through the Antichrist and demonic deception and power to create an apostate religious system that will be ultimately destroyed. Clearly, in whatever age God's people live, they must avoid religious movements which result in unnatural spiritual unions with the world that defile Christ's headship.

The Leaven (vv. 33-35)

Three symbols: meal, leaven (yeast), and the woman, are used in this parable to depict the progressive corruption of the kingdom by the enemy through false doctrine. Warren Wiersbe summarizes the enemy's effort in this and the previous parable: "The mustard seed illustrates the false *outward* expansion of the kingdom, while the leaven illustrates the *inward* development of false doctrine and false living."[45]

Christ's divine character is typified in the meal offering of Leviticus 2. Meal (ground grain) is used to bake bread, a timeless food staple for humanity. Thus, in Scripture, bread is often likened to the receipt of and internalizing of God's Word. Scripture is God's spiritual food for us and without it there can be no spiritual growth. For example, at the end of his life, Moses admonished his countrymen: *"So He [God] humbled you, allowed you to hunger, and fed you with manna which you did not know nor did your fathers know, that He might make you know that man shall not live by bread alone; but man lives by every word that proceeds from the mouth of the Lord"* (Deut. 8:3). The Lord Jesus affirmed the necessity of internalizing God's Word to live for Him (4:4). Likewise, the apostles taught that believers must feed on God's Word to be nourished and strengthened (1 Cor. 3:1-2; Heb. 5:12-14).

Metaphorically speaking, leaven in Scripture is always used to speak of sin, corruption, or evil doctrine (v. 33; 1 Cor. 5:8). The Lord Jesus warned His disciples against the influence of humanized traditions that oppose sound doctrine: *"Beware of the leaven of the Pharisees, which is hypocrisy"* (Luke 12:1). He also warned them concerning *"the leaven ... of the Sadducees"* (16:6). The Sadducees were materialists who denied the existence of the supernatural, the spiritual nature of man, and the idea of a future resurrection. Lastly, the Lord Jesus warned His disciples not to be influenced by *"the leaven of Herod"* (Mark 8:15). Herod, a Jew, was in cahoots with the Roman Empire, and was, therefore, a friend of the world (Jas. 4:4).

Leaven is used to symbolize corruption in the Old Testament also. During the *Feast of Unleavened Bread*, the Jews were not to eat leavened bread, nor were they to look upon it, or even have leaven in any of their houses during the seven-day feast (Ex. 13:7).

Despite the consistent negative connotation of leaven in Scripture, some have applied an unscriptural meaning of leaven in this parable in at least two ways. First, after leaven is introduced into the meal, its influence will spread throughout the lump unhindered. This is supposed to represent the unstoppable spread of the gospel through the world. Second, the meal is said to represent all of humanity and the leaven the spread of the gospel; thus, the gospel message will spread around the world until everyone is saved. This would be the thinking of those holding a post-millennial view of the Lord's second coming. The main components in the parables must be understood with how each is consistently used in the whole of Scripture, or a wrong interpretation of the story will follow. Though these dynamics are reasonable similes of leaven, leaven is never used in Scripture to denote a positive influence.

What does the woman represent in the parable? In a prophetic vision, Zechariah saw a woman restrained in a basket having a lead lid, which was being carried back to Babylon by two winged women. In this scene, the constrained woman symbolizes the idolatry in Israel that God was removing from His people. He was returning this corrupting influence among His people to where it had originated, Babylon.

In God's original plan, woman was created to be Adam's helper and companion; however, she led Adam to disobey God in Eden (Gen. 3:1-6). Likewise, as seen throughout Israel's history, foreign women often enticed Jewish men to depart from the Lord and to embrace false gods (e.g., Num. 25:6-8). So, although women are no more inherently wicked than men, a woman is used at times in the Bible to picture an evil or seductive influence on men (e.g., Rev. 2:20). This highlights the spiritual weakness of men to be seduced into error by sensual means. For this reason, we observe systems of evil being assigned to expressions such as *"the daughter of Zion"* and *"the daughter of Babylon"* (Zech. 2:7; Jer. 6:2).

The key components of this parable are:

The leaven = the introduction of and spreading sway of corruption.

The meal = God's Word – God's food for His people.

The woman = wickedness or evil influence.

Learning of the opposition to the kingdom in the previous three parables and the symbolic meanings of the meal, leaven, and the woman permits us to properly understand this parable: The enemy is introducing evil into good meal to corrupt the food of God's people. By design, this parable follows the imagery of an advanced state of the kingdom, as pictured in the mustard tree – Christendom. This means that, in the latter days of the Church Age, we should expect a number of unsound Bible translations and theological frameworks to be misleading. Satan will readily attack God's Word (Scripture) by perverting, changing, and diluting it. Some have suggested that the leaven represents the unstoppable growth of false professions, the evil presence within Christendom, but if this understanding were correct the dynamic of leaven influence would corrupt all those who have identified with Christ.

Rather, the enemy knows that if he can corrupt the food of God's people, they will not thrive spiritually. Thankfully, as shown in Zechariah's vision, God is quite capable of limiting and removing wicked influences and corruption from among His people. The Lord's people need not be deceived, for God has preserved His truth for us in Scripture to live by.

The Hidden Treasure (v. 44)

The crowd dispersed after the telling of the fourth parable. The remaining parables in Matthew 13 were spoken privately by the Lord to His disciples. There was an enemy present in the previous parables, but he is gone also in the final *Kingdom Parables*. It was as if the Lord was saying to His disciples, "There has been much opposition to God's kingdom, but now let me tell you the rest of the story." The final parables symbolize how God will save refined Israel, the Church, and Tribulation saints despite what the enemy does!

The parable of *The Hidden Treasure* addresses God's relationship with His covenant people (Israel) and His plan for saving and restoring a refined Jewish remnant to Himself in a future day. God has and does consider Israel a special treasure to Himself (Ex. 19:5; Ps. 135:4). Moses reminded his countrymen of this fact again before his death and their entrance into Canaan – their inheritance from God:

> *Also today the Lord has proclaimed you to be His special people, just as He promised you, that you should keep all His commandments, and that He will set you high above all nations which He has made, in praise, in name, and in honor, and that you may be a holy people to the Lord your God, just as He has spoken* (Deut. 26:18-19).

The prophet Zechariah proclaimed that any nation which harms the Jewish people (beyond what God permits for discipline) will ultimately be judged by God: *"For thus says the Lord of hosts, 'He sent Me after glory, to the nations which plunder you; for he who touches you touches the apple of His eye'"* (Zech. 2:8). The Jews are the apple of God's eye.

Because of Israel's past stubborn idolatry, God did punish His people and scatter them among the Gentile nations (Ezek. 36:16-26). However, after several centuries of being dispersed, the Lord Jesus came into the world to personally offer the kingdom to the Jewish people, but they rejected His offer. Thus, the treasure (the Jewish nation) was found by Christ, and then hidden again after they rejected His Kingdom message. The Lord then bought the entire field (the world) which contained the hidden treasure for His own. As God's Lamb for sacrifice, Christ paid the price for the sin of the world at Calvary by shedding His own blood (John 1:29; Heb. 2:9; 1 Jn. 2:2). Today, the Jewish people remain scattered throughout the world. But in a coming day, Christ will return to reclaim His treasure, His purchased possession, and the spiritually revived Jewish nation will never be lost in the world again.

The key components of this parable are:

The land or field = the world – where Jewish people reside.

The man that bought the field = Christ.

The payment for the field = Christ's judgment at Calvary.

The hidden treasure = the Jewish nation (Israel).

This parable highlights the rejection of Christ and the resulting spiritual blindness of the nation of Israel (Rom. 11:7; 2 Cor. 3:14-15).

Israel was cut off from God for rejecting Christ, who then began to woo a Gentile bride for Himself. Israel, the treasure, was consequently hidden again among the nations of the world. Yet, at the Lord's second coming to the earth, He will be gladly accepted by the Jewish nation (Zech. 12:10), and the Jewish people will then receive the Holy Spirit and be restored to God as His people forever. God will regather the Jews to the land of Israel; He will not leave one of them among the nations (Ezek. 39:28-29). In that day, God's *peculiar treasure* will be fully recovered.

The Pearl of Great Price (vv. 45-46)

This parable represents the Kingdom in relationship to the Church. The Church Age is the Kingdom in its interim spiritual state. The Church is not the same as the Kingdom, as the Church will be removed from the earth before Christ returns to establish His kingdom on earth. Then the Church will rule and reign with Christ during the Kingdom Age (Rom. 8:17; 2 Tim. 2:12), as will the Tribulation saints (Rev. 20:4).

In His story, the Lord Jesus said that there was a merchant searching for beautiful pearls to purchase. One day he found one superb pearl that he had to have, no matter the cost. He went and sold everything he had to purchase that one exquisite pearl.

Pearls come from oysters which dwell in the sea. When spoken of metaphorically, seas in Scripture typify the Gentile nations (Rev. 17:1, 15). While gems usually gain value when properly cut, pearls only have value in their entirety. In the Lord's mind, there is one particular special pearl (the Church), coming from the seas (i.e., the Gentile nations), which must be His in its complete wholeness. To secure and preserve this pearl, the Lord gave His all, including His life at Calvary to purchase it (2 Cor. 5:19).

The key components of this parable are:

The merchant = Christ.

The great price = Christ's judgment at Calvary on our behalf.

The pearl = the Church.

This lovely allegory is further enhanced when we understand that pearls are created by the oyster's natural response to an irritation within its shell, such as a grain of sand. The pearl slowly forms around the grain of sand and may require as much as four years to fully develop. The sacrifice of Christ at Calvary is the means by which He is likewise slowly building His Body, the Church, saved souls mainly from Gentile nations, but with a few Jews trusting in Him also.

Christ is at the center of everything that the Church is and does. The Church has value only in its full oneness; from a relationship standpoint, the Lord cannot lose part of His Body and still be complete (Eph. 4:4, 15-16). Perhaps this is why there are twelve gates of pearl in the capital city heaven, the New Jerusalem: Whosoever will from any nation on earth can enjoy eternal communion with God through Christ.

The Dragnet (vv. 47-50)

This parable represents the kingdom in relationship to the Gentiles who are saved during the Tribulation Period. The net represents the influence of the kingdom gospel that will be preached by the faithful during the Tribulation Period (24:14). This message consists of a warning not to worship the Antichrist and a declaration that judgment of the wicked and Christ's kingdom is coming soon (Rev. 14:6-12).

The fish caught in the sea represent surviving Gentiles who lived through the Tribulation Period. As previously mentioned, seas figuratively represent Gentile nations in Scripture (Rev. 17:1, 15). The sorting of the good and the bad caught in the dragnet refers to the gathering of survivors by the angels to stand before Christ in *The Judgment of the Nations.* This same judgment is spoken of in Matthew 25:31-46, but in that passage, Christ is actively separating the sheep (Tribulation saints) from the condemned goats (the followers of the Antichrist). The meaning is the same: "the good" in this parable and "the sheep" in Matthew 25 will enter Christ's righteous kingdom.

This activity is also pictured allegorically in Daniel 2:35, 44-45 and has its literal, prophetic realization in Revelation 19:20 at Christ's second coming to the earth. In the latter reference, Christ ensures that "the bad," all those who followed the Antichrist (i.e., those who took his mark) and persecuted the Jews are executed and committed to eternal judgment by an angel escort – these people will not enter Christ's kingdom.

The key components of this parable are:

The sea = the Gentile nations.

The dragnet = being divinely gathered for judgment.

The fishermen ("they") = the holy angels.

The sorting = the Judgment of the Nations by Christ.

The good = the Tribulation saints.

The bad = the followers of the Antichrist.

The furnace of fire = Hell.

The net represents the outcome of preaching the kingdom gospel worldwide during the Tribulation Period (Matt. 24:14). This message consists of a warning to people not to worship the Antichrist because Christ is coming soon to judge the wicked and establish His kingdom (Rev. 14:6-12). The net's contents represent those Gentiles who survived the Tribulation Period, and the holy angels will ensure that no one will escape Christ's judicial authority. *The Judgment of Nations* is done suddenly, and the general populace will not be expecting it (Matt. 24:36-41). Those unfit for the kingdom (i.e., those who ignored the Kingdom Gospel message) will be abruptly removed from the earth.

Reflecting on Kingdom Truth (vv. 51-52)

After speaking the seventh Kingdom Parable recorded in Matthew 13, the Lord asked His disciples if they had understood *all* that He had told them (v. 51). Their reply of "yes" is surprising, as the Lord had supplied them with a lot of new information and He had only explained the meaning of the first, second, and seventh parables. Certainly, the disciples did not comprehend the full implications of all that the Lord Jesus had just taught them in allegory. Their questions to Him later prove this assessment to be true (e.g., 16:6-12).

Regardless, in addition to Old Testament Scripture, the disciples had now been entrusted with new revelation from Christ. Their stewardship of divine truth was likened to that of a householder who could show off both old and new treasures stored in his home (v. 52). The disciples were to dispense in tandem both Old Testament truth and the principles of truth just received, the latter being the fulfillment of the former. The *new* is in the *old* contained, but by the *new* the *old* is explained. Truth cannot contradict itself, but the new revelation given by Christ to His disciples would enable them in time to understand what had been previously prophesied in Scripture.

The Second Nazareth Visit and Rejection (vv. 53-58)

Luke records Christ's first visit and rejection in His hometown of Nazareth (Luke 4:16-30). On this occasion, the Lord Jesus ventured into a synagogue. He was handed a scroll of Isaiah to read from. After announcing that the Spirit of the Lord was upon Him, He read Isaiah 61 verse 1 and half of verse 2 and then closed the book, returned it to the attendant and sat down. With every eye fixed on Him, the Lord said, *"Today this Scripture is fulfilled in your hearing"* (Luke 4:21).

The Jews understood that the Lord was claiming to be the One Isaiah was prophesying of, that is, the Messiah. They became so enraged by His claim that after putting Him out of the synagogue and leading Him out of town, they sought to push Him over a cliff (Luke 4:29). But it was not His time to die, and He walked away through the crowd unharmed.

The Lord did not read the remaining portion of verse 2 or verse 3, as that pertained to His second advent, when He will return to judge the nations and to restore Israel to honor: *"And the day of vengeance of our God; to comfort all who mourn, to console those who mourn in Zion..."* (Isa. 61:2-3). For Israel, the Lord's promise to comfort those who mourn will occur after the Tribulation Period.

A few months later Matthew and Mark record a second visit to Nazareth by the Lord and His disciples (vv. 53-58; Mark 6:1-6). This was a bold decision by Christ, as earlier those in Nazareth sought to kill Him for what He taught in the synagogue. But His second visit to Nazareth during His Galilean ministry shows the Lord's compassion and tenacity for reaching the lost sheep of Israel.

On the Sabbath, the Lord returned to the synagogue and taught the people (v. 54). Those listening were astonished at His ability to teach and to do mighty works. The Lord's audience could not reconcile in their minds how a lowly carpenter's son, that they had watched grow up could have such wisdom and ability to teach and to do mighty works. They asked among themselves, "Is this not the son of Mary, whose brothers are James, Joses, Simon, and Judas and whose sisters are with us also" (vv. 55-56)? God had blessed Mary and Joseph with a large family and the reference is to Jesus' half-brothers and half-sisters through Mary. The people could not see past Christ's upbringing and were thus offended at Him – who are you, a carpenter's son, to teach us anything? They were literally "repelled" by His words, His wisdom, and His works.

The Lord responded to their disdain by saying, *"A prophet is not without honor except in his own country and in his own house"* (v. 57). Because of their unbelief (i.e., rejection of the truth), He only did a few miracles in Nazareth (v. 58). The Lord and His disciples departed Nazareth and there is no record that He ever returned there again.

Matthew Chapter 14

The Death of John the Baptizer (vv. 1-14)

After hearing of the miraculous feats that Jesus was performing in Galilee, Herod concluded that John, whom he put to death had risen from the grave and was working in Jesus (vv. 1-2). Matthew now conveys the story of John the baptizer's murder.

Herod the Great had at least fourteen children by eight different wives. Antipas and Philip were sons of Herod the Great, but were half-brothers. Herod Antipas apparently had an affair with his brother Herod Philip's wife, Herodias, after Philip settled permanently in Rome. Herodias left Philip and remained with Antipas in Palestine. Antipas divorced his wife (the daughter of Aretas, the king of Petra) to illegally marry his brother Philip's wife, and Herodias divorced her husband, which the Law did not permit. Herodias (the feminine form of Herod) was the granddaughter of Herod the Great, thus the niece to both her husbands, Philip and Antipas.

John rebuked their adultery publicly (vv. 3-4). Although Herod esteemed John as a just and holy man (Mark 6:20), he considered putting John to death, to silence his public ridicule of his illicit relationship with Herodias. However, because he feared the people, who believed that John was a prophet, Herod chose to imprison John (v. 5). It is generally believed that John was imprisoned in Herod's royal palace/fortress at Machaerus, which faced Arabia on the southeast border of Herod's domain. Herod had several such residences.

John's imprisonment was unacceptable to Herodias, who had been publicly humiliated by John's rebuke (Mark 6:19). She schemed with her daughter Salome to trick Herod into granting her a request (v. 8). The young girl danced before Herod and his guests on his birthday, which pleased the tetrarch greatly (v. 6). Herod, with an oath, asked the girl to make a request of Him and he would do it to show his appreciation (v. 7). The girl, following her mother's prompting, asked for John's head on a platter (v. 8). The pompous king had fallen into the feminine trap, and to save face, Herod had John executed (vv. 9-10). His head was brought to Herodias' daughter who then brought it to her mother (v. 11). John's disciples claimed the prophet's body and buried it, then went and told the Lord Jesus what had happened (v. 12).

At this same time the disciples were returning with joyous news concerning their Galilean ministry (Luke 9:10). Given all that had just happened, the Lord told His disciples that it was time to come aside to rest for a while (i.e., time to separate themselves from the crowds and daily ministry). The Lord teaches us that there should be a legitimate time to grieve the loss of a loved one and that we need times of physical and mental rest from ministry also. Proper grieving requires time away from life's normal responsibilities to reflect and settle one's soul in prayer and reading His Word. The disciples departed in a boat *together* to journey to a deserted place to achieve solitude (v. 13; Luke 6:32). Notice that they did not isolate from each other during this time. To be free from responsibilities and distractions during the grieving process is important but isolating from friends and family is dangerous. It is at such times as this that we need our closest friends and family members nearby to anchor our minds in the truth and to weep with us. To give a grieving person a hug from the Lord when the bottom has dropped out of their world is a tremendous blessing.

After an unknown time of solitude, the crowds became aware of their location and sought them. When the Lord saw the multitude, He was moved with compassion and began to serve them (v. 14; Mark 6:34). Indeed, we should take time to mourn the death of a loved one, but the Lord shows us that there is also a time to get back to serving others.

Five Thousand Fed (vv. 15-21)

On two different occasions, the Lord Jesus performed miracles to feed the multitudes that had gathered in remote locations to hear His message. Matthew records the first event here and the second miracle in the next chapter. The feeding of the five thousand is the only miracle recorded in all four Gospels and signals the close of Christ's two-year Galilean ministry. After this, Christ will travel to Phoenicia, Decapolis, Caesarea-Philippi, Judea, Perea, and then back to Jerusalem for His final days of ministry, culminating with His death, burial, and resurrection.

The first miracle occurred in "a deserted place" (v. 15) that was remotely near Bethsaida according to Luke (Luke 9:10). However, John refers to the location being near Tiberias, a city on the western shore of the Sea of Galilee (John 6:23). Bethsaida is the hometown of Peter, Andrew, and Philip (John 1:44). But there were two towns that went by this name: Bethsaida Galilee (Tabgha) on the northwest side of the Sea of Galilee and Bethsaida Julias on the north-northeast side of the sea. Luke is apparently referring to Bethsaida Galilee as the location of the miracle, which is just north of the area that John identities for the event. Two towns named Bethsaida are mentioned: Luke says that the miracle occurred near Bethsaida and Mark states that the Lord told His disciples afterwards to cross the sea to Bethsaida. Yet, the information in the Gospels is not sufficient to emphatically identify the exact location of this miracle; we can, however, speculate about its most likely location.

John, an eyewitness of these events, states that the feeding of the 5,000 occurred near Tiberias (John 6:23). The disciples departed from this location in a boat without the Lord and were told by Him to go to Bethsaida (Mark 6:45). If Bethsaida Julias was meant, that would be an eight-mile journey to the northeast of Magdala directly across the sea, which would be a risky venture at night. John records that the disciples rowed towards Capernaum, which would be in the direction of Bethsaida Galilee (John 6:17). This would be a safer trek north-northwestward as the shoreline would remain in sight (John 6:17).

However, a windstorm throughout the night hindered their progress northward until the Lord came to them walking on the sea in the fourth watch. After He entered the boat, He calmed the sea, and instantly moved the boat to a location just southwest of Capernaum (John 6:24), which allowed them to do ministry in Gennesaret the next day (v. 34; Mark 6:53). This agrees with John's statement that people came in boats from Tiberias to Capernaum looking for Jesus the next day and found Him (John 6:23-24). If the miracle occurred at Magdala (about four miles south of Bethsaida Galilee and three miles northwest of Tiberias), it might be possible for the news to have spread down to the people from Tiberias overnight, but it seems more likely that these seekers from Tiberias had witnessed the miracle themselves and sought Jesus in the most likely place they might find him, Capernaum. Capernaum was the Lord's home base, so to speak, during His Galilean ministry.

Returning to the text at hand, after a long day of ministry, the disciples came to the Lord and asked Him to send the people away, so that they could journey to surrounding villages and purchase food for themselves before nightfall overtook them (v. 15). The Lord informed His disciples that there was no need to send the people away, but rather they should feed them (v. 16). John's account affirms that there were neither sufficient funds available, nor nearby resources to feed a crowd of this size. Moreover, the only food that the disciples had found was a boy's sack lunch of two fish and five loaves which Andrew had spied out (v. 17; John 6:9). The Lord told His disciples to cause the people to sit down in the grass and to bring Him the fish and the loaves (v. 18). After receiving what was available, the Lord gave thanks for the fish and the bread, broke the bread, and gave the fragments to the disciples to be passed out to the people (v. 19). After everyone had eaten their fill, there were twelve baskets full of fragments that remained.

Three helpful applications are suggested from this story. First, serving will always precede the reward for service, and the reward will be far more than we deserve! There was a basket for each serving disciple, and each received an abundant portion after their service was completed. Second, everyone was completely satisfied with the Lord's provision. He fed an estimated 20,000 people (5,000 men, plus women and children; v. 21). The Lord Jesus satisfies all genuine need when we rest in Him. Help may not always come the way we expect it to or when we think it should, but the Lord's provision will never leave us disappointed! Third, the pattern of service in this story is a good one for us to follow: Understand what the Lord has given each of us, be willing to give it back to the Lord, obey how He says to use it, and then preserve the blessing that God supplies afterwards as a testimony of His goodness.

Walking on Water and Calming a Storm (vv. 22-33)

After a long day of ministry, which included feeding a large crowd, it was time for the crowds to disperse. The Lord desired to be alone with His Father, so He told His disciples to enter into a boat and cross the sea towards Capernaum without Him (John 6:17). He would send the people away by Himself (vv. 22-23). At dusk, the Lord saw His disciples in the sea and struggling to row against a contrary wind (Mark 6:48). The Lord continued praying throughout the night and in the early dawn hours (i.e., the fourth watch was between 3 and 6 a.m.) the Lord came towards them walking on the rough sea (vv. 24-25). John says that they had rowed only three to four miles since entering the boat (John 6:19).

Although it was not the Lord's intention, it seemed to the disciples that the Lord was going to pass them by, so they cried out to Him (Mark 6:48). At first, they were terrified by His presence, thinking He was a ghost, but He comforted them with these words, *"Be of good cheer! It is I; do not be afraid"* (v. 27). Peter then said, *"Lord, if it is You, command me to come to You on the water"* (v. 28). The Lord said, "come" and Peter exited the boat and walked towards Him on the water (v. 29). But Peter took his eyes off the Lord to notice the turbulent sea and boisterous wind and began to sink into the sea. He frantically cried out, *"Lord, save me"* (v. 30). The Lord responded by immediately stretching out His hand to catch a sinking Peter. The Lord then admonished Peter, *"O you of little faith, why did you doubt"* (v. 31)? The map below is a possible scenario derived from the Gospel accounts as to the disciples' boat journey.

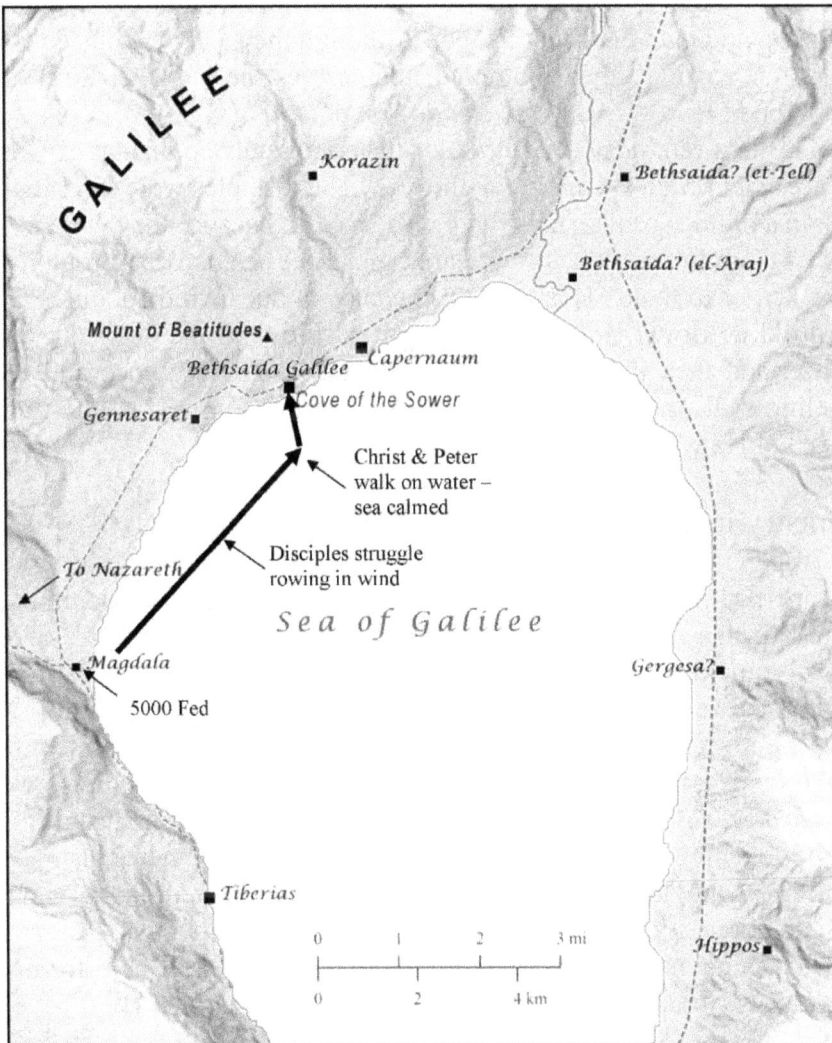

When by faith our eyes are fixed on Christ, He delights to demonstrate His abilities and goodness. Unless it is frozen, walking on water is difficult anytime. Similarly, sojourning on a wicked, sin-cursed planet as a child of God is not easy anytime. We need the Lord every moment of every day. On this side of glory, our faith is not perfect, but what a consolation to know that in times of distress we can cry out to the Lord, "save me," and He will immediately respond.

The Lord then entered the boat and the impeding wind ceased and the boat was instantly moved across the sea to a place near Capernaum, its intended destination (v. 32; John 6:21). Their half-day arduous trial was over. Mark notes that the disciples were "greatly amazed ... beyond measure, and marveled" at this feat. Although they were exhausted from hours of rowing, they humbled themselves before the Lord and worshipped Him, *"Truly you are the Son of God"* (v. 33).

This text reminds us that the Lord is completely cognizant of where we are at and what we are going through. The disciples were safer in that boat in a raging sea than anywhere else on earth because they were in the will of God. In fact, what they feared most, the sea, is what brought the Lord nearer to them. This is often the case in our own difficulties. The Lord did not force Himself into their hardship until they called out for Him; when they did, they were comforted by His presence and their grueling trial was over. The Lord longs to show Himself strong in our lives, but He will wait to be invited to do so.

Ministry in Gennesaret (vv. 34-36)

Apparently, the Lord conveyed their boat to the shoreline southwest of Capernaum in *"the land of Gennesaret"* so that they could do ministry there that day (v. 34). Many recognized the Lord, and the news of His arrival quickly spread throughout the region (v. 35). Those with infirmities were brought to Him for healing. They had such faith in the Lord's ability that they believed if they merely touched the garment that Jesus was wearing, they would be healed. And as many that did so were *"made perfectly well"* (v. 36). There was no actual power in the garment, but by touching it, they were signifying in whom they were trusting for a miracle. Only the sick and impaired desire to be healed; those who are well do not need the care of a physician. Likewise, only those discerning their desperate spiritual need to be made well, will seek help from the Lord Jesus Christ.

Matthew Chapter 15

God's Commands and Man's Traditions (vv. 1-9)

Scribes and Pharisees from Jerusalem arrived in Gennesaret to confront the Lord concerning a purification ritual that His disciples were ignoring, the washing of hands before they ate (vv. 1-2). This symbolic ritual of pouring water over one's hands before eating was not about good hygiene but rather remaining ceremonially clean by obeying Rabbinical law (i.e., man-made traditions). The two leading rabbis of this age, Hillel and Shammai, were rival teachers of Jewish tradition. Both lived during the reign of Herod the Great. Hillel was the liberal, while Shammai wanted to protect Judaism from being influenced by Rome. These men held little in common, but they both agreed that water should be poured on the hands and allowed to run down the wrists. The practice was intended to keep Jews from having close contact with Gentiles.

The Lord responded to the Pharisees' inquiry with His own question: *"Why do you also transgress the commandment of God because of your tradition"* (v. 3)? He then reminded them of the honor they should have for one's parents by quoting the fifth of the Ten Commandments (v. 4; Ex. 20:9). Next, the Lord referred to the judgment that the Law required for those who dishonored their parents (Deut. 27:16).

The Lord then provides them an example of how their non-biblical traditions were undermining God's commands. He refers to their practice of Corbin, a transliteration of the Hebrew and Greek words, meaning "an offering" (vv. 5-6). The rabbis taught that it was acceptable to give to God the funds needed to care for (honor) one's aging parents. Besides making God appear as an ogre, the scribes were directly negating God's command of honoring one's parents by their traditions. How foolish they were to rebuke the disciples for neglecting to ceremonially wash their hands before they ate when they were disregarding God's Law to fill their own coffers.

Warren Wiersbe explains how these religious traditions developed:

From where did these human traditions come? They were handed down from the teachers of previous generations. These traditions were originally the "oral law" which (said the rabbis) Moses gave to the elders, and they passed down to the nation. This oral law was finally written down and became the *Mishnah*. Unfortunately, the *Mishnah* became more important and more authoritative than the original Law of Moses.[46]

The Lord calls these legalistic zealots "hypocrites" to their faces (v. 7). The term hypocrite(s) is found twenty times in the New Testament and fifteen of those occurrences are in Matthew. As in this instance, it is always the Lord Jesus who applies the condescending term to others. The Lord continues His rebuke by quoting Isaiah's message to the Northern Kingdom seven centuries earlier to indicate God's adamant disgust over the foolish religiosity of His people:

These people draw near to Me with their mouth, and honor Me with their lips, but their heart is far from Me. And in vain they worship Me, teaching as doctrines the commandments of men (vv. 8-9; Isa. 29:13).

Because God's covenant people were prone to dead religiosity and offering the Lord mere lip service, instead of heartfelt admiration, He had no desire to be present in their religious gathering. Isaiah put the Lord's revulsion this way: *"Wickedness and the solemn meeting I cannot bear"* (Isa. 1:13; JND). He utterly despised their sacrifices, offerings, prayers, and observances! The seriousness of Israel's offense is bluntly expressed by the phrase *"My soul hates"* in the next verse, which literally means, "I hate with all my heart!" God keenly feels the offense of exchanging His commandments for the traditions of men – He utterly hates it!

Much of the Old Testament contains the sad history of God's people languishing under human traditions instead of being taught Scripture. Verse 9 offers us a good definition of what "legalism" is: *"Teaching as doctrines the commandments of men."* Whether in Israel previously or in the Church today, there are always consequences when men lord themselves over God's people and burden them with their own rules. Approaching God in any other manner than humble sincerity and in obedience to His revealed will is utter vanity. He is not pleased with such religiosity; rather, His wrath is invoked against those offering to Him what He considers putrid.

The Heart Diagnosis (vv. 10-20)

After rebuking the vain religiosity of the Pharisees, the Lord offered an axiom of wisdom to the multitude listening to Him: *"Not what goes into the mouth defiles a man; but what comes out of the mouth, this defiles a man"* (v. 11). What we say reflects what is in our hearts. It is not what we eat that defiles us, but our words. Food eaten without first performing the ceremonial purification ritual did not affect the body's digestion of it.

Afterwards, the disciples came to the Lord privately and told Him that the Pharisees had been offended by His speech (v. 12). The Lord was not concerned about their hurt feelings, but rather He affirmed that Israel's blind leaders and those who impetuously followed them would be under God's judgment in a coming day (vv. 13-14). God would uproot and remove every plant that did not belong in His kingdom.

Peter then requested that the Lord further explain what He meant about what goes in and out of the mouth (v. 15). The Lord wondered why Peter did not understand the simple truth that He had stated (v. 16). What one eats goes into the mouth, then passes through the gastrointestinal tract and is then eliminated from the body as waste (v. 17). We are to give thanks to God for the food He provides for us to eat. This activity sanctifies the food we eat to strengthen our bodies to serve the Lord (1 Cor. 10:30-31). However, what one speaks reflects what he or she is thinking about. If carnal or evil thoughts are lurking in our heart, our own speech will inevitably condemn us (vv. 18-19). The Lord then summarized that it is not what is eaten or the eating with unwashed hands that defiles us, but rather our unwholesome speech (v. 20).

The Faith of a Syro-Phoenician Woman (vv. 21-28)

The Lord and His disciples then journeyed northwest to the Mediterranean coastal region of Tyre and Sidon in Phoenicia (v. 21). As far as we know, this is the only time that the Lord ventured outside of Israel. While in Phoenicia, "a woman from Canaan" urgently requested that the Lord heal her demon-possessed daughter. She addressed the Lord Jesus as "Lord, Son of David" (v. 22).

The Lord did not answer her request, but this did not stop her asking for assistance. The Lord's silence was not to show disdain for the woman who was a Gentile, but to provide an opportunity for her faith to be publicly drawn out, so that the Lord could then bless her. However, her ongoing pleading annoyed the disciples, who asked the Lord to send her away (v. 23). In response to their request, the Lord said in the hearing of the woman, *"I was not sent except to the lost sheep of the house of Israel"* (v. 24). The Canaanite woman then came before the Lord to worship Him and said, *"Lord, help me"* (v. 25). The Lord again affirms His heavenly mission by stating an allegory: *"It is not good to take the children's bread and throw it to the little dogs"* (v. 26). Currently, the Lord and His disciples were preaching the kingdom gospel message to the lost sheep of Israel ("the children"). The Lord was not sent to preach to the Gentiles ("the dogs") initially.

The Canaanite woman seemingly understood what the Lord was saying, and added, *"Yes, Lord, yet even the little dogs eat the crumbs which fall from their masters' table"* (v. 27). The Lord marveled at her statement and said, *"O woman, great is your faith! Let it be to you as you desire"* (v. 28). The woman's daughter was immediately healed. In Christ, Gentiles would become a second benefactor of the New Covenant established with Judah and Israel through Christ's shed blood (Heb. 8:8). Through trusting the gospel message preached in the Church Age, Jews and Gentiles would be fellow members in Christ's Body and fellow heirs to the unconditional blessings God promised to Abraham as obtained in Christ (Gen. 12:3; Eph. 3:6).

Paul employs an olive tree analogy in Romans 11 to reveal God's plan to ultimately restore the Jewish nation and to also bless the Gentiles through the Abrahamic covenant. God's covenant with Abraham which promised blessing to all families of the earth is the root of the olive tree. Christ is represented in the olive tree (Jer. 11:16-17) that draws up blessing from its root (i.e., God's covenant with Abraham).

It would be natural for the blessings of the root to pass through the tree to nourish its branches (picturing the two houses of Israel and Judah), but these were cut off by disbelief. God then grafted in a wild olive tree, the Gentiles collectively speaking, to receive the blessings of Christ during the Church Age. Such grafting is an intervention in the natural growth of the tree which highlights the nature of the illustration. Later, God will graft the original branches back into the tree when the Jewish nation comes to faith after the conclusion of the Church Age, signaled by the Rapture of the Church. This also signals "the fullness of the Gentiles" (Rom. 11:25), that is, when the last Gentile is saved during the Church Age. All the goodness God intends for Gentiles and Israel comes through Christ – our blessed Olive Tree.

The Canaanite woman's description of "little dogs" eating the crumbs of bread that fell from the master's table (i.e., the bread of life, that God had provided for the Jewish people) beautifully conveyed God's plan of saving both Jews and Gentiles in Christ. At this point in His ministry, the Lord was seeking the lost sheep of Israel to receive Him as their Messiah; His efforts were not directed to the Gentiles.

This explains why the Lord performed only two miracles in association with Gentiles. Both healings were performed at a distance on behalf of a Gentile who had great compassion for someone else who was suffering and great faith in the Lord to resolve the issue. The other occurrence is when a Centurion showed faith in understanding who Christ was and where His authority came from (8:5-13). The Lord was thrilled by their sincere faith and granted both their requests. Why did the Lord travel outside of Israel to Phoenicia? Perhaps to merely test the faith of one distressed Canaanite woman. The Lord yearns to demonstrate His compassion and ability to bless others for those who will seek Him in faith.

Further Healings in Northern Galilee (vv. 29-31)

After healing the Canaanite mother's daughter, the Lord journeyed east and then south through Decapolis to the Sea of Galilee. He and His disciples then skirted the eastern shoreline northward until they came to a mountain (v. 29). Seeking some solitude for prayer, the Lord ascended this mountain alone. However, it was not long before those seeking Him for help found Him. The people brought the lame, blind, mute, maimed, and those with other infirmities to the Lord to be healed (v. 30). The crowd marveled at the Lord's ability to heal every sort of illness and disability and they responded by praising "the God of Israel" (v. 31). This indicates that many Gentiles had now heard about Israel's Messiah and were praising God for His good works.

Four Thousand Fed (vv. 32-39)

The Lord's preaching and healing ministry in this wilderness location extended into a third day (v. 32). The Lord Jesus had compassion for the people and told His disciples that He did not want to dismiss them while they were hungry, lest they faint on their journey. Apparently, the disciples had forgotten how the Lord had previously multiplied a boy's sack lunch and fed 5,000 men, plus women and children. They concluded that there were no nearby locations to purchase bread for this "great multitude" (v. 33).

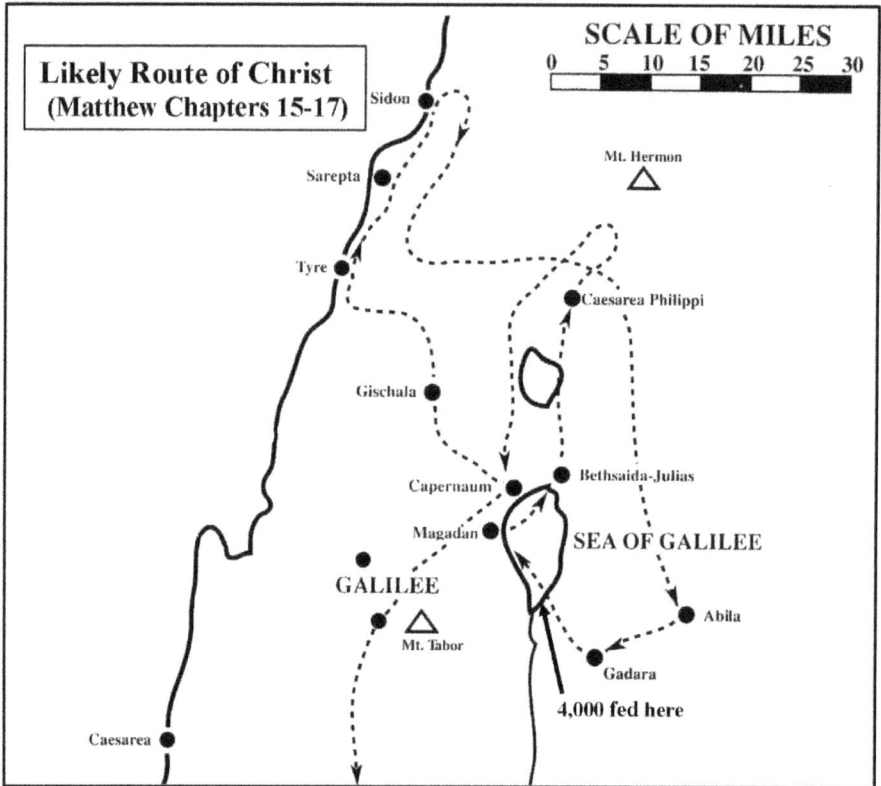

The Lord asked His disciples how many loaves of bread they had. They responded, "We have seven loaves and a few little fish" (v. 35). The Lord then commanded that all the people sit down. He then took the loaves and the fish, gave thanks for them, and broke them into small pieces, which He gave to the disciples to be distributed among the people (v. 36). All the people ate their fill and there were seven large baskets full of the fragments afterwards (v. 37). Matthew then provides the approximate size of the crowd: 4,000 men, plus women and children, perhaps 15,000 people total (v. 38).

After everyone had eaten their fill, the Lord dismissed the crowd. Then, He got into a boat and journeyed to the region of Magdala. Magdala was located about 3 miles north of Tiberias on the western shoreline of the Sea of Galilee. Matthew does not mention that the disciples were with Christ in the boat, but Mark does (Mark 8:10).

148

Matthew Chapter 16

The Blind Seek a Sign (vv. 1-4)

Although the Pharisees and Sadducees held doctrinal extremes, they found common ground in the necessity of challenging the Lord Jesus (v. 1). They asked Him to show them "a sign from heaven" to validate the authority of His ministry. The word "miracle" is not found in Matthew's Gospel; rather, the miracles that the Lord performed are referred to as "signs." These signs were irrefutable evidence to Israel to prove that Christ was who He claimed to be – the Messiah.

The Lord's preaching and signs composed the kingdom message to the Jews. Though the signs provided proof that Jesus was the Christ, they would prove insufficient to cause the people to trust the Messiah for salvation. *"Without faith it is impossible to please Him* [God]*"* (Heb. 11:6), and faith requires us to venture beyond what our senses and human intellect can verify. Therefore, the Lord Jesus had declared that it was the unrighteous who wanted to see a "sign or a wonder" to believe in Him. Previously, He had called these "sign seekers" an evil generation (12:38-39), and while addressing Israel's religious leaders, He does so again.

Some of Israel's religious leaders had witnessed the Lord heal people, but now they were asking Him to work some spectacular sign in heaven that they might see and then believe in Him. The Lord uses a meteorological illustration to point out the fallacy of building one's faith on what is visible in the heavens. When they observed a red sky in the evening, they would forecast fair weather for the next day, but a red sky in the morning meant stormy weather for that day (v. 2). The Lord then called the Pharisees and Sadducees hypocrites, because they could discern the face of the sky, but not the signs of the times (v. 3). He then stated that a wicked and adulterous generation seeks after signs (v. 4).

These religious leaders had memorized significant portions of the Old Testament, and yet they could not discern by Scripture that their prophesied Messiah was standing before them. Because of their willful, spiritual blindness, the Lord would not work any signs in their presence, other than "the sign of the prophet Jonah." Just as Jonah was in the belly of a great fish for three days, the Son of Man would be crucified, buried, and rise from the grave on the third day. What sign could be greater than someone causing his own resurrection? But even after Christ's resurrection, the religious leaders largely did not believe in Him. This shows that although signs may be used to confirm Scripture, it is faith in God's Word alone that builds one's faith.

Beware of Leaven (vv. 5-12)

Given the dialogue that follows in this passage, the disciples may not have been with the Lord during His interchange with the Pharisees. Regardless, they were with the Lord again about the time He was wrapping up His conversation with Israel's religious leaders.

The Lord left the Pharisees and got in a boat with His disciples to cross the sea northward towards Bethsaida and then to travel on foot to Caesarea Philippi (vv. 5, 13). The disciples realized after getting into the boat that they had forgotten to buy bread (v. 5). Mark states that there was only one loaf of bread in the boat (Mark 8:14). The Lord then issued a warning to His disciples: *"Take heed and beware of the leaven of the Pharisees and the Sadducees"* (v. 6). As leaven is necessary to cause loaves of bread to rise, the disciples believed that the Lord was admonishing them for not buying bread. Rather, His allegorical warning was prohibiting them from obtaining bread from the Pharisees (v. 11).

Both sects of the Pharisees and Sadducees came to prominence during the Maccabean period. The Pharisees were called "separatists" because they separated themselves from the Hellenizers, the political opportunists and liberals of their day. The Pharisees saw themselves as the guardians of the Law and the traditions of the oral law. The Sadducees were the aristocrats and politicians among the Jews; they were the theological liberals and humanists of their day. They had yielded to the Hellenizing influences of the Greeks and adopted the principles of Aristotelian philosophy. Consequently, they rejected any doctrine that could not be proven by reason.[47]

The disciples' preoccupation with food caused them to completely miss the spiritual lesson that the Lord was providing them concerning leaven. He was not questioning them about where their next meal was coming from, but rather warning them against the doctrines being taught by Israel's religious leaders to the people (v. 12).

On the matter of literal bread, the Lord wondered why His disciples were weak in faith, so He called their attention to the previous two miracles in which He had fed the multitudes. Did they not remember how He had multiplied a few loaves and fish to feed the masses all that they could eat (vv. 8-10)? Consequently, the Lord was not rebuking their negligence in buying bread but warning them where not to go to obtain spiritual food for the soul.

Leaven, in Scripture, speaks of sin, corruption, or evil doctrine (13:33; 1 Cor. 5:8). Because leaven (yeast) is used in the fermentation process, it is a perfect symbol of decay and corruption, which is why, spiritually speaking, we should not be contaminated by it.

The leaven to be avoided in the believer's life comes in diverse varieties. The Lord Jesus warned His disciples against the influence of humanized traditions that oppose sound doctrine: *"Beware of the leaven of the Pharisees, which is hypocrisy"* (Luke 12:1). Church traditions have caused many professing Christians to ignore Christ's command to remember Him often through the Lord's Supper or to transform the memorial feast into some unscriptural practice. Some, for example, associate the eating of the bread and the drinking of the wine in the Lord's Supper with receiving or maintaining their salvation. This kind of leaven (i.e., false teaching) undermines the gospel message of grace declared repeatedly in the New Testament (e.g., Gal. 1:6-9).

The Lord spoke about the leaven of the Sadducees. The Sadducees were materialists who denied the existence of the supernatural, the spiritual nature of man, and the idea of a future resurrection. In our present day, the ideologies of the Sadducees live on in intellectualism, humanism, higher criticism, post-modernism, and naturalism.

The Lord Jesus also warned His disciples not to be influenced by *"the leaven of Herod"* (Mark 8:15). Herod, a Jew, was in cahoots with the Romans, and was, therefore, a friend of the world (Jas. 4:4). In the case of Herod, and those like him, love for God and His Word had been supplanted by the love for materialism, fame, and political ambition.

Peter's Confession of Christ (vv. 13-16)

The Lord with His disciples then journeyed to Caesarea Philippi about 25 miles north of the Sea of Galilee (v. 13). This was the capital city of the region ruled by the tetrarch Philip (not to be confused with Herod Philip). Caesarea Philippi is at 1,147 feet above sea level, a lush location hidden at the base of Mount Hermon and amid three valleys. Several springs around the city are the upper sources for the Jordan River.

After arriving, the Lord Jesus asked His disciples a question: *"Who do men say that I, the Son of Man, am?"* The disciples responded by saying that some believed that He was John the baptizer (14:2; Luke 3:15), others thought Him to be Elijah, or Jeremiah, or another of the Old Testament prophets (v. 14). While anyone else would have been honored to be considered alongside these great men of faith from the past, these views of Jesus were lacking. He was not Messiah's forerunner prophesied by Isaiah (Isa. 40:3) or merely one of God's prophets; rather, He was "the Prophet" that Moses foretold would come to show Israel the way back to God (Deut. 18:15-19). He was God-incarnate, Israel's Messiah, and any other view of Him was deficient and insulting.

Then the Lord asked a more important question, *"Who do you say that I am?"* (v. 15). Peter did not hesitate to answer, *"You are the Christ, the Son of the living God"* (v. 16). Although Peter was still learning the greatness of His Savior, he did understand that Jesus Christ was the Son of God and had come from heaven to the earth to do His Father's will.

There are seven important events pertaining to Christ's ministry that are recorded in all four Gospels: The ministry of John the baptizer as the forerunner of Christ, the feeding of the 5000, Peter's confession of Jesus being the Christ, the Triumphal Entry presentation of Messiah, and the crucifixion, burial, and resurrection of the Lord.

Christ Will Build His Church (vv. 17-20)

Peter understood who Christ was and that He had come from heaven in obedience to His Father's will. He was the Son of God in the flesh. John says that it is the spirit of antichrist to deny this truth (1 Jn. 4:2-3). Anyone having a diminished view of the Savior, such as denying His deity (i.e., that He is the great I Am), will perish in their sins (John 8:24).

The Lord rejoiced in Peter's answer, for human reasoning could never render such a conclusion. Accordingly, on this occasion, the Lord addressed Peter as "Simon Bar-Jonah," that is, his natural or given name (John 1:42). The natural man, what is "flesh and blood," cannot understand spiritual truth (1 Cor. 2:14), but the Lord told Peter that His Father who is in heaven had revealed this truth to Him (v. 17). Because of Peter's faith, God the Father had blessed him with understanding of who Jesus Christ really was.

Then the Lord said, *"You are Peter, and on this rock I will build My church"* (v. 18). Peter was the spiritual name that the Lord had assigned him on their first meeting (John 1:42). What the natural man fails to understand, the spiritual man embraces in faith. The Lord said that on this "rock" (i.e., Peter's spiritual profession of who Christ is) He would build His Church and the gates of Hades would not prevail against it. Peter's name in the Greek text is *petros*, meaning a stone or rock fragment. Some have taught that Peter, himself, would be the foundation for building the Church (and thus he is supposed to be the first Pope). However, the Greek word for the "rock" that the Church would be founded on is *petra*, meaning a massive rock. Petros is in the masculine gender and *petra* is in the feminine, so the two words cannot be equated. Later, Peter said that he was one of many living stones in the spiritual temple called the Church that Christ was building on the foundational statement that Peter had previously declared (1 Pet. 2:4-5).

This new Temple of God would be created by the Holy Spirit and therefore would not be physical, but spiritual in nature (Eph. 2:22). The foundation for this mysterious temple is the gospel truth first declared by Peter and further explained by the Apostles (Eph. 2:20; Heb. 2:3-4). Before His crucifixion, Christ declared that on the "rock" of Peter's confession that He was the Christ, the Son of the Living God, He would build His Church and the gates of Hades would not prevail against it. The tense of the Greek verb *oikodomeo*, rendered "I will build," is future. But before Christ could start building His Church, He must complete His program for saving Israel – He must establish the New Covenant that would ensure the restoration of the Jewish nation in a future day.

This is the first time that Christ has mentioned His Church, which would be composed of both Jews and Gentiles beginning at the Feast of Pentecost fifty days after His resurrection (Acts 2). The Greek word for Church is *ekklesia*, which means "called out ones." The Church is a company of believers who are *kaleo* (called) – *ek* (out of or from something). But what are God's people called out from? Randy P. Amos explains, and may believers live accordingly:

- They are called *out of* the world's thinking and system (John 15:19).
- They are called *out of* the perishing nations (Acts 15:14).
- They are delivered *from* this present age (Gal. 1:4).

- They are delivered *from* the power of Satan's darkness (Col. 1:13).
- They will be physically delivered *out of* this world into Heaven (Rev. 3:10).
- They are commanded to come *out of* wicked Babylon (Rev. 18:4).[48]

Because Peter had been forthright in rightly declaring who Jesus was, the Lord blessed Peter with *"the keys of the kingdom of heaven"* (v. 19). Those holding the keys to something have authority over it. Peter would have heaven's authority to open new doors of gospel opportunity from Jerusalem to the uttermost parts of the world. The book of Acts records three times that Peter turned the key, so to speak, to advance the work of the Lord in building His Church. The first key related to the Jews, the second key to the Samaritans, and the third key to the gospel work among the Gentiles.

The Jews: Peter is speaking to a large group of Jews gathered at the temple for the feast of Pentecost and three thousand souls came to Christ (Acts 2:41). To ensure that these believing Jews were identifying with Christ and not Judaism, the apostles laid hands on those who had confessed Christ in baptism. These then received the Holy Spirit.

The Samaritans: The second key unlocked gospel expansion among the Samaritans (Acts 8:12-16). Phillip had informed the apostles that the Samaritans were receiving the gospel message. Peter and John were sent to investigate the matter. They laid hands on the Samaritans (after their confession through baptism) to receive the Holy Spirit. This act demonstrated that Samaritans could be saved by the same message that the apostles were preaching to the Jews.

The Gentiles: Through a vision of a sheet containing various unclean creatures coming down from heaven, God taught Peter that "w*hat God has cleansed you must not call common"* (Acts 10:15). Immediately after this, messengers from the house of Cornelius in Caesarea arrived where Peter was lodging to request his presence. Peter departed with them and shared the gospel message with the household of Cornelius, and immediately the Gentiles started speaking in tongues, just as the Jews did at Pentecost when the Holy Spirit came upon them to indwell and fill them (Acts 10:47-48). The speaking in tongues provided evidence to Peter that the Gentiles could be saved by the preaching of the gospel message. The third key to the kingdom had been turned – the gospel had come to the Gentiles (e.g., Acts 16:14-15, 30-33, 18:8). By one gospel message, Christ was building one Church, not a separate Jewish and Gentile church.

The Lord Jesus had been preaching with His disciples in northern Israel for about two years but had been widely rejected. Consequently, He instructed His disciples not to publicize that He was the Christ (v. 20). The people enjoyed His stories and benefited from His miracles, but generally they were not interested in the spiritual ramifications of His message. The Jews longed to be delivered from the Romans, but not from themselves through inward reflection, humble repentance, and subjection to Christ. This was the deliverance God wanted for His covenant people, but they were blind to it. Christ's early popularity had waned, and going forward, His course was steadfast to Calvary.

Christ Foretells His Death (vv. 21-23)

Often Scripture provides its own outline of a particular passage or book. The phrase *"from that time,"* found only twice in Matthew's Gospel (4:17 and 16:21), properly divides the book into three main sections: *"From that time ... Repent for the Kingdom of heaven is at hand"* (Matt. 4:17). *"From that time forth began Jesus to show unto His disciples, how that He must...suffer"* (Matt. 16:21). Accordingly, Matthew 1:1 – 4:16 forms an introduction, while Matthew 4:17 – 16:20 presents the Jewish Messiah, and Matthew 16:21 – 28:20 records the rejection of the Jewish Messiah. The last section begins after Peter's confession of Jesus as Christ and the Son of God and just prior to the Lord's transfiguration.

It is at this time that the Lord plainly informs His disciples that He must go to Jerusalem and suffer many things by Israel's religious leaders, including being put to death. But this was not the end of the story; He would be raised from the dead on the third day (v. 21).

Peter, who had just declared Christ to be the Son of the living God and received the keys to the kingdom, took the Lord Jesus aside privately to correct Him, *"Far be it from You, Lord; this shall not happen to You!"* (v. 22). The Father had revealed to Peter who His Son was, but Peter did not understand the Son's mission as God's Lamb of sacrifice for human sin (John 1:29). Peter was now speaking in the ignorance and carnality of the flesh and the Lord abruptly rebukes him. What is contrary to God's will is from the devil, so the Lord says to Peter, *"Get behind Me, Satan! You are an offense to Me, for you are not mindful of the things of God, but the things of men"* (v. 23).

There is no doubt that Peter loved the Lord Jesus and did not want Him to suffer any harm, yet He was not speaking for God on this matter. The Lord had already taught His disciples that there was no middle ground in spiritual matters: either we are doing God's will and experiencing His power, or we join ranks with the devil to oppose God (12:30; Mark 9:38-40). This scenario reminds us not to permit natural affections to undermine what Scripture commands us to do or not do.

> And shall I pray Thee change Thy will, my Father,
> Until it be according unto mine?
> But, no, Lord, no, that never shall be, rather
> I pray Thee blend my human will with Thine.
>
> I pray Thee hush the hurrying, eager longing,
> I pray Thee soothe the pangs of keen desire –
> See in my quiet places, wishes thronging –
> Forbid them, Lord, purge, though it be with fire.
>
> — Amy Carmichael

The Cost of Discipleship (vv. 24-28)

After speaking of what doing God's will would cost Him, the Lord spoke of what following Him would cost the disciples: *"If anyone desires to come after Me, let him deny himself, and take up his cross, and follow Me"* (v. 24). The Lord speaks of three critical mindsets that those identifying with Him must have: self-denial, taking up one's own cross, and following Him.

First, a true disciple of Christ must deny himself. Complete identification with Christ means that we practically reckon who we were in Adam (i.e., in our unregenerate state) is dead and gone, and we are alive in Christ. Paul put the matter this way: *"I have been crucified with Christ; it is no longer I who live, but Christ lives in me; and the life which I now live in the flesh I live by faith in the Son of God, who loved me and gave Himself for me"* (Gal. 2:20; also see Gal. 6:14). The Greek verb rendered "crucified" in this verse has a passive voice and a perfect tense, meaning that God has once and for all carved us out of the world by the cross of His dear Son, and we are now to live for Him. We are one with Christ forever and must seek to live out His life in the way that He desires us to. This new calling precludes self-ambition, self-sufficiency, self-exaltation, and self-gratification (i.e., beyond what has God's approval).

Second, a true disciple must take up his or her cross daily. Anyone being nailed to the cross in ancient days meant that he or she was going to die a slow, agonizing death. Those crucified had nothing on their daily planners for the following week. Dying daily means, "Not my will, but your will be done, Lord." Additionally, when one's hands were nailed to the cross, it made it impossible to grab anything. Bearing one's cross daily means that believers cannot engage in carnal appetites or get sidetracked by worldly pursuits.

Paul identifies what is necessary for Christians to adequately display the name of Christ: *"Let everyone who names the name of Christ depart from iniquity"* (2 Tim. 2:19). Believers cannot pretend to be holy; their conduct will either honor a sin-hating Savior or endorse a Savior-hating system. To declare the name of Christ is a great privilege, but to fully associate with His name is the highest honor. To be identified as a "Christian" is one and the same as acknowledging Christ's call to live as He did – a holy, consecrated life to God.

Accordingly, we come to Christ's cross and leave with our own cross. The cross is a symbol of shame and death, and Christ asks those who believe in Him to follow His selfless example of faithfulness, even unto death. On the night before His crucifixion, the Lord told His disciples that by identifying with Him, they would also experience the world's hatred and persecution (John 15:18-20). The gospel message pleads for the hell-bound sinner to embrace the cross of Christ, and no less so for the heaven-bound saint to take up his or her cross that he or she might enjoy His life now.

> The cross of popular evangelicalism is not the cross of the New Testament. It is, rather, a new bright ornament upon the bosom of a self-assured and carnal Christianity. The old cross slew men; the new cross entertains them. The old cross condemned; the new cross amuses. The old cross destroyed confidence in the flesh; the new cross encourages it.
>
> – A. W. Tozer

Third, a true disciple of Christ must forsake to follow the Lord. Forsaking must occur before following. Otherwise, there are too many anchors to the old life, which will hinder close exposure to the Savior. Our desire to follow Christ is a measure of how much we truly love Him and believe His message. The reason we hold back from being fools for Christ, and thus from seeing the mighty hand of God in our lives, is disbelief – we don't trust God. Through disbelief, the One who was offended for us becomes an offense to us. Those associating with Christ superficially will ultimately find Him loathsome. A true disciple of Christ esteems Him more important than anything this world has to offer: career, wealth, education, prestige, fame, following peers, going with the flow, and even natural relationships.

> To be a follower of the crucified Christ means, sooner or later, a personal encounter with the cross. And the cross always entails loss.
>
> – Elisabeth Elliot

Many come to Christ's cross for salvation but then neglect to go on with Him and bear their own cross; this is an affront to the discipleship message He taught. The believer was never to flee the cross, but rather is to die daily upon it – only then does his or her life count for eternity (v. 25). Taking up one's cross means that we will follow Christ no matter the personal cost. The Lord Jesus is a perfect gentleman; He will not force us to bear our cross or obey His calling for our lives. However, to ignore His calling is to pursue an existence which has no meaning or no eternal value. Christ likens this ideology to man who gains all the world has to offer, but still loses His own soul in the end (v. 26). What is the profit in that – trading brief luxury and sensual pleasure for an eternal abode without God?

May each of us learn the necessity of denying ourselves, taking up our cross, and following the Lord with all our heart. There is a coming day in which all true disciples of Christ will be rewarded for following the Savior (v. 27). For those in the Church Age, this will occur at the Judgment Seat of Christ directly after the Church is raptured from the earth (Rom. 14:10-12; 2 Cor. 5:10). The Lord then said something that certainly perked up the ears of the disciples, *"There are some standing here who shall not taste death till they see the Son of Man coming in His kingdom"* (v. 28). We learn later that the Lord was speaking of what Peter, James, and John witnessed on the Mount of Transfiguration – a preview of Christ's glory in His kingdom (2 Pet. 1:16).

Additionally, as the last living disciple, an elderly John was banished to the isle of Patmos as a Roman prisoner. While there, John witnessed the apocalypse, the revelation of Jesus Christ in various visions. For our benefit, he recorded what he witnessed in heavenly realms. His chronicle of future events has been preserved for us in the book of Revelation.

158

Matthew Chapter 17

The Transfiguration of Christ (vv. 1-9)

About six days after the incident in Caesarea Philippi, the Lord took Peter, James, and John up to a high mountain in Galilee (v. 1). Luke states that it was after about eight days (Luke 9:28). As neither apostle uses exactness in the record, and Luke may be including the terminal days as well as the intervening days, we may conclude that the transfiguration occurred approximately a week after Peter's confession of faith at Caesarea Philippi.

Mount Tabor, about fifteen miles southwest of Tiberias, is the traditional site for Christ's transfiguration, but this seems unlikely as there was an ancient, fortified city on top of Tabor (1 Chron. 6:77) that was garrisoned by Roman soldiers during the time of Christ. Furthermore, the Lord and His disciples had been in the region of Decapolis for some time and recently as far north as Caesarea Philippi. This region, loosely considered to be Galilee, boasted many high mountains in which this event may have occurred. Given that the Lord had been in Caesarea Philippi (16:28) and was back in Capernaum directly afterwards (17:24), a trip to Mount Tabor (about twenty miles southwest of Capernaum and fifty miles south of Caesarea Philippi) seems unlikely. Scripture is silent on where this event occurred.

Luke infers that the Lord and His three disciples spent the night on the mountain and came down the next day (Luke 9:37). This means that the following events may have occurred during nighttime hours.

When applied metaphorically, mountains in Scripture symbolize governmental authorities or kingdoms. Both Isaiah and Micah foretold of God's glorious mountain on earth, speaking of Messiah's future earthly kingdom (Isa. 2:2; Micah 4:1-3). This future reality is momentarily displayed when the brilliance of Christ's intrinsic glory is revealed on a mountaintop in Galilee. Matthew describes the scene: *"He was transfigured before them. His face shone like the sun, and His clothes became as white as the light"* (v. 2). One can only imagine the dazzling glory of the Lord on this high, remote mountain and apparently at night.

In the preceding chapter, the Lord Jesus had said, *"Assuredly, I say to you, there are some standing here who shall not taste death till they see the Son of Man coming in His kingdom"* (16:28). Years later, Peter confirmed what was represented by this incident: *"the power and coming of our Lord Jesus Christ"* – the revealing of *"His majesty"* (2 Pet. 1:16). For a brief moment the disciples were given a foretaste of the coming kingdom.

Matthew explains what happened next: *"And behold, Moses and Elijah appeared to them, talking with Him. Then Peter answered and said to Jesus, 'Lord, it is good for us to be here; if You wish, let us make here three tabernacles: one for You, one for Moses, and one for Elijah'"* (vv. 3-4). The presence of both Moses and Elijah is significant, as Moses represents the Law and Elijah the prophets. All that the Law and the prophets reveal about Israel's coming Messiah will be fulfilled by Jesus Christ. Just as the disciples saw Christ on earth in His glory, in a coming day the entire world will see Christ in His glorious kingdom!

But it was not time for His kingdom to come. Peter's suggestion of erecting three tents showed a lack of discernment for the Lord's proper place in the kingdom. Yet, his unintentional blunder was immediately checked when a sudden bright cloud overshadowed them and God the Father declared, *"This is My beloved Son, in whom I am well pleased. Hear Him"* (v. 5). The disciples fell to the ground in fear, but the Lord touched them and when they looked up, they only saw the Lord and in His normal appearance (vv. 6-8). There is a glorious earthly kingdom coming in which Jesus Christ will be wonderfully recognized as God's only begotten Son. He will rule the earth with the full glory, honor, and authority as God's faithful Son.

The Lord asked Peter, James, and John not to reveal what had happened on the mountain until after His resurrection (v. 9). The establishment of His kingdom would occur after His second advent to the earth, but His redemptive work of Calvary was yet unfinished business that must be attended to. Suffering must precede glory!

Elijah Must Come (vv. 10-13)

Having just witnessed a preview of Christ's coming in power and glory, the disciples asked the Lord about the appearance of Messiah's forerunner, Elijah, before the kingdom could be established (v. 10). The prophet Malachi foretold that God would send the prophet Elijah again just prior to the Day of the Lord: *"Behold, I am going to send you Elijah the prophet before the coming of the great and terrible day of the Lord"* (Mal. 4:5).

The Lord confirmed that the spirit of Elijah was in John, who faithfully called that nation to repentance before Christ began His ministry during His first advent (vv. 11-12). Likewise, 144,000 Jews will be sealed and empowered by the Holy Spirit to again preach the Kingdom Gospel message just before Christ's second advent. Their mission will be similar to Elijah's previous ministry to apostate Israel; it is also possible that Elijah himself will be one of the two powerful witnesses spoken of in Revelation 11:3-14.

F. B. Hole summarizes how Malachi's references to God's messenger (3:1) and to Elijah (4:5) tie together:

> At His first advent the messenger sent in advance was clearly John the Baptist, who prepared the way of the Lord, and came in the spirit and power of Elijah, though not the Elijah of which Malachi 4:5 speaks, for he is to come before the great and dreadful day of the Lord in judgment. John came after the fashion of Elijah, but before the coming of the Messiah in grace, who is the Master, identified here with Jehovah.[49]

Clearly, John the baptizer was not Elijah in person (John 1:21-23), but he was God's messenger (3:1) who came in the spirit of Elijah's ministry to call the nation to repentance, hence preparing the way of the Lord. An angel confirmed that this would be the focus of John's ministry even before he was born (Luke 1:17). Then, years later, the Lord Jesus affirmed John's Elijah-like ministry: *"For all the prophets and the law prophesied until John. And if you are willing to receive it, he is Elijah who is to come. He who has ears to hear, let him hear!"* (11:13-15).

As in the days of Elijah, Israel did not receive John's message of repentance either (vv. 12-13). So, while John fulfilled the prophecy in the execution of an Elijah-type ministry, it was not successful; therefore, Elijah must yet come in such a way that results in national revival of the Jewish nation (Mal. 4:6). Since that will not occur until the Tribulation Period, many believe that Elijah, who did not previously experience death, but must (Heb. 9:27), will be one of the two witnesses for Christ in Revelation 11. (Perhaps Enoch will be the other for the same reason.)

These two men, whoever they are, will preach repentance, will withstand the Antichrist, and will perform great wonders (Rev. 11:1-13).

Whether this will be Elijah himself (as possibly indicated in verse 11) or another who comes like John in the spirit of Elijah's ministry is debated. However, the prophecy predicts that Israel will not come to Christ without a supernaturally empowered ministry like Elijah's to call them to repentance. It is with this promise of Christ's coming to judge the wicked, to reward the righteous, and to restore the nation of Israel to Himself that the Old Testament closes. God is not finished with the Jewish nation. Their hope is in Christ, and He is coming in power and in glory. May the Sun of Righteousness rise soon (Mal. 4:2)!

Lack of Prayer – Lack of Power (vv. 14-21)

The twelve disciples had just returned from preaching the kingdom message throughout Galilee. The Lord had given them authority over demons and the power to cure infirmities as they went (Luke 9:1). Immediately after the Lord and His disciples descended the mountain, they were met by a large crowd. A man came to the Lord and kneeled before Him with an urgent request: *"Lord, have mercy on my son, for he is an epileptic and suffers severely; for he often falls into the fire and often into the water. So, I brought him to Your disciples, but they could not cure him"* (vv. 15-16).

To have Christ's authority and not reflect His ability in ministry is an offense to the Lord. Accordingly, the Lord publicly chided His disciples for lacking faith to heal the man's son. They were acting like the general Jewish populace, from which they had been called, *"a faithless and perverse generation"* (v. 17). The Lord then asked the father to bring his son to Him, which he did. The epileptic symptoms were resulting from demon possession, so the Lord rebuked the demon residing within the boy and he was instantly cured (v. 18).

Afterwards, the disciples came to the Lord Jesus privately and asked, *"Why could we not cast it out?"* (v. 19). The Lord answered their inquiring by stating that they lacked faith to cast out the demon. Even a little faith in God, as likened to the small size of a mustard seed, can move mountains. Mountains here speak of seemingly insurmountable difficulties. True faith that discerns the will of God will lay hold of the power of God through prayer and fasting (v. 21).

The Critical Text does not include verse 21; however, the expression is found in the parallel account of Mark 9:29, less the phrase "and fasting." The Majority manuscripts speak of prayer and fasting in both passages. The Lord had already instructed His disciples about appropriate fasting, *"when you fast"* (5:17). This affirms that fasting should be a normal part of the believer's life. Paul later highlighted the importance of prayer and fasting in the Christian experience (Acts 13:2-3, 14:23; 1 Cor. 7:5). This means that prayerless believers will be powerless failures in serving the Lord! The Christian life should be marked by prayer and fasting. A believer who fails to pray will fail at everything.

Christ Foretells of His Death and Resurrection (vv. 22-23)

While still in Galilee, the Lord again reminded His disciples of the sorrow that awaited Him in Jerusalem. This is the third time that the Lord Jesus has spoken of His forthcoming betrayal, death, and resurrection in Matthew's record. The two previous occurrences were Matthew 16:21 and 17:9. It is doubtful that the disciples fully understood the meaning of the Lord's statement, but after hearing His words, they were "exceedingly sorrowful" regardless (v. 23).

Temple Tax Miraculously Paid (vv. 24-27)

The Lord and His disciples traveled back to Capernaum. While there, an individual who collected the half-shekel tax to maintain the temple challenged Peter, *"Does your Teacher not pay the temple tax?"* (v. 24). Hoping to avert a conflict with Jewish religious leaders and perhaps to prevent an embarrassing situation, Peter affirmed that the Lord would pay the tax.

According to the Mishnah, Jewish men (excluding the priests) over the age of twenty were required to pay a half-shekel annually to support temple maintenance.[50] What had been a one-time requirement by Moses when the liberated Israelites were numbered in the wilderness (Ex. 30:12-15) had been enlarged by human command. God's house was supposed to be a place of worship and of prayer and was to be supported by the tithes and gifts of the people (Neh. 10:38-39). The activities at Herod's temple were governed by ritualism, legalism, and commercialism. Consequently, the Lord was not burdened to pay a tax devised by religious men who wanted money from their subjects.

After Peter returned to the house where the Lord and His disciples were residing, the Lord preempted Peter's inquiry about the tax with His own question to Peter: *"From whom do the kings of the earth take customs or taxes, from their sons or from strangers?"* (v. 25). Peter answered correctly, *"From strangers"* (v. 26). The Lord added, *"Then the sons are free."* The point being that a king taxes the subjects of his kingdom to gain his support, not his own family. To tax his family would not gain him anything, as what was already his would just come back to him. Since the temple was technically God's house, and the Lord Jesus was God's Son, it would not be proper for Him to pay tribute to Himself.

However, to make for peace and not offend those who did not understand this truth, the Lord agreed to pay the temple tax. He then instructed Peter to go to the sea and cast a hook and line into the water and the first fish that he caught would have a piece of money in its mouth (v. 27). The "piece of money" was a "shekel" (*stater*), a silver coin worth twice the value of the temple tax. Peter was to pay the tax on behalf of the Lord and himself with the money found in the fish's mouth.

Laurence Laurenson describes the lesson depicted in the story for believers to grasp and what the Lord wanted Peter to learn from it:

> Though the believer is placed by grace in the highest possible position as a child of God, even while here, yet the same grace enables him to walk through this world seeking no place in it, and accepting no place from it, other than the place given to the Lord Himself – that of being both despised and rejected. And just in proportion as he is true to the Lord, so will he find that the world will treat him as it treated his Master. Here we find that this truth is developed as the outcome of Peter's hasty assumption that the Lord, as a good Jew (for Peter's appreciation of the Lord here rises no higher), would necessarily pay the temple tribute. But the Lord takes occasion to teach Peter three lessons.
>
> *First,* that when the kings of the earth levy tribute, they take it from strangers: their own children are free.
>
> *Second,* that He, though He was the Son of God and Lord of the temple, yet claimed no right and demanded no place, but maintained His position of lowly grace, and was willing to be treated even as the kings of the earth treat "strangers," as indeed He was – the Heavenly Stranger upon the earth.
>
> *Third,* He would associate with Himself, His followers, providing for them at the same time and meeting every need of their pathway.[51]

Matthew Chapter 18

Must Have Childlike Faith to Enter the Kingdom (vv. 1-6)

The disciples came to the Lord Jesus with a question, *"Who then is greatest in the kingdom of heaven?"* (v. 1). The Lord then called a little child to Him and set him in the midst of them (v. 2). Apparently, the child came to the Lord without hesitation, which was the behavior the Lord wanted to apply in His object lesson:

> *Assuredly, I say to you, unless you are converted and become as little children, you will by no means enter the kingdom of heaven, therefore whoever humbles himself as this little child is the greatest in the kingdom of heaven* (vv. 3-4).

Additionally, the Lord told His disciples that *"he who is greatest among you shall be your servant. And whoever exalts himself will be humbled, and he who humbles himself will be exalted"* (23:12). The physical kingdom would not be established for some time, but the inward or spiritual realities of the kingdom would be revealed in Spirit-filled believers during the Church Age. This is what the Lord is speaking of now. Greatness is obtained in the kingdom by assuming a humble attitude before others to best serve them: Do we willingly serve others before ourselves? Do we quickly sacrifice our rights for the good of others (1 Cor. 9:19)? Do we serve to insert our personal opinions? Do we desire visibility or recognition for serving? How do we respond when treated like a servant (John 3:29-30)? Do we complain while serving? Do we gloat over our doings? Do we listen or seek to promote ourselves?

In verse 4, the Lord says that greatness in His kingdom would be achieved by humbling oneself, but in Luke 9, He adds the necessity of demonstrating His love and humility to the lowliest believer. Our esteem for the lowliest believer in the Church shows how much we love the Lord Jesus (25:40). From the parallel account of this incident in Luke, we learn that the disciples had been thinking of their own greatness (Luke 9:46). As a result, they lacked power in the Lord's work, and they lacked wisdom and commitment to properly do what the Lord tasked them to do (Luke 9:40, 54-56).

Although there is no example of infant baptism in the New Testament, this passage and Matthew 19:13-15 have been used as a proof text by some to assert its necessity. Notice that baptism is not mentioned, there is no example in Scripture of anyone being baptized without repenting and confessing Christ first, and there is also no water referenced in this story. The Lord merely used a small child as an object lesson to teach His disciples about having childlike faith in following Him and exhibiting childlike humility in serving others. The idea that baptizing an infant somehow washes away the original sin of a child to save him or her from hell or that it somehow makes the child safe until salvation is received later is an affront to the gospel message. The Lord Jesus said, *"Come! And let him who thirsts come. Whoever desires, let him take the water of life freely"* (Rev. 22:17). We may choose to come or not to come to Christ for salvation, but we cannot decide for others.

Having addressed the childlike humility that servants must have towards each other to advance spiritually in the kingdom, the Lord seamlessly transitions to caring for those young in the faith (vv. 5-6). In verses 2-5, the Greek word *paidion* is repeatedly used to speak of a "little child" or "little children," but a different Greek word, *mikros*, is used in verses 6, 10, 14. *Mikros* means "little" and the plural form is used here to speak of those young in the faith – babes in Christ. Anyone receiving (assisting) those who are His will receive a reward as if he or she were serving Christ Himself (v. 5). Anyone who harms those who have come to Him in childlike faith will, however, be punished (v. 6).

Obviously all those who harm innocent children will be punished by the Lord, but our Savior here is speaking of those who would harm the spiritual children (true believers) of His kingdom. Those who bless them will have His blessing, but those who harm them will be severely judged. Harm here speaks of robbing a believer's innocence, or seducing him or her to sin, or corrupting a believer's testimony or ministry through false doctrine. Believers can either lead others into a higher experience with the Lord through faith, humility, and obedience or cause them to stumble in their faith through fear, pride, and disobedience. For example, Peter caused Barnabas and other Jewish and Greek believers to stumble in their faith in Antioch (Gal. 2:11-13). Paul then rebuked Peter for doing so.

A millstone was a heavy stone used for grinding grain and was often turned by an animal during milling operations. Having a millstone strapped to one's neck and then being thrown into the sea pictures God's zeal for punishing those who harm His children. On this point, William MacDonald writes, "It is bad enough to sin against oneself, but to cause a believer to sin is to destroy his innocence, corrupt his mind, and stain his reputation. Better to die a violent death than to trifle with another's purity!"[52]

Do Not Offend Children (vv. 7-14)

While living in a sin-cursed world that is plagued with all sorts of evils, secular philosophies, and flesh-controlled behaviors, offenses to God's children are inevitable. But the Lord warned that it would be much better to suffer in righteousness than to be an agent of evil that offends those who are His (v. 7). Believers therefore should take drastic measures to discipline themselves, rather than to tempt other believers to stumble in their faith and experience God's chastisement for doing so.

Whether the offending member is a hand, a foot, or an eye, it would be better to have these removed by a surgeon's scalpel than to permit any member of our body to undermine God's work in someone else's life. A hyperbole is then used to amplify this point: It would be better to endure life without limbs than to be cast into hell with all of them. This statement does not suggest that there will be some without limbs after experiencing bodily resurrection. Rather, the Lord is referring to one's physical condition at the time of death, as determined by the choices we made during our lifetime to harm or to not harm children of the kingdom (other believers).

To affirm the fact that God has great concern for His own children, the Lord again refers to the small child before them. God has assigned guardian angels in heaven to watch over children (v. 10). The point being that whether human children on earth or spiritual children of the kingdom, God has a great concern for the young. Apparently, guardian angels provide a certain level of protection against the forces of evil which work in various ways to prevent them from understanding divine truth and turning to God.

Just as a shepherd with one hundred sheep is concerned about one lamb that strays from the fold, God is concerned about each child of His and desires that none should stray away from Him (vv. 11-13). Our heavenly Father desires the unregenerate to come to Him with childlike faith and for those who have done so to continue before Him with the same spirit of humility and sincerity (v. 14).

Resolving Offenses With Christ's Authority (vv. 15-20)

The Lord provides some timeless instruction in how to resolve personal offenses. If an offense is taken, we must be sure to gather all the facts before responding. Often the first appearance of a situation is not correct. Additionally, our minds tend to fill in missing information with negative thoughts, so we must stay positive in our thinking or at least give the benefit of the doubt until we know the facts.

Once the facts are known, we then decide if this is an offense that should be addressed to benefit the offender or if it should be released to the Lord without taking any personal action. If the former course of action is determined, then we must "go and tell" the offender privately and inform him or her of the "fault" (v. 15). "Go and tell" means no letters, text messages, emails, or even phone calls. Face-to-face communication is the best means of resolving conflict. The word "fault" is singular, so do not take a list of grievances to someone and expect a favorable outcome. The Lord's people need to keep short accounts with the Lord and with each other. This requires us to work through problems and offenses one at a time.

If the offending party accepts the claim and asks for forgiveness, then we must declare our forgiveness (Luke 17:3) and the matter should be forgotten. If the claim is rejected, then we must decide whether to continue to pursue the matter further (v. 16). We must ask ourselves if doing so would be beneficial to the offender by correcting a sin or bent? If the matter is pursued, then we must take one or two trusted persons with us as witnesses to the conversation.

If the issue is still not resolved, then we must decide if it should be taken to the church (i.e., the church elders) or dropped. It is important to realize that if a personal issue is taken to the church for a ruling, we are not expecting the fellowship of the offender with other believers to be affected by that decision. A one-time offense between two people is not a matter that should impact everyone. The "you" in verse 17 is singular; therefore, we are not forcing uninvolved people to have an issue with someone else because we do.

If the church agrees with offended person's position, then everyone understands that he or she has a right to relate to the offending party as "a heathen and a tax collector." These people were outside the fellowship of Jewish society. Likewise, having received confirmation of the matter through the local church, a believer would be correct in not associating with another believer who had sinned against him or her and would not repent and apologize for the offense. However, it is important to remember that the outcome cannot be considered as a matter of Church discipline (excommunication) unless there is proof of unrepentant sin by the offender. Then the fellowship of all those in the local church with the one in sin would be affected. Believers cannot have fellowship with those who are not in fellowship with the Lord, so the action of church discipline is acknowledging the spiritual reality which already exists.

A public statement by the church would put extra pressure on the affronting party to resolve the outstanding offense. Believers are not to take each other to civil court to resolve their differences, as this causes disdain on Christ's name (1 Cor. 6:1-8). During the Church Age, the highest court for resolving issues among Christians is to be the local church. Thus, a decision rendered by a local church is bound by God's authority (v. 18). But God will only honor those decisions that are just and righteous. If church elders abuse their delegated authority for personal gain, or by being a respecter of persons, or for achieving personal vengeance, then God will render justice on those who have brought dishonor on His Son's name (Heb. 13:17; Jas. 1:20).

While verses 19-20 have general application for applying Christ's authority in corporate prayer, the specific context of the passage is for the judicial situation just discussed. The size of the local church in issuing such judgments between believers is not important. If two or three believers come together in Christ's name (i.e., invoking His authority that is consistent with His Word and His character), then whatever is decided on in unity will be bound in heaven (v. 19). This would include judicial judgments and matters of prayer.

The power of believers collectively praying in unity is witnessed several times in the book of Acts (e.g., 1:14, 4:24-31, 12:6-11). In each case there was a wonderful work of God in response to the prayers of the saints. In response to the corporate prayers in Acts 1, the Holy Spirit came in Acts 2, and the Church Age began with spectacular signs and miracles. The result was 3,000 souls were won to Christ.

In Acts 4, the believers with one accord exalted the Lord and prayed for boldness to preach the Word of God. What was the result of their praying? *"And when they had prayed, the place where they were assembled together was shaken; and they were all filled with the Holy Spirit, and they spoke the word of God with boldness"* (Acts 4:31).

Then, in Acts 12, we read of another situation prompting the Church to gather for corporate prayer:

> *Peter was therefore kept in prison, but constant prayer was offered to God for him by the church. ... So, when he had considered this, he came to the house of Mary, the mother of John whose surname was Mark, where many were gathered together praying* (Acts 12:5, 12).

Herod intended to have the apostle publicly executed the next day, but the Lord had different plans and sent an angel to rescue Peter from prison. He then went to a house where he knew the saints would be gathered to pray, and indeed they were. The apostle was then able to inform everyone how God had wonderfully answered their prayers.

The Lord promises to answer those prayers asked of the Father in His name (John 14:13, 15:16, 16:23). Additionally, He promises that when two or more agree on prayer requests, He will honor His Son's name by answering them (v. 20). Having immediate access to God should prompt Christians to labor together in prayer, wherever and whenever they can (Heb. 4:14-16). Never resist the urge to pray!

How Often Should We Forgive Others (vv. 21-35)

After listening to the Lord's instruction in how offenses between those in God's family should be resolved, Peter had a question: *"Lord, how often shall my brother sin against me, and I forgive him? Up to seven times?"* (v. 21). The Lord had given instruction in how to deal with an offender, but how should the offended party behave? Peter's question indicates a lack of understanding and perhaps humility also on the topic of forgiveness. First, he presents himself as the offended party and not the offender. Second, Peter thought that seven times was more than sufficient to forgive someone that had offended him.

Although Peter thought seven times was sufficient to demonstrate grace, the Lord had a quite different idea. He said that "seventy times seven" was a better disposition to have (v. 22). The Lord was not suggesting that forgiveness should be limited to 490 tallied infractions, but rather, by combining the two numbers, we are to maintain an open-ended attitude.

Paul gives us the motivation to release the offenses of others immediately when we have been wronged: *"And be kind to one another, tenderhearted, forgiving one another, even as God in Christ forgave you"* (Eph. 4:32). Releasing the offenses of others to God frees our minds to serve God appropriately. Because we fully trust Him to handle the situation, we move these released offenses from the foreground to the background of our minds; this permits us to live for God without being hindered by them. Believers are to have a releasing spirit and are to not limit mercy if the offender admits his or her wrongdoing and asks to be forgiven. At such times we are commanded to declare forgiveness to the offender (Luke 17:3-4). We are to maintain such matters in the background of our minds until we can verbally declare forgiveness to the repentant, then the matter should be forgotten. Given what we have been forgiven by Christ, we are not to withhold forgiveness from others when they have repented of the wrongdoing and asked to be forgiven.

The Lord then spoke the parable of the Unforgiving Servant (vv. 23-35) in response to Peter's question as to how often forgiveness should be extended to someone requesting it. This parable was spoken in Capernaum towards the end of Christ's Galilean Ministry, about a year before Calvary.

The story reveals the proud heart of the debtor in several ways. First, he was sorry that he got caught embezzling his master's wealth, but he did not acknowledge his sin or ask for forgiveness – he merely asked for mercy (because he did not want to be imprisoned for life).

Second, the debt he owed was enormous. At this time, the region of Galilee's total annual revenue was only about 300 talents, and this man owed over thirty-three times that amount.[53] The metal is not mentioned but it is generally assumed to be silver and not gold. Given present-day prices of silver, 10,000 talents (i.e., 330 to 375 tons) of silver would be worth more than a quarter billion U.S. dollars. If the metal was gold, this amount would be multiplied by ninety to obtain its present value. Clearly, there was no way that the embezzler could ever hope to work and repay such an amount. These two behaviors indicate that his motives were fostered in pride and insincerity.

Third, after experiencing the king's immense mercy through forgiveness, he was unwilling to forgive another who owed him merely 100 denarii. This was pocket change in comparison to the debt the man had just been forgiven, yet he grabbed the debtor by the throat and demanded payment in full. The debtor begged for mercy and asked for more time to pay his outstanding balance, just as the forgiven servant had done before the king. But the forgiven servant would not relent – he wanted what was his and he wanted it immediately. Unable to pay, the man owing the smaller debt was put into prison until his account could be settled.

The king's actions reflect God's merciful character in wanting to grant forgiveness to those who are undeserving of it. He is a God of tender mercies who is slow to anger and quick to forgive. The embezzler rightly deserved to be thrown into prison, but when the king heard the guilty party beg for mercy, he was prompted to forgive him, erase the enormous debt, and not put him in prison.

However, the king's servants who understood and appreciated their master's merciful spirit were outraged by the incident and informed the king of the matter. God is also just and righteous, so when the king heard that the forgiven thief had coldly cast a fellow servant into prison over a minor debt, the servant was called before the king again. The king sharply rebuked his "wicked servant" with a question: *"Should you not also have had compassion on your fellow-servant, just as I had pity on you?"* (v. 33).

The thief had not responded properly to the king's mercy and thus invoked his wrath. The unforgiving man was thrown into prison until he could pay his original debt, which was approximately 600,000 times greater than the debt he was unwilling to forgive. In the end, he did receive what was his – the enormous debt that he had no hope of ever repaying. How unreasonable is such a callus behavior? Yet, we mimic this wicked servant anytime that we are unwilling to release the offenses of others to the Lord, who has forgiven us of so much more.

God is a forgiving God, but He judges those who willfully trample on His mercy with unthankful and unforgiving hearts (v. 35). In light of the enormous debt of sin forgiven us through the work of Calvary, let us release to God the lesser ills that we have suffered by others. Bitterness and rejoicing are both choices: The former is a decision to swallow a poison that rots the soul, while the latter choice delights in the character and attributes of our great God, who is always faithful to do good and judge all injustice. To be unforgiving of others is to behave like a wicked servant who is out of touch with the heart of God.

Frequently the enemy entices Christians to harbor an unforgiving spirit, a very common symptom indeed among God's children. Such bitterness and fault-finding and enmity inflict a severe blow upon spiritual life.

– Watchman Nee

Matthew Chapter 19

Christ's Teaching on Divorce (vv. 1-12)

Neither Matthew nor Mark provide details concerning the Lord's Judean ministry from the time of the Feast of Tabernacles (in late September) to the Feast of Dedication celebrated in December. However, Luke dedicates nine chapters of his gospel record to the timeframe (chs. 10-18), while John includes five chapters (chs. 7-11) in his account. The Lord will spend the next four months in Perea and then depart for Jerusalem about a week prior to His passion.

As the Lord trekked southward through Perea (on the eastern side of the Jordan River), a crowd of people followed Him, and He healed many of their infirmities (vv. 1-2). But the Pharisees were also among the multitude. They did not seek to hear Christ's teachings or to be healed by Him. Rather, they came to test Him, hoping to somehow catch Him in His words to accuse Him of wrongdoing. The Pharisees asked a question which they thought might serve this purpose: *"Is it lawful for a man to divorce his wife for just any reason?"* (v. 3). Even among Israel's leaders there were some who took a stringent view of divorce and remarriage, while others held a liberal attitude towards the teachings of Moses. So regardless how the Lord answered this question, some would not be pleased with the answer.

Historically speaking, the Old Testament indicates that children were crucial to Jewish family life. Inheritance and clan leadership were passed down to male children. This is why Elkanah likely married Peninah; Hannah, his first wife, could not bear him children (1 Sam. 1). At this time, men did what was right in their own eyes (Judg. 17:6). Later, kings often had multiple wives to ensure there were plenty of males who could survive, if a rival tried to seize the throne by massacring the kingly line. Though a practical solution from a human perspective, polygamy was not God's intention for marriage.

God instituted His Law with the Israelites to show them that they were inherently sinful, condemned before God, and needed a Savior (Rom. 3:20; Gal. 3:24). The Law put constraints on their sin and warned them against behaviors that displeased God. For example, God's design for marriage did not allow for divorce, but because of the hardness of man's heart, God permitted divorce in the Law with constraints (v. 8). Likewise, polygamy was not God's plan for marriage, but at that time He only warned against it and put constraints on it (Deut. 17:17, 21:15). Through the Mosaic Law, God proved to the Jews that they were Law-breakers and thus deserved judgment. However, with the Holy Spirit's coming to indwell believers in the Church Age, the Lord Jesus again confirmed God's standard for marriage:

> *He who made them at the beginning 'made them male and female,' and said, 'For this reason a man shall leave his father and mother and be joined to his wife, and the two shall become one flesh'? So then, they are no longer two but one flesh. Therefore, what God has joined together, let not man separate* (vv. 4-6).

This divine design for marriage was given to our first parents in Eden, before sin entered the world and centuries before the Law was given. Divorce did not originate with God; rather, it is a consequence of human sin. The Mosaic Law put boundaries on divorce to limit its destructive repercussions among God's people. Moses did not command divorce, but it was permitted with limitations (Deut. 24:1-4).

Having confirmed God's original design of permanence for marriage, the Lord said that if a divorce occurs for any other reason than "sexual immorality," anyone marrying one of the divorced persons will be committing adultery (v. 9). The Greek noun *porneia* is rendered "sexual immorality" in this verse and it is singular in number. *Porneia* is usually translated as "fornication" in Scripture, which speaks of any sexual activity outside of a marriage covenant between a husband and a wife. Hence, the sin of adultery is a subset of fornication. The Greek verb rendered "commits adultery" is in the present tense to indicate an ongoing situation.

Because Matthew is written to a Jewish audience and the exception clause is not found in the parallel accounts in Mark and Luke, some view Matthew's statements relating to the period of marital purity – that is, the time between the marriage betrothal and the physical consummation of the marriage covenant by the bride and groom. While this understanding is possible, the Lord does not uphold the Mosaic Law or developed Jewish traditions, but God's original design for marriage. Under the Law,

174

unfaithfulness during the time of purity was to be punished by death and divorce was not an option (Deut. 22:23-24).

Mary and Joseph were in the time of purity when the Lord Jesus was conceived in her womb by the power of the Holy Spirit. There is no example in the Old Testament of a convicted adulterer being stoned, and Joseph's example of wanting to divorce Mary quietly (1:18-25) indicates that the Jews favored divorce instead of stoning. However, the Jewish leaders understood that the Law demanded stoning for the offense of adultery (John 8:1).

The Lord was affirming God's original design for marriage which was for one biological man and one biological woman to be bound by a marriage covenant until separated by death. Furthermore, the idea of polygamy was not what God intended for marriage. The fact that a man would be disqualified from church leadership if he was a polygamist tells us what marital pattern is important to God. The apostles only had one wife or no wives (1 Cor. 9:5) and those in church leadership or in the office of deacons could not be polygamists (Tit. 1:6; 1 Tim. 3:2, 12). Scripture records no example of any Christian engaging in the practice of polygamy; monogamy, however, is repeatedly shown to be the proper pattern for marriage (Eph. 5:31-33).

Under the Law, adulterers were to be put to death if found guilty of violating the seventh of God's Ten Commandments. This would permit the innocent party to remarry if desired. In the Church Age, we do not put adulterers to death, but the sin breaks the marriage covenant, nonetheless. Civil divorce for any other reason than adultery is not biblical. Those who divorce for other reasons and remarry afterwards would be guilty of ongoing adultery, for the Lord views them as still married to their previous spouse. Such offenses can be forgiven through repentance and the blood of Christ, but there are always consequences for disobeying God. We choose our sin and God chooses the consequences of our sin to better us and to honor Himself.

Paul presents a high standard for Christians to follow in this matter: remain with your spouse until death ends your marriage covenant, but if you cannot live together, you may separate and live in purity, but divorce should not be sought (1 Cor. 7:10-11). Each situation is different, and there may be safety issues or financial concerns that necessitate a civil divorce, but in God's eyes that does not free the husband and wife from their vow to each other and to God. It is important to realize that civil divorce and biblical divorce have different criterion.

After hearing the Lord's teaching about marriage and that divorce was only permitted for the offense of adultery, they wondered if it would be safer not to marry to avoid any possibility of having a failed marriage and sinning against God (v. 10). This was an absurd position, as God instituted marriage for the purpose of companionship and to produce a godly seed for Him (Mal. 2:14-15). This meant that without marriage there would be no children born to be raised up for Him. Therefore, God never intended the general populace to remain unmarried. Hence, the Lord said that only a few would be able to accept a celibate lifestyle: those born as eunuchs, those made eunuchs by men, and those who chose to be eunuchs to serve the Lord (v. 12).

Blessing the Children (vv. 13-15)

Little children were being brought to the Lord that He might touch them and pray over them (v. 13). The disciples saw this activity as a waste of time and tried to stop it. However, the Lord never turned away genuine seekers, no matter how much they irritated His disciples. The Lord responded to their angst by providing an object lesson as to how one enters into His kingdom – by exercising childlike faith in Him: *"Let the little children come to Me, and do not forbid them; for of such is the kingdom of heaven"* (v. 14). Children do not need to become adults to be saved, but adults must become like children to become God's children.

Consequently, the Lord continued to lay His hands on the children and bless them (v. 15). As mentioned in the previous chapter (18:1-6), the Lord is not granting these little children access to heaven by touching them and praying for them. Those old enough to understand that they have an inherent sin problem and need for a Savior could then exercise faith in Christ and be saved by Him (John 3:18). Those too young to understand this were blessed by Christ's presence and may have received His healing and further protection from evil.

The Rich Young Ruler (vv. 16-26)

Matthew records the dialogue of a rich young man who wanted to be justified before God and thereby be assured of heaven. Many think that they are good by their own standards of evaluation, but since only God is *good*, the Lord Jesus challenged the young man to think of goodness according to *divine standards* (vv. 16-17). The Lord then used God's Commandments to bypass the intellect to speak to the inquirer's conscience (vv. 18-19). He referred to the last six of the Ten Commandments (which are manward in application). However, He placed the fifth commandment concerning honoring one's parents behind the ninth, and then represented the tenth concerning not coveting by its application of loving one's neighbor as yourself. If you truly love your neighbor, you will selflessly give to your neighbor, not lust for what he has for yourself. Why did the Lord order the commandments in this way? The purpose of the Law is to show us our sin and that we might understand that only God is good (Rom. 3:9-12). The Lord knew all about the sin of this young man, so He placed the most applicable commands last to convict him of what the Lord knew that he had failed to do.

Sadly, the Law did not achieve its intended purpose in the rich young ruler's heart. Instead of feeling guilt and impending judgment, he pompously declared that he had kept all of the Law, which he ironically broke by that false assertion (v. 20). Our gracious Lord did not rebuke the young man for his audacious statement, but instead set about to show him who his god really was. After being told that he needed to sell his possessions, give the proceeds to the poor, and follow Him, the young man departed in sorrow, for he was wealthy (vv. 21-22). Money was his god; he valued it more than treasure in heaven and following the Lord.

For those of us who have reckoned ourselves as needy sinners and have received the Savior, we can exclaim with David: *"O taste and see that the Lord is good: blessed is the man that trusts in Him"* (Ps. 34:8). Truly, God is good and does good (Ps. 119:68).

After the rich young ruler departed, the Lord informed His disciples, *"Assuredly, I say to you that it is hard for a rich man to enter the kingdom of heaven"* (v. 23). He then supplied a hyperbolic illustration to accentuate His point: *"It is easier for a camel to go through the eye of a needle than for a rich man to enter the kingdom of God"* (v. 24). Some have suggested that this analogy references the act of camels walking on their knees to get under a low archway. However, the Lord's point is not one of difficulty, but impossibility. The Greek word *rhaphidos* rendered "needle" speaks of a sewing or surgical needle. Luke uses the same description in the parallel account (Luke 18:25). The idea of a large camel fitting through the eye of a surgical needle was impossible. Likewise, anyone trusting in their riches for security or esteeming what they have as more important than pleasing God by doing His will cannot enter into heaven.

The phrases "the kingdom of God" and "the kingdom of heaven" are used interchangeably in this text by the Lord. Some believe the terms are synonymous. While this is possible, it is noticed that the kingdom of heaven contains evil components (e.g., the first four parables of Matthew 13), but the kingdom of God refers to willful submission to God's sovereign rule. Hence the kingdom of God would likely be a subset of the kingdom of heaven, which explains why the terms can be used interchangeably in the passage, without being completely synonymous.

The disciples were astonished at the Lord's statement concerning those who value their riches above the One who gave them. They asked, *"Who then can be saved?"* (v. 25). The Lord responded, *"With men this is impossible, but with God all things are possible"* (v. 26). The Lord again emphasizes that in matters of salvation it is not merely difficult for men to earn heaven by their doings; it is impossible. The work of salvation which God brings about through humble, childlike faith in the Savior is how God ushers redeemed sinners into heaven.

Reward for Faithfulness Now and Later (v. 27-30)

The Lord Jesus had previously told His disciples of the divisive outcome of gospel preaching:

> *Do not think that I came to bring peace on earth. I did not come to bring peace but a sword. For I have come to "set a man against his father, a daughter against her mother, and a daughter-in-law against her mother-in-law"; and "a man's enemies will be those of his own household"* (10:34-37).

Those who freely chose Christ as Lord and Savior would be isolated and persecuted by those who had not believed on Him. This dynamic is exceptionally painful when the division happens within a family. It is evident from Paul's instructions to the saints at Corinth that even marriages were being split apart by the gospel message (1 Cor. 7:12-16).

The rich young ruler had departed the Lord's presence sorrowfully because he was not willing to part with his wealth to follow Christ. This was the opposite response of the disciples, who had identified with Christ and had been willing to forsake all to follow Him. Peter felt that he and the other disciples were doing much better than the rich young ruler, so he asked the Lord, *"See, we have left all and followed you. Therefore what shall we have?"* (v. 27). Later, Peter would learn that what *we get* for following Christ was not as important as *having* the crucified life so that Christ can live within us and work through us (Gal. 2:20).

The Lord could have responded to Peter's not so humble inquiry with a mild rebuke, "How do you know you will have anything in the kingdom?" But He did not. Rather, the Lord affirmed that they would be highly honored and given authority in His coming kingdom (v. 28). Additionally, they would possess eternal life and even now could expect a hundredfold increase for every relationship severed by the gospel (v. 29).

It is the same for believers today. For every person who persecutes a believer, there will be a hundred more believers to extend him or her a helping hand. Christian love is a powerful weapon against the enemy, for it conveys the reality of the gospel message to the lost. May we all give thanks to the Lord for all the gracious benefits of a loving community of saints during our earthly sojourn. Indeed, rewards will be received at the *Judgment Seat of Christ*, but we can assist each other to be faithful to Christ until that day.

The Lord then reminds His disciples that they must maintain a right attitude in service now to receive His reward later: *"But many who are first will be last, and the last first!"* (v. 30). To illustrate the meaning of His statement, the Lord will tell the parable of *The Laborers* in the next chapter. It suffices here to say that believers should consider any personal sacrifices for Christ now are merely privileged investments for eternity.

People talk of the sacrifice I have made in spending so much of my life in Africa. It is emphatically no sacrifice. Say rather it is a privilege.

– David Livingstone

Love always involves responsibility, and love always involves sacrifice. And we do not really love Christ unless we are prepared to face His task and to take up His Cross.

– William Barclay

Matthew Chapter 20

The Workers in the Vineyard (vv. 1-16)

Peter had just asked the Lord Jesus a bold question concerning rewards for being loyal to Him: *"We have given up everything for you. What shall we have?"* (19:28-29). Surprisingly, the Lord did not rebuke Peter, but merely cautioned him about his motives. The Lord then affirmed that they would be highly honored and given authority in His kingdom. Moreover, they would have eternal life and could expect a hundredfold increase for every relationship severed by the gospel.

The Lord spoke *The Workers in the Vineyard* parable to accentuate the proper motives that servants of the Lord should maintain during their earthly sojourn. This story was told in the Spring of 30 A.D. during the Perean ministry as an additional response to Peter's question, "What shall we have?" The Lord and His disciples were nearing the Jordan River on their way to Jericho.

A landowner, looking for laborers to work in his vineyard, negotiated with several laborers at 6:00 a.m. to work a full day in his vineyard for a denarius (vv. 1-2). Afterwards, the landowner found men standing in the marketplace at 9 a.m., Noon, 3 p.m., and 5 p.m. These men wanted to work, but no one would hire them, so the landowner compelled them to go and work in his vineyard and he would pay them "what was right" (vv. 3-6). These workers eagerly went to the vineyard and labored for various lengths of time without knowing what they would receive at the end of the day as a wage (v. 7).

At the end of the workday, the foreman paid the laborers in the reverse order that they had been summoned (v. 8). Surprisingly, everyone received the same wage – a denarius (vv. 9-10). Those who had worked an entire day in the vineyard supposed that they would have received more from the landowner, since the latecomers were paid a full day's wage (v. 11). These workers therefore complained against the landowner, but he reminded them that they had received what they had agreed to earn for their laboring (vv. 12-13). What he paid other servants that labored for him was none of their business, for he was the master of the vineyard. Why did they think evil of him because he had extended grace to others (v. 15)?

The Lord concludes the story by saying, *"So the last will be first, and the first last. For many are called, but few are chosen"* (v. 16). Those things done in pride or for selfish reasons will not be rewarded. All those demoted by others for their honorable service will be promoted by the Lord for their faithfulness. There will be many surprises in the matter of rewards when we stand before Christ's judgment seat in a coming day.

There are at least three important applications from this parable that we should consider. First, we understand that believers are given different opportunities to serve the Lord. Some receive Christ later in life, while others are hampered by mental and physical limitations. It is comforting to know that at the *Judgment Seat of Christ*, the Lord will reward saints for faithfulness to the opportunities into which they have been entrusted. A middle-aged convert who lives vibrantly for Christ the remainder of his or her life will not receive a diminished reward. It is our faithfulness to the opportunities Christ gives to further His kingdom that is important, not how long we have been a Christian or even how faithful we were to the more glamorous opportunities afforded to us. We cannot pick and choose what we want to do for Christ. Rather, He rewards us for faithfulness to do what He puts before us in the season that He provides for us to accomplish it.

Second, the Lord Jesus will reward us far beyond what we deserve for being faithful to the opportunities that He does give us to serve Him. We need not compare our ministries to those of others, for servants are not to judge each other in this manner – only the Master will judge the value of our service (Rom. 14:4). Each of us must give an account to Christ for what we do, not what others do.

Third, we should not presuppose to what extent the Lord will reward each of us for faithful service. What rewards that He does bestow at the *Judgment Seat of Christ* will be a reflective glory of Himself that will give us a greater appreciation of heaven and opportunity to worship Christ forever. While all believers in the Church have been positionally declared righteous in Christ, each believer has the opportunity to labor in righteousness for Christ. Those things which are done in accordance with revealed truth and in the power of the Holy Spirit have eternal value. The outshining of these righteous acts is what the believer is adorned with throughout eternity (Rev. 19:7-8).

After glorification, some saints will shine brighter than others, just as some stars at night are more brilliant than others (1 Cor. 15:40-42). This acquired glory directly reflects the righteous acts (good works) that are done for Christ now (Rev. 19:8). Eternal glory has a weight to it; in other words, its quality is measurable (2 Cor. 4:17) and can be earned by believers through selfless service for Christ now. May we be faithful to all the opportunities Christ affords us to serve Him!

The Lord Predicts His Death Again (vv. 17-19)

The Lord Jesus had concluded His Perean ministry and was beginning His westerly journey to Jerusalem through Jericho (v. 29). After concluding the parable of *The Workers in the Vineyard*, He paused with His disciples to speak of His forthcoming suffering in Jerusalem (v. 17). According to Matthew's account, this is the fourth time that Christ had foretold His upcoming death and resurrection.

He knew that He would be betrayed into the hands of Israel's religious leaders, who would condemn Him to death (v. 18). Because the Jews did not have the authority to judicially execute the condemned, the Lord knew that He would be given over to the Gentiles (the Romans), who would mock, scourge, and crucify Him (v. 19). But on the third day, He would rise again from the grave.

Christ Response to James' and John's Mother (vv. 20-28)

The wife of Zebedee kneeled before the Lord to ask Him a favor. Her sons James and John were with her (v. 20). After the Lord prompted her, she requested that her two sons might sit on either side of Him in His kingdom (v. 21). After hearing her petition, the Lord affirmed that she did not fully understand the ramifications of her request. The Lord's response in verse 22 is directed to James and John, as they were clearly the ones who had prompted their mother's request. He asked them if they were able to drink from the same cup of suffering and undergo the same baptism of sorrow that He was about to undergo. They answered with self-confidence, *"We are able."*

The Lord did not deny their intentions of identifying with Him and suffering for doing so, but future reward in the kingdom must be determined by proven faithfulness, not good intentions (v. 23). Time proves the validity of the heart and His Father in heaven knew who would be faithful to live for Christ. These would be rewarded appropriately. Some are sovereignly chosen for specific roles of personal greatness, such as John the baptizer and Mary the mother of Christ, but most will earn greatness in the kingdom through personal faithfulness.

The timing of Zebedee's wife's request must have somewhat grieved the heart of the Lord. He had just spoken of His future agony and death, but His disciples were thinking about their own glory and not His suffering. Yet, the Lord graciously responded to her inquiry.

However, after the other disciples overheard the request of James and John through their mother and the Lord's response to them, they were displeased with the two brothers (v. 24). The Lord then called His disciples together to teach them that true greatness from God's perspective was using authority to humbly serve others (vv. 25-27). The disciples were not to follow the example of Gentile rulers who lorded their authority and status over others. Rather, they were to follow His example of exercising authority – sacrificially giving to serve others (v. 28). Greatness is not obtained by having position and power, but by revealing the character of Christ in what we do.

What the Lord taught in word and deed was counter to the world's philosophies of success. Worldlings will say, "save your life at all costs," but the Lord taught, "lose your life to gain one worth living." The world exclaims, "live for the moment," but Christians are to "live for eternity." Worldlings want to be served by others, but Christ taught His disciples to humble themselves and serve others, for that was the true path to greatness in His kingdom.

Biblical leadership is not one of lordship or heavy-handed tactics of control, but rather is a style that serves God's sheep and upholds them so that they flourish. The Gentile kings were often dictators, who oppressed their subjects, but those who would lead God's people must not do so. Those who love Christ must follow His sacrificial example. Christ stated that He had not come into the world to be served, but rather to die – to give His life as a ransom for those who did not deserve God's favor in any way, shape, or form. If the Lord of Glory can do that for others, should not we be able to serve those who are difficult to serve?

One must be a submitted servant before he or she can be a true leader of others. The Lord Jesus humbled Himself to serve and develop others into profitable leaders. He devoted three-plus years of His life to train twelve men, one of which was a traitor. A true mark of Christlike leadership is the ability to develop greatness in others by serving them.

The Lord's meek and humble character, His compassion for the suffering, and His resolute spirit in the face of opposition invite us to follow His example – He was a true Servant of God. Christ's selfless ministry shows us that true love needs no title to serve, just the power to do so, which is supplied by Him alone. Those who follow His example of selfless service will have the appreciation of the saints now and will be joyfully honored by the Lord Jesus in the future.

Two Blind Men Healed (vv. 29-34)

A great multitude of people followed the Lord and His disciples out of Jericho as they journeyed towards Jerusalem (v. 29). Under the Mosaic Law, at least two witnesses were required to substantiate a legal claim or allegation (Deut. 19:15). While offering instructions on how to reconcile an offense with a brother, the Lord acknowledged the importance of two witnesses to confirm the truth. *"But if he will not hear, take with you one or two more, that 'by the mouth of two or three witnesses every word may be established'"* (Matt. 18:16). Matthew is the only Gospel writer to record these statements of Christ.

As Matthew is mainly addressing a Jewish audience, he is conscious of this legal regulation in his writing. Though the other Gospel writers neglect this detail, he often identifies the existence of *two* witnesses to legally substantiate important events of the Lord's life. Although both Mark and Luke record a blind man being healed near Jericho, neither mentioned that two blind men were actually healed, but Matthew does to uphold his Jewish vantage point of two witnesses. Mark states that a blind man was healed when the Lord departed Jericho, but Luke indicates that the miracle happened just before the Lord entered the city. It is possible that there were two separate miracles, but it seems more likely that Matthew and Mark are speaking of the old city Jericho and Luke the new Jericho; both were on the Lord's route. If this is one incident, then one of the two blind men healed would be Bartimaeus as identified by Mark. His name was mentioned because of his personal dialogue with the Lord.

Two blind men were sitting on the road out of Jericho and engaged in begging when they heard the commotion. After learning that Jesus was nearing their position, they cried out as loudly as they could even after being warned by the crowd to be quiet, *"Have mercy on us, O Lord, Son of David"* (vv. 30-31). But the Lord Jesus heard their cries for help and paused to speak to them, *"What do you want Me to do for you?"* (v. 32). They quickly responded that they might gain their sight (v. 33). The Lord had compassion on them, touched their eyes, and immediately both men gained their sight and followed Him (v. 34).

Matthew Chapter 21

The King's Triumphant Entry Into Jerusalem (vv. 1-11)

The Lord and His disciples traveled towards Jerusalem. John informs us that after departing Perea that the Lord had briefly gone to Jerusalem and then to the wilderness near the city of Ephraim to escape hostility (John 11:54). Now the Lord is returning to Jerusalem for the final time of His earthly ministry, just a few days before His passion.

As the Lord and His disciples drew near the village of Bethphage on the eastern side of Mount Olivet, the Lord sent two of His disciples on a mission (v. 1). The Lord again shows the importance of the two-by-two principle in ministry for the benefit of encouragement and accountability (Mark 6:7; Luke 10:1). The two disciples were to go into the nearby village where they would immediately find a tied-up donkey with her colt (v. 2). The disciples were to loosen the donkey and bring both animals to Him. If anyone confronted them for taking the animals, they were to reply, *"The Lord has need of them"* (v. 3). After hearing this, there would not be an objection. Everything occurred just as the Lord said. Although Matthew does not record the protest of the owner, Luke does, but the owner immediately released the animals into the care of the disciples after hearing that the Lord had need of them (Luke 19:33). As noted by the "them" in verses 3 and 7, both the donkey and her colt were brought to the Lord. The other Gospels do not mention that detail.

Both Bethphage, meaning "a place of young figs," and Bethany, meaning "house of figs," were two villages on the eastern slope of Olivet. The Lord and His disciples often resided with beloved friends in Bethany (John 11:18, 12:1). Luke mentions both villages (Luke 19:29), but we are not informed which village supplied what the Savior was looking for, the colt of a donkey. These villages stand in stark contrast to the barren fig tree that the Lord cursed en route to Jerusalem to illustrate His sorrow over Israel's barren spiritual state (Matt. 21:19).

Matthew has been faithfully noting in his account the various Old Testament prophecies that Christ has fulfilled. He now refers to a prophecy declared by Zechariah four centuries earlier:

> *Tell the daughter of Zion, "Behold, your King is coming to you, lowly, and sitting on a donkey, a colt, the foal of a donkey"* (vv. 4-5; Zech. 9:9).

Here the idea of "daughter" means an "inhabitant," that is, those dwelling in Jerusalem, Israel's capital. Matthew's quotation of Zechariah's prophecy reveals the general disposition of Israel towards the One riding on the foal of a donkey. Zechariah says for Israel to "rejoice greatly," but Matthew says "tell" the nation, which underscores the lack of joy and anticipation for the One who was entering Jerusalem. In fact, many did not know who Jesus was, or thought Him to be merely a prophet from Nazareth (vv. 10-12).

On the Sunday prior to His crucifixion (John 12:1,12), the Lord Jesus descended the Mount of Olives and entered Jerusalem on the colt of a donkey (Mark 11:7; Luke 19:35). This fulfilled Zechariah's prophecy. Christendom often refers to this event as *Palm Sunday*, but this scene has little to do with the palm branches being placed on the road ahead of the Lord. This was the triumphant entry of Christ into His kingdom's capital.

Kings usually mounted horses in time of war (Rev. 19:11) but rode donkeys in time of peace. At this juncture, the Lord Jesus was offering genuine peace to the nation of Israel, but they must receive it on His terms through repentance and submission to His Father's will.

A large multitude quickly assembled as the Lord descended the Mount of Olives. They laid their clothes and freshly-cut palm branches before the colt the Lord was riding on. Palm branches were tokens of victory and of peace (Rev. 7:9) and a display of righteousness (Ps. 92:12). The multitude, referring to Psalm 118:25-26, shouted, *"Hosanna to the Son of David! Blessed is He who comes in the name of the Lord! Hosanna in the highest!"* (v. 9). In this brief moment, the Lord was rightfully declared to be the long-awaited Jewish Messiah.

Psalm 118:25 reads, *"Save now, I pray, O Lord; O Lord, I pray send now prosperity."* The Greek form of the Hebrew *yasha na* (meaning "save now") is "Hosanna." In John's account of this event, he notes that the people called the Lord Jesus, "the King of Israel." This is also how Zechariah identified the one riding a foal of a donkey. Mark states that the people said, *"Blessed is the kingdom of our father David that comes in the name of the Lord"* (Mark 11:10). All this highlights the intense desire of the Jewish people to be freed from Gentile oppression. They clearly wanted to be immediately liberated from Rome, but not to be saved from their sins. Many shouting "Hosanna" were merely curious seekers who got caught up in the fanfare of the moment without truly believing in Christ (John 12:18).

Matthew states that the entire city was moved with wonder and curiosity concerning the One who rode on the colt of the donkey. *"Who is this?"* (v. 10). Could this be the One prophesied by Zechariah four centuries earlier? But the far majority believed that Jesus was merely a prophet from Nazareth of Galilee, thus implying that He was not the expected Messiah (v. 11). Even after three years of preaching the kingdom gospel message throughout Israel, there was still much confusion concerning who Jesus really was.

The Pharisees were greatly agitated by the immense crowd that were shouting "Hosanna" to the One they believed was threatening Judaism (John 12:19). Luke tells us that the Pharisees demanded that Jesus should rebuke His disciples for making such a declaration. But the Lord said to them, *"I tell you that if these should keep silent, the stones would immediately cry out"* (Luke 19:40). John later notes that he and the other disciples did not understand the significance of Christ's entry into Jerusalem until after His resurrection (John 12:16). For three years Jesus' identity as Israel's Messiah had been kept secret, but now, five days before His crucifixion, His grandeur was to be emphatically publicized. What had been considered dangerous to state earlier was now necessary to boldly publish. Ironically, however, only the Lord Jesus fully understood the significance of the incident.

Christ Cleanses the Temple Again (vv. 12-17)

Mark records that the Lord and His disciples departed from Jerusalem to Bethany after Christ's triumphant entry into Jerusalem and then they returned to Jerusalem the next day, on Monday (Mark 11:11-12). Mark refers to Christ cleansing the temple on Monday (Mark 11:15), while Matthew and Luke indicate that it was on Sunday. It is plausible that when the Lord returned to the temple on Monday, the merchants and moneychangers had not learned the lesson from the previous day and the Lord had to cleanse the temple again.

Although the Lord Jesus is rarely spoken of in Scripture as being angry, it is evident that His righteous anger, His holy zeal for God, flared up on some occasions. After arriving at the temple, He made a scourge to drive the animals and their masters from the temple and He threw over the tables of the moneychangers (v. 12). These racketeers had turned the temple, God's house, into a place of commerce and thievery, but the Lord restored it to a house of prayer (v. 13). The Lord Jesus cleansed the temple twice, once at the beginning of His earthly ministry (John 2:14-17), and then again a few days before His death.

Previously, while confronting the Pharisees, the Lord healed a man on the Sabbath day to challenge their shallow spiritual existence (Mark 3:5). With utter contempt, He later warned them of impending judgment (23:13-36). At other times, the Lord's anger did not result in direct action; instead, He relinquished the offense into His Father's care (Luke 23:34). The Lord shows us that there are times to defer from righteous anger to accomplish a greater good: *"The discretion of a man makes him slow to anger, and his glory is to overlook a transgression"* (Prov. 19:11).

After cleansing the temple, the Lord resumed His ministry there. The blind and the lame were healed by Him (v. 14). However, when the chief priests and scribes saw the wonderful things that He was doing and how the children were crying out "Hosanna to the Son of David," they became indignant (v. 15). They challenged the Lord concerning what the children were saying. He told the priests that He was aware of it and then declared His approval of their behavior by quoting Psalm 8:2, *"Out of the mouth of babes and nursing infants You have perfected praise"* (v. 16). Since Israel's religious leaders suffered from spiritual blindness and could not discern who the Lord Jesus really was, God would use the zealous assertions of children to honor His Son.

Afterwards the Lord departed the temple and again journeyed about two miles east to the village of Bethany and lodged there (v. 17). He would repeat the same trek to Jerusalem and back again on the following day, Tuesday.

The Barren Fig Tree (vv. 18-22)

The next morning, the Lord began the trek back to Jerusalem. Matthew places this incident on Tuesday morning, but Mark prefers Monday morning, just prior to the cleansing of the temple. Regardless, the Lord was hungry and sought fruit from a fig tree that was along the roadway (v. 18). The main fig crop did not ripen until the summer months and Mark tells us plainly, *"it was not the season for the figs"* (Mark 11:13). Clearly, the Lord was applying a spiritual significance to the incident, rather than attempting to satisfy His hunger.

Fig trees in Israel produced an early crop of fruit prior to the leaves appearing in the spring. This was a harbinger of the regular crop, which meant that if there were no early figs, there would be no main summer crop. John Heading explains how the Lord used this fig harvesting dynamic to reveal Israel's present spiritual condition and to foreshadow God's future plan for the nation:

> There can be two crops of figs. Those in spring were called "the hasty fruit before the summer" (Isa 28:4), or "the firstripe fig before the summer" (RV). This former crop precedes the leaves, which in turn precede the summer crop. These details reflect upon the many facets of interpretation found in the incident where the Lord found no fruit but only leaves. The Lord longed for early fruit from His people but, apart from the remnant previously noted, there was none. There may have been leaves produced over the years since then, and more certainly will be produced in the future days; these leaves will herald the future restoration when "summer is nigh" (Matt. 24:32).[54]

After seeing that there were only leaves on the tree and no fruit, the Lord cursed the tree, *"Let no fruit grow on you ever again"* (v. 19). The tree instantly began to wither. About four months earlier Christ had spoken a parable concerning an unfruitful fig tree, which represented the fruitless religiosity of Israel at that time (Luke 13:6-9). The Jewish nation is allegorically likened to a foliage trilogy in Scripture: the vine, the fig tree, and the olive tree. Each one represents a distinct aspect of Israel's existence. The nation of Israel, as a political reality, is likened to a noble vine (a grape vine; Jer. 8:13), which God planted in the world (Jer. 2:21, 12:10); Israel was to be God's vineyard.

At the end of the Tribulation Period, the refined Jewish nation will receive the Holy Spirit and obtain spiritual life in Christ (Zech. 12:10). The work of the Holy Spirit in Israel is similarly depicted by the oil flowing to a lampstand from the olive tree in Zechariah's vision (Zech. 4:4-7). In this spiritually fruitful state, the Jews will be known as the olive tree which provides a testimony of God's goodness to the entire world (Hos. 14:6; Rom. 11:17-24).

When Israel is spoken of as a fig tree in Scripture, the metaphor relates to Israel's religious veracity, which often was fruitless for God (Jer. 8:13). This reality, including Judaism today, is what the Lord Jesus is addressing in this parable. After preaching the Kingdom message for three-plus years to the lost sheep of Israel, Christ cursed the fruitless fig tree just before His death at Calvary (vv. 18-21). He sought spiritual fruit from the Jewish nation and found none. Less than forty years later, Jerusalem and the temple were destroyed, and the Jews have not sacrificed since. The Old Covenant was replaced by the New Covenant, sealed with Christ's blood, and God would not permit the Jews to continue in what was now obsolete (Heb. 8:8-13).

One of the signs that the Tribulation Period and the Second Advent of Christ are nearing is that the fig tree (i.e., religious Israel) will again shoot forth leaves after a long winter season of deadness (Luke 21:29-31). Leaves must precede the main crop of fruit, but the fig tree will bear no fruit until the spiritual rebirth of the nation occurs in the latter days of the Tribulation Period. What might the new leaves speak of? This is likely a reference to the Jews reviving the old sacrificial system during, and perhaps just prior to, the Tribulation Period.

We know from various prophecies that the Antichrist will desecrate the Jewish temple and put a stop to animal sacrifices at the midpoint of the Tribulation Period (24:15; Dan. 9:27; 2 Thess. 2:3-7). Therefore, logically speaking, a temple will have to be erected and animal sacrifices will have to be reinstituted by that point. The generation that sees these activities will certainly see the coming of the Lord Jesus in His glory (24:32-35). But presently, the fig tree, Israel's religious system, is leafless (i.e., no animal sacrifices) and fruitless (void of spiritual vitality).

The disciples marveled at how quickly the tree withered after Christ cursed it (v. 20). The Lord answered their inquiry by affirming that what was declared in the will of God by faith and without doubting could move mountains, let alone wither a tree (v. 21). In a few days, the Lord would be leaving His disciples. He wanted them to understand that through *believing* prayer they would have all the power of heaven to assist them in fulfilling their mission for Him (v. 22).

The Challenge of the Priests and Elders (vv. 23-27)

The Lord arrived at the temple for *Super Tuesday*. On this day, the Lord would silence multiple challengers, speak three parables to the multitudes, deliver a *woe* message to the Pharisees, and privately teach His disciples about things to come on the Mount of Olives.

The chief priests and Jewish elders were the first to confront the Lord, *"By what authority are you doing these things? And who gave you this authority?"* (v. 23). The Lord chose to answer their two-part question with a two-part question of His own, which, if they answered, then He promised that He would answer their inquiry concerning the origin of His authority (v. 24). So, the Lord asked them, *"The baptism of John – where was it from? From heaven or from men?"* (v. 25).

The priests discussed that matter and decided that there was no safe answer to the Lord's questions. If they said that John's authority came from heaven, then they would be guilty of ignoring His message as the Messiah's forerunner. However, if they said that John was not from God, then they feared that the people would revolt against them, because they believed that John was a true prophet of God (v. 26). So, they declined to answer the Lord's question, but their silence rather affirmed the answer to their own questions to Him. Therefore, the Lord was neither obligated to, nor did He need to, answer their challenge with a response (v. 27).

The Two Sons (vv. 28-32)

The parable of the *Two Sons* is the first of three parables spoken together in the temple on the Tuesday before Christ's Crucifixion. The clarity of content and directness of focus in the Lord's final parables are noteworthy. A man had two sons; he commanded the first son to go to his vineyard and work (v. 28). The first son said he would not go, but later repented and labored in the vineyard as requested (v. 29). The man then gave the same command to his second son, who said he would go to the vineyard, but did not do so (v. 30).

The Lord then asked those listening to His story, *"Which of the two did the will of his father?"* (v. 31). Those listening answered correctly, "the first." The Lord, speaking directly to the Pharisees, *"Assuredly, I say to you that tax collectors and harlots enter the kingdom of God before you"* (v. 31). John the baptizer had presented God's message to Israel. Tax collectors and harlots had heard his message and repented before God – they needed to be saved from their sins. However, Israel's leaders ignored his warnings and clung to their humanized religion of doings. They were righteous before God and did not need to repent.

It is suggested that the first son represents the overall disposition of the Gentiles in Scripture. The Genesis record shows that the nations were rebellious from the beginning. The rebel behavior of Cain's descendants (Gen. 4), the vast wickedness of humanity during Noah's Day (Gen. 6), and the widespread rebellion of Nimrod at Babel (Gen. 10) all show the disobedient nature of the nations from the beginning.

However, as Hosea prophesied long ago, God would ultimately find a way to call those who were "not His people" – "His people" (Hos. 2:23). Paul explains that this prophecy was fulfilled in the Church Age, when Christ sought a Gentile Bride, the Church, for Himself (Rom. 9:25-26; Eph. 5:25-30). Through repentance and regeneration, Gentiles have become one with Christ and are now obedient to His will.

In contrast, the second son in the parable said that he would labor for his father, but then did not go into the vineyard as he had promised to do. The second son represents the Jewish nation. After being delivered from slavery in Egypt, Israel entered into a covenant with God at Mount Sinai. The Jews promised to do all that God had requested of them in His Law: *"All that the Lord has spoken we will do"* (Ex. 19:8). Yet, only a few days later they were dancing around and revering a golden calf that Aaron had crafted. This was in direct disobedience to the first two of the Ten Commandments.

This unfaithfulness to Jehovah was characteristic of the Jewish people throughout most of the Old Testament record. This same rebel spirit was alive and well in Israel in Christ's day also. Therefore, the Lord rebuked the religious leaders; they were the unfaithful second son. What they said they would do and what they taught others to do, they did not do themselves (Rom. 2:21-23). They were hypocrites of the worst kind because they had the most revelation of what God wanted from them, but they had ignored His Law. Through the parable, Christ was indicating that the Pharisees were being disobedient, unrepentant, unbelieving, and thus dead in their sins.

The Landowner and the Wicked Vinedressers (vv. 33-46)

This is the second of three parables spoken together in the temple on the Tuesday before Christ's Crucifixion. In short, a landowner planted a vineyard and leased it to tenants, who would not render to him its fruit and, in fact, the tenants injured or killed the owner's messengers, including his only son, who came to collect what was owed to the landowner. The tenants, therefore, would receive the wrath of the landowner who afterwards would lease the vineyard to others.

The nation of Israel, as a political reality, is likened to a noble vine (a grape vine; Jer. 8:13), which God planted in the world (Jer. 2:21, 12:10). In fact, several Old Testament prophets refer to Israel as God's special vine that He had planted (e.g., Isa. 5:1-7; Ezek. 15:2-4).

The prophet Hosea rebuked Israel because, though it (as a vine) had lush foliage, its fruit was worthless because it was self-produced for itself, and was not from God or for God: *"Israel empties his vine; he brings forth fruit for himself"* (Hos. 10:1). Two centuries later, the prophet Jeremiah told his fellow countrymen that God had planted a beautiful vineyard (speaking of the Jewish nation), but Israel's shepherds had made it desolate (Jer. 12:10). Israel was God's vineyard, but even in Christ's day, corrupt leaders were keeping it from being fruitful to God.

God repeatedly attempted to restore the vine to a fruitful condition by sending prophets to rebuke Israel's wayward and carnal leaders, but to no avail. Finally, God sent His beloved Son to plead with Israel to repent and be restored to God, but the Jewish nation rejected Him and had Him put to death. As Paul explains to the Ephesians, the offer of grace in Christ has been presented to the Gentiles, who through faith have been brought into the commonwealth of blessing promised to Israel (Eph. 3:2-12). Gentile believers in the "dispensation of the grace of God" (Eph. 3:2) are now bearing spiritual fruit to God. This is what God wanted from Israel, but having rejected Christ, the opportunity was given to those who were not God's covenant people (Rom. 9:25).

The key components of this parable are as follows:

The certain landowner = God.

The vineyard = Israel.

The vinedressers via lease = Israel's leaders.

The servants = the former prophets and John the baptizer.

The Son = the Lord Jesus.

The other vinedressers = Gentiles trusting Christ in the Church Age.

Paul's analogy of the olive tree in Romans 11 parallels Christ's teaching in this parable. In this analogy, the root of the tree is the Abrahamic covenant, and the olive tree is Christ; through Him the promises of God will bless Israel, the natural branches. Yet, disbelief leads to rebellion and the loss of God's blessings and fellowship. Willful sin and rebellion will always invoke God's chastening hand. God did to Israel exactly what He told them He would do if His people erred from the Law and abandoned Him (Deut. 28); thus, the natural branches (the

Jewish people) were removed from the opportunity to be nationally blessed by God through Christ.

Yet, the analogy shows us that God will restore Israel to Himself. The fact that the Jews (the natural branches) could be, and indeed will be, grafted back into the olive tree indicates that the focus of the illustration is not eternal salvation per se, but rather the blessings that God desires to share with those who exercise faith in Christ. Gentile believers (the wild branch) are a second benefactor of the New Covenant and thus are permitted to share in the blessings promised Israel (Eph. 2:11-3:7). Gentiles are grafted into the olive tree, indicating the blessings of Christ rooted in God's covenant with Abraham. The New Covenant permits individual Jews to be saved now and the Jewish nation to be reconciled to God after the Church Age ends.

However, when Christ spoke this parable, proud Israel was in rebellion against God, His prophets, and His Son, whom they put to death (vv. 35-39). The tenants wanted the inheritance (to control the people and receive their honor and praise) instead of giving it to the rightful owner – God. The scribes and Pharisees condemned themselves when they answered the Lord's question as to what should be done with the rebellious tenants. They adamantly stated that the tenants should be killed for their brutal insolence and the vineyard should be leased to others who would render to the owner the fruit of his vineyard (v. 41).

After answering Christ's question correctly, the Lord quoted Psalm 118:22 to affirm that God would provide the Gentiles an opportunity to be tenants of His vineyard to receive the desired fruit He longed for (vv. 42-43). At that time, the Jewish nation had no place for Christ; He was the rejected Stone that they tripped over and were thus broken up. God then used Christ, the rejected cornerstone, to create and build the Church (i.e., a Gentile bride for His Son). Those who repent and receive Christ alone for salvation in the Church Age (i.e., become broken on the Stone) will be saved and have the opportunity to bear fruit to God (v. 44). But those who reject Christ will be eternally judged by Christ at His second advent to the earth (i.e., they will be crushed to powder by the Stone from heaven; Dan. 2:45).

The scribes and Pharisees were infuriated by this conclusion because it was obvious that Christ was likening them to the proud, murderous tenants who would be destroyed (v. 45). These religious leaders would have arrested the Lord Jesus but declined to do so for fear of how the crowds listening to Him might respond (v. 46).

Matthew Chapter 22

The Marriage Feast (vv. 1-14)

This parable was spoken to a crowd in Jerusalem directly after the parable of *The Landowner and Wicked Vinedressers* on the Tuesday before Calvary (v. 1). The Jewish religious leaders were enraged after hearing the previous parable and would have arrested the Lord Jesus, but they feared the reaction of the multitude that was gathering for the Passover.

It is observed that both Matthew and Luke record this parable, but Matthew upholds his authority theme in his account, while Luke advocates Christ's humanity. Accordingly, Luke refers to the prominent character as *"a certain man"* (Luke 14:16), whereas Matthew is more specific: *"a certain King"* (v. 2). Both accounts were accurate but different. Matthew upholds the kingly assertion of Christ in his Gospel, while Luke is careful not to distract from the humanity of Christ and the social appeal of the Savior.

A king desires to hold a marriage feast at his home for his son, and sends out messengers with invitations, but many make excuses for declining to come (v. 3). The king then sends out his servants again to invite guests to the feast, but again the invitation is largely rejected and some of the kings' messengers were treated spitefully, and some were killed (vv. 4-6). The king is greatly insulted by these events and brought his army to bear on the insolent and the murderers of his servants (v. 7). Judgment was swift and without mercy, even to the utter destruction of the cities where the rebels dwelt. These were not worthy of attending the king's feast (v. 8).

Afterwards, the king sent out invitations to the byways and highways to ensure that his house would be full of guests (vv. 9-10). As a result, *"both the bad and good"* came to the wedding hall. The bad and the good represents Christendom, which is composed of true believers that have been born again and those who have merely identified with Jesus Christ. As those responding to the invitation were off the street, the king provided everyone wedding garments upon their arrival. Those who chose not to wear the proper attire – that is, "the bad" – made an outward show by attending, but inwardly they did not appropriate what the king (God) provided. These people were rejected and put out of the wedding festivities (vv. 11-13). The key components of this parable must be properly identified if we are to understand its meaning:

The King of heaven = God.

The Son to be married = Christ.

The wedding feast = the celebration of Christ with His redeemed.

The first invitation = by prophets, John, and Christ Himself.

The second invitation = by disciples to Jews in Jerusalem (Acts 1-8).

City of murderers destroyed = destruction of Jerusalem in 70 A.D.

The third invitation = general decree to all nations (fulfills Gen. 12:3).

The wedding hall = heaven.

The proper wedding garment = being adorned with Christ's righteousness.

The guest without a wedding garment = a false professor.

The meaning of this parable is plain. The Jewish nation had repeatedly rejected the offer of God's Son, the Lord Jesus, as their Messiah. After Christ's death and resurrection, God would take His offer of grace in Christ to the Gentiles. After the Church Age began, the message was first proclaimed in Jerusalem and then quickly swept across the Roman Empire. The Holy Spirit wooed a Gentile Bride to Christ, a work that He is still engaged in today. Favored and privileged Israel was judged by God in 70 A.D. The Romans destroyed much of Jerusalem and the temple, and the entire Levitical system that Christ replaced was put away. Israel will remain in spiritual blindness until Christ's second coming to the earth. But before the Jewish nation is restored to God, redeemed Gentiles from all over the world will be blessed to feast at God's banqueting table in heaven. This will occur after the Church experiences the *Judgment Seat of Christ* in heaven.

The faithful servants in verse 3 are clearly saved as shown by their good works; however, as the Lord had already taught (7:21-23), not everyone professing Christ is truly saved. How is this shown in this parable? The answer is in the wedding garments of the attendees.

A believer who is justified in Christ has God's righteousness imputed to his or her account (2 Cor. 5:21). Figuratively, then, true believers are clothed in God's righteousness. It was customary for the host to provide the guest with a wedding garment if they had none – without Christ this guest was spiritually naked and thus deserving of God's judgment. In Revelation 19:8, the Bride of Christ is wearing white linen garments which reflect the righteousness of Christ. Because the garments in this text refer to the righteous acts of those in Christ, both the positional and practical righteousness of believers are portrayed, for true faith has good works to substantiate it (Jas. 2:17). The parable indicates that though all are called by God through the gospel message, some willfully reject it, and others do not fully trust in Christ only for a righteous standing before God. Hence, *"Many are called, but few are chosen"* (v. 14). Only those who sincerely choose Christ are chosen in Christ to commune with God.

The Challenge of the Herodians (vv. 15-22)

Previously, the Lord Jesus warned His disciples not to be influenced by *"the leaven of Herod"* and by implication, others with the same ideology (Mark 8:15). Herod Antipas the tetrarch, the infamous son of Herod the Great, was a ruling Jew in cahoots with the Romans to preserve his power. James would refer to him as "a friend of the world" (Jas. 4:4). In the case of Herod, and those like him, love for God and His Word had been supplanted by the love for materialism, fame, and political ambition. Such individuals are prone to skepticism, immorality, and worldliness and thus close association with them was to be avoided.

The prophet Zechariah speaks of three shepherds in Israel that will abhor the Messiah at His first advent, and that the Messiah will loath them also and will publicly dismiss them for not properly tending to God's flock in Israel (Zech. 11:8). J. J. Stubbs suggests that the three shepherds dismissed (or "cut off"; KJV) are identified in Matthew 22 as the Pharisees, the Herodians, and the Sadducees:

> The Lord as the true Shepherd must deal with three groups of leaders of the people and authoritatively, by His teaching, cut them off. The words "cut off" do not mean to destroy or put to death, but rather to disavow (M. F. Unger). In Matthew 22 the Lord is seen disowning and renouncing the teaching of the three false shepherds.[55]

On the Tuesday before Christ's crucifixion, the Pharisees, the Sadducees, and the Herodians all challenged Christ's authority. By articulating divine wisdom, the Lord not only stopped the mouths of His objectors, but He also denounced them as corrupt leaders of God's covenant people. These shepherds had not cared for God's sheep in Israel, but rather had led them away from the Lord into a miserable spiritual condition.

After the Lord spoke *The Marriage Feast* parable, the Pharisees began plotting how they might entangle Jesus in His words (v. 15). After they devised what they thought would be foolproof questions to accomplish this goal, the Pharisees came with the Herodians to pose their inquiry (v. 16). These two parties were bitter foes, but they had a common enemy, the Lord Jesus, which temporarily caused them to work together. The objective was to dupe Jesus into uttering a political statement against Rome that would then force the Roman authorities to act against Him.

In the true form of politicians, the Herodians first complimented the Lord before moving to spring their trap. They claimed that He was a true teacher who taught the way of God accurately despite what men might say about what He taught. Their mistake was thinking that wicked men could ever appeal to the ego of a righteous man. Their praise would not entice the Lord to say something that they wanted to hear; rather, their empty praise just revealed the deceit harboring in their hearts.

The question was then posed to the Lord, "Is it lawful to pay taxes to Caesar, or not?" (v. 17). If He said "yes," then He would be viewed as affirming Gentile oppression over Israel, and many of His countrymen would refuse to listen to His message. This position would oppose the Abrahamic covenant which promised Gentile liberation. This would be ultimately achieved by the coming Jewish Messiah. Certainly then, if Christ was the Jewish Messiah, He would not endorse paying taxes to Rome. If the Lord said "no" to the question, then He would certainly be arrested by Roman authorities for leading a rebellion against the empire.

But the Lord perceived their wickedness and addressed them as hypocrites for testing Him with such an inquiry (v. 18). How did the Lord answer their question? He said, *"Show Me the tax money"* (v. 19). He was shown a denarius and asked His audience, *"Whose image and inscription is this?"* (v. 20). They responded by saying that it was Caesar's image and inscription on the coin. The Lord then said, *"Render therefore to Caesar that things that are Caesar's, and to God the things that are God's"* (v. 21).

If they were using Roman coinage, then they were admitting that they were under Roman rule. But given the warnings of Moses (e.g., Deut.

28:47-48), Israel would only be under Gentile rule because they had rebelled against Jehovah. So, the Lord was reminding them that they were paying taxes to Rome because they were under the chastening hand of God. When the Lord's oppressors heard His response, they marveled at His wisdom and departed from Him without asking any more questions (v. 22). He had thwarted their best attempt to hoodwink Him into saying something that would be viewed as controversial or dangerous.

The Challenge of the Sadducees (vv. 23-33)

The next group to challenge the Lord's authority were the supernatural-denying Sadducees. This religious sect formed part of the Jewish judicial court called the Sanhedrin. They did not believe in the angels, miracles, or in resurrection (v. 22). These were the liberal theologians of Christ's day and touted ideologies such as higher-criticism and skepticism that negated the proper interpretation of Scripture.

The Sadducees asked the Lord Jesus about a woman who had been married to seven different men (she was widowed seven times and never married to more than one man at once; vv. 24-27). As the Sadducees did not believe in a bodily resurrection, their question to the Lord was clearly a test: *"In the resurrection, whose wife of the seven will she be? For they all had her"* (v. 28). The Lord's rebuke of the Sadducees was threefold: they were mistaken, they did not know the Scriptures, and they did not know the power of God (v. 29).

They were mistaken, because in the resurrection, people would not be given to marriage, in the same way angels were not given to marriage (v. 30). Rather than reiterating what they had already rejected, the Lord used the opportunity to affirm the truth of resurrection. The Sadducees did not know the Scripture, for Jehovah was the God of the living (vv. 31-32). They also did not know the power of God, for God was the God of the living, not the dead (v. 32). How could God keep His unconditional covenants with Abraham, Isaac, and Jacob, all of whom had died, unless their souls were eternal, and they each would experience bodily resurrection in the future?

Contrary to the Mormon and Islamic views of heaven, people in heaven will neither be male nor female, at least in the way we understand the genders to exist today. There will be no marriages (save the Lamb with His saints) or sexual activities in heaven as some world religions tout. The Lord confirmed this truth while responding to a fictitious scenario posed by the Sadducees. Those listening to His teaching on this matter were astonished at His wisdom (v. 33).

Those who experience resurrection will not be gender-significant in eternity, but will be like the angels, who do not reproduce. Angels are neither male nor female, although when they deliver God's messages to humans, they always appeared as men when taking a human form (e.g., Gen. 18). Male and female genders were God's design to provide complementing companionship in marriage and for the purpose of procreation (Gen. 1:28, 2:18). In heaven, the need for reproduction will be eliminated as everyone will be eternal. Moreover, our communion with God in heaven will far exceed anything we could have ever experienced in an earthly relationship. Accordingly, we will be completely satisfied with being in fellowship with God and desire nothing else, including marital relationships. One of the clear warning signs of a false teaching is the notion that fleshly desires will be satisfied in heaven, or even worse, that such things are a part of some supreme deity's reward system.

The Challenge of the Pharisees (vv. 34-40)

After hearing that the Lord Jesus had silenced the Sadducees, the Pharisees decided it was time to confront the Lord with their test as presented by one of their esteemed lawyers (vv. 34-35). The Pharisees were the dominant party in the Sanhedrin and thus had the most sway in how the Law was interpreted.

The lawyer asked, *"Teacher, which is the greatest commandment in the Law?"* (v. 36). The Lord Jesus did not hesitate to answer this important question. However, instead of providing the single Godward response that the lawyer was looking for, the Lord supplied a dual response to give a balanced answer to a biased question. To love God with all your heart, soul, and mind was the greatest commandment and to love your neighbor as yourself would be the second greatest commandment (vv. 38-39). The Lord then explained that all that was in the Law and declared by the prophets hung on these two commandments (v. 40). That is, to love God above all and to sacrificially give to others was the basis for all other laws.

The first two of the Ten Commandments relate to the subject of recognizing God as Creator and not worshipping creation. The first commandment is: *"You shall have no other gods before Me"* (Ex. 20:3). Moses explained how one obeys this commandment – it is by believing in the one true God and giving Him first place in your life (Deut. 6:4-5). The Lord reiterated this teaching to the Pharisees: *" 'You shall love the Lord your God with all your heart, with all your soul, and with all your mind.' This is the first and great commandment"* (vv. 37-38). On another occasion, the Lord Jesus explained the commandment's meaning: *"He who loves father or mother more than Me is not worthy of Me. And he who loves son or daughter more than Me is not worthy of Me. And he who does not take his cross and follow after Me is not worthy of Me"* (10:37-38). When it comes to having no other gods besides the Creator, it means that He has first place in everything.

The Lord Challenges the Pharisees (vv. 41-46)

While the Pharisees were still gathered before Him, the Lord asked them some questions, *"What do you think about the Christ? Whose Son is He?"* (vv. 41-42). They answered correctly, *"The Son of David."* Then the Lord asked them how it was possible for David, speaking by the Holy Spirit, to call His descendant "Lord" (v. 43)? The Lord then quoted David (Ps. 110:1) to validate His question: *"The Lord said to my Lord, Sit at My right hand, till I make Your enemies Your footstool"* (v. 44).

In Psalm 110, as the writer of Hebrews proclaims (Heb. 1:13), God the Father is speaking to God the Son, whom David calls his "Lord." Given this understanding, the Lord Jesus poses His final question to the Pharisees, *"If David then calls Him 'Lord,' how is He his Son?"* (v. 45). The only logical answer to this question is that David's Son, the future Jewish Messiah, must be both God and a descendant of David. But the Pharisees would not answer this question, for to do so would validate the Lord Jesus' claims as being God's Son and the rightful heir to the throne of David.

Through wisely conveying the truth, the Lord soundly defeated all those who had come to test Him. Afterwards, no one challenged Him with further questions (v. 46).

No mind, no wisdom – temporary mind, temporary wisdom – eternal mind, eternal wisdom.

– Adoniram Judson

Matthew Chapter 23

The Marks of a Pharisee (vv. 1-12)

Having silenced the Pharisees by His questions concerning David's Son also being his Lord, the Lord Jesus spoke to the multitude (including His disciples) about the hypocrisy of the Pharisees. He mentions several negative behaviors of the scribes and the Pharisees to show why they had been rejected by God as His shepherds in Israel. The scribes were the teachers and protectors of the Law.

First, the Pharisees considered themselves to have equal authority with Moses in declaring God's Word to Israel (v. 2). While generally teaching the written Law correctly to the people, they also added their own teachings which were not inspired by God.

Second, they were hypocrites. They instructed the people as to what they must do to be obedient to the Mosaic Law but failed to adhere to their own commands (v. 3). The Lord told His audience to not follow their disingenuous example. We are to "observe and do" what Scripture commands, regardless of what men say or do.

Third, they went beyond the written Law to levy heavy burdens (human traditions) on the people (v. 4). Yet, they felt no burden to hold to such legalism themselves or to assist the people in following their customs.

Fourth, what the Pharisees did in public (e.g., religious observances, long prayers, holy attire, etc.) was for the appreciation of men, rather than by an inward compulsion to please God (v. 5). To appear spiritual to others they developed practices that went beyond what the Law required. William MacDonald explains how the Pharisees latched on to portions of the Mosaic Law to magnify themselves before men, rather than benefiting from the intended spiritual purpose of the directives:

> Their use of phylacteries was an example. In commanding Israel to bind His words as a sign upon their hands and as frontlets between their eyes (Ex. 13:9, 16; Deut. 6:8; 11:18), God meant that the law should continually be before them, guiding their activities. They reduced this

spiritual command to a literal, physical sense. Enclosing portions of Scripture in leather capsules, they bound them to their foreheads or arms. They weren't concerned about obeying the law as long as, by wearing ridiculously large phylacteries, they appeared super-spiritual. The law also commanded the Jews to wear tassels with blue cords on the corners of their garments (Num. 15:37–41; Deut. 22:12). These distinctive trimmings were intended to remind them that they were a distinct people, and that they should walk in separation from the nations. The Pharisees overlooked the spiritual lesson and satisfied themselves with making longer fringes.[56]

But the wearing of enlarged phylacteries and long blue tassels on the fringes of their garments did not make the Pharisees more spiritual, but rather exposed their carnal desire to be honored by men, rather than to have God's approval and blessing. A phylactery was a piece of parchment that was attached to the forehead or left arm by a strap. Quotations from the Law were written on the parchment to ensure that the wearer would be reminded of God's Word throughout the day. The goal was to have a personal testimony of God's goodness and greatness, but the Pharisees were self-glorying in the ritual.

Fifth, the Pharisees sought the chief seats in the synagogues, so that they would have a high position above the common people (v. 6). In their own minds, they were rulers of the people and therefore above them, but as demonstrated by the Good Shepherd, God's idea of a spiritual leader is to humble oneself to serve others (v. 11; John 10:11).

Sixth, the Pharisees desired to have exalted titles among men. They were thrilled when people greeted them in the marketplaces by recognizing their religious position, *"Rabbi, Rabbi"* (v. 7). Interestingly, there is no example of a disciple of Christ anywhere in Scripture having a title of position before his or her name, for all such titles are reserved for Christ. "Lord" and "Christ" are predominantly associated with the name Jesus after His resurrection.

Men covet titles so that they might be honored by others – it is a natural pull of our fallen nature. But those who worship Christ must not dishonor Him by stealing His glory. Hence, disciples of Christ do not seek the praise of men or titles of position before their names. John the baptizer, speaking of Christ, declared the proper obligation of all true believers: *"He must increase, but I must decrease"* (John 3:30).

Many of the common expressions we use to refer to each other or to individuals in Scripture do not conform to the same scriptural etiquette upheld by the Holy Spirit in conveying honor to the Lord. For example, we do not read of "Doctor Luke," but "Luke, the beloved physician." Nor do we read of "the Apostle Paul" but "Paul an apostle of Jesus Christ." No "Saint Matthew," no "Elder Peter," no Pastor ..., no Minister ..., no Deacon.... Men love titles, yet Scripture provides none, except for the Lord Jesus Christ.

Terms of association or endearment for believers, such as "brother" or "sister," are warmly permitted: Paul is referred to as "brother Paul" (Acts 9:17, 22:13; 2 Pet. 3:15), Apollos as "brother Apollos" (1 Cor. 16:12), and Timothy is spoken of as "brother Timothy" in Hebrews 13:23. The Holy Spirit shows us that how we address the Lord and others does matter. May each of us esteem the Lord more and human titles and praise less; only Christ is to be revered by us.

Consequently, the Lord forbids His disciples from adopting such nomenclature as "Teacher" or "Father" (vv. 8-10). We understand that the Lord is referring to titles that should be reserved for the Godhead. These are spiritual designations which rise above natural, professional, or academic associations. There is nothing wrong with a child calling out to his daddy for help. Or a patient referring to his or her physician as "Doctor ...".

However, the Lord was prohibiting the use of titles which exalted man at God's expense. The Lord Jesus was their Teacher and taught them nothing but the truth; there was no one else that they could better learn God's will from than Him. They also only had one spiritual Father, His Father, God the Father who was in heaven; therefore, why revere an imperfect man on earth with a title that belongs to God the Father? Rather, if we want God's approval, we are to humble ourselves before others and serve them as Christ would (vv. 11-12). God's true shepherds will exhibit this quality. Sadly, the Pharisees sought to be honored by men at the expense of God's honor before men.

Titles of status and honor in Scripture belong to God, with most titles of honor being reserved for Christ. This helps ensure that we continue to regard Him as the only Lord of the Church, and ourselves as merely brethren. Men covet titles so that they might be honored by others – it is natural to our fallen nature. But those who worship Christ must not dishonor Him by stealing His glory. The believer's allegiance is to Him alone: we are His priests, His brethren, His friends, and His bondservants. The Lord Jesus said that He alone was Master of all believers, who formed one class of people called "brethren." *"Let me not, I pray you, accept any man's person, neither let me give flattering titles unto man. For I know not to give flattering titles; in so doing my Maker would soon take me away"* (Job 32:21-22; KJV).

Woes Pronounced on the Pharisees (vv. 13-36)

Having identified the carnal tendencies of the Pharisees, the Lord proceeds to pronounce eight "woes" on the scribes and the Pharisees. The scribes were copiers and teachers of the Old Testament Scripture.

The first woe pronounced against the scribes and Pharisees was for their spiritual obstructionism (v. 13). Not only did they reject Christ's kingdom message, they aggressively hindered others from believing it also. The idea that one needs to repent to receive God's grace is putrid to the natural man, so those rejecting Christ's message could not enter the kingdom of God.

The second woe pronounced against Israel's religious leaders was for devouring widows' houses (i.e., the finagling of widows out of their property for a religious cause) and then covering their crime by uttering long prayers (v. 14). The Critical Text does not contain this verse, but both Mark and Luke include it in their accounts; however, the word "beware" is substituted for "woe" to announce the various offenses (Mark 12:40; Luke 20:47). Regrettably, many people today are still being swindled out of their possessions and livelihood by those posing as religious leaders promoting some religious crusade that God has no part in. These con-artists become rich by hoodwinking undiscerning believers into bequeathing their wealth for God's glory or to get His blessing. It is often the elderly and widows that are taken advantage of, but the Lord promised that such pious profiteers *"will receive a greater condemnation."*

The third woe condemns their misdirected zeal in making one religious convert that would be twice as wicked as he was before (v. 15). Some of the cults today expend incredible resources to knock on doors and to advertise their claims in various ways. Yet, an ignorant, unregenerate person is closer to being saved than one who has emphatically embraced a lie that opposes receiving salvation in Christ through grace alone.

The fourth woe pronounced on the scribes and Pharisees was for being blind guides of spiritual truth (vv. 16-22). They taught the people traditions and practices which undermined scriptural truth, such as honoring vows made to the Lord. The Pharisees taught that, depending on how you swore to the Lord, you may not have to honor what you promised to give to Him. But this hypocritical act of swearing degraded the value of the Lord's name in the minds of the people.

In esteeming the gold band that adorned the pinnacle of the temple more than the temple itself, the Pharisees were demonstrating disdain for God. Where is the value? In the gold or the temple? In the offering or the altar? The Lord bluntly told them that the altar gave value to the sacrifice, and that the temple bestowed the honor to the gold. The altar and the temple were patterned after holy, heavenly realities (Heb. 9:23); each was directly connected to God. In placing the value on the offering and the gold, the Pharisees had disassociated themselves from God, but the Lord was telling them that only that which is connected with God has value; their traditions and swearing were just human nonsense and an insult to God.

The highest honor for gold would have been to be used in the house of God. The highest honor of a lamb was to be used as a sacrifice on the bronze altar. If gold and sheep had ambition, this would have been their highest calling. Christ was teaching that man apart from his connection with God is nothing; ambition apart from God is nothing; abilities apart from God are nothing! The only reason believers can be honored before God is because of their association with Christ.

Christ wants our motives, our abilities, and our entire life to be connected with Him. It is possible for us to ignorantly commit the same form of blasphemy that the Pharisees did (i.e., undervaluing our association with Christ). For example, the reader might have a brilliant mind and be prompted to think, "The Lord would be fortunate to have a mind like mine in His service." Wrong! That which is in association with Christ is what has the value. The right thinking is: "My greatest privilege in life is to use my talents for the Lord." Your intellect does not sanctify Jesus Christ, but He sanctifies your mind for His purpose and glory. Likewise, all of our abilities must be submitted to Him.

As believers, we only have value because of our association with Christ. We should not mock His Lordship and defame His name by thinking we have some ability or talent that He would do well to value and use. Such thinking is nothing less than hypocrisy and a pharisaical expression of pride – a form of blasphemy! Our highest service to the Lord is to be a living sacrifice, an emptied vessel of honor (2 Tim. 2:21) fitted for His sovereign use. If we live a holy, consecrated life, He will honor Himself; we need not presuppose our profitability to God.

The fifth woe pronounced was for focusing on minor rituals and neglecting the weightier matters of Scripture (vv. 23-24). They were meticulous to render to God one tenth of the most insignificant herbs that they grew, but then exonerated themselves from displaying the greater matters of the Law, such as justice and mercy. The Lord was not saying that they should not pay their tithe to the Lord as required by the Law, but rather heretical teaching is typified by out-of-balanced thinking. Majoring on a minor or majoring on one truth at the exclusion of other truth will eventually cause division among God's people. The truth is in the whole of God's Word, and nothing should be neglected. The Pharisees were focused on the minutiae of the Law, but blind to the justice, honesty, generosity, and holiness, which were foundational aspects of the Law.

The sixth woe pertained to externalism (vv. 25-26). The Pharisees were more concerned in maintaining an outward moral and religious facade than exercising introspection that would lead to repentance and humility before God. They were more concerned about what others thought of them than God's evaluation of their spirituality. The Lord likened this disposition to that of a cup or a dish that had been thoroughly washed on the outside but was full of impurities on the inside, such as extortion and self-indulgence. Who wants to drink out of a cup that is filthy on the inside? Spiritually speaking, the Pharisees did not care about the inside condition of the cup if it appeared outwardly clean. The Lord rebukes their externalism. The Pharisees needed to get their hearts right with the Lord, rather than worrying about what the people thought of them.

The seventh woe pronounced on the scribes and Pharisees, like the sixth, condemned their externalism (vv. 27-28). Where the sixth woe rebuked their secret greediness and lusting, the seventh woe condemned their covert hypocrisy and lawlessness. Previously, the Lord likened the Pharisees to *"graves which are not seen"* (Luke 11:44). The Pharisees were dead in trespasses and sins, but they and those who followed them failed to recognize their spiritual condition. By acting righteous, when they were spiritually dead, they were being like an unmarked grave. Now, the Lord reversed the metaphor; the Pharisees were like whitewashed sepulchers with a rotting corpse inside. The Pharisees looked good on the outside, but inwardly they were full of corruption. They strived to appear upright before men, but God saw directly into their depraved hearts and what He found there was as putrid as a rotting body.

The eighth and final woe against the scribes and Pharisees pertained to their homage to God's murdered prophets to justify themselves before the people (vv. 29-36). To honor the Old Testament prophets, the Pharisees maintained their tombs and monuments and decorated them with wreaths. What did this activity indicate to the people? The idea being that if those prophets had been speaking to them, they would have received their message and not put them to death.

First, the Lord reminded them that, by their own admission, their forefathers had murdered God's prophets, therefore the judgment of God was not only on their forefathers but would have repercussions for their sons (descendants) also. Second, just as their forefathers had rejected God's messengers and put them to death, they were rejecting Him, God's Messenger, and were plotting His death at that moment. Nothing had changed; they were just as rebellious as their forefathers.

The Lord Laments Over Jerusalem (vv. 37-39)

It had been a long day of ministry in which the Lord had shut down various groups opposing Him, spoken several parables, and delivered a "Woe" message to the scribes and Pharisees. Before departing the temple for the Mount of Olives with His disciples, the Lord Jesus laments over Jerusalem: *"O Jerusalem, Jerusalem, the one who kills the prophets and stones those who are sent to her! How often I wanted to gather your children together, as a hen gathers her chicks under her wings, but you were not willing!"* (v. 37).

The Lord's anguish and tears over His rebellious people were foretold long ago when Joseph wept over his deceitful brothers in Egypt (Gen. 45). The tears of Joseph were both a testimony of the sorrow of his rejection and the forgiving love he desired to show in restoration. Likewise, the Lord Jesus was heartbroken over Jewish rejection and wept over His countrymen in sorrow, knowing the consequence of their rejection – the destruction of Jerusalem (Luke 19:41). Hence, He says, *"Your house is left to you desolate"* (v. 38). This is likely a reference to the temple, which had not been God's house for a long time in the same way that the feasts of Jehovah had become the "feasts of the Jews" (John 5:1). God was not with His people and His Messenger was leaving them.

The turtledove (the hen) likely represents mourning in Scripture (Isa. 38:14, 59:11). The Lord Jesus was grieved over Israel's rejection of Himself as their Messiah and this is symbolized by the turtledove gathering her chicks under her wing, but the chicks would not come to the place of intimacy and safety. J. G. Bellett suggests that Christ's lamentation over Jerusalem was foreshadowed by Jeremiah's lament over the city's destruction by Babylon for stubborn rebellion:

> Through this long, unmeasured age of His absence, it is the Lamentations of Jeremiah that are heard by the ear of faith, amid the desolations of Zion. ... "What thing shall I take to witness for thee? what thing shall I liken to thee, O daughter of Jerusalem? what shall I equal to thee, that I may comfort thee, O virgin-daughter of Zion? for thy breach is great like the sea: who can heal thee? Thy prophets have seen vain and foolish things for thee: and they have not discovered *thine iniquity, to turn away thy captivity;* but have seen for thee false burdens and causes of banishment" (Lam. 2:13-14). This is the utterance of a broken heart vindicating God. ... Jerusalem must account to herself for her captivity and banishment. Her iniquity has been her ruin. And so, with the lamentation of Jesus over her. She had killed the prophets, and stoned the messengers of God, and after all, she "would not." Her wound is incurable, but herself has done it. Her iniquity has been her captivity, says the prophet. Because she would not, therefore she is not gathered, says the Lord.[57]

Speaking of the Lord Jesus, John says, *"He came to His own, and His own did not receive Him"* (John 1:11). As a result, the nation of Israel would experience war and desolation until a future day, when they would recognize Jesus as their Messiah at His second advent to the earth (v. 39; Dan. 9:26). Then when the people see Christ, they will shout, *"Blessed is He who comes in the name of the Lord"* (v. 39) and mean it!

Thankfully, there is a coming day when Israel will be restored to God. There will be great weeping on that day also, but these will be the tears of restoration and joy (Hos. 2:19-23; Zech. 12:10). The Bible does not say that there will be no tears in heaven, as some have taught. What the Bible states is that God will wipe away our tears once we are in His presence (Rev. 7:17, 21:4). What believer could possibly have a dry eye when they behold their Savior face-to-face for the first time!

Matthew Chapter 24

The Temple to Be Destroyed (vv. 1-2)

The Tuesday before Calvary (three days prior to the Lord's death) was an incredibly busy day for the Lord Jesus. Besides mastering the verbal challenges of the Herodians, the Sadducees, the Pharisees, the scribes, and a lawyer, He also delivered the "Woe" message to the Pharisees and spoke several parables. After these events, the Lord departed with His disciples to the Mount of Olives for a time of private ministry. At this time, He proclaimed to them important details concerning the future of Israel and the time of His Second Advent to the earth. Because this teaching was privately given on the Mount of Olives, it is often referred to as "The Olivet Discourse."

As with the "Sermon on the Mount," Matthew records the specific details of this incident more prominently than the other evangelists (Matthew 24 and 25). Both Mark and Luke devote one chapter each to the narration (Mark 13 and Luke 21), while John does not mention the discourse at all. Much of the detail contained in Matthew 25 is completely unique to Matthew.

The Olivet Discourse again is *strictly* Jewish, for the Church will already be in heaven before the events of the Tribulation Period begin to unfold. The Olivet Discourse provides escalating signs of the coming Tribulation Period and describes events in the first half, mid, and last half of this horrendous time on earth. Then the Lord spoke of His Second Coming to the earth to judge the wicked.

Only in Matthew do we read: *"Then the King will say to those on His right hand, 'Come, you blessed of My Father, inherit the kingdom…'"* (25:34). *"And the King will answer and say… to them on the left hand, 'Depart from Me, you cursed, into the everlasting fire prepared for the devil and his angels'"* (25:40-41). The message resounds with a theme of watchfulness throughout: The Jews should not be deceived by the forthcoming Antichrist but should instead wait for the Lord Jesus to return to judge the wicked and to establish His kingdom. *"Watch therefore, for you do not know what hour your Lord is coming"* (24:42).

After arriving on the Mount of Olives, the Lord called the attention of His disciples to the temple now directly west of them across the Kidron Valley (v. 1). He then told His disciples that this temple would be completely destroyed; not one stone would remain on another (v. 2). This prophecy was fulfilled when Roman armies under Titus' command destroyed the temple and much of Jerusalem with fire in 70 A.D. The extreme heat crumbled the stones of the temple and melted the gold band around the top of the temple. After the rubble cooled down, Roman soldiers then removed each stone to retrieve the precious metal.

But the destruction of the temple was also necessary to ensure that a prophecy by Haggai five centuries earlier (pertaining to the coming Messiah) would be fulfilled. Although the temple constructed by Jews under Zerubbabel's leadership in sixth century B.C. was smaller than Solomon's temple destroyed by the Babylonians in 586 B.C., the prophet Haggai predicted that it would be more glorious than its predecessor.

Why would the new temple be more glorious than Solomon's temple? Haggai answers this question in part: *"'The glory of this latter temple shall be greater than the former,' says the Lord of hosts. 'And in this place I will give peace,' says the Lord of hosts"* (Hag. 2:9). In short, the coming temple would have a greater glory than Solomon's temple. This may refer to either the millennial temple spoken of in Haggai 2:6-8 or it may be alluding to a future, glorious event which occurred in the temple that the Jews were erecting at that time. Possibly both are in view, as there is an increasing glory associated with God's temple, from His perspective.

For example, the temple under construction would be greater because the Jewish Messiah, the Prince of Peace, would present Himself in *"this latter temple"* some five centuries in the future. John tells us that on the same day that Haggai issued this prophecy (i.e., the final day of the Feast of Tabernacles), the Lord went to the temple to teach (John 7:28). We read that the Lord Jesus addressed the crowd at that time: *"On the last day, that great day of the feast, Jesus stood and cried out, saying, 'If anyone thirsts, let him come to Me and drink'"* (John 7:37).

So when the Lord Jesus entered the temple 2000 years ago, God did uphold His promise, *"I will fill this temple with glory"* (Hag. 2:9). Simeon confirms this perspective in his prayer after the Holy Spirit came upon him in the temple and while holding the baby Jesus in his arms:

Lord, now You are letting Your servant depart in peace, according to Your word; for my eyes have seen Your salvation which You have prepared before the face of all peoples, a light to bring revelation to the Gentiles, and the glory of Your people Israel (Luke 2:29-32).

The glory of Israel, Jehovah's salvation (the literal meaning of Jesus' name), had now entered the temple constructed in the sixth century B.C. Then, about 38 years after Christ's coming, that temple was destroyed, meaning that no one else claiming to be Messiah could ever fulfill Haggai's prophecy.

With surety, then, we can proclaim to every Jew, "Your Messiah has already been in Jerusalem." Though His essential glory was veiled by flesh, Christ's divine moral glory was declared in Herod's temple on several occasions. The message He spoke was how to have peace with His Father through Himself. Though the offer of peace was extended to Israel in the temple in Jerusalem, the Jewish nation rejected it.

The Beginning of Sorrows: Pre-Tribulation Signs (vv. 3-8)

While the Lord Jesus was speaking to His disciples on the Mount of Olives, they asked Him to reveal to them, *"What will be the sign of Your coming, and of the end of the age?"* (v. 3). The Lord then identified many signs associated with the coming of the Tribulation Period, the first half of the Tribulation Period, the Abomination of Desolation in the middle of the Tribulation Period, then the Great Tribulation (speaking of the last half of the Tribulation Period), and of His second Advent to conclude this horrific time. He desires that Christians throughout the Church Age, as indicated by the phrase *"the end of the age,"* would not be deceived by false prophets or false Christs (v. 4).

He first speaks of the Beginning of Sorrows (vv. 3-8). This would be an era marked by specific prophetic fulfillment which would alert the Jews to the forthcoming Tribulation Period. These troubling events are of an escalating nature and are meant primarily to be signs to Israel that the time of *Jacob's Trouble* is nearing. But as the Church will be removed from the earth prior to this seven-year period of Israel's final chastening, believers in the Church Age can be excited about these signs also. However, Christians should remember that there are no signs given to the Church for Christ's imminent return. The rapture of the Church is the next eschatological event on God's calendar.

First, the Lord explains that in the era just prior to the Tribulation Period there would be a dramatic increase in those claiming to be sent from God, especially claiming some type of Messianic authority (v. 5). Since the 1830s there has been an explosion of false cults, many of which tout their own prophets from God and their own Christs, but not Jesus Christ. For example, Sun Myung Moon was born in North Korea in 1920 and founded The Unification Church. According to Moon, Jesus is not coming back to the earth, but another Messiah, who will be born in the flesh in Korea.[58] Moon says that he is that Messiah and will return to the earth in a future day to the Mount of Olives.

Second, there will be wars and rumors of wars before the Tribulation Period (v. 6). The twentieth century saw the first two wars that were worldwide, which ushered in the Nuclear Age and the resulting Cold War – the constant threat of nuclear annihilation. It is not likely that there will be another world war until the Tribulation Period.

Third, nation will rise against nation, and kingdom against kingdom (v. 7). The Greek word rendered "nation" in this verse is *ethnos*, which is root for our English word "ethnic." As the Tribulation Period nears there will be a dramatic increase in ethnic violence. A shift from large numbers of soldiers perishing in warfare to ethnic genocide is likely indicated by this prophecy. For example, from April 7 to July 19, 1994, somewhere between 500,000 to a million people of the Tutsi ethnic group and 10,000 of the Twa ethnic group were slaughtered in Rwanda by Hutu militias.[59] Since 1980, similar genocidal attacks have occurred in Angola, Bosnia, Burundi, the Democratic Republic of Congo, Iraq, Somalia, and in the Darfur province of Sudan. Millions died in these ethnic massacres.

It is estimated that the military casualties during WWI were 10 million, while civilian casualties were about 500,000. There is a 20:1 ratio between these two numbers. In WWII, there were about 26 million military casualties in comparison to 24 million civilian deaths, or about a 1:1 ratio. During the Korean War (Police Action) there were approximately one million military personnel deaths to five million civilian casualties, or a 1:5 ratio. Then, in the Vietnam War there were roughly 150,000 military deaths to three million civilian casualties, a 1:20 ratio.[60] Since the Vietnam War ended in 1975, this ratio of civilian to military deaths has further increased. Throughout human history, conquering empires were intent on defeating opposing armies and then putting the populations of the defeated into subjection to profit from them. However, during the twentieth century a shift from merely defeating military personnel to slaughtering non-combatants (often motivated by racial hatred) has been observed. As the Lord said, ethnic group shall rise against ethnic group!

Fourth, there will be a dramatic increase in famines, pestilences, and earthquakes in various locations throughout the planet (v. 7). The United Nations World Food Programme states that famine is declared when malnutrition is widespread, and when people have started dying from starvation through lack of access to sufficient and nutritious food[61]. With the growing world population, there is an increasing difficulty of everyone receiving adequate nourishment. According to the World Health Organization (WHO), hunger is the gravest threat to the world's public health. WHO presently estimates that approximately 733 million people worldwide are undernourished.[62] During the twentieth century, an estimated 70 to 120 million people died from famines worldwide, with over half of those deaths in China.[63]

With the rapid rise of expedient transportation in the twentieth century also came the opportunity to rapidly transmit viruses over great distances. Given the earth's growing and mobile population, global pandemics may occur today in days instead of months as in previous centuries.

Last, the Lord spoke of a time marked by increased earthquakes just prior to the Tribulation Period. The National Earthquake Information Center in the US locates about 20,000 earthquakes around the globe each year. According to long-term records (since about 1900), we may expect about sixteen major earthquakes in any given year. That includes fifteen earthquakes in the magnitude 7 range and one earthquake magnitude 8 or greater. In the past 40-50 years, their records show that we have exceeded the long-term average number of major earthquakes about a dozen times.[64] While seismic activity waxes and wanes over time, we are presently witnessing a period of increased incidents. Some areas of the U.S. have recently experienced a dramatic increase in earthquakes resulting from the hydraulic fracturing (fracking) process used to obtain crude oil from the earth.[65]

The previous escalating signs prior to the commencement of the Tribulation Period were referred to by the Lord as "the beginning of sorrows" (v. 8). The eschatology timeline presented in Matthew 24 is chronological. The Tribulation Period begins in verse 9.

214

The First Half of the Tribulation Period (vv. 9-14)

The Lord then informed His Jewish brothers that when the time of *Jacob's Trouble* began, the Jews (the "you") would be hated by the Gentiles (the "they") and be delivered up to tribulation and killed (v. 9). The word translated "afflicted" in the KJV or "tribulation" in the RV and NKJV is the same Greek word *thlipsis* used in verses 21 and 29. These latter verses pertain to the Great Tribulation and events afterwards. This indicates that the Olivet Discourse (Matthew 24 and 25) pertains to the Jewish people who are in tribulation before and after the Abomination of Desolation that occurs in the middle of Jacob's Trouble (Dan. 9:27; Rev. 12:6). The "elect" in verse 22 then refers to the refined Jewish remnant who will survive this seven-year slaughter by the Antichrist. According to Zechariah, two-thirds of all Jews worldwide will perish during this timeframe (Zech. 13:8-9).

During the first half of the Tribulation Period many will be offended by the gospel of the kingdom being preached throughout the world (v. 14). This message will cause much division, betrayal, oppression, and hatred among those living on the earth (vv. 9-10). There will even be a loss of trust in and love for one's own family members (v. 12). Many false prophets will rise at this time to confuse and deceive the inhabitants of the earth from believing the truth (v. 11).

There will be 144,000 divinely chosen and sealed Jewish evangelists that will be preaching this kingdom message throughout the earth at this time (Rev. 7:3-8, 14:1-5). The Kingdom message is what Christ preached to Israel initially but was rejected; she was offered a literal, earthly, political kingdom (4:17). Today, the Church preaches the gospel of grace: Christ crucified and raised from death for our justification. Only believers are tasked by the Lord with sharing this message with the lost (28:19-20). There is no example in Scripture of even angels intruding on this responsibility. After the Church Age has concluded, the Kingdom message will be preached again in Israel and indeed throughout the world. John foretold that angels would then fly over the earth to publicly declare its validity – the true King is coming to judge; do not worship the Antichrist (Rev. 14:6-12). These gospel distinctions show that Christ's plans for His Church and for restoring Israel are different. The Church has a heavenly citizenship, calling, and inheritance, while Israel has earthly promises and inheritance.

All those who endure through the Tribulation Period and believe that Christ will come to the earth to avenge His name and set up His kingdom will be delivered by Him at His second advent. These individuals will not worship the Antichrist or take his mark (Rev. 13:11-18; 19:20). In fact, a great multitude will not identify with the Antichrist and will be put to death during the Tribulation Period (Rev. 7:9-15). These Tribulation saints will be resurrected to rule and reign with Christ in His earthly kingdom (Rev. 20:4).

Mid-Tribulation: The Abomination of Desolation (vv. 15-20)

The Lord Jesus then referred to Daniel's prophecy concerning the abomination of desolation committed by the Antichrist in the temple of God in Jerusalem. Namely, he will stop the Jewish sacrifices and declare himself as God incarnate (2 Thess. 2:4). God moved the prophet Daniel to declare His ultimate timetable for the final restoration of the Jewish nation (Dan. 9:24-27). The prophecy is broken into two major parts: sixty-nine weeks, which consists of two portions of seven weeks and sixty-two weeks, and then the final section of one week. The word translated "week" is literally "seven." But seven what? Based on how the final week is described elsewhere in Scripture, we can conclude that a week is speaking of seven years.

The abomination of desolation committed by the Antichrist (the one who will make a peace covenant with the Jewish nation for one week) occurs in the middle of the week (v. 15; Dan. 8:25, 9:27; 2 Thess. 2:4). But Scripture elsewhere provides the exact timing of this event. It occurs "a time (1), times (2), and half a time (1/2)" after the start of the week of years (Dan. 7:25, 12:7; Rev. 12:14). This three and a half times is also equal to 1260 days (Rev. 12:6) or 42 months (Rev. 13:5). As just witnessed in the fulfillment of Jeremiah's seventy-year prophecy, a Jewish prophetic year in Scripture is consistently 360 days (12 months x 30 days/month = 360 days). Three and a half years would then be equal to 1260 days (3.5 years x 360 days/year = 1260 days). Thus, Daniel's prophecy is unmistakably speaking of seventy weeks of years or, literally, "seventy sevens."

When the abomination of desolation occurs at the midway point in the Tribulation Period, there will also be war in heaven. The archangel Michael, along with his angels, will war against the devil and his fallen angels to constrain evil to the earth (Dan. 12:1; Rev. 12:7-10). Satan, knowing that his time is short, will be enraged and seek to exterminate the Jewish people (Rev. 12:12-15). However, the Lord will preserve and protect a remnant of His covenant people from harm (v. 16; Rev. 12:16-17). The slaughter will be so severe and widespread that Lord warns His countrymen not to tarry for any reason but to journey to places of hiding in the mountains as quickly as possible (vv. 17-18). The Lord then acknowledged the difficulties of accomplishing this in wintertime, or those who were pregnant or who were caring for young children (vv. 19-20).

The Last Half of the Tribulation Period (vv. 21-28)

While speaking of signs associated with the Great Tribulation, the time when the Antichrist will be gaining followers on the earth and slaughtering those who will not take His mark (v. 21; Rev. 13:15-18), the Lord gave a warning concerning the powerful signs of the Antichrist to deceive the masses (vv. 21-25). The Lord then stated that during this time the slaughter on the earth would be so great that no one would survive the Great Tribulation if it lasted longer than three and a half years (v. 22). But for "the elect's sake" this terrible era would not be permitted to go beyond the appointed time. "The elect" are those redeemed during the Tribulation Period including the refined Jewish remnant; these will enter Christ's kingdom.

During this era, the beast, the false prophet, and other deceivers will be working great signs and wonders to deceive the inhabitants of the world (Rev. 13). The devil is a powerful being that can do what from our lowly viewpoint seems impossible. This is why saints are challenged to trust Scripture and not their senses to judge all things. The truth is in the whole, so if we rightly divide Scripture and hold to it, we will not be deceived (1 Pet. 5:8-9). Hence, the Lord told the sign-seeking Pharisees that *"An evil and adulterous generation seeks after a sign"* (12:39). Signs (what our senses affirm) can be fabricated by the devil, but God's Word is from Him alone and thus is always truth. The deception at this time will be so powerful that the Lord warned against listening to anything that men proclaim as truth. Yield to God's Word alone.

The Great Tribulation will conclude with the second advent of Christ to the earth. Like lightning that flashes across the sky, the Lord's coming will be sudden and visible to all (v. 27). Furthermore, just as vultures and eagles gather to devour a dead carcass, no religious corruption or evil will escape the judgments of God at Christ's appearing. Apostate Judaism, Christendom, and all the people that the Antichrist has mustered together as a part of his one-world occult system will be destroyed (v. 28).

Tribulation Period Ends: Christ's Second Advent (vv. 29-31)

Christ will return to the earth to destroy the Antichrist and liberate surviving Jews in Jerusalem (Zech. 14). Matthew states that this will be a time of great upheaval in heaven and in earth (v. 29). Christ's return will be a visible coming in which the entire world will see the glory of Christ (v. 30; Luke 17:24).

When the Jews see Jesus Christ returning to the earth in glory and power, they will mourn as a family would if they had lost their firstborn son or their only son (v. 30; Zech. 12:10). With Christ's Second Advent to earth, the spiritual blindness of the Jewish nation will come to an end. They will trust in the Lord Jesus Christ, their Messiah, the One they had pierced two thousand years earlier (Zech. 12:10). Although we see that individual Jews in the Old Testament were filled by the Holy Spirit to speak for the Lord or to serve Him effectively (e.g., Ex. 35:30-35; 1 Sam. 10:10), the Jewish nation has never been indwelt by the Spirit of God (Zech. 4:4-7). This will not happen until Christ's second coming to the earth (Isa. 59:21).

Immediately after Christ's arrival to the earth, there will be a blast of a trumpet and the angels will gather all of God's covenant people remaining in the world back to the land of Israel (v. 31). The prophet Ezekiel states that the Lord will not leave one Jew anywhere in the world; all should be brought back to Israel to witness the complete fulfillment of the Abrahamic covenant (Ezek. 39:28-29).

Those who hold a Mid-Tribulation Rapture view of the Church point to the Church being taken up to heaven at the last trump of 1 Corinthians 15:51-52, which they associate with the last of seven trumpet judgments in Revelation 8-11. However, the seventh trumpet judgment of Revelation 8-11 is not the last trumpet blast to be heard during the Tribulation Period; there is another trump at the end of the Tribulation Period which is used to re-gather all Jews back to Israel, not the Church to heaven (v. 31).

Jehovah used silver trumpets to call an assembly of His people together while they were wandering in the wilderness. In Exodus 19, a long blast of a trumpet, perhaps of a ram's horn, was used to signal the Israelites to gather at the base of Mount Sinai to meet the Lord. The mount quaked exceedingly, it burned like an overheated furnace, and thick billows of smoke ascended from it into heaven. From the thick darkness, a deafening voice, which increased in volume, uttered words as if blasted from a trumpet. The people feared and were in awe of the Lord. This will be Israel's response when they are called to and restored to Jehovah at the end of the Tribulation Period.

The Parable of the Fig Tree (vv. 32-35)

The Lord spoke a prophetic parable concerning the fig tree. The generation that sees the fig tree shoot forth leaves again after being dormant over the winter will see all the things that Christ has just foretold about the Tribulation Period and His second coming to the earth (vv. 32-34). The Lord reminded His disciples that though heaven and earth will pass away, His words were eternal and would come about (v. 34). But what is symbolized by leaves (not fruit) appearing on the fig tree?

As previously explained (ch. 21), the Jewish nation is allegorically likened to a foliage trilogy: the vine, the fig tree, and the olive tree. Each one represents a distinct aspect of the nation's existence. For example, the prophet Jeremiah told his fellow countrymen that God had planted a beautiful vineyard (Israel), but Israel's shepherds had made it desolate (Jer. 12:10). The nation of Israel, as a political reality, is likened to a noble vine (a grape vine; Jer. 8:13), which God planted in the world (Jer. 2:21; 12:10); Israel was God's vineyard. Jeremiah explains that the destruction of Israel in his day would be like livestock moving freely through God's vineyard and trampling the vines. It would consequently have no productivity, bearing only the fruit of sowing to sin, that is, the thorns of affliction and a harvest of shame (Jer. 12:11-13).

When Israel is spoken of as a fig tree in Scripture, the metaphor relates to the religious element of Israel, which often was fruitless for God (21:19-21; Jer. 8:13). This reality, Judaism today, was identified during one of the events in the life of the Lord Jesus (Luke 13:6-9). After preaching three years to the lost nation of Israel, Christ cursed the fruitless fig tree just before His death at Calvary. Less than forty years later, Jerusalem and the temple were destroyed, and the Jews have not sacrificed since then. The Old Covenant was replaced by the New

Covenant, sealed with Christ's blood, and God was determined not to allow the Jews to continue in what was now obsolete.

One of the signs that the Tribulation Period and the Second Advent of Christ are nearing is that the fig tree (i.e., religious Israel) will again shoot forth leaves after a long winter season of deadness (Luke 21:29-31). Leaves must precede fruit, but the fig tree will bear no fruit until the rebirth of the nation occurs in the latter days of the Tribulation Period. What might the new leaves speak of? This is likely a reference to the Jews reviving the old sacrificial system during, and perhaps just prior to, the Tribulation Period.

We know from various prophecies that the Antichrist will desecrate the Jewish temple and put a stop to animal sacrifices at the midpoint of the Tribulation Period (24:15; Dan. 9:27; 2 Thess. 2:3-7). Therefore, logically speaking, a temple will have to be erected and animal sacrifices will have to be reinstituted by that point.

Therefore, we see that, during the Tribulation Period, the Jews will again offer sacrifices under the Levitical system. This reality could commence just prior to the Tribulation period. The Lord Jesus said that the generation permitted to witness this event would also visibly see His coming to the earth in glory (Luke 21:32). It is worth noting that the Temple Institute in Jerusalem has already recreated most of the temple vessels and furnishing and has performed "educational" animal sacrifices in anticipation of this historic event.

> Rabbi Yisrael Ariel, one of the leaders of the Temple Institute in Jerusalem, has stated that everything is now ready for recommencement of the sacrificial system. All that remains is for the government of Israel to give them the permission to go onto the Temple Mount and perform the sacrifice. While Israel does control the Temple Mount, it is administered by the Islamic Waqf of Jordan, and the Israeli Police generally prohibit any action that might cause contention with the Muslims.[66]

Many orthodox Jews are anticipating an imminent day when they will again perform the sacrifices as specified in the Mosaic Law.

At this juncture, there are leaves upon the tree, depicting a religious reality, but there is no fruit. Spiritual fruit can only be produced through spiritual rebirth which coincides with the Holy Spirit being poured out upon the Jewish nation at the end of the Tribulation Period. At that time, they will know and worship Jesus Christ as Messiah (Joel 2:25-3:21; Zech. 12:10-13:1). At the end of the Tribulation Period, the refined Jewish nation will receive the Holy Spirit and obtain spiritual life in Christ. Once the Jewish nation has experienced spiritual renewal, the vineyard of the Lord (the house of Israel; Isa. 5:7) will be again planted in Israel as a testimony to the nations of God's glory (Isa. 4, 60:1-5).

During the Kingdom Age, which begins shortly after Christ's Second Advent to the earth, the fig tree will bear fruit. The Jewish millennial activities will occur in Jerusalem at the newly erected temple, the detailed dimensions and construction of which the prophet Ezekiel specified (Ezek. 40-43). Thus, the fig tree of the Old Testament, the visible religious system of the Jewish nation, will become fruitful in the millennial kingdom because it will have Christ as its true spiritual focus. Judaism, with all its extra-biblical traditions and interpretations, will have no part in the worship of the Jewish Messiah.

Watchfulness Is Required (vv. 36-44)

Speaking of Christ's second advent and establishing His kingdom on earth, the Lord states that no one knows the day and hour in which that will occur (v. 36). Not even the angels in heaven are let in on this secret; only God the Father had this knowledge. This was a mystery that the Father did not want His Son to reveal. Obviously, Christ, who is God incarnate, knows all things, but in His humanity, He also learned through experience (e.g., Luke 2:52; Heb. 5:8). Apparently, at this juncture, the Jewish Messiah was to yet learn when He would come into His kingdom. By reviewing the Jewish betrothal and marriage customs of that day, we realize why this detail is mentioned by Matthew.

In the historical Jewish betrothal custom, a man would approach a virgin's father to ask for her hand in marriage. If the father was agreeable to this, they would then negotiate the bride's price (i.e., the virgin's dowry). Once this had been finalized, the virgin's parents would have the prospective groom over for dinner. At this meal he would pour a glass of wine and offer it to the daughter, the prospective bride. If she accepted the glass from the suitor's hand, it meant that she accepted his proposal. If she did not accept the glass, his offer was rejected. If the marriage offer was accepted, the couple was then considered betrothed – they were bound by a marriage covenant. This began an interval called a "time of purity" in which the groom built a house near his father's house or added on a room to his father's house for him and his bride.

During this time of purity, the bride was not idle either, for she was preparing her wedding gown and had to be ready to be called away by her husband when he came for her. Once the groom's father was satisfied that the new home was finished and furnished, he would instruct his son to go get his bride. When arriving at the bride's home, he would shout for her to come; she would quickly join him, and they would return together to the new home. After this, they enjoyed personal intimacy together, and then a marriage feast to celebrate their marriage and new home was held with their friends and relatives.

The parallels between Christ's relationship with the Church and that of the groom to the bride in the Jewish betrothal custom are impressive. When an individual accepts the gospel invitation, the dowry is applied (the blood Christ shed at Calvary). The night before He died, the Lord poured a glass of wine and gave it to His disciples to drink. He told them: *"This cup is the new testament in My blood, which is shed for you"* (Luke 22:20). They received it and drank it and a new covenant was acknowledged. Each time a believer drinks of the cup at the Lord's Supper, he is reaffirming "I do" to the Lord Jesus. The Lord promised His disciples later that evening that though He was leaving to prepare a place for them, He would return for them (John 14:2-3). When will the Lord come? While still on earth, the Lord said that only His Father knew (v. 36). So, the Son is busy preparing a home for His bride. When it is complete, the Father will tell His Son, "It is time to receive Your bride." The Church must always be ready for His sudden appearance to take her home, which means doing righteous works in the name of Christ, illustrated by the glorious gown of the bride (Rev. 3:18, 19:7-8).

Next, the Lord said that the world would be surprised by His coming to the earth to judge the wicked (vv. 37-44). In fact, at the Lord's second advent, the behavior of man will be like that in Noah's day. Sexual perversion and unceasing wickedness will characterize man prior to judgment. Man will be living for all the pleasure life can offer and have no remorse for the Creator's grieving heart. Noah's contemporaries lived as if they had flood insurance, but the only insurance was the ark. Likewise, today, in our post-Christian society, man lives for the day, not realizing that judgment is coming and that the good news of Jesus Christ is the only means of escape. Much of the world will be suffering from stubborn spiritual blindness when Christ returns to judge them.

One man taken from the field and the one woman removed from the grinding stone refer to those who followed the Antichrist (vv. 40-41). As part of judging the nations, all those who took his mark will perish in judgment and not be permitted to enter Christ's kingdom (13:47-50; Rev. 19:21). This analogy does not refer to the rapture of the Church to Heaven but is a judgment of the wicked occurring at Christ's second advent. On this point, Louis A. Barbieri, Jr. writes:

> Clearly the church, the body of Christ, cannot be in view in these statements. The Lord was not describing the Rapture, for the removal of the Church will not be a judgment on the Church. If this were the Rapture, as some commentators affirm, the Rapture would have to be posttribulational, for this event occurs immediately before the Lord's return in glory. But that would conflict with a number of Scriptures and present other problems that cannot be elaborated on here (e.g., 1 Thess. 4:13-18 and Rev. 3:10). The Lord's warning emphasized the need to be prepared, for judgment will come at a time when people least expect it.[67]

As Matthew explains in the next chapter, those suddenly taken away here are referred to as goats that must be separated from the sheep. The goats are slaughtered, and the sheep are permitted into Christ's kingdom (25:31-46). Regrettably, many commentators insert the Church into this Jewish-focused text because of the sudden taking of people from the earth. In the Rapture of the Church, that occurs before the Tribulation Period commences, redeemed saints are removed from the earth to be with the Lord in heaven, but in the event that Matthew describes here, it is the wicked that are removed from the earth in judgment. In this former situation, being left behind is a bad thing, but in the latter, to "be left behind" is a good thing as these believers will enter Christ's kingdom.

The Lord then warns that it would be prudent for humanity to realize that judgment is coming. If a man knows that his home is going to be broken into by thieves, he will be watching and waiting for them, even though he does not know when they are coming (vv. 42-43). The world will not be expecting Christ's sudden appearance to set up His kingdom, but His servants (the Jewish remnant and perhaps Tribulation saints) should be watching and waiting with great expectation for that event (v. 44). A true servant is known by how they behave concerning Christ's coming. Whether it is to snatch the Church from off the earth to heaven or to later rescue the remnant of Israel out of the Antichrist's clutches, faithful servants will be watching and waiting for Christ.

The Lord Jesus never told His disciples to be looking for the Antichrist, but rather to be intently watching and waiting for His unannounced return to the air to take the Church home (1 Cor. 1:7-8; Phil. 1:6, 10; 1 Thess. 5:9; 2 Thess. 1:10). It is noted that a few Christians hold to a Partial Rapture view, a position that states that only those believers "watching and waiting" for the Lord's coming will be raptured at various times prior to and during the seven-year Tribulation Period. But both the Lord and Paul confirm that Christ is coming for the Church in its entirety (John 14:1; 1 Cor. 12:13, 15:51-52).

Around the dial of a clock in a church in Strasburg, Germany, are these words: "One of these hours the Lord is coming." We do not know when; it may be today; it may be now! Therefore, let us be watchful servants while we wait for our Beloved to come.

The Two Servants (vv. 45-51)

Both Matthew and Luke record the parable of *The Two Servants* spoken privately to the disciples on the Mount of Olives the Tuesday before Christ's crucifixion (vv. 45-51; Luke 12:42-48). The disciples did not understand that there would be a long period of time between the Lord's advents to the earth. Several of the Lord's final parables emphasized that His disciples should not lose heart during this interim which would be marked by hardship.

This story was told to exhort the disciples to be faithful to Him after His departure. They and the following generations of disciples that would believe their message were to show love to Christ by properly caring for His people. Loyal and wise servants would be amply rewarded when He returned to examine their reliability in what had been entrusted to them. The Lord's sheep (His people) are not always easy to love and to serve with joy, but they are His Beloved; thus we should care for them regardless of how much they glare, smell, kick, bite, and wander.

There will be some who identify with Christ, but their lackadaisical attitude towards Christ's return and the way they treat His servants will reveal that they were not His disciples. These imposters will be put to death at Christ's coming and will be destined for eternal judgment in the Lake of Fire after experiencing resurrection to stand before Christ at the Great White Throne Judgment (v. 51; Rev. 20:11-15).

Matthew Chapter 25

The Ten Virgins (vv. 1-13)

While the Lord Jesus was speaking to His disciples on the Mount of Olives, they asked Him to reveal to them, *"What will be the sign of Your coming, and of the end of the age?"* (24:3). He then proclaimed to them important details concerning the future of Israel and the time of His second coming to the earth. The Lord identified signs associated with the coming of the Tribulation Period and events that would occur during the Tribulation Period, which would conclude with His second advent. The Lord's teachings in this passage are generally chronological and *strictly* Jewish in nature. Because the Church will already be in heaven before the events of the Tribulation Period begin, the events of this passage do not pertain to the Church Age (i.e., except for the escalating signs occurring just prior to the Tribulation Period).

In the Tribulation, the beast (the Antichrist) and the false prophet will be working great signs and wonders to deceive the inhabitants of the world (Rev. 13) – so much so that at the Lord's second advent, the behavior of man will be similar to that in Noah's day. Sexual perversion and unceasing wickedness will characterize humanity's behavior prior to God's judgment, which is not expected.

Therefore, the Lord did not tell His disciples to be looking for the Antichrist, but rather to be intently watching and waiting for His unannounced return to the air to take the Church home (1 Cor. 1:7-8; 1 Thess. 4:13-18, 5:9; 2 Thess. 1:10). During the Tribulation Period, many Jews will be living for the moment and not expecting Jesus Christ to return as their Messiah. These are pictured by the five virgins without oil who will perish during the Tribulation Period.

The key components of this parable are as follows:

The groom = Christ.

The lamps = a testimony of truth.

The ten virgins = those with Messianic hope in the Tribulation Period.

The oil = the working of the Holy Spirit.

The five virgins with oil = the true remnant at Christ's coming.

The five virgins without oil = superficial faith, do not enter the Kingdom.

The bride = the Church (not mentioned because She returns with Christ).

Given the Jewish context of this passage, the bride (the Church) is not mentioned as she is in heaven with the Groom, but the Jewish people are still on earth. The "then" in verse 1 ties this parable with the events revealed by Christ in Matthew chapter 24. The Jewish people are still waiting for Messiah to come. At the end of the Tribulation Period, He and His Bride (all His redeemed in heaven) will return to the earth with Him (Rev. 19:11-16). The Vulgate version of the Bible states that the Bride is with her Groom when He comes in this parable. This suggests that the wedding has already occurred in heaven and that the Bride and the Groom are returning to the earth for the marriage supper, and all that will enter Christ's kingdom will be attending the festivities.

Given the Jewish tenor of this passage, it is likely that the ten virgins represent the Jewish people scattered among the nations during the Tribulation Period. However, given that the Kingdom gospel is preached throughout the world at this time, the ten virgins may have a wider representation of all those who have Messianic hope, including repentant Gentiles. While this is possible, there is nothing in Scripture that suggests that Gentiles refusing to worship the Antichrist receive the Holy Spirit before entering the Kingdom Age. Many Old Testament prophets do, however, foretell that God will pour out His Spirit on the entire Jewish nation at that time (Joel 2:28-29; Ezek. 37:1-14, 39:25-29).

It is noted that all ten virgins slept prior to the Groom's return, which indicates that there was not much difference in their outward behavior while they were waiting for the marriage feast. The critical difference is that five virgins had true Messianic hope in Jesus Christ and had received the Holy Spirit, while others had a mere profession of that truth. No doubt some of these "oil-less" virgins were holding to an erroneous view of the Messiah, which much of Judaism embraces today.

The prophet Zechariah foretold that two-thirds of all Jews will die during this timeframe (Zech. 13:8-9), but those remaining will receive the Holy Spirit and gladly worship Jesus Christ at His second coming (Zech. 12:20). This realization would bolster the idea that the ten virgins (as a minimum) represent the Jewish nation during the Tribulation

Period. That is, many Jews will not believe that Jesus Christ is their Messiah and will perish.

Olive oil is a type of the Holy Spirit in Scripture (Zech. 4:2-6). The light from one's lamp speaks of his or her testimony for God (5:14-16). It is only possible to have a true testimony for God when the Holy Spirit is enabling us to live for Christ. The Holy Spirit indwells those who are Christ's; His presence cannot be purchased with money (Eph. 1:13-14).

The five Spirit-filled virgins were watching and waiting for Jesus Christ's return. These true believers were welcomed to celebrate with Christ and His Bride at the wedding feast. At this time Christ will vindicate His name on earth and punish all those who followed the Antichrist; this is called *The Judgment of Nations* (Rev. 19:17-21). *The Judgment of Nations* is done suddenly, and the general populace will not be expecting it (24:36-41).

This same judgment is pictured in the analogy of Christ separating the sheep and the goats in verses 31-46. Those following the Antichrist (the goats) will be executed, while Gentile survivors who were kind to the oppressed Jewish peoples and did not take the beast's mark (the sheep) will enter Christ's Kingdom. The goats suffer death and will wait in Hades for their resurrection and final judgment at *The Great White Throne Judgment* (Rev. 20:11-15). The other five virgins, though waiting for Messiah to come, were not looking for Jesus Christ to return to rule over them. These individuals did not receive the Holy Spirit and hence were not saved from wrath; they did not enter Christ's Kingdom as the five virgins with oil (i.e., those having the Holy Spirit) did.

Most of the prophetic books in the Old Testament foretell a future day when the Messiah will come and restore the nation of Israel to Himself. From this viewpoint, Jehovah is the faithful Husband waiting for the restoration of His unfaithful wife, Israel (Jer. 3:8; Hos. 3). In this sense, the ten virgins in this parable seem to equate with the *"daughters of Jerusalem"* referred to in the Song of Solomon (Song. 1:5, 2:2, 2:7, 3:5…). These represent the Jewish nation, which is presently spiritually estranged from Jehovah, while the Church is the spotless Bride patiently waiting to be united with her Beloved, the Lord Jesus Christ (Eph. 1:6).

The Talents (vv. 14-30)

The Lord was still on the Mount of Olives the Tuesday evening before Calvary when He spoke this parable to His disciples. He had been teaching them about the Tribulation Period and His second coming, in response to their question to know more about future events.

In the story of *The Talents*, a man was preparing for an extended journey into a far country. He set his household in order and committed his substance into the hands of his servants. He gave one servant five talents, another two, and another one, *"to each according to his particular ability"* (v. 15, Darby). There would be much accountability for each servant's stewardship, as a talent was 58 to 80 pounds of silver worth 6000 denarii. A talent represented about twenty years of wages for a common laborer.

After the master departed, the servant with five talents earned double that amount through wise investments. The servant who had been given two talents also doubled his talents in the same way. However, the servant who had received one talent buried it in the earth. He decided to reserve and return what his master had given to him, but without any benefit of having received it.

When the householder returned, the first two servants reported the increase and delivered the ten and four talents, respectively. The master heartily praised each of them with the same words: *"Well done, good and faithful servant; you were faithful over a few things, I will make you ruler over many things. Enter into the joy of your lord"* (v. 21, 23). Then the last servant came before the householder. After calling his master harsh and unfair, he returned the single talent that he had received without any earnings.

The master then addressed him as a *"wicked and lazy servant,"* and rebuked his slothfulness. If he personally did not want to use the talent to earn a profit, he should have deposited it in a bank, so at least the talent would have earned some interest. In the end, the last servant's lone talent is entrusted to the one who had ten, and the servant himself is thrown out into the outer darkness where there is weeping and gnashing of teeth (this speaks of eternal judgment in Hell).

As previously mentioned, the *Olivet Discourse* of Matthew 24-25 is Jewish in focus and is speaking of the Tribulation Period and Christ's second coming. During the Tribulation Period the Kingdom gospel message will be preached throughout the world (24:14). The Jewish people will be refined and restored to God during this horrific time.

The time setting in which this parable is associated is crucial to understanding its meaning. Every person has been given abilities by God to be used for His honor and glory. Those who reject His offer of salvation will not use their natural abilities to serve God and thus live a wasted life. In this parable the third servant represents this type of person. Someone who is ignorant of God's character, attributes, word, etc. will not live for Him. God does not force Himself on anyone, but permits us to choose life in Him or death apart from Him.

This coldhearted servant did not want to do anything to benefit his master. Unfaithful servants are so because they do not trust their Lord's character and they do not realize the Lord's claim on them. This is why the unfaithful servant grudgingly returned the single talent and said, *"There you have what is yours."* The servant was smugly declaring to his master, "You own the talent, but you do not own me!"

During the Tribulation Period, those living on the planet will have to choose God and His Lamb or the Antichrist; those aligning with the Antichrist will ultimately be cast into Hell (speaking of the *Lake of Fire*). This understanding explains why the unprofitable servant in this parable, an unbeliever, was cast into eternal judgment, but the unprofitable servant in the parable of *The Minas* (a despondent believer in the Church Age) only lost his reward. The parables relate to two different economies of truth in which man has been entrusted to respond by faith (this is called a "dispensation" in Scripture; Eph. 1:10, 3:2).

The parable shows us that God bestows different "talents" (natural abilities) to each person as He chooses, but everyone has an opportunity to please God with what they have received. Likewise, in the Church Age, Christ has given different individuals to the Church for its edification (Eph. 4:11-12), and the Holy Spirit bestows spiritual gifts to each believer as He wills (1 Cor. 12:4-11). The tendency of our flesh is to compare our abilities and ministries to each other, but as we learn from this story, eternal reward is given in accordance with faithfulness to use what we have been given, rather than what was accomplished.

Paul posed three questions to exhort the carnal Corinthian believers to cease comparing God's servants and their ministries to each other: *"For who makes you differ from another? And what do you have that you did not receive? Now if you did indeed receive it, why do you boast as if you had not received it?"* (1 Cor. 4:7). The answers to these questions respectively are: "God," "Nothing," and "It is foolish to compare or boast about what we have received in God's sovereignty." Hence, believers should be faithful to use what God entrusts to each individual and should not question, compare, or boast about what has been received or what others have received from Him. What God alone gives, He alone enables through faith and that is all that matters!

In summary, we are not to compare what we have received by divine grace and wisdom to what others have received. No one should compare the ministries of a one-talent preacher to a five-talent preacher; all that is important is that both preachers faithfully use their God-given abilities for Him. All of our talents received (resources, natural abilities, and spiritual gifts) should be fully devoted to the work of the Lord. When God gives more, He expects more. Accordingly, we see that the first two servants in the parable received the same praise from their master, despite having differing abilities to serve him. We can expect the Lord to behave in this gracious manner at the *Judgment Seat of Christ*.

Judgment of Nations: The Sheep and the Goats (vv. 31-46)

The Lord followed the parable of *The Talents* with specific teaching about *The Judgment of Nations* (the sorting of the sheep and the goats) at the end of the Tribulation Period. The Sheep, the righteous who are permitted to enter Christ's kingdom in the analogy, did not understand the King's accolade about them caring for Him, so He clarified the matter: *"And the King will answer and say to them, 'Assuredly, I say to you, inasmuch as you did it to one of the least of these My brethren, you did it to Me'"* (v. 40). William Kelly identifies the three groups of people in this analogy:

> We have had the sheep and goats – the righteous and the unrighteous Gentiles; but who are the King's brethren? Those whom the Lord will send out before He comes in the glory of the kingdom; men sent to announce that He is coming in His kingdom. The sheep showed them love, care, and sympathy in their sorrows. So that these brethren of the King must have been exposed to tribulation before the King appears. The conclusion is that, in that day, the ground on which He will deal with the nations will be this, "How did you behave to My messengers?" The King's messengers, immediately before He appears in glory, will go forth preaching the gospel of the kingdom everywhere; and when the King takes His throne, those that received the gospel of the kingdom among the nations are recognized as "sheep," and the despisers perish as "goats." Those that honor the message treat the messengers well, caring for them, and identifying themselves with them.[68]

Those who trusted the kingdom message and consequently aided the Jewish people, Christ's brethren (Acts 9:24), during the Tribulation Period will enter His kingdom. These individuals are referred to as sheep. Those who did not, but chose to align with the Antichrist, will be destroyed at Christ's coming. These are the goats. The Jewish remnant are neither the goats nor the sheep in this analogy.

In application, it is good for us to remember that the way we treat the lowliest believer in the Body of Christ shows our true esteem for the Lord Jesus Christ. Our tendency is to rub shoulders with those of status and that are well-to-do and snub those of humble estate. We tend to avoid identifying and associating with those who are burdened, persecuted, and suffering. But all believers are one in Christ; we all are members of His Body, of His Church, and compose His Bride. When one member of the Body suffers – all its members suffer. This spiritual reality must compel us to have the same care for one another that Christ would have for us.

The Millennial Kingdom of Christ will begin directly after *The Judgment of Nations* at the conclusion of the Tribulation Period. The Lord Jesus also taught about this judgment in the seventh of the Kingdom Parables (13:47-50). In that parable, the Lord casts a net into the sea (depicting the nations – Rev. 17:1, 15) and sorts through that which is caught. Those who did not follow the Antichrist are separated from those who did. The "good" are permitted into His kingdom; the "bad" are committed to eternal judgment. The net represents the influence of the kingdom gospel message that will be preached worldwide during the Tribulation Period (24:14). This message consists of a warning not to worship the Antichrist and a declaration that judgment of the wicked and Christ's kingdom is coming soon (Rev. 14:6-12).

The Judgment of Nations is done suddenly and those unfit for the kingdom will be removed from the earth. The Judgment of Nations is also pictured in Daniel 2:35, 44-45 and described in Revelation 19:20.

> He came the first time to die; He is coming again to raise the dead. When He came the first time, they questioned whether He was King; the next time the world will know that He is King of kings and Lord of lords. The first time He wore a crown of thorns; the next time He will be wearing a crown of glory. The first time He came in poverty; the next time He is coming in power. The first time He had an escort of angels; the next time He will come with ten thousands of His saints. The first time He came in meekness; He is coming again in majesty.
>
> – Adrian Rogers

Matthew Chapter 26

Christ's Death and Resurrection Again Foretold (vv. 1-5)

The Lord Jesus concludes His instruction on things to come to His disciples by again foretelling of His death, but this time He states that it will happen in association with the feast of Passover in two days (vv. 1-2). This is the fifth time that Matthew records the Lord informing His disciples of His death, burial, and resurrection. The "you know" statement in verse 2 must have shocked the disciples. Indeed, they were quite familiar with the Passover timing, but they knew nothing about the Lord's death. But John says, "Jesus knew" all about it (John 13:1).

Prophetic events are in rapid motion now. Matthew notes that the Christ-humiliated Pharisees were already plotting with the high priest Caiaphas as to how they might capture Jesus through trickery and put him to death without creating a public uproar (vv. 3-5).

Christ Anointed for His Burial (vv. 6-13)

The Lord was in Bethany at the home of a cleansed leper named Simon (v. 6). Matthew and Mark state that this incident occurred on Wednesday, two days before the Passover. The circumstances which John describes are similar, but he places the anointing just prior to Christ's triumphant entry into Jerusalem on Sunday (John 12:12). John names the woman who anointed the Lord, Mary (Lazarus' and Martha's sister), but Matthew and Mark do not identify the woman. Matthew and Mark state that the woman anointed the Lord's head (v. 7; Mark 14:3), while John indicates that Mary anointed the Lord's feet (John 12:3). It is therefore possible that there were two separate anointings by two different women in the final week of the Lord's ministry. However, to simplify the discussion, we will consider both accounts as one incident, as most commentators do.

Lazarus, who had been raised from the dead, was sitting with the Lord at a table, while Martha was serving (John 12:2). Their sister Mary arrived with a flask of costly fragrant oil (v. 7). John tells us that it was a pound of spikenard oil (John 12:3). She then anointed the Lord's head (and perhaps His feet) with the ointment. This is a beautiful scene of Christian fellowship, service, and worship all in the Lord's presence.

Judas, the betrayer, condemned Mary for her wastefulness (John 12:4), as did some of the other disciples, saying that the oil could have been sold and the proceeds used to assist the poor (vv. 8-9). But the Lord defended Mary and acknowledged her good work towards Him. *"Let her alone; she has kept this for the day of My burial"* (v. 10; John 12:7). The Lord reminded His disciples that the poor would always be with them, but He was about to depart from them (v. 11).

Mary apparently possessed a deeper understanding of what was coming than the disciples and she wanted to show her utmost appreciation (v. 12). She gave her best to the Lord and kept none of the oil for herself. It would be inappropriate to speak of personal cost or limiting gratitude for the One possessing all things and yet was willing to give His life for her to live. John notes that the house was filled with the sweet fragrance of Mary's worship. Genuine, selfless worship will refresh the hearts of all those who love the Lord Jesus. Let us remember that *"Christ came, who is over all, the eternally blessed God"* (Rom. 9:5) and He deserves our best. As a result of her sincere and selfless act towards the Lord Jesus, wherever the gospel was preached, she would be remembered as someone who truly loved the Lord (v. 13).

Judas Agrees to Betray the Lord (vv. 14-16)

Directly after Mary's anointing of the Lord, Judas *"went to the chief priests"* to negotiate Christ's betrayal (v. 14). This was likely Wednesday evening. No doubt that Judas, who pilfered the ministry money box (John 12:6), was put out by the terrible waste of the spikenard oil, as he could have secretly profited from its sell. Concerning Judas' treachery, John Heading observes:

> If there was worship within, then there was evil and treachery without. Judas is described as "one of the twelve," a unique designation to single out a unique man. In v. 47 he is again described as "one of the twelve," while in John 6:70 the Lord called him "one of you," v. 71 ending with "being one of the twelve." This man "went unto the chief priests." Note the four occasions on which Judas "went." Here he "went" to the chief priests; in John 13:30 he "went" immediately out: and "it was night." In Matt 27:5 he "went and hanged himself." In Acts 1:25 he went "to his own place" as the son of perdition.[69]

During the next two days, two symbols of redemption in Scripture will be used to signify what Christ would be securing on our behalf at Calvary. Both silver and barley symbolize redemption (Ex. 30:12-16; Lev. 23:9-14, 25:9). The Lord Jesus was betrayed for thirty pieces of silver, which was later referred to by the Pharisees as "blood money" and indeed it was (v. 15, 27:3-9). Additionally, in keeping with the Passover meal, the Lord broke unleavened barley bread the night before His crucifixion (Luke 22:14-20).

The prophet Zechariah uttered a messianic prophecy stating that the Lord would be betrayed for thirty pieces of silver. This prophecy was inserted between the breaking of the first and second staffs by the prophet to ensure that the meaning of both acts would be associated with the rejection of God's Shepherd by the Jewish nation:

> *Then I said to them, "If it is agreeable to you, give me my wages; and if not, refrain." So they weighed out for my wages thirty pieces of silver. And the Lord said to me, "Throw it to the potter" – that princely price they set on me. So I took the thirty pieces of silver and threw them into the house of the Lord for the potter* (Zech. 11:12-13).

Indeed, the chief priests decided that it would be worth thirty pieces of silver to get rid of Jesus, and Judas also agreed that this would be a fair price! But according to Zechariah's prophecy, not only would the Jewish Messiah be betrayed for thirty pieces of silver, but also this money would be returned to the temple and be used to buy a potter's field. Matthew confirms that Judas and the Pharisees fulfilled every detail of this prophecy (27:3-10).

The phrase *"a princely price they set on me"* in the prophecy reveals how deeply the Lord felt this scornful denunciation by His own people – those whom He came to deliver. David foretells the Lord's anguish over His betrayal and desertion:

> *Reproach has broken my heart, and I am full of heaviness; I looked for someone to take pity, but there was none; and for comforters, but I found none. They also gave me gall for my food, and for my thirst they gave me vinegar to drink* (Ps. 69:20-21).

Judas' betrayal indicated just how much he valued the Lord, who had abandoned the supreme glory of Heaven to be the incarnate man born of a virgin, to live in a sin-cursed world, to endure the contradiction of sinners for thirty-three-plus years, to endlessly serve those in need to the point of exhaustion, to lay down His life and to be cursed of God to save others from Hell that they might enjoy the abundant life of God. What an insult for Judas, who had been with the Lord for more than three years, to value Christ for a mere thirty pieces of silver.

> Thirty pieces of silver
> For the Lord of life they gave;
> Thirty pieces of silver –
> Only the price of a slave!
> But this was the priestly value,
> Of the Holy One of God;
> They weighed it out in the temple,
> The price of the Savior's blood.

> — William Blane

Preparation for the Passover Feast (vv. 17-19)

The next day, the first day of the Feast of Unleavened Bread, the disciples asked the Lord, *"Where do You want us to prepare for You to eat the Passover?"* (v. 17). The disciples understood that the Lord would be hosting the Passover for them and wanted to get everything ready for the meal later that evening.

The Lord answered their question by instructing two of them (Peter and John; Luke 22:8) to go into the city and when they saw a man carrying a pitcher, they were to follow him (v. 17, Mark 14:13). Then they were to say to the master of the house in which the man entered, *"The Teacher says, 'My time is at hand; I will keep the Passover at your house with My disciples'"* (v. 18). Luke and Mark provide the most details concerning the interchange, and both writers tell us that the master of the house showed the disciples a large, furnished, upper room that he would make available for the Lord to eat the Passover with His disciples (v. 15; Luke 22:12).

Typically, women retrieved water for the household, so it would be an unusual sight to see a man carrying a pitcher of water. But this would be how the disciples would meet their contact, who then would show them where the Lord wanted to host the Passover meal for His disciples. All was accomplished just as the Lord foretold them (v. 19).

The Last Passover Feast (vv. 20-25)

Around sundown on Nisan the fourteenth the Lord gathered with His disciples to keep the Passover in a large, furnished, upper room (v. 20). After they began eating the Passover feast, the Lord stated that one of them would betray Him (v. 21). The disciples began asking Him, *"Lord, is it I?"* (v. 22). There is no evidence in Scripture that Judas ever addressed the Lord Jesus as Lord, but clearly the other disciples did. John records that while leaning on the Lord's breast, he specifically asked the Lord who the betrayer was (John 13:25).

The Lord responded to his question by referring to the prophecy of Psalm 41:9 and saying, *"He who dipped his hand with Me in the dish will betray Me"* (v. 23). Judas had just hours earlier agreed to betray Christ for thirty pieces of silver. The realization that a betrayer sat with Him at the table troubled the Lord's spirit (John 11:33). It was customary for the host to dip a piece of bread in gravy or vinegar and give it to the honored guest (sitting to his left) during the feast. It is likely, given Christ's private charge to Judas, that Judas occupied this place of honor (John 13:27, 30). Christ gave Judas the sop and thus identified him as the betrayer (John 13:26).

John says that Satan entered Judas after he received the sop (John 13:27). Judas, then asked the Lord, deceitfully, *"Rabbi, is it I?"* (v. 25). Judas did not dare to address the Savior as "Lord," for he was in utter rebellion against His lordship. The Lord confirmed that he was the betrayer and told Judas, *"What you do, do quickly"* (John 13:27). Judas then departed the upper room; the other disciples did not discern what Christ meant by these words. They assumed that Judas, having the purse, was taking care of a feast-related matter (John 13:28-29).

The Lord's Supper Is Instituted (vv. 26-30)

Towards the end of the Passover feast, the Lord did something that did not follow the Seder tradition: *"Jesus took bread, blessed and broke it, and gave it to the disciples and said, 'Take, eat; this is My body'"* (v. 26). *"Then He took the cup and gave thanks, and gave it to them, saying, 'Drink from it, all of you. For this is My blood of the new covenant, which is shed for many for the remission of sins'"* (v. 28).

The Greek root verb for "blessed" in verse 26 is *eulogeo* and means "to speak well of something," that is, to give praise for or to bless something, in a religious sense. In the parallel account, Luke says that

236

the Lord "gave thanks" for the bread (Luke 22:19). The Lord was not putting some spiritual blessing on the bread that would then be internalized when eaten by the disciples. Rather, He was following His normal practice of giving God thanks for the food about to be eaten.

Likewise, the Lord "gave thanks" for the contents of the cup before passing it to His disciples to drink. The Greek root verb *eucharisteo* is rendered "gave thanks." In the Roman Catholic Church, the eucharist (or holy communion) that members consume after being blessed by a priest is taught to no longer be bread and wine, but the literal body and blood of Christ. But the Lord was merely providing two symbols for believers to regularly use to remember Him and His sacrifice.

Paul later reiterates the words of the Lord on this occasion to the Corinthians: *"'Take, eat; this is My body which is broken for you; do this in remembrance of Me.' In the same manner He also took the cup after supper, saying, 'This cup is the new covenant in My blood. This do, as often as you drink it, in remembrance of Me'"* (1 Cor. 11:24-25). "As often as" means every time it is kept. Believers are to keep the Lord's Supper often, in the way specified, but no specific regularity was stated. The first Lord's Supper was not held in a church building; in fact, the Church did not exist at that time. The first Christians obeyed the Lord's command by continuing steadfastly in the breaking of the bread (Acts 2:42), and they did so often from house to house (Acts 2:46). Christians were meeting informally and often to remember the Lord (not just on Sundays or as a local assembly).

Years later, the practice of the local church gathering on Sundays to break bread became the pattern of the Church. For example, on one occasion, Paul waited a week in Troas to break bread with the saints there on Sunday (Acts 20:7). Yet, because Paul preached long, they did not break bread until early Monday morning and that was acceptable.

To summarize, *the commands* for the Lord's Supper are to do it often and to preserve its protocol and purpose. The *developed pattern* of the Church was that saints gathered in local assemblies each Sunday to break bread together. The latter point is a scriptural observation, which means there is no prohibition in Scripture preventing saints from remembering the Lord on other days of the week or in smaller groups. While following the scriptural pattern is safe for guiding our behavior, not following what is observed should never negate what is commanded. So, no matter what our circumstances might be, let us follow the Lord's command and remember Him the best possible way that we can!

The Lord Jesus did not drink from the cup that He passed to the disciples, but He promised to drink it with His disciples at a future day in His Father's kingdom (v. 29). By drinking the contents of the cup, the disciples were accepting the full test to be faithful to Christ. They were following Christ's example of drinking down to the dregs the cup of wrath to be received from His Father at Calvary.

Having instituted the Lord's Supper on the eve of His crucifixion, Matthew records that the Lord sang a hymn with His disciples before departing to the Mount of Olives (v. 30). If following the Jewish tradition, this hymn would have been the final song in the Jewish *Hallel* – Psalm 118. This song celebrates God's patient faithfulness to Israel and previews a future day when Israel will be restored to God and honored by all nations. Fittingly, it is also the final Messianic poem in the book of Psalms. The psalmist concludes by requesting continued salvation and prosperity for the people at the hand of the one who *"comes in the name of the Lord"* (Ps. 118:25-29). Because this psalm was sung at Passover, its lyrics would have been on the minds of the people when Christ entered Jerusalem on what is commonly referred to as Palm Sunday. Thus, it was no accident that the psalm was openly shouted by the people when the Lord descended the Mount of Olives into Jerusalem a few days before His crucifixion: *"Blessed is He who comes in the name of the Lord"* (Ps. 118:26). Jesus Christ is the one who comes in the name of the Lord, offering life and blessing.

Psalm 118:22 is quoted several times in the New Testament, where it is evident the reference to the rejected Cornerstone relates to Israel's refusal of Jesus Christ as their Messiah. The psalmist says, *"this is the day which the Lord has made"* (Ps. 118:24). The Lord Jesus Himself acknowledged that this verse spoke of Him (21:42; Luke 20:17), as did the apostles (Eph. 2:20; 1 Pet. 2:6-7). After being rejected by the Jewish nation, the Lord suffered and died at Calvary and was resurrected to the highest station in heaven, and in a future day He will return to the earth to establish His throne as Israel's King.

The Hebrew word *yowm*, normally translated as "day," appears frequently in the Old Testament; however, only about twenty times is it used in the Hebrew expression that correlates to the English phrase, "on that day" or "this is the day." In Psalm 118:24, the specific day referred to had been marked on God's calendar since before the foundations of the world were laid – it would be the day in which propitiation for humanity's sins would be offered by His own Son (Heb. 2:9; 1 Jn. 2:2).

If following the Jewish tradition, it seems likely that the Lord with His disciples sang of this special day, just hours before Calvary.

It is hard to imagine what thoughts went through our Savior's mind when He with His disciples sang Psalm 118 at the conclusion of the first Lord's Supper. The day that the Lord had made was the day that redeeming blood was to flow from Immanuel's veins to ensure the redemption of all those trusting in His message of salvation. Animal sacrifices were bound by a cord on the north side of the Bronze Altar before their throats were slit and the blood was collected and applied to its horns or poured out at its base. Incredibly, the psalmist wrote of this spectacular day:

> **The stone which the builders rejected** *has become the chief cornerstone.* **This was the Lord's doing***; it is marvelous in our eyes.* **This is the day the Lord has made***; we will rejoice and be glad in it* (Ps. 118:22-24).

> **Blessed is he who comes in the name of the Lord!** *We have blessed you from the house of the Lord. God is the Lord, and He has given us light;* **bind the sacrifice with cords to the horns of the altar** *(Ps. 118:26-27).*

After rehearsing in song with His disciples what was about to happen to Him at the cross, the Lord then expressed His resolve to honor God: *"You are my God, and I will praise You; You are my God, I will exalt You"* (Ps. 118:28). And the Lord Jesus did just that!

Ironically, the Church often sings the latter portion of this Psalm as a praise chorus, without regard to its proper context. In other words, we are applying a different meaning to it than what the Holy Spirit intended. While it is true that the Lord is sovereign over each of our days, the focus of our joy is not *our day*, but *the day* Christ was rejected of men and judged by God for our sins. The content of this psalm is a capstone on the revelation of all the fullness of Christ and His work mentioned in the other Messianic Psalms. May we treasure the full value God breathed into the text of Psalm 118 three thousand years ago and, like the psalmist, let us rejoice and be glad in what God has accomplished through Christ!

Christ Foretells of Peter's Denials (vv. 31-35)

According to John, after the Lord Jesus instituted His remembrance feast, the Lord informed His disciples that He would soon be leaving them (John 13:36-38). Matthew, who has been diligent to refer his Jewish audience to the Old Testament prophecies concerning the Messiah throughout his gospel account, states that the Lord quoted Zechariah 13:7 to inform His disciples that they would all scatter from Him that night. God was about to strike His Shepherd with a sword at Calvary and all the disciples would stumble before the Lord because of it. But the Lord then promised that after His resurrection He would see them again in Galilee (v. 32).

Peter specifically asked where the Lord was going (John 13:36). The Lord answered his question by saying that where He was going Peter could not follow Him then, but implied that he would later. Christ was going to the cross and then on to heaven. Peter would do the same in about thirty-five years.

Peter then declared his allegiance to the Lord and that he would follow Him now even if all others stumbled at Him (v. 33). But the Lord informed Peter that before the early morning watch was over (known by the cock's crowing), he will have denied him three times (v. 34; John 13:38). Peter responded to this statement, *"Even if I have to die with You, I will not deny You!"* (v. 35). The other disciples also affirmed the same allegiance to the Lord.

Luke also records Peter's willingness to die with the Lord (Luke 22:49-50). John states that the Lord then warned Peter with a question, *"Will you lay down your life for My sake?"* (John 13:38). In a few hours, Peter would learn just how impossible it was to serve Christ in the strength of the flesh.

Christ in the Garden of Gethsemane (vv. 36-46)

After leaving the upper room, the Lord and His disciples meandered through the streets of Jerusalem, trekked eastward across the Kidron brook and up the Mount of Olives to the Garden of Gethsemane, a place the Lord often resided with His disciples. He asked His disciples to sit in a particular place and then He went a little farther into the garden with Peter, James, and John (vv. 36-37).

It was at this juncture that the Lord informed the three disciples with Him that His soul was "exceedingly sorrowful" (v. 38). He then asked them to stay with Him and watch with Him while He prayed. The Lord then went a little farther and fell on His face and prayed, *"O My Father, if it is possible, let this cup pass from Me; nevertheless, not as I will, but as You will"* (v. 39). Luke says that He prayed, *"Father, if it is Your will, take this cup away from Me"* (Luke 22:42), and *"being in agony, He prayed more earnestly"* (Luke 22:44).

A similar scene is recorded in Mark, but not in John, who presents Christ in His deity. Thus, there is not one word in John's account about Christ's anguish of soul or perspiration while praying in Gethsemane, but Luke writes, *"Then His sweat became like great drops of blood falling down to the ground"* (Luke 22:44). These statements describe the Son of Man as the Man of Sorrows. John is the only one to present the heavenly view of Christ that night; thus, he highlights Christ's great expectation of being received into heaven, regaining His glory, and being with His Father forevermore (John 13:1, 17:1-5).

The Lord returned to find Peter, James, and John sleeping. At the most critical moment in the Lord's ministry, even His closest friends were not there for Him. He said to them, *"What! Could you not watch with Me one hour?"* (v. 40). He then exhorted them to watch and pray lest they be given over to temptation (i.e., solicitations to do evil). But the Lord also acknowledged what Paul later confirmed in his own life: None of us can do what pleases God in the power of the flesh (v. 41; Rom. 7:15-18). Peter had claimed to be the tough guy that would never deny the Lord, but when the Lord needed him most, he was sleepy.

A second time the Lord departed from the three disciples to privately pray with His Father, *"O My Father, if this cup cannot pass away from Me unless I drink it, Your will be done"* (v. 42). After a while, the Lord returned to where Peter, James, and John were and found them sleeping again, *"for their eyes were heavy"* (v. 43). The Lord understood their weariness and therefore did not wake them again. Despite being disappointed, the Lord's grace amid human failure is astounding.

The Lord returned to His previous place to continue praying as He did before (v. 44). There is no evidence in Scripture that the Lord slept at all the night before His passion. His human soul was "exceedingly sorrowful," and He spent the night preparing His disciples for what was coming and in prayer. Luke, who upholds the humanity of Christ in his gospel account, informs us that angels ministered to Christ in the garden. None of the other writers mentions that detail.

The Lord returned to His sleeping disciples a third time and aroused them because the hour had now come for Him to be betrayed "into the hands of sinners" (v. 45). But prayer had accomplished its work, despite His previously expressed distress; the Lord declared that He would continue to please His Father no matter the personal cost to Himself: *"Rise, let us be going. See, My betrayer is at hand"* (v. 46).

Christ's Betrayal and Arrest (vv. 47-56)

While the Lord was speaking, His betrayer arrived in Gethsemane. Judas knew the place that the Lord often resided with His disciples, and he had led a great multitude having clubs, torches, and swords to that location, with the Jewish leaders also (v. 47). Why so many people to arrest someone that had never hurt anyone? Apparently, Christ's arrestors thought that He would be hiding, and they would have to search him out. The moon would have been full at the Paschal Feast, so there would have been plenty of light to find a hiding Jesus. But John states that seeing His arrestors approaching Him, He stepped forward and asked them who they were looking for (John 18:4). The Lord Jesus already knew what was going to happen to Him at Calvary and did not resist being arrested, though He had the power to do so.

Judas had told the mob that he was leading, *"Whomever I kiss, He is the one; seize Him"* (v. 48). He then went up to the Lord and said, *"Greetings, Rabbi!"* and kissed Him. The Greek verb for "greetings" is in the present tense, indicating that Judas likely spoke to the Lord more than once (and likely kissed Him repeatedly) to ensure that everyone knew who should be arrested. Kenneth Wuest's *Expanded Translation of the New Testament* renders what Judas did in verse 49 this way: "He [Judas] embraced Him and kissed him tenderly and again and again."

How did the Lord respond to such blatant betrayal? He said to Judas, *"Friend, why have you come?"* (v. 50). Fully knowing what Judas was doing, our Savior still extended kindness and compassion to Judas. Although under Satan's control, the Lord still felt it was necessary to appeal to Judas' conscience one last time. When it seems like everything around you is dark and evil, remember individual souls still need to be reached by compassion and with the truth. But Judas did not respond to the Lord's tenderness; rather the Lord was arrested. John says that they first bound the Lord before taking Him away (John 18:12).

As Christ's arrestors stepped forward, Peter drew his sword and was ready to face down a band of soldiers to protect His Lord. Peter struck one of the high priest's servants named Malchus and sliced off his ear. The Lord Jesus told Peter to put his sword away, lest he perish by it, and then He repaired the damage that Peter's sword did to Malchus' ear (v.

52; John 18:10-11). Peter needed to learn that the Lord did not want Peter to die once to serve Him, but to die daily to self to live for Him. It is easy to swing a sword when one is ignorant of God's will and make a mess of things. It is entirely another matter to fully rest in the Lord to witness God accomplish what only He can.

The Lord then reminded Peter that everything that was happening was under His control and fulfilling Scripture (v. 54). If He needed protection, He could request that His Father send twelve legions of angels to assist Him (v. 53). That would be between 36,000 and 72,000 angelic warriors – no human agency would survive such an angelic force.

The Lord's response to those arresting Him was noteworthy (v. 55). He clearly states the facts to appeal directly to the consciences of those arresting Him: "I was with you daily in the temple without any expression of hostility; why then are you coming against Me now with clubs and swords?" "What have I done that now justifies you treating Me like a robber?" The Lord does not try to escape what He knows is necessary, but He still has a compassionate heart towards those under the enemy's control. He chooses to reason with them, not attack or retaliate against them in any way.

Indeed, the situation was being incited by wickedness in high places, yet the Lord's compassion for those individuals under its influence is paramount. Additionally, He told His arrestors that all that was happening was to fulfill what the prophets had foretold, as recorded in Scripture (v. 56). Then, as the Lord had previously predicted in the upper room, all His disciples forsook Him and fled.

Why did the Jewish leaders want to arrest Jesus in the middle of the night and in a private place, like Gethsemane? The Roman historian Tacitus stated that Jerusalem's population was 600,000 when Rome assaulted the city in 70 A.D. Yet, this number seems high as compared with archeological information relating to that timeframe. Examining this evidence, Geva offers a minimal estimate of the city's population to be 20,000 at this time.[70] Others, such as Wikinson[71] and Broshi,[72] put the population of Jerusalem in 70 A.D. to be between 70,000 and 80,000 persons. Though estimates vary, it seems likely that Jerusalem's population at the time of Christ's crucifixion was likely between 50,000 and 80,000 people. However, during religious festivals this number often increased three- to fourfold.

The Jewish leaders knew the possibility of social unrest was high at such times and even a riot was a distinct possibility. Because the

Pharisees feared the people (for many had high thoughts of Jesus), and of Roman repercussions for a riot, they chose to arrest Jesus of Nazareth in a private place, which the betrayal of Judas made possible.

Christ's Religious Trials (vv. 57-68)

The Lord would endure three religious trials and three civil trials in less than nine hours. Quirinius, the governor of Syria appointed Annas as the Jewish high priest in 6 A.D. However, the Romans did not want a long-standing high priest. Limiting the high priest's tenure would reduce the priest's sway among the people. So Annas had been replaced in 15 A.D. by Valerius Gratus, procurator of Judea and then each of his five sons were appointed the high priest and then Caiaphas, his son-in-law.[73] Luke confirms that both Annas and Caiaphas were high priests currently (Luke 3:2). From the Jewish perspective, Annas was the true high priest, though Caiaphas was the acknowledged leader to pacify Roman rule.

John states that Christ first appeared before Annas and then was interrogated by a larger gathering of Jewish leaders with Caiaphas present (v. 57; John 18:13). Interestingly, night gatherings of the Sanhedrin for a capital trial were illegal.[74] The introduction of false witnesses at the trial and the declaring of a verdict before the trial commenced were also forbidden (John 7:51). As F. B. Hole observes, the worst part was not the presence of false witnesses, but that Israel's leaders, who were to represent God's justice, sought false witnesses:

> The mob delivered Him to the leaders of Israel, and these men, who claimed to represent God, had thrown away any pretense of seeking righteousness. We are not told that they were *misled* into accepting false evidence, nor that they were *tempted* into receiving it because it was thrust upon them. No, it says, they *"sought* false witness against Jesus, to put Him to death." They SOUGHT it. Has there ever, we wonder, been another trial upon this earth where the judges started by hunting for liars, that they might condemn the accused? Thus, it was here; and in the presence of it, Jesus held His peace. Judgment being utterly divorced from righteousness, He met them with a dignity that was Divine, and He only spoke to affirm His Christhood, His Sonship, and to affirm His coming glory as the Son of Man.[75]

Moreover, the Defendant was not permitted any time to prepare His case. This was a sham trial from start to finish, and one that violated Sanhedrin protocol on several points. At first light, the Lord would be brought before the full Sanhedrin to determine how He should be put to death.

Peter followed the Lord at a distance, but after arriving at the high priest's courtyard, he sat down to see what would happen and warmed himself by a fire with Caiaphas' servants (v. 58). John tells us that he spoke on Peter's behalf so that he would be permitted into the courtyard.

The chief priests and elders were soliciting false witnesses to testify against Christ before Caiaphas, so they could put Him to death, but initially they could not find two that agreed (vv. 59-60). Finally, two witnesses agreed that the Lord Jesus had said, *"I am able to destroy the temple of God and to build it in three days"* (v. 61). Caiaphas asked the Lord to answer this charge, but He said nothing (v. 62).

Then Caiaphas, being the high priest, put Christ under oath to implore Him to answer whether He was the Christ, the Son of God (v. 63)! Under the Mosaic Law, the Lord Jesus would bear guilt if He did not answer the high priest who put Him under oath (Lev. 5:1). The Lord's response affirmed that He was the Christ, the Son of God. Speaking to Caiaphas who had put Him under oath (the first "you" in verse 64 is singular), the Lord said he would not see Him again. However, all Israel (the second and the third "you" are plural) would see Him when He returned from heaven in power and glory to establish His kingdom (v. 64). The Lord was claiming Daniel's prophecy for Himself (Dan. 7:13); He was "the Son of Man" returning from heaven in glory and the high priest understood the connection (Dan. 7:13).

Caiaphas responded by tearing his priestly apparel, which was forbidden, for such was considered holy before the Lord (v. 65; Lev. 10:6, 21:10). Caiaphas declared that the Lord Jesus spoke blasphemy and that there was no need of further witnesses, for they had heard the offense themselves. His constituents agreed saying, *"He is deserving of death"* (v. 66). In a fit of rage, they spit in Christ's face and struck Him with their fists. Laurence Laurenson describes the scene of judicial corruption and religious hatred at this moment:

> No sooner has He been unjustly condemned than His judges step down from the bench to spit in His face (Mark 14:65).... It is neither the rude soldiers of the governor, nor the Gentile executioners here. It is the leaders of Israel; they are seen seeking *false* witnesses: condemning the *guiltless* and setting an example in hatred and cruelty. The Son of Man

thus stood before the leaders of Israel. What a moment when the leaders of Israel shall stand before the Son of Man.[76]

As the Lord was being beaten, they mocked His testimony by saying, *"Prophesy to us, Christ! Who is the one who struck You?"* (v. 68). Considering that He could have quickly ended all their lives, the Lord demonstrated incredible restraint in not swiftly judging His oppressors. Furthermore, the Lord Jesus maintained the molecular integrity of the very human fists that were battering His face! Paul writes, *"In Him all things consist"* (Col. 1:17) and thus He was able to demonstrate the "fullness of the Godhead bodily" (Col. 2:9) in all that He did.

Peter Denies the Lord (vv. 69-76)

While Peter was sitting outside in the courtyard with others by a fire, a servant girl saw him and said, *"You also were with Jesus of Galilee"* (v. 69). Peter utterly denied this assertion in front of everyone (v. 70). Strike one. Whether or not Peter heard the warning, we do not know, but Mark states that a rooster crowed after his first denial. Apparently, Peter became uncomfortable with his surroundings and ventured towards the porch by the courtyard gateway (Mark 14:68).

A little later, another girl saw him and stated that he was with Jesus of Nazareth (v. 72). Peter promptly replied, *"I do not know the Man!"* (v. 73). Strike two. So far, the tough fisherman has been taken down by two girls. A while later Peter was challenged by those waiting on the outcome of the trial, *"Surely you also are one of them, for your speech betrays you"* (v. 73). Next, a relative of Malchus recognized Peter as having been in the garden with Jesus. Peter, while cursing and swearing, adamantly declared, *"I do not know the Man!"* (v. 74). Strike three.

No sooner had the words departed Peter's lips, when he heard the rooster crow (all four Gospel writers record that event). It was normal for roosters to crow in the fourth watch (3 a.m. to 6 a.m.). Mark notes that the rooster had sounded his warning previously, but only now did Peter recognize it and remember the Lord's prediction, *"Before the rooster crows, you will deny Me three times"* (Mark 14:72). Luke states that at this moment Peter's eyes and the Lord's eyes briefly met (Luke 22:61). It was a sorrowful look that Peter would never forget. The defeated fisherman immediately went out of the courtyard and wept bitterly.

Matthew Chapter 27

Christ Before the Sanhedrin (vv. 1-10)

The full Jewish Sanhedrin gathered at first light to determine *how* they should put Jesus to death (v. 1). He had already been found guilty and deemed worthy of execution by the high priest and some of the Sanhedrin (26:66). The Romans did not permit the Jews to execute anyone according to their laws and tradition, so if Christ was to be executed, He must be taken to the Roman governor of the region, Pontius Pilate (John 18:31), which they did immediately (v. 2).

Judas felt remorse for betraying the Lord and returned the silver to the temple just before hanging himself (vv. 3-5). Judas' act was not one of repentance; otherwise, he would have gone to the cross to seek forgiveness instead of conversing with Israel's false shepherds at the temple. By hanging himself, Judas again proved that man can never get right with God through his own methods. The wages of sin is death!

The Pharisees could not return blood money to the temple treasury, so they used the silver to purchase a potter's field – a location to bury the unidentifiable dead (vv. 6-8). The irony of their action was that these religious leaders were more concerned about following their traditions than obeying the Law that commanded that those indicted with crimes receive a fair and impartial trial.

J. J. Stubbs suggests that by buying the potter's field, the Pharisees provided a perpetuating memorial of their evil actions:

> The thirty pieces of silver were thrown down in the temple, the very place where Judas cast them. They are said to be cast to the potter, because it is to him they were appointed by the Lord ultimately to go. God, whose secret operations and sovereign power extend over all men, had so arranged this matter that Judas threw down the money in the temple to bring it before the face of God as blood-money and to call down the judgment of God on the nation. The high priest, by purchasing the potter's field for this money, which received the name of "The field of blood, unto this day" (Matt. 27:8), thus perpetuated the

memorial of their sin against their Messiah. So the statement of Zechariah that he took the thirty pieces of silver and "cast them to the potter in the house of the Lord" was in this way literally fulfilled. Messiah in the person of Zechariah says, "I took, I threw." Matthew says, "They took, they gave them" (see Matt. 27:6-7). The reason for this is that the act of Judas and the Jews together was the Lord's appointment (Matt. 27:10; Acts 2:23).[77]

By providing Judas the exact amount and type of currency and then using what he returned to the temple to buy a potter's field, the Pharisees had unknowingly confirmed that Jesus of Nazareth was the promised Messiah. Every detail of Zechariah's prophecy had been literally fulfilled (v. 9; Zech. 11:12-13). Matthew ties the prophecies of Zechariah and Jeremiah together. By buying the potter's field with blood money, Christ had redeemed the discarded marred clay to put back on the Potter's wheel to be remade again (Jer. 18:1-11). The unmalleable clay in Jeremiah's prophecy was the nation of Israel. During the Tribulation Period, God will again begin to work with His covenant people to refine and restore them to Himself through Christ.

Christ Before Pilate (vv. 11-14)

The Lord Jesus was brought before the Roman Governor of Judea, Pilate, to be questioned. It did not take the Sanhedrin long to decide Jesus' fate for when He arrived at the Praetorium, it was still early morning (John 18:28). The chief priests and elders informed Pilate that Jesus was subverting the nation by denying that the Jews should pay Caesar tribute and by claiming Himself to be King instead of Caesar (Luke 23:2). Pontius Pilate then interrogated the Lord to discern if these charges of sedition were legitimate.

Pilate asked Jesus if He was *"the King of the Jews"* (v. 11)? The Lord affirmed that what he had asked was correct. John records a lengthier dialogue between Pilate and the Lord Jesus. John tells us that Pilate was also told by Jesus Christ that though He was a king, His kingdom was not of this world; if it were, His servants would have fought for Him, and the Jews would not have arrested Him (John 18:36).

While before Pilate, the chief priests and Jewish elders accused Jesus of many things, but Christ did not defend Himself, even when Pilate extended an opportunity for Him to do so (vv. 12-14). Pilate marveled greatly at the Lord Jesus' restraint and Luke tells us that he told the

Jewish leaders, *"I find no fault in this Man"* (Luke 23:4). This may have been the first time that Pilate had an accused offender at his judgment seat that made no effort to defend himself.

Pilate's statement rallied the Jewish elders to become fiercer in their accusations against Jesus, saying that He was a Galilean and had incited trouble from Galilee to Judea (Luke 23:5). After hearing this, Pilate sent Jesus to Herod to be examined. Galilee was Herod's jurisdiction as a tetrarch, and he was in Jerusalem at that time for the feast (Luke 23:7). This was Christ's second civil trial. Although Herod asked Jesus many questions, the Lord answered him nothing. After Herod's soldiers had mocked and abused the Lord Jesus, Herod sent Him back to Pilate.

Barabbas or Jesus of Nazareth? (vv. 15-26)

As explained in the previous chapter, there were likely between 150,000 to 300,000 people in Jerusalem for the Passover Feast. The potential for a riot was high and Pilate wanted to avoid that scenario, lest he be called to Rome and questioned by Caesar for the uprising. To encourage a peaceful situation, it was Pilate's custom to pardon a Jewish prisoner of the people's choosing during the feast (v. 15). As an attempt to release Jesus, Pilate offered the Jewish assembly a choice of whom he would pardon. They could choose to free Jesus of Nazareth or a notorious prisoner, Barabbas, who had been found guilty of inciting rebellion in Jerusalem and of murder (vv. 16-17; Luke 23:19-25).

The Roman governor chose to contrast the worst convicted criminal available to him with an accused Man that, in his judgment, was completely innocent, to expose the envy of the Jewish leaders in indicting Jesus (v. 18). It was at this moment, while Pilate sat on the Pavement (the Roman judgment seat), that his wife sent a private message to him: *"Have nothing to do with that just Man, for I have suffered many things today in a dream because of Him"* (v. 19).

There were many false witnesses that appeared during Christ's religious and civil trials, but there were also true witnesses of His righteousness. Matthew notes two witnesses of aristocratic influence (Pilate and his wife), who both proclaimed Christ's innocence. Luke adds two testimonies from those of a common station declaring the same conclusion. The repentant thief proclaimed, *"This Man has done nothing wrong"* (Luke 23:41). Having watched the way in which the Lord suffered on the cross, a Roman centurion declared after the Lord expired,

"Certainly this was a righteous Man" (Luke 23:47). Even in the matter of witnesses, the writers maintain their vantage points of Christ: Matthew, Christ's royalty; Luke, Christ's humanity, but grace abounds in both.

Pilate was unable to persuade the Jews to turn from their bloodthirsty intentions. They wanted Barabbas released and Christ crucified (vv. 20-22). Pilate again asserted that Jesus had done nothing worthy of death, but the crowd cried out the more, *"Let Him be crucified"* (v. 23). Fearing a riot, Pilate washed his hands in a basin and proclaimed, *"I am innocent of the blood of this just Person. You see to it"* (v. 24). The Jewish crowd answered, *"His blood be on us and on our children"* (v. 25). In effect, they had put themselves under a blood curse for condemning a righteous man to death (Acts 2:23, 3:14-15, 5:28). The Jewish nation had no idea the centuries of pain and sorrow that would result from this proclamation. But the consequences of cutting off their Messiah were foretold by the prophet Daniel long ago: War and desolations would be determined against them until the end of the Tribulation Period, when, by grace, the blood of expiation will erase the blood of the curse (Dan. 9:24-27). The Jews crucified God's incarnate Son and their Messiah.

Pilate then released the notable murderer Barabbas and had Christ scourged. Perhaps, Pilate thought that by having Christ severely whipped, the hostile crowd might then show Him sympathy and His life would be spared. But the Jewish crowd had no sympathy for Jesus Christ. To prevent a riot in a city likely having four times its normal population because of the Passover, Pilate sentenced Christ to death by crucifixion.

A common punishment under the Law and practiced in both the Old and New Testaments by the Jews was that of scourging (Lev. 19:20). According to Deuteronomy 25:1-3, up to forty stripes could be administered, but to ensure compliance with the Law, the Jews limited themselves to "forty stripes minus one" or *thirty-nine* stripes (2 Cor. 11:24). However, there were no such limitations of abuse during a Roman scourging, which typically preceded public executions to speed up the dying process of crucifixion.

The Roman whip did much more than put stripes on the condemned; it was designed to rip the flesh wide open. A Roman flogging resulted in deep lacerations which exposed muscles and caused excessive bleeding. Church historian Eusebius of Caesarea recounts the horror of a Roman scourging: "For they say that the bystanders were struck with amazement when they saw them lacerated with scourges even to the innermost veins and arteries, so that the hidden inward parts of the body, both their bowels and their members, were exposed to view."[78] The term "half-dead" was commonly associated with a Roman scourging, as many who endured its wrath died afterwards. Yet, the idea of scourging was to stop the beating before death resulted to ensure that the victim was still able to undergo public crucifixion.

Isaiah foretold that the Messiah, God's Servant, would be faithful to live out what He was asked to do no matter the personal cost to Himself. In the prophecy, the Servant conveys His determination to expend Himself on Israel's behalf (and on ours too) despite the human brutality and divine judgment He knew He would suffer:

> *I gave My back to those who struck Me, and My cheeks to those who plucked out the beard; I did not hide My face from shame and spitting. For the Lord God will help Me; therefore, I will not be disgraced; therefore, I have set My face like a flint, and I know that I will not be ashamed* (Isa. 50:6-7).

This prophecy tells us that Christ knew beforehand that He would be scourged, beaten in the face, and spat on. Matthew records the direct fulfillment of these prophecies in his gospel account (26:67, 27:26, 30). Thankfully, two thousand years ago, the Lord Jesus did not enter into His rest until He had secured ours, through the shedding of His own blood. We worship a brave, tenacious, and sacrificial Savior!

Christ Stripped, Mocked, and Beaten (vv. 27-32)

In the previous hours, the Lord Jesus had been abused by the servants of the chief priests and by Herod's men. He has already received many blows from human fists. After being scourged, Matthew informs us that the Lord was taken into the Roman Praetorium, and an entire garrison of soldiers (typically comprised of 200 to 300 men) gathered to have sport with Him (v. 27). They stripped Him of His clothes and put a scarlet robe or cloak on Him, which likely revealed His nakedness (v. 28). Scarlet and purple were colors of royalty. They also twisted a crown of thorns and placed it on His head and put a hollow reed in his right hand (v. 29). Thorns resulted after God cursed the ground (i.e., the earth; Rom. 8:20-22) because of Adam's sin (Gen. 3:17-18). Now the Creator was bearing on His brow the very curse He levied on humanity in Eden.

Being adorned with a mock robe, crown, and scepter, the Roman soldiers then bowed the knee to Jesus in mock worship, *"Hail, king of the Jews!"* (v. 29). The Lord had been rejected and abused by the Jewish authorities; now the Gentiles also were guilty of disdaining the Savior. They spat on Him and took the reed out of His hand and beat the crown of thorns into His brow with it (v. 30).

Afterwards, the soldiers put His own clothes on the Lord and led Him away to be crucified (v. 31). In His physically weakened state, the Lord was not able to bear his own cross (bar or beam) on His shoulder. Such a beam typically weighed between 75 and 125 pounds. The Romans compelled Simon from Cyrene (a city in northern Africa with a significant Jewish population) to bear Christ's cross to the place of public execution (v. 32).

Jesus Christ Is Crucified (vv. 33-44)

The Lord Jesus was brought to Golgotha, the "Place of the Skull," to be crucified (v. 33). John Heading describes the meaning of Golgotha and what it symbolized:

> Golgotha and the corresponding Roman name Calvary (Luke 23:33) both mean "skull" – hence Matthew's interpretation "a place of a skull." Various reasons have been suggested why the place had this name – for example, because the shape of the place resembled a skull. Typically, however, the name speaks of the apex of human wisdom, for those who crucified the Lord of glory possessed this wisdom, the opposite to the wisdom of God (1 Cor. 2:6–8). It speaks of the unsanctified intelligence of men who still reject Christ in unbelief.[79]

Before the nails were driven through His wrists to the cross bar, Christ was offered wine mingled with gall (a narcotic to numb the senses to reduce pain), but after tasting the mixture, He would not drink it to fulfill the Messianic prophecy of Psalm 69:21 (v. 34). The Roman soldiers then stripped the Lord of His clothes and crucified Him. They cast lots for His outer garment that was woven without seam and tore his inner garment into four pieces, so that each soldier would receive a portion (v. 35). After the soldiers had crucified two condemned men on either side of the Lord, they placed a placard over the Lord's head that read, *"This is Jesus the King of the Jews,"* and then they sat down to watch over the pitiful sight (vv. 36-38).

Both Luke and John document that the superscription hanging above the Lord's head was written in Greek, Latin, and Hebrew. As Luke is an appeal to humanity and John is writing to the whole world, it makes sense that the use of all three languages was recorded by these two evangelists. If Matthew had written concerning this detail, perhaps he would have only focused on the Hebrew language. Likewise, Mark would have likely referred to the language of the Roman Empire, Latin.

Those passing by blasphemed Him, the chief priests mocked Him, and even both robbers initially reviled Him (vv. 39-44). His oppressors quoted back to the Lord Jesus His own words to cast doubt on their validity, given His situation. Let us see you build the temple in three days now! If you are the Son of God and the King of Israel, prove it by saving yourself! If God was really your Father, He would deliver you!

Victory in Death (vv. 45-56)

Mark informs us that Christ was crucified at the third hour (9 a.m.; Mark 15:25). Matthew does not record any of the Lord's statements or intercession during His first three hours on the cross. He states that at the sixth hour (noon in Roman time) until the ninth hour (3 p.m.) there was an intense darkness "over all the land" (v. 45). The judgment of human sin was a private matter between the Son and the Father; nothing would be permitted to intrude into the work of eternal propitiation.

After suffering for three hours in darkness, the Lord cried out with a loud voice, saying, *"Eli, Eli, lama, sabachthani?"* meaning, *"My God, My God, why have You forsaken Me?"* (v. 46). This quotation of Psalm 22:1 was declared just prior to His death at 3:00 p.m. The Lord affirmed that while He was being our Sin-bearer, fellowship with His Father was severed. The Lord also wanted to ensure that Psalm 22 would be associated with His redemptive work. The English expression "loud voice" is derived from the Greek *megas phone*. A megaphone effectively amplifies sound for all to hear. While the Lord Jesus was hanging from a cross, He was fully aware and in complete control of His situation. He astutely fulfilled every Old Testament prophecy so there would be no question that He was Israel's promised Messiah.

Some standing by thought that Jesus was calling for Elijah to assist Him (v. 47). One of them immediately got up and filled a sponge with sour wine and placed it on a reed and lifted it up to the Lord to drink from it (v. 48). However, the other onlookers rebuked the actions of this man, and said to leave Jesus alone to see whether Elijah would come to assist Him (v. 49).

After finishing the required suffering for all human sin (Heb. 2:9; 1 Jn. 2:2), the Lord Jesus *"cried out again with a loud voice, and yielded up His spirit"* (v. 50). "Loud voice" is again derived from the Greek phrase *megas phone*. The Greek verb rendered "cried out again" is *krazo*, which means "to scream." This was the kind of loud shrill scream that one would not soon forget. John tells us what the Lord said, before commending His spirit into His Father's care: *"It is finished!"* (John 19:30). John uses the perfect tense verb *teleo* to declare that what Christ had just accomplished at Calvary could never be undone – it was an eternal propitiatory and redemptive work. Afterwards, there would never be another offering for the offence or damages of human sin (Heb. 9:28, 10:12-14).

The Lord fulfilled dozens of Old Testament prophecies at His first advent, but ten specific Psalm 22 prophecies can be identified as being fulfilled by Christ at Calvary; clearly, these do not apply to David.

Psalm 22 Prophecies Pertaining to Calvary	OT Reference/NT Fulfillment
"My God, My God, why have You forsaken Me?"	Ps. 22:1/ Mark 15:34
Time of darkness	Ps. 22:2; Amos 8:9/ Matt. 27:45
Mocked and insulted	Ps. 22:7-8/ Matt. 27:39-43, 45
Scoffers to mock: "He trusted in God, let Him deliver Him"	Ps. 22:8; Ps. 31:14-15/ Matt. 27:43
Be thirsty during execution	Ps. 22:15/ John 19:28
Hands and feet pierced	Ps. 22:16/ Matt. 27:31, 35
Stripped of clothes	Ps. 22:18/ Luke 23:34
Soldiers cast lots for outer coat	Ps. 22:18/ Matt. 27:35; Mark 15:24
Soldiers divided inner garment	Ps. 22:18/ Matt. 27:35; Mark 15:24
Committed Himself to God before dying	Ps. 22:20-21/ Luke 23:46

Christ was made *"the reproach of men and despised by the people"* and *"a worm"* (Ps. 22:6). "Worm" is rendered from the Hebrew word *tolaath*. The *tola* worm was smashed to yield a scarlet-colored dye; this pictures the humble servant nature of Christ and how He was crushed to produce the blood of our redemption. Praise the all-wise Lamb!

Just after Christ gave up His spirit, Matthew tells us the inner veil of the temple (a sixty-foot-tall hanging tapestry) was torn from top to bottom and that there was a great earthquake causing rocks to split (v. 51). Jewish tradition upholds that the temple veil was as thick as a man's hand and was so heavy that it took 300 priests to manipulate.[80] Albert Edersheim affirms this description to be correct.[81] The point being that tearing the veil from the top downward while it was hanging in the temple was an impossibility, humanly speaking.

In the Old Testament, access to God was limited. Only the high priest could enter the Most Holy Place of the tabernacle and temple once a year on the Day of Atonement, and he did so with trepidation and not without the blood of a goat and of a bull. After the completion of Christ's work at Calvary, the inner veil of the temple was rent from top to bottom to illustrate that through Christ, God could have full fellowship with man, and man could have full access to God. No doubt the priests worked diligently to repair and rehang the veil, but God removed it by fire when the temple was destroyed in 70 A.D. by the Romans.

Matthew then refers to an event that happened directly after Christ rose from the grave on the third day after His death:

The graves were opened; and many bodies of the saints who had fallen asleep were raised; and coming out of the graves after His resurrection, they went into the holy city and appeared to many (vv. 52-53).

This detail is not recorded by the other gospel writers, but clearly Matthew wanted to show that Christ was the firstfruits from the dead and also the King of the saints, ever leading them heavenward (1 Cor. 15:20; Rev. 15:3). Not having divine revelation on the topic of heaven, Old Testament saints, like David, hoped to enjoy God's presence on the earth after escaping the cold confines of Sheol through resurrection (e.g., Job 19:26; Dan. 12:2). Old Testament saints understood that death was unavoidable and that beyond the grave their souls would be sequestered in a spiritual abode called Sheol.

The Hebrew word translated "Sheol," but sometimes rendered "grave" in the Old Testament, is the general equivalent of the Greek *Hades*, used in the New Testament. The Lord Jesus taught that this spiritual domain houses disembodied spirits in one of two compartments (Luke 16:19-31). Abraham's Bosom is where faithful souls consciously await resurrection unto life through Christ, and the second is a place of torment where the wicked reside until their resurrection unto final judgment in the Lake of Fire. It is the author's opinion that Christ and the repentant thief went to Abraham's bosom after dying and that this realm of disembodied spirits was emptied after Christ's resurrection and joined Him in heaven. Apparently, at least some of these saints experienced the First Resurrection after Christ's own glorification (Rev. 20:6). In the Church Age, the souls of departed saints join Christ in heaven immediately after death (2 Cor. 5:8).

When the centurion who was overseeing Christ's crucifixion saw all that had happened, he and those with him feared greatly, saying, *"Truly this was the Son of God"* (v. 54). The three hours of intense darkness, the Savior uttering gracious intercession for His oppressors, and the great earthquake convinced them that Christ was who He proclaimed Himself to be. Matthew then notes that many of the women who had served Christ during His three-plus-year ministry were watching from afar (v. 55). Among these were Mary Magdalene, Mary the mother of James the less, and Salome, the mother of James and John (v. 56; Mark 15:40).

The Body of Christ Is Buried (vv. 57-61)

A rich man named Joseph, a secret disciple of Christ from Arimathea, went to Pilate and requested the body of Jesus (v. 57). He was a just man, a member of the Sanhedrin, but had not consented to the Lord's death (Luke 23:51). Pilate was surprised that Jesus had already expired and asked the centurion in charge of His execution to confirm the matter (Mark 15:44). Learning that the claim was true, Pilate granted Joseph's request (v. 58). There was not much time to bury the body as the Sabbath was at hand. As the Lord's death was at 3:00 p.m. and the dialogue between Pilate, Joseph, and the centurion occurred afterwards, there was likely less than 90 minutes to take the body off the cross (Luke 23:53), transport it to the tomb, wrap it, and seal it in the tomb. Nicodemus, another secret disciple of Christ, joined Joseph in the task. He brought a hundred pounds of myrrh and aloes to the tomb (John 19:39).

Joseph and Nicodemus quickly wrapped Jesus' body with the spices in strips of clean linen (John 19:40). Then both men placed the Lord's body in Joseph's own tomb hewn out of rock (v. 59; John 19:42). This new tomb was in a garden near the crucifixion site (John 19:41). After the body was placed in the tomb, the men sealed it with a large rolling stone (v. 60). The two Marys before mentioned observed where Christ's body was placed and then came to the tomb Sunday morning to properly prepare the body after the Sabbath had concluded (v. 61).

The Tomb Is Sealed and Guarded (vv. 62-66)

On the next day, which traditionally speaking would be Saturday, the chief priests and Pharisees came to Pilate with a concern (v. 62). They informed him that while the deceiver was alive (speaking of Jesus), He said that He would rise again from the dead after three days (v. 63).

In comparing different statements in the Gospels that Christ made about His resurrection, there seems to be a contradiction. For example, the Lord said that He would *"be raised the third day"* after being killed (16:21), but also that He would *"be killed, and after three days rise again"* (Mark 8:31). But in fact, these are interchangeable Jewish expressions, though appearing contradictory to us in the English. Most references to the resurrection state that it would occur on the third day (17:23, 20:19; Luke 9:22, 18:33) or in the third day (John 2:19-22). However, while speaking to the Pharisees, the Lord referred to the sign of Jonah to foretell His death and resurrection: *"For as Jonah was three days and three nights in the belly of the great fish, so will the Son of Man be three days and three nights in the heart of the earth"* (12:40).

The Pharisees later repeated Christ's statement to Pilate, *"after three days I will rise"* (v. 63), but then they asked for a guard *"until the third day"* (v. 64). If the term, "after three days," was not interchangeable with "the third day," then the Pharisees would have asked that the tomb be guarded for four days. The term "one day and one night" was a Jewish idiom indicating a day, even when only a part of a day was indicated (e.g., Gen. 42:74; 1 Sam. 30:12). In summary, the terms "three days and nights" and "three days" were terms the Jews used interchangeably.

The Pharisees were concerned that Jesus' disciples would steal the body of Jesus to fake His resurrection. So, they asked Pilate to secure the tomb to ensure that this would not happen. Pilated granted their request and gave them a guard (likely four soldiers) to make the tomb as secure as they could (v. 65). The Jewish leaders went to the tomb where Christ's body was laid and put a seal on the rolling stone and ensured that the Roman guard was placed before the stone (v. 66).

Matthew Chapter 28

While there is some debate as to whether Christ was crucified on Thursday or Friday, the Scripture clearly informs us that He experienced resurrection early on Sunday morning. Traditionally speaking, Christ was crucified on Friday as indicated by the combined weight of the Gospel accounts. The argument for a Thursday crucifixion arises from John's account in which the Pharisees were before Pilate prior to the Passover (John 18:28) and the reference to the forthcoming Sabbath as "a high day" (John 19:31). This may indicate that at the time of Christ's passion, two Sabbath days followed each other (i.e., on Friday and Saturday). As the feast of Unleavened Bread began on the fifteenth day of the first month, that day was a special Sabbath day no matter what day of the week it fell on (Lev. 23:5-7).

Those who propose this position take the Lord's reference to the Pharisees of the sign of Jonah literally, that is, Christ's body would be in the grave "three days and nights." However, the Lord spoke more often that He would rise on the third day. Furthermore, as discussed at the conclusion of the last chapter, "a day and night" was a Jewish idiom for any part of a day. Because the Passover and feast of Unleavened Bread were connected, the terminology referring to these feasts was often used interchangeably. Hence, since the first day of Unleavened Bread was a holy day, this may explain why the Pharisees did not want to defile themselves at Passover by coming inside the Gentile judgment hall. Luke quoted the Lord who plainly said that He was eating the Passover meal with His disciples the night before His crucifixion, not a preparation meal (Luke 22:15). Given the above understanding and this specific statement by Christ, the evidence best affirms a Friday crucifixion date.

Christ's Resurrection (vv. 1-10)

Matthew had previously noted that Mary Magdalene and Mary the mother of James the less observed where the body of Christ was entombed. Now that the Sabbath had passed, they and other women were going to the tomb at the earliest possible moment to properly prepare the

Lord's body for burial (v. 1). How these women were going to get past the Roman guard, open a tomb that had been officially sealed, and move the large rolling stone to gain access to the tomb is unknown; regardless, they came to show their love and respect for the Savior.

Matthew states that the Marys were en route to the tomb at the starting of dawn. Mark's account has three women (Salome is included with the Marys) arriving at the tomb near sunrise (Mark 16:1). John states that Mary Magdalene came to the tomb when it was yet dark (John 20:1). Luke mentions at least five women that came early to the tomb that morning (Luke 24:10). Putting the accounts together, we have various women arriving at the tomb early Sunday morning at various times. Since the women were coming from Bethany, and likely Jerusalem, it would have taken some time to get to the tomb. Some arrived while it was still dark, while others arrived at sunrise.

We then learn what happened just prior to the women arriving at Christ's tomb; an angel from heaven descended from heaven and rolled away the stone that sealed the tomb and then sat on it (v. 2). This feat was accompanied by, but not caused by, an earthquake. A great earthquake had occurred at Christ's death and now another announced His resurrection. The countenance of the angel was like lightning and his clothing as white as snow (v. 3). The guards were terrified at the angel's presence and fell to the ground like dead men (v. 4). When the women arrived at the tomb, that angel spoke to them, saying, *"Do not be afraid, for I know that you seek Jesus who was crucified. He is not here; for He is risen, as He said. Come, see the place where the Lord lay"* (vv. 5-6).

As the women were coming forward to peer into the tomb, the angel instructed the women to go and inform the disciples that Christ had risen and would meet them in Galilee, as He had previously stated (v. 7). As the women departed the tomb in different directions to accomplish their task, the risen Savior appeared to them and said, "Rejoice!" The women immediately fell at His feet to worshiped Him (v. 9). The Lord comforted them and then instructed the women to complete the task that the angel had given them to do. It is noted that Matthew and Mark describe one angel speaking to the women, while Luke and John state that two angels were in the tomb. We may conclude that, indeed, there were two angels at the tomb, but only one served as the spokesman.

It is important to realize that each Gospel writer presents Christ from a different perspective. If all the writers gave the same story, same order, same details, we would immediately become suspicious that the records were the copies of a single account. But because some events are recorded in some Gospels and not others, we have proof of multiple accounts and not one story repeated. For example, only Matthew records Christ's first appearance to the women, while only Luke records the events transpiring on the Emmaus Road. Luke does not record Mary Magdalene's visit to the tomb. Only John and Luke record Christ's appearance in the upper room on resurrection day. Given all the information recorded in the Gospels, there is a reasonable construction of all that took place on resurrection morning without contradiction.

New Testament Scripture confirms at least ten separate post-resurrection appearances of Christ prior to His ascension. Five of these incidents occurred on the day of Christ's resurrection. None of the Gospel writers record all of these appearances. The following is the likely order of Christ's post-resurrection appearances to those loved by Him:

First, to Mary Magdalene after telling Peter and John that Christ had arisen and having returned to the tomb (John 20:11-18).

Second, to women returning from the tomb after they had heard the angel's declaration and instructions (28:8-10). These women had apparently departed the tomb after Mary Magdalene had left.

Third, to Peter to deal with his sin of denial privately and to restore him (Luke 24:34; 1 Cor. 15:5). Peter's sin would be publicly dealt with later (John 21).

Fourth, to the two disciples on the Emmaus Road (Luke 24:13-32). The Lord became known to them in the breaking of the bread.

Fifth, to ten of His disciples, plus others, who were together behind locked doors listening to the men who had walked with Christ on the Emmaus Road (Luke 24:36-43). Thomas was not present.

Sixth, to the disciples, with Thomas present (John 20:26-31).

Seventh, to seven disciples who had fished all night on the Sea of Galilee (John 21). The Lord cooked them breakfast.

Eighth, to the apostles and above 500 brethren (1 Cor. 15:6). It seems likely that this event coincides with Matthew's account but may refer to a separate post-resurrection experience, such as Christ's ascension (vv. 16-20).

Ninth, to Christ's half-brother James, which led to his conversion as well as of His other half-siblings (1 Cor. 15:7; Acts 1:14). The timing of this resurrection appearance is unknown.

Tenth, to the disciples and many other followers on Mount Olivet before ascending into Heaven forty days after His resurrection.

Besides these eyewitness accounts, there is more evidence for the resurrection of Christ. For example, logically speaking, who would want to steal the body of Christ from His tomb? The Romans would not want to remove Jesus' corpse from its tomb, as their main objective was to maintain civil order during the Jewish feasts. Because Jesus publicly foretold of His resurrection, the Jews wanted to ensure His body did not go missing after three days, which is why they requested Pilate to place guards at His tomb. Christ's disciples had no reason to steal His body; otherwise, they would have suffered a lifetime of misery for a lie. Fanatics may die for a religious cause, but not for what they know is not true. Additionally, lying would have grieved the Holy Spirit (Eph. 4:29-30); why then did the Holy Spirit so wonderfully bless their ministries and enable them to perform miracles?

Another evidence of Christ's resurrection is the radically changed lives of His disciples. The disciples were transformed from common laborers to zealous men that thought nothing of losing their lives for Christ – they saw, heard, and felt the risen Savior and never got over that experience. They willingly risked their lives in obedience to Christ's command to be His witnesses throughout the world.

John was banished and imprisoned on the Isle of Patmos. James was executed by Herod. Nero crucified Peter upside down. Andrew was crucified in Greece. Thomas was pierced by spears. Philip was put to death for converting the wife of a Roman proconsul. Matthew was stabbed to death in Ethiopia. Simon was killed in Persia for refusing to sacrifice to the sun god. James, the half-brother of Christ, was stoned and then clubbed to death at the temple. He was not converted until after he personally spoke to his resurrected half-brother and Savior (John 7:5; Acts 1:14; 1 Cor. 15:7). He penned the book of James before his death. Then we have Paul, a prominent Jewish leader that had Christians imprisoned and executed for their faith. But after meeting the glorified Savior on the road to Damascus (Acts 9), he converted to Christianity, was appointed an apostle to the Gentiles by Christ, and then suffered much persecution fulfilling that calling. He wrote at least thirteen books in our Bibles and, after finishing his course, was beheaded by Nero.

Additionally, the signs and wonders occurring at Pentecost are proof that Christ did rise from the grave. Peter explained to the Jews that Jesus' ministry had been approved by God through the evidence of miracles. The signs and wonders that they were witnessing at Pentecost were a continuation of Christ's authority, which meant God had raised Him from the dead (Acts 2:22-24). If Christ did not experience resurrection, from where did the Apostles get the power to do the miracles recorded in the book of Acts?

Jesus Christ declared to the Pharisees that His resurrection would prove that He was the Son of God (12:39-40; Rom. 1:4). Jesus Christ, the only begotten Son of God, was the firstfruits of eternal resurrection and is now with His Father in heaven (Heb. 1:5; Rev. 3:21). There have been many skeptics (e.g., Frank Morrison, Josh McDowell, and C. S. Lewis) who have tried to disprove the resurrection of Jesus Christ and in the process came to the truth and confessed Christ as Lord. The doctrine of Christ's resurrection is essential to the Christian faith and the evidence for the resurrection of the Lord Jesus Christ is overwhelming!

The Soldiers Are Bribed (vv. 11-15)

The sudden appearance of the angel who removed the stone sealing the tomb as an earthquake occurred cause the guards to quake also (v. 4). They fell to the ground as dead men, which may mean they passed out. After they recovered from the incident, they went into Jerusalem and informed the chief priests all that had happened (v. 11). The Jewish leaders now have a huge problem. Jesus, whom they called a "deceiver," said He would rise from the dead after three days, and now His body was missing from the tomb. Rather than heeding the miracle, they sought to protect their own interests by instigating a coverup story.

They paid the guards a great sum of money to lie about what had happened (v. 12). When questioned, the guards were to say that the disciples had secretly stolen the body of Jesus while they were sleeping (v. 13). But if the soldiers were sleeping, how would they know who took the body of Jesus? If a soldier was caught sleeping on his watch, it was normal protocol to put him to death for his negligence (Acts 12:19, 16:27). The Jewish leaders therefore promised to protect the soldiers if they were questioned about the matter by their commanders (v. 14). As the Jewish leaders had much to lose if the truth was made known, the soldiers believed what they had been told and agreed to the bribe (v. 15).

The Great Commission (vv. 16-20)

Matthew's overall framework has been to present Christ as the King of the Jews. In upholding Christ's nobility, Matthew has invoked several unique key words and phrases that are either peculiar to Matthew or more prominent than in the other Gospels: "king," "throne," "righteousness," "kingdom of heaven," and "son of David." Matthew now closes his account also in a peculiar way as compared to the other Gospels.

Matthew began his gospel record by proclaiming that the Lord Jesus, as the Son of David, was the rightful heir to David's throne. He will close his Gospel in a figurative manner that beautifully climaxes this realization. Does he conclude, as Mark did, by recording the ascension of Christ back to heaven? No. You will find no ascension of Christ in Matthew.

What we do observe is Christ, in His glorified body, positioned on a mountain in Galilee imparting directions to His disciples. Mountains, in the figurative sense, symbolize kingdoms in the Bible. From a Jewish perspective, this scene is the climax of Matthew and completes the theme that he began in the very first verse and became possible through Christ's redemptive work at Calvary. Just before the curtain draws closed, we get a futuristic representation of Christ's kingdom established on earth.

The disciples have journeyed to a particular mountain in Galilee as previously instructed (v. 16). The subjects of the kingdom are before Christ and worshipping their King. Regrettably, some had doubts about what the future held for them, while others, who had not witnessed Christ's crucifixion, may have wondered if Christ had actually died, as He looked so full of life now (v. 17). Despite human doubts, God will keep His promise to Abraham, to David, to the Jewish people, and to all those who heed the gospel and enter by faith into the kingdom of heaven.

The Lord Jesus said that all authority had been given to Him in heaven and on earth (v. 18). Being under His authority, the disciples were being sent to the nations to preach the gospel message, to baptize those who responded to the gospel in the name of the Father, Son, and Holy

Spirit, and then to teach them all the things that Christ had taught them (vv. 19-20). This is how one makes disciples of Christ. This is Christ's evangelistic plan to reach the masses with the truth and to build His Church. This activity will continue until the end of the Church Age.

The Great Commission demonstrates God's great love for the lost and the fact that He wants to see as many as possible redeemed by the blood of His dear Son (2 Pet. 3:9). Believers are to be witnesses for Christ in the world (Acts 1:8). The Greek verb in verse 19 conveys the idea, "as you are going make disciples." There was never any doubt in the Lord's mind that His disciples were going.

The Lord Jesus instructed His disciples to teach new converts to observe all the things that He had commanded them, as well as those things which the Holy Spirit would teach them after Christ's ascension into heaven (John 16:13-15). Scriptural doctrines and practices are to be the illumination of Christ's glory in the life of the believer.

Just as we do not expect a newborn to be earning income for the family two weeks after birth, spiritual growth in new converts requires time and care. Paul gives us a good pattern to follow in discipling those who profess Christ: consistent tender care but also only committing to reliable people who will be faithful with what they are taught (1 Thess. 2:7-8; 2 Tim. 2:2).

Paul had a nurturing ministry with the Thessalonian believers, yet he exhorts Timothy to invest only in those who would be faithful to the truth. Striking the balance between these two bookends is one of the difficult tasks of discipleship. Those who profess Christ as Savior will require tender care and regular feedings of the sincere milk of the Word (i.e., the rudiments of the Christian faith; 1 Pet. 2:2; Heb. 5:12) to encourage their growth, yet maturity must be realized. Maturity is evidenced by a deepening devotion to Christ, being a witness for Him, spending time in Bible study and prayer, repenting and forsaking sin, and faithfully attending church meetings.

May we continue to labor with Christ as He builds His Church. May we be true disciples living for Him and see generations of disciples thoroughly equipped to do the same. This is where Matthew draws the curtain on his record. We are left with the impression in our minds of the King of David, in His Kingdom, with His faithful subjects before Him. This scene will be fully realized in the Kingdom Age after Christ descends from heaven to vindicate His name and judge the wicked that are on earth.

Mark

Mark Overview

Introduction

About ninety percent of Mark's gospel record has similar content to that contained in Matthew and Luke. However, Mark portrays these commonalities from a unique perspective and the best chronological order. Mark is the most condensed of the Gospel accounts, which means that key words or phrases are not largely repeated to accentuate certain points or to provide an outline of his work. In Matthew and Luke, angelic messengers and prophetic pronouncements through human agents introduced the Savior, but not in Mark. His introduction is concise: a few verses to describe the ministry of John the baptizer and the Lord's baptism and temptation, but by verse 14 of the first chapter, the Lord is preaching the kingdom gospel and tirelessly serving the lost sheep of Israel. The fact that Mark so abruptly brings us to the beginning of Christ's ministry fits well with his theme – Christ the humble and industrious Servant of God.

Mark contains only four parables, whereas Matthew contains many more. Mark focuses more on the busy life of Christ in doing miracles and ministering to the needy and brokenhearted. Mark depicts Christ ministering to God's chosen people, while Matthew reveals Christ as testing Israel. Mark is addressed to a wider audience, the Romans, while Matthew is distinctly Jewish. At the time that Christ walked upon the earth, the Roman Empire numbered about 120 million people, and half of these were slaves. Slavery was a social reality of that day; therefore, his Roman audience would readily understand and relate to the tenor of Mark's record.

Because Mark presents Christ as a lowly servant, almost no authoritative decrees by the Lord are presented; that would be out of place in Mark. No sentence is passed on Israel. No "woe" message to Pharisees or stinging "woe unto you" decrees are issued by Christ in Mark; these well mark Matthew. There is no Christ weeping over Jerusalem, as in Matthew. The Lord Jesus cleansed the temple twice during His three-plus years of public service, once at the beginning and once at the end of His ministry. Concerning the first event, Mark merely records that the Lord entered into the temple, but nothing is said of His driving out the moneychangers or turning over their tables. In Mark, Jesus is serving man, not pronouncing judgment upon him.

Author

Mark was a Jew and a native of Jerusalem; his mother's name was Mary (Acts 12:12). Although referred to in Mark 14:51, his name is not specifically mentioned in the Gospels. His name does appear ten times in Acts and the Epistles. The first significant reference to Mark is when Paul and Barnabas (Mark's uncle) took him on the first missionary journey into Asia Minor. John Mark withdrew from the team at Perga and returned home (Acts 13:13). However, Barnabas later took him on another missionary journey to Cyprus (Acts 15:39), and Scripture confirms that he was faithful to serve the Lord afterwards (Col. 4:10; 2 Tim. 4:11). Peter refers to John Mark as his spiritual son, which may mean that Peter was instrumental in Mark's conversion (1 Pet. 5:13). Accordingly, it is generally believed that Mark's gospel is a strong reflection of Peter's view of Christ.

Date

Mark was likely the second of the four gospels written, Matthew being the first. A date between his restoration to service in 50 A.D. (Acts 15:38-40) and 68 A.D. (four years after Peter's execution) is generally accepted.

Mark's Omissions

Examination of the four Gospels reveals that Mark chose not to include certain material in his account to better maintain his theme of *The Lowly Servant of Jehovah*. Perhaps the first obvious omission is that Mark includes no genealogies. In fact, no mention is made of Christ's birth or childhood. This omission is in keeping with the perspective of Christ's serving ministry. In Mark, it would not be genealogies or childhood history, but what the Lord did for others that established His credentials as the Servant of Jehovah.

Because the Lord Jesus is presented as ministering to instead of commanding others, no mention is made in Mark of the *Sermon on the*

Mount; no Kingdom Manifesto is declared. Hence, authoritative expressions are seldom found in Mark, as compared to the other Gospels. Divine or exalted titles pertaining to the Lord Jesus are also rare in Mark. He is not called Emmanuel – "God with us." Of the twenty-eight times Jesus is referred to as "the Son of God" in the four Gospels, only three are found in Mark.

In Mark, the Lord is referred to by the reverent title "Christ" only twice. Matthew refers to Jesus as Christ four times in the first chapter alone. The Lord Jesus is referred to as the "Son of David" only once in Mark; Matthew applies the title ten times.

Also, no enlisting of Jesus as king is found in Mark. Mark is the only writer to refer to the Lord as *"the son of Mary"* (6:3). The Lord was born into His mother's low social status, ensuring He was acquainted with a simplistic and austere way of life. The Lord Jesus, as God's Servant, knew firsthand about hard work and redeeming time.

Though brief in introduction, Mark safeguards against having a degraded view of God's lowly Servant in his opening verse: *"The beginning of the gospel of Jesus Christ, **the Son of God**."* Humanly speaking, it is natural to adopt a smug attitude about someone serving you, but Mark ensures that his readers understand that this was willful condescension by the Son of God. For this reason, the Lord never speaks of "My Father" or "Our Father" in Mark's record; His humble service to man, not His relationship with the Father, is paramount. But to ensure no confusion on the matter, Mark immediately guards against undermining the deity of Christ.

A Busy Servant

Twelve of Mark's sixteen chapters begin with the word "and," and the far majority of the verses in Mark begin with conjunctions and adverbs such as "and," "now," and "then." For example, Mark 1 contains 45 verses, and 35 of them begin with "And...." More specifically, many verses in Mark begin "And Jesus..." or "And He...." Mark is careful to present a serving Savior to his audience: "And Jesus was doing this, and Jesus was doing that."

But he doesn't stop there. For the reader to gain a higher sense of the Lord's exhausting ministry, he adds further description to the verbs describing the Lord's service, employing words such as "forthwith" and "immediately." This is accomplished by repeatedly applying two Greek adverbs: *eutheos* meaning "directly," and *euthus* meaning "at once." How are these adverbs applied in the other Gospels? Here is the breakdown. Keep in mind that Mark has only sixteen chapters compared to Matthew's twenty-eight.

Adverb	Matthew	Mark	Luke	John
Eutheos	*15*	*40*	*8*	*4*
Euthus	*4*	*6*	*2*	*3*
Total	**19**	**46**	**10**	**7**

The frequency of usage in Mark is unmistakably distinctive! Those of the Lord's servants who are involved in various "full-time" ministries understand, in a measure, non-stop ministry exhaustion. (Many elders and other saints know this all too well also.) Can you imagine the life of the Lord Jesus? Day in and day out, at any time of day or night, people were coming to Him with their problems and ailments. Those rejecting His message confronted Him continuously. No wonder He fell asleep in the stern of a boat and did not wake up when the boat was being tossed to and fro in a violent storm. Add to this His fervent prayer life. Even though His life was marked by a constant state of physical exhaustion, He still arose early, often while it was yet dark, to spend time conversing with His Father. Mark presents to us not just a serving Savior, but One that incessantly, steadily, and promptly served others. The Lord Jesus poured His life out to satisfy the needs of others and in so doing left us a lowly example to follow.

A Serving Savior

In depicting the Servant of Jehovah, Mark provides the perfect character sketch of a godly servant. The Lord Jesus teaches us through His selfless example what true servanthood is all about. Just prior to his death, Paul's final exhortation to his spiritual son Timothy was to fulfill his ministry: *"Preach the word! Be ready in season and out of season"* (2 Tim. 4:2). Christ knew all about "in season" and "out of season" ministry; He was on duty at all times! How might the Lord's service to others be described? Mark provides a complete character sketch.

The Lord's service was motivated by love. *"Then Jesus, moved with compassion"* (1:41). The Lord teaches us that the only true motive for Christian service to God is love and, nonetheless, that the only reason to serve others is love. Biblical love initiates sacrificial giving! *"For God* *so loved* the world that *He gave* His only begotten Son." Mark notes the Lord's self-sacrificing example throughout his Gospel (3:20, 4:35-36, 4:38, 6:31, 7:34, and 8:12). Love is discerning and understands what is best for those who need help. Love, not pity, must be our reason to serve others, or we may unknowingly enable their sin or interfere with God's chastening hand in their lives.

The Lord served others before Himself. *"Then the multitude came together again, so that they could not so much as eat bread"* (3:20). *"For there were many coming and going, and they did not even have time to eat"* (6:31). The Lord was so busy serving others, so disposed to mankind, so available to the distressed, that He often had no time to properly care for Himself. On one occasion, we find the Lord asleep in the stern of a boat, during daytime and while in the midst of a raging storm – physical exhaustion and emotional fatigue frequented His body, yet we never read of Him complaining once.

The Lord served with tenacity. *"Then He healed many who were sick with various diseases, and cast out many demons; and He did not allow the demons to speak, because they knew Him"* (1:34, also 3:10). The disciples said to the Lord, *"Everyone is looking for You"* (1:37). This statement highlights the immensity of Christ's counseling and healing ministry. Who wouldn't want to go to a physician who had a one hundred percent success rate of curing patients and mending families?

The Lord did not seek popularity. What was the Lord's response when His disciples informed Him that *"everyone is looking for You?"* The Lord replied, *"Let us go into the next towns"* (1:38). He could have used the opportunity to promote Himself and gain a fan club, but He was more interested in the quality of His disciples than the quantity of the followers. Mark reveals Christ's progressing humility in response to his instant fame. At first, He tolerated the popularity, then He shunned it, and finally He avoided it altogether: *"And immediately His fame spread throughout all the region around Galilee"* (1:28). *"But Jesus withdrew with His disciples to the sea. And a great multitude from Galilee followed Him"* (3:7). Later, the Lord even requested of those that He had healed to keep quiet about it (7:35-36, 8:25-26, 9:30). It is evident from Mark's various healing accounts that the Lord did not desire fame or popularity, but rather that He desired to demonstrate that genuine service is veiled in secrecy. May each of us learn of Christ and pursue His meek and lowly example.

The Lord served compassionately. The Lord Jesus had His eyes open to the needs of others; He was discerning – *"He looked upon them."* What do a leper, four blind men, and three disciples have in common? They were all touched by Christ to satisfy a need. The leper was a social outcast and longed to be embraced. For the blind, every clumsy step ventured into the unknown, but the Lord lifted this darkness and gave their souls security. At His transfiguration, the fearful disciples were comforted in a time of panic: *"But Jesus came and touched them and said, 'Arise, and do not be afraid.' When they had lifted up their eyes, they saw no one but Jesus only"* (Matt. 17:7-8). Why didn't the Lord just speak a good word to these individuals? He understood that a loving touch could convey what words couldn't. Let us not fear to reach out and touch those in need, so they, too, might see *no man save Jesus!* The Lord cared about the possessed, the sick, the blind, the deaf, the mute, the paralyzed, the diseased, the suffering, and the dead. He often touched those He healed (1:30-31). There is a whole world of needy people, and Christ teaches us to open our eyes to see them and not to be afraid to share some skin with those in need. Listening and touching are important gestures of love.

The Lord continued serving despite constant opposition. Before the events of Calvary, nearly twenty references of the Lord doing ministry in the face of challenges, disdain, and rejection are found in Mark (2:6-7, 2:16, 2:24, 3:2, 3:6, 3:22, 5:17, 5:40, 6:3, 6:5, 7:1-2, 8:11, 10:2, 11:27-28, 12:13, 12:18, 12:28, 14:4, …). Christ shows us that if we are doing anything for the Lord, we will be criticized and suffer for it, so expect it. The same pharisaical attitude that existed during Christ's first advent continues unto this day. The Lord Jesus left us a self-sacrificing example to follow. A true servant cares nothing for himself, about what he is asked to do, or about what others think of him; the only focus must be to do the Master's bidding (1 Pet. 2:19-21).

The Lord was a good administrator. The Lord redeemed the most out of His time on earth and showed good managerial skills while serving. Concerning evangelism, the Lord sent His disciples *"forth two by two"* (6:7). In accomplishing the miracle of feeding the 5000 (plus women and children), the Lord had the people sit down in ranks of hundreds and fifties (6:39-40).

In application, might we, before taking on new ministries and responsibilities, learn discipline, good organizational skills, and efficient and frugal means of accomplishing God-directed ministry. Why would the Lord give us more to do for the kingdom of God, if we have not learned to be efficient in accomplishing what He has already requested of us? Many of the Lord's people today cannot respond with their time or finances to the urgent needs of the mission field because they are strapped with debt and, thus, enslaved to an employer or business. May we all learn from the Lord's example of managing every task to an efficient and profitable conclusion. He did all things well!

The Lord prayed before serving. *"Now in the morning, having risen a long while before daylight, He went out and departed to a solitary place; and there He prayed"* (1:35). *"And when He had sent them away, He departed to the mountain to pray"* (6:46). Matthew records Christ praying on only three separate occasions, but Mark and Luke often refer to the Lord's prayer life. This difference is in keeping with the Gospel themes, as the exalted King would be less dependent upon help from above than the lowly human Servant.

How often do we surge ahead of the perfect plan of God? Waiting is often harder than working, for we feel compelled to do something, but often it is not to pray. Prayer demonstrates complete faith in the Lord to initiate, direct, and complete each matter of our lives according to His will (1 Jn. 5:14). Besides moving the hand of God to exhibit His glory, prayer transforms our hearts by conforming our thinking to the mind of Christ.

Hudson Taylor, who labored for the kingdom in China, had three important principles concerning prayer: "You can work without praying, but it is a bad plan. You cannot pray in earnest without working. Do not be so busy with work for Christ that you have no strength left for praying. True praying requires strength."[82]

Warren Wiersbe writes, "Prayer is not an escape from responsibility; it is our *response* to God's *ability*. True prayer energizes us for service and battle."[83]

Before choosing His disciples, the Lord spent an entire night in prayer (Luke 6:12). The Lord prayed before feeding the 5000, just prior to Peter's pronouncement that He was *"the Christ, the Son of the living God,"* and before raising Lazarus from the dead. The Lord's final hours before Calvary were spent in prayer. The prayer life of the Lord Jesus was so intense and so fruitful that on one occasion the disciples asked the Savior to teach them how to pray. They wanted in on the blessings of prayer. How about you? How is your prayer life? We should follow the Lord's example: prayer preceded service and followed accomplishments – prayer preceded crisis and followed achievements. The Lord Jesus exhorted *"that men always ought to pray and not lose heart"* (Luke 18:1).

Outline

I.   The Servant's Introduction (1:1-13)

II.   The Servant's Early Galilean Ministry (1:14-3:12)

III. The Servant's Galilean Ministry With His Disciples (3:13-7:30)

IV.   The Servant's Ministry in Decapolis (7:31-9:50)

V.   The Servant's Perean Ministry (10:1-52)

VI.   The Servant's Ministry in Jerusalem (11:1-12:44)

VII. The Servant's Olivet Discourse (13:1-37)

VIII. The Servant's Passion and Death (14:1-15:47)

IX.   The Servant's Resurrection and Ascension (16:1-20)

Mark Chapter 1

The Ministry of John (vv. 1-8)

Scripture reveals that God rarely refers to individuals as His servants. For example, the explicit title "The Servant of the Lord" is only extended to two individuals in the Bible, Moses and Joshua, and predominantly applied after their deaths. Despite their faults, they were remembered by the Lord for finishing well. The less formal expression "My servant" is assigned by God to only ten individuals: Abraham, Job, Moses, Caleb, David, Isaiah, Eliakim, Israel (speaking of the nation as His servent), Zerubbabel, and the Lord Jesus.

As we ponder the Lord Jesus as God's lowly servant, it must be emphasized that the revealed character of the servant of God is as important as what that servant does. The servant of the Lord represents God in character and conduct. Mark will show us the gentle, kind, humble nature of the Lord Jesus while enduring distress, rejection, and hardship in His God-given ministry. When the Father proclaims to all "Behold My Servant" (Isa. 42:1; Matt. 12:18), it is an invitation to admire the Person as much as His tenacious ministry.

Yet, God's request for us to admire His Servant also invites the accusations and challenges of the wicked, which Christ endured without ever neglecting His lowly service to humanity. God's Servant willingly and selflessly spends and is spent for others and will be attacked and rejected for doing so. From this vantage point, Mark attests to man's superficial claim on Christ, not Christ's rightful claim on men. Thus, he begins his record by eliminating any confusion: Jehovah's lowly Servant is *"the Son of God"* (v. 1). Mark did not want his audience to interpret Christ's meek and lowly disposition in serving others as somehow discrediting His deity. The Lord Jesus is the Son of God incarnate.

Mark then refers to Malachi 3:1 and Isaiah 40:3 to affirm that God the Father was sending a forerunner before His Servant to prepare the way for His ministry (vv. 2-3). This forerunner was John the baptizer, the cousin of Jesus through Mary.

The Gospel of John is packed with *sevens*, a number speaking of perfection and completeness. It is used in John to declare the perfections of Christ's work and person. The Holy Spirit includes a sevenfold witness in the first thirteen verses of Mark's Gospel for the same purpose. Before beginning His lowly service to humanity in verse 14, *"the way of the Lord"* was prepared beforehand. Mark ensured that his audience knew that the One who was in the form of a Servant was none other than God Himself. Hamilton Smith summarizes the seven testimonies of the divine glory of Christ:

v. 1	The first witness is the writer of the Gospel – Mark – by reminding us that He is *"Jesus Christ, the Son of God."*
vv. 2-3	Second, the prophets are quoted, as being witness of the glory of His Person.
vv. 4-8	Third, we have the witness of John, the Forerunner, to the glory of the perfect Servant.
vv. 9-11	Fourth, we have the witness of the voice from Heaven to the glory of Christ.
vv. 12-13	Fifth, we have a brief allusion to the temptation in the wilderness. The temptation of our Lord in the wilderness became a witness to His infinite perfection whereby He overcame Satan.
v. 13	Sixth, creation itself bears witness to the glory of His Person, for we read He was *"with the wild beasts."* However much the beasts may fear men, they have no fear of this blessed Man, for He, indeed, is their Creator.
v. 13	Last, we read, *"the Angels ministered unto Him."* The One who came to be the Servant is, Himself, served by angelic hosts. He is none less than *"the Son," "the First Begotten,"* of whom, when He comes into the world, it is said, *"Let all the angels of God worship Him."*[84]

We are introduced to Christ's forerunner, John, in verse 4. His miracle birth to elderly parents (for his mother Elizabeth was barren) was foretold by the angel Gabriel while speaking to John's father, Zacharias, in the temple (Luke 1:13). As a divinely chosen vessel, John was filled with the Holy Spirit at his conception (Luke 1:15). Luke informs us that after John's birth he *"grew and became strong in spirit, and was in the deserts till the day of his manifestation to Israel"* (Luke 1:80).

John maintained a self-denying lifestyle in the wilderness. He clothed himself with a cloak of camel's hair secured by a leather belt about his waist and ate locusts and wild honey (v. 6). When called into ministry, he began declaring the kingdom gospel message to Israel, *"Repent, for the kingdom of heaven is at hand!"* (Matt. 3:2). But one could not enter God's kingdom without repenting of sin and receiving the One who was coming, speaking of Israel's Messiah (v. 4). John said that he was not worthy to even loosen His shoe strap (v. 7).

Repentance of sin was to be demonstrated through water baptism (v. 4). The first step to salvation is to acknowledge one's unrighteous standing before God and need to be redeemed and cleansed. This is how John was preparing the way for the Lord. When the Lord did come, those who had received Him would receive the Holy Spirit (v. 8).

The Baptism of Christ (vv. 9-11)

Mark informs us that the Lord Jesus departed Nazareth in Galilee and traveled to Bethabara where John was baptizing those repenting of their sins in the Jordan River (v. 9; John 1:28). Matthew informs us that Christ wanted to be baptized by John, but as he knew the identity of Jesus, the prophet initially refused to do so (Matt. 3:13-17). John said that he needed to be baptized by Christ.

Obviously, the Messiah had no sins of His own to confess, but what John did not understand was that the Lord had come to publicly identify with those He came to save (i.e., those who had publicly confessed their sins through baptism). Thus, the Lord told John to baptize Him, for *"it is fitting for us to fulfill righteousness"* (v. 15). Notice, the Lord said to John that it was fitting for "us to fulfill righteousness" (both men were needed to perform His baptism). Baptism was not taught in the Law, so there could be no association of it with righteous Law-keeping.

If the Lord had not been baptized by John, it would have hindered the people from listening to Christ's message, for by His action He would be saying to everyone that He was more righteous than them. Although this was true, it was necessary for Him to first be accepted as a teacher, so that He could both proclaim and demonstrate the righteousness of God to the people. In time, the Lord would show His fitness as God's righteous Savior and Messiah.

Not only was Christ identifying with those He came to save in water baptism, but the event would also reveal Him as the Son of God, for John had been divinely informed previously that the Holy Spirit would descend like a dove and alight on the One who was the Son of God (John 1:32-34). Directly after His baptism, the Spirit of God descended on Him in the form of a dove, and the voice of His Father was heard from Heaven praising His Son, *"You are My beloved Son, in whom I am well pleased"* (vv. 10-11).

On three separate occasions during the Lord's earthly sojourn, God the Father spoke from heaven to express His pleasure in His Son, Israel's Messiah. The first was directly after Christ's baptism, as we have been considering. A similar statement was uttered from heaven at Christ's transfiguration (Matt. 17:5). The third time is after the Lord foretold His death and asked His Father to glorify His name. God affirmed that He would do so again through Christ's work at Calvary (John 12:28).

Luke tells us that the Lord Jesus was approximately 30 years of age when He was baptized and now His years of quiet obscurity were over. Peter later confirms that the Holy Spirit anointed Christ at this time to set Him apart for and to empower His ministry that His Father had sent Him to accomplish (Acts 10:38). This is the *kickoff*, so to speak, of the Lord's three-plus-years' ministry to the lost sheep of Israel.

The Holy Spirit's anointing of Christ fulfilled a prophecy of Isaiah which would involve all three persons of the Godhead.

> *The Spirit of the Lord God is upon Me, because the Lord has anointed Me to preach good tidings to the poor; He has sent Me to heal the brokenhearted, to proclaim liberty to the captives, and the opening of the prison to those who are bound* (Isa. 61:1).

The person (identified as *"Me"*) in this passage is Messiah Himself. He was sent by the Father to preach tidings of good news to the lost sheep of Israel. The Father anointed the Lord Jesus with the Holy Spirit to enable His work to be effectual.

The Testing of Christ (vv. 12-13)

Immediately after His baptism, the Lord was led into the wilderness by the Holy Spirit (v. 12). For forty days He fasted and was externally solicited by the devil to act contrary to God's will (Matt. 4:2). Matthew and Luke record the final exchange between the Lord and the devil at the conclusion of the forty-day trial. During this testing period, the Lord dwelt in a solitary place with wild beasts. Mark states that the Lord was ministered to by angels, but Matthew indicates that this angelic assistance occurred directly after the forty days of testing concluded (Matt. 4:11). After being proven to be righteous, the Lord commanded Satan to leave Him and the devil obeyed the Lord (Matt. 4:10-11).

The number *forty* is used dozens of times in Scripture to convey the idea of a *probationary test or trial*. *Forty* is often the duration that God tests the obedience of His people before passing judgment upon them, if found guilty. For example, Moses lived in Egypt for *forty* years, then was morally refined in the wilderness of Midian for *forty* years, before leading the Israelites out of Egypt and into the wilderness for another *forty* years. There were also three occasions in which Moses was on Mount Sinai in God's presence *forty* days and nights (Ex. 24:18, 34:1-28; Deut. 8:18). At Kadesh Barnea, Moses sent twelve Jewish spies into Canaan for *forty* days, to investigate the land God had promised them (Num. 13:25, 14:34).

The Bible records a few occasions when individuals went *forty* days without food or drink through the supernatural care of God: Elijah during his wilderness experience (1 Kgs. 19:8), Moses before Jehovah on Mount Horeb (Ex. 34:28), and Christ during His testing in the wilderness while He fasted (v. 13; Matt. 4:1-11). After His resurrection, the Lord also appeared to encourage and commission His disciples over a *forty*-day period before ascending into heaven (Acts 1:1-11).

It is likely that Christ's baptism and the subsequent forty days of testing by the devil occurred in late Summer or early Fall of 26 A.D. (this assumes the traditional date of 30 A.D. for Christ's crucifixion). John the baptizer, Christ's forerunner, had already been calling Israel to repentance for some time (perhaps one to two years) when Christ was anointed by the Holy Spirit after His baptism.

Christ's Ministry Commences in Galilee (vv. 14-15)

Shortly after the first cleansing of the temple at Passover (John 2:13-22), Christ departed Jerusalem through Samaria and returned to Galilee (John 4). At this juncture (the Spring of 27 A.D.), an approximate two-year ministry began throughout Galilee. Capernaum was the Lord's home base of operation during this time.

After hearing that John, the baptizer, was put into prison, the Lord relocated from Nazareth to central Galilee, often residing at Capernaum (v. 14). It was at this time that the Lord Jesus began to offer a literal, earthly, political kingdom to Israel: *"The kingdom of heaven is at hand. Repent, and believe in the gospel"* (v. 15). The long-awaited Messiah had come, and it was time for God's people to get right with Him.

Christ Calls His First Disciples (vv. 16-20)

Mark then recounts how the Lord called His first disciples into His kingdom preaching ministry. While walking along the shore of the Sea of Galilee, the Lord saw two brothers, who were fishermen, Simon called Peter, and Andrew (v. 16). They were fishing with nets at the time, but when the Lord called them to follow Him to become fishers of men, they immediately left their nets and followed Him (vv. 17-18). Continuing to walk along the shoreline, the Lord saw two more brothers, James and John, who were also fishermen (v. 19). They were in a boat with their father Zebedee mending their nets when they were called by the Lord, and instantly they left their father in the boat and followed Christ (v. 20).

The Lord Jesus exhibited tremendous patience in calling His disciples. Initially, He invited two of John's disciples, including Andrew (Peter's brother), to His home to spend some time with Him, but at the end of the day they departed (John 1:39). Andrew then told Peter that he had found the Messiah, but Peter did not come to Christ on his own. The Lord had to repeatedly call Peter to follow Him, but after each time, Peter dedicated more of himself to Christ.

Initially, Peter forsook his fishing nets to follow Christ at His bidding (v. 20). Later, Peter forsook all to pursue the Savior (Luke 5:11). After Peter's denial of Christ and Christ's resurrection, the Lord again called Peter to follow Him with the understanding that it would cost Peter his life (John 21:15-19). The Lord's patience with Peter is an encouragement to all those who are involved in training others. Those who mentor younger believers must be patient and tender.

Christ Casts Out Demons in Capernaum (vv. 21-28)

Christ and His disciples journeyed to Capernaum, and shortly after arriving, they entered a synagogue on the Sabbath (v. 21). The Lord began to teach the people, who were astonished at His ability, for He taught as if He owned the Scriptures. Christ's knowledge of Scripture and His passion for God exuded an authority that the scribes, who simply taught the Law's regulations, were missing (v. 22).

There was a man in the synagogue who had an unclean spirit and in fact was indwelt by several demons (v. 23). Using the man's vocal cords, the demons cried out, *"Let us alone! What have we to do with You, Jesus of Nazareth? Did You come to destroy us? I know who You are – the Holy One of God"* (v. 24). The demons knew who Christ was, that He had authority over them, and that they would ultimately be destroyed by Him. The Lord commanded the evil spirits in the man to be silent and to come out of him (v. 25). After the man convulsed and cried out with a loud voice, the demonic spirits departed their host (v. 26).

Those at the synagogue had never seen anything like this before and they inquired among themselves who Jesus was and about His unfamiliar teachings (v. 27). Christ taught with authority and exercised authority over unclean spirits – could Jesus of Nazareth be the Holy One of God as the demons had declared? The news of what He had done in the synagogue that day quickly spread throughout Galilee (v. 28).

Christ Heals Peter's Mother-in-Law (vv. 29-31)

Mark informs us that Simon Peter and Andrew lived in the same house in Capernaum, that Peter was married, and that his mother-in-law also resided in their home. There is no evidence in Scripture that any of the other disciples were married at this juncture, which might explain why so much of the Lord's Galilean ministry was at Capernaum and the surrounding villages.

The Lord and his disciples departed the synagogue and went to Peter and Andrew's home (v. 30). The Lord Jesus was made aware that Peter's mother-in-law lay sick in bed with a fever (v. 31). He went to her and took her by the hand and lifted her up and immediately she was well. Being well, she immediately began serving their many household guests. Her service refreshed the Lord and His disciples, who would be engaging in long hours of ministry throughout the remainder of the day.

This is a good reminder that those who are born again are healed and strengthened to serve the Lord. This often begins with bearing one's daily burdens to bless others. What the Lord does, He does perfectly. Not only was Peter's mother-in-law's fever gone, but her body was enabled to serve without any diminished capacity after being ill.

More Healings as the Gospel Is Preached (vv. 32-40)

The news of Christ's arrival at Peter's home spread quickly through the city. By evening, there was a line at the door of many sick and demon-possessed people to be healed (vv. 32-33). The Lord healed everyone that journeyed to seek His assistance that evening, and He also prohibited the demons from speaking in His presence (v. 34). The demons knew who He was, but because He was God's Message and Messenger to Israel, no infringement on His mission would be tolerated. He would reveal His identity and the reason of His earthly sojourn according to God's sovereign timing.

The next morning, the Lord rose long before daylight and quietly went to a solitary place to pray (v. 35). To ensure privacy, the Lord often spent the early morning hours communing with His Father. The Lord received His marching orders for the day during these intimate times of prayer. His soul was refreshed by the presence of His Father despite the heavy ongoing demands of ministry. This is a good routine for all believers to follow. Service without enjoying God's presence will be burdensome to our souls, for *"the joy of the Lord is our strength."*

After dawn came and went, Simon Peter and others began searching for the Lord Jesus (v. 36). After finding Him, Peter said, *"Everyone is looking for you"* (v. 37). The disciples were likely wondering, "Why is Jesus spending so much time in prayer when people are trying to find Him? Doesn't He want to have followers and be famous?"

It is evident from Mark's account that the Lord served the people tenaciously and compassionately, but He was not seeking popularity. What was the Lord's response when Peter informed Him that *"everyone is looking for You"*? The Lord replied, *"Let us go into the next towns"* (v. 38). He could have used the opportunity to promote Himself and gain a fan club, but as Arthur Pink notes, that was not His way:

> We like to boast of the crowds that attend our ministry. But the perfect Servant of God never courted popularity; He shunned it. And when His disciples came and told Him – no doubt with pleasurable pride – *"All men seek for Thee,"* His immediate response was, *"Let us go!"*[85]

Mark shows the advancing attitude of humility by the Lord in response to His instant fame. At first, He tolerated the popularity, then He shunned it, and finally He avoided it altogether:

And immediately His fame spread throughout all the region around Galilee (1:28).

But Jesus withdrew with His disciples to the sea. And a great multitude from Galilee followed Him, and from Judea (3:7).

Immediately his ears were opened, and the impediment of his tongue was loosed, and he spoke plainly. Then He commanded them that they should tell no one; but the more He commanded them, the more widely they proclaimed it (7:35-36, see also 8:25-26).

Then they departed from there and passed through Galilee, and He did not want anyone to know it (9:30).

Clearly, the Lord did not desire fame for helping others, though He deserved it. Rather, He showed through a selfless example that genuine service for others is veiled in secrecy. Thus, he continued preaching throughout Galilee, healing the sick, and liberating the demon-possessed without seeking a following (v. 39). The Lord had the approval of His Father and that was all that mattered. May each of us keep small and keep hidden as we follow His example.

A Leper Is Cleansed (vv. 40-45)

The prophet Isaiah predicted that when the Messiah arrived in Israel, He would heal blindness, deafness, lameness, dumbness, and various diseases (Isa. 35:5-6, 53:4). Having concluded His lengthy *Sermon on the Mount* (which Mark does not record), the Lord descended the mount and was followed by a large crowd (Matt. 8:1). A leper saw Jesus Christ and came to worship, saying, *"Lord, if You are willing, You can make me clean"* (v. 40; Matt. 8:2). The Lord was moved with compassion and stretched out His hand and touched the leper and said to Him, *"I am willing; be cleansed"* and immediately his leprosy was gone (vv. 41-42).

The Lord then told the cleansed leper not to tell others of what had happened, but to immediately go to the temple and be inspected by the priests and offer the gift required by the Law (Lev. 14). This would serve as a testimony of Himself before all the priests (vv. 43-44). It is likely that the cleansed leper eventually arrived at the temple to undergo the cleansing ritual after being healed, but he also largely published the miracle along the way – so much so that Christ and His disciples had to depart the city for a remote region to avoid the swelling numbers of people desiring His assistance (v. 45). Many still came to Him in the wilderness for healing. However, being in a deserted place made His ministry more manageable, as only those who really believed that He could help them would make the journey to find Him.

Whether the Lord did not want the cleansed leper to speak of the miracles to others or just not to be delayed in going to the temple by doing so is unclear. However, the Lord often instructed those He had healed or who had observed a healing to keep quiet about the miracle. This was most likely to avoid being prematurely enthroned by the Jewish populace wanting relief from Roman rule. His countrymen must understand and accept the spiritual aspects of His kingdom offer before He could ever sit on a throne in Israel.

While today there is effective treatment for leprosy, there was none in Old Testament days, meaning that if someone contracted the disease, he or she was isolated from the Jewish society to suffer a slowly deteriorating and miserable existence. To prevent the spread of the disease, lepers normally communed together in remote colonies and were dependent on loved ones to supply their necessities. For this reason, leprosy was intensely feared and caused understandable paranoia among the Jews. (See Matthew 8 for further commentary on leprosy.)

Besides healing the leper, the Lord Jesus showed compassion in two additional ways. First, He was not afraid to convey love to the leper by touching him, even though the Law declared him to be untouchable. Not only did the Lord have power to heal the disease, but also He showed that He could not be brought under its corrupting power. He thus remained a fit and clean sacrificial Lamb for God. Second, by sending the healed leper immediately to the priests, He was able to declare the gospel message to hard-to-reach religious leaders sequestered in the temple. Healing a blind or lame person would not accomplish this, as there was no requirement in the Law for them to be inspected and ceremonially cleansed.

There is no Old Testament record of a healed leper ever going through the ceremonial purification process as supervised by Levitical priests (Lev. 14). This meant that there was something new in Israel. Did this mean that Isaiah's prophecy had been fulfilled? Was Messiah in Israel? The Lord Jesus sent a steady stream of healed lepers to the temple over the next three years. As a result, a multitude of Jewish priests believed on Him and were saved (Acts 6:7).

Mark Chapter 2

A Paralytic Is Healed and Forgiven (vv. 1-12)

Mark does not record Christ's rejection by the Gergesenes, but rather that He returned with His disciples to Capernaum after some days (v. 1). The Lord was teaching a large group of people in a house when four men brought a paralyzed man on a stretcher to the Lord to be healed but they could not gain entrance to the house because of the crowd (vv. 2-3). Therefore, they carried the paralytic to the roof top, broke through the roof (perhaps removing tiles) and then lowered the disabled man down to Christ through the hole (v. 4). When the Lord saw the faith of the four men and that of the paralytic who desired to be lowered down to Him, despite the possibility of injury, He said to the paralytic, *"Son, your sins are forgiven"* (v. 5).

When the scribes heard this statement, they said within themselves, *"This Man blasphemes!"* for only God can forgive sins (vv. 6-7). Because the Lord Jesus said that He had the authority to forgive sins, He was claiming to be God, which infuriated Israel's religious leaders. The Lord, overhearing their thoughts, asked them two questions (v. 8). First, He asked them why they thought evil of Him for this declaration; if they truly understood who He was, then they would not think that He was blaspheming God. Second, He asked them, *"Which is easier, to say to the paralytic, 'Your sins are forgiven,' or to say, 'Arise, take up your bed and walk'?"* (v. 9). The Lord was implying that it was easier for man to engage in religious jargon than to produce spiritual change in one's life.

As the forgiveness of sins was a spiritual matter, it could not be humanly verified. Hence, one could say, "Your sins are forgiven" without knowing if it were true or not (v. 10). Therefore, to prove that He did have the authority to forgive sins, the Lord commanded the paralytic, *"arise, take up your bed, and go to your house"* (v. 11). This activity could be visually verified. The paralytic was instantly healed and gained the ability to use his muscles in such a way as to carry his bed while walking to his home. The healed man did not have to struggle to do what the Lord commanded him to do (i.e., he did not have to learn to walk). Again, we see the Lord not just healing someone, but also fully equipping them to obey what He said to do. When the multitudes saw the miracle, they marveled and glorified God that a mere human could have such power to heal (v. 12).

This scene conveys a wonderful truth about repentance and faith. The Lord Jesus said that unless people repent of their sins, they cannot be saved (Luke 13:3, 5). Confession of sin is necessary for forgiveness to be granted (e.g., Luke 17:3). We also know that unless someone believes on Christ as Savior, he or she cannot be saved (John 3:16-18, 5:24). Repentance and faith swing on the same hinge of gospel truth. Repentance agrees with God on the matter of sin and turns away from what displeased God and could never earn His favor. But one must turn from sin to embrace in faith God's solution for sin, Christ. So, although the paralytic did not confess his sin before receiving forgiveness, the Lord knew the condition of the man's heart by the evidence of his faith in Him. The Lord used the incident to again declare to Israel's leaders that He was God's Son and their Messiah.

The Call of Matthew (vv. 13-17)

The Lord then went to the Sea of Galilee at Capernaum to teach the multitudes (v. 13). His teaching ministry was ongoing in that city, and one day He walked by a tax office and saw a man named Levi (Matthew) sitting within. The Lord said to him, *"Follow Me"* (v. 14). Matthew instantly obeyed the invitation and was a tax collector no more. Because tax collectors were notoriously crooked and collected for personal gain more from the people than Rome required, they were hated by the Jews. Matthew had probably been disavowed by his Jewish parents for engaging in this occupation. But on this day, he left a lucrative and hated occupation to become a poor but beloved disciple of Christ, who wrote the Gospel according to Matthew for us to appreciate.

After being called to be a disciple, Matthew (Levi) hosted a large gathering in his own home in or near Capernaum so that others, including tax collectors, could hear Christ's teachings (v. 15; Luke 5:29). The sight of Christ eating a meal with tax collectors and sinners infuriated the Pharisees who asked His disciples why He did so (v. 16). When the Lord heard their indictment, He said, *"Those who are well have no need of a physician, but those who are sick. I did not come to call the righteous, but sinners, to repentance"* (v. 17).

The Pharisees believed that they were spiritually well and righteous before God; therefore, they did not need to repent and be saved by Jesus Christ. However, the outcasts of society, like the tax collectors, being less hindered by self-righteousness, were more open to listen to the Lord's message. These sinners were more willing to acknowledge the true condition of their souls and seek God's forgiveness through Christ. The fact is, wherever the Lord went, He associated with sinners, for He came to seek and to save the lost. The self-righteous Pharisees did not want what the Lord was offering them, so He did not waste time speaking to those who had no interest in His message of salvation.

For this reason, Matthew informs us that the Lord told the Pharisees, *"But go and learn what this means: 'I desire mercy and not sacrifice.' For I did not come to call the righteous, but sinners, to repentance"* (Matt. 9:13). This quotation from Hosea 6:6 was to prove that God did not want ritualistic worship and cold religiosity from those who called upon Him, but rather inward humility, righteousness, and holiness. The Pharisees looked good outwardly, but inwardly, they were just as lost as the tax collectors; they were in a much more dangerous situation, as they did not believe that they were lost before God.

The Disciples Do Not Fast (vv. 18-22)

John the baptizer was likely in prison when John's disciples came to the Lord Jesus with a question about fasting (v. 18). Apparently, they were fasting often, as were the Pharisees, but they had noticed that the Lord's disciples were not fasting. The Lord affirmed that His disciples were not given to fasting because the bridegroom (Himself) was still with them, but soon He would not be – then they would regularly fast (vv. 19-20). His answer indicated that a new dispensation was coming.

A dispensation in Scripture is not an era of time per se, but rather an economy of truth that God reveals to man and holds him accountable to obey. Dispensations do have their outworking in time and may overlap to some extent. For example, the dispensation of human government established in Genesis 9 was concurrent with the dispensation of the Law instituted with Israel at Mount Sinai and is still in effect during the present dispensation of grace (i.e., the Church Age).

The Lord cited two examples (these were likely His first spoken parables), a new cloth on an old garment and new wine in an old wineskin, to show that the purposes of the dispensations of the Law and of Grace were quite different (vv. 21-22). The Law of Moses was rigid in that, if broken, it did not offer mercy, only condemnation. Accordingly, Paul explains that the purpose of the Law was to show sin (Rom. 3:20) and point guilty sinners to the solution – Christ (Gal. 3:24). The Law only brought condemnation, as no one could keep all of its precepts. But grace through Christ was offered to those who realized that they had fallen short of God's righteousness and needed to be justified by Him to be acceptable before Him (1 Tim. 2:3-6). Grace is receiving the unmerited favor of God.

In summary, lost souls may approach God through law-keeping (i.e., by self-justification) and be found wanting, or by humbly acknowledging their sinful state and receiving redemption and justification through Christ by grace. Consequently, the purpose of both parables was to show that one can choose to live by the Law or by Grace, but not both; the two systems cannot be mixed (Rom. 4:4-5). The purpose of the first was to show the necessity of the second for salvation.

Both parables illustrate this point. A piece of new cloth (unshrunk material) is a poor patch for an old garment, for after it becomes wet and dries, it will shrink and pull away from the old cloth. The latter situation creates a worse outcome than the original problem. Likewise, those trying to mix efforts of self-reformation with God's work of grace will become more resistant to the truth of the gospel message, which has its basis in grace alone.

For the same reason, putting new wine in an old wineskin (which has no elasticity) will result in a bad outcome. As the new wine ferments, it will expand and burst the old wineskin, making it unusable. It would have been better to hold to the law alone than to try to mix Law-keeping with God's grace for salvation. Grace plus a nickel is not grace!

The Law was stringent and rigid; its purpose was to condemn, not to save. The Law was designed to highlight man's lost state before God and show his need for God's Savior. Because Christ was born under the Law and completely kept the Law, He was proven an acceptable substitute for sacrifice on the account of the guilty (i.e., everyone). Through the process of substitution, then, God was able to righteously judge human sin and offer forgiveness and acceptance through Christ. This means that those who resort to Law-keeping to earn God's favor instead of believing in Christ's redemptive work alone are telling God, "Your Son did not do enough to save me; You need my help too." This is an offensive notion to God. Let us be careful of mixing any elements of the Law with all that God wants us to appreciate in grace!

Laboring on the Sabbath Controversy (vv. 23-28)

While venturing through ripened grainfields near Capernaum on the Sabbath Day, the Lord's hungry disciples plucked and ate a few heads of grain (v. 23). Their actions were abruptly challenged by the Pharisees who said, *"Look, why do they do what is not lawful to do on the Sabbath?"* (v. 24). The Pharisees' accusation afforded the Lord Jesus with an opportunity to rebuke their religious pride, which had blinded them from comprehending who He really was. He was not the son of a fornicator, nor a Samaritan, nor a man possessed by demons, as they claimed. Rather, He was their Messiah – the Son of God. The Lord's rebuttal contained one historical illustration and a reference to priestly temple service.

First, the Lord Jesus reminded them of what David and his men had done to alleviate their hunger; they entered the house of God (the tabernacle located at Nob) and ate the showbread (vv. 25-26). Only the priests were allowed into the house of God and only the priests could eat the twelve unleavened cakes, and then only on the Sabbath Day. Yet, David and his men were not punished by God for their actions. Why? It was because David was a righteous man, God's chosen man, who had been rejected by the nation under King Saul's reign. Given their dire and unjust situation, their necessary action was permitted – it would never have occurred if David had been treated properly by Saul.

This historical example was chosen for its direct correlation between David and his men and the Lord and His disciples. Just as David's leadership had been rejected by the nation under Saul's reign, the Pharisees had prompted the people to reject Jesus Christ as their Messiah. If the Pharisees had received Jesus as their Messiah, His disciples would not have been scavenging for food.

It is at this juncture that Matthew informs us that Christ addressed the key matter: *"But if you had known what this means, 'I desire mercy and not sacrifice,' you would not have condemned the guiltless"* (Matt. 12:7). God is not heartless; He values mercy, compassion, and kindness much more than mechanical rituals and pious traditions. *"The Sabbath was made for man, and not man for the Sabbath"* (v. 27). The Sabbath forced man to regularly pause and remember his Creator.

The Pharisees had become uncaring; they valued cold religious formality more than pursuing the heart of God and making Him rightly known among the people as a good and generous God. The Lord punctuated this point by declaring Himself as the Lord of the Sabbath (v. 28). Since He was the one who had instituted the Sabbath, He was the best one to declare its meaning. In both an authoritative and a practical sense, He was doing what the Pharisees had failed to do – display the full merciful and gracious character of God. Yes, there was One standing before them who was greater than the temple – He was the Lord of the Sabbath and the rightful heir to the throne of David.

Is it possible for believers today to fall into the same religious snare which hindered the Pharisees from more fully knowing God? Though Christians understand that the Lord Jesus is their Savior, they may still suffer from pharisaical pride and misrepresent His character to others. Regrettably, some Christians value symbolic truth and Church order to the extent that commonsense would not rule their actions in unusual situations. In the normative sense, symbolic truth, scriptural principles, and God-ordained order are to be demonstrated in meetings of the Church. But in some circumstances, there may be weightier matters to consider than form.

For example, if a sister noticed that one end of the Church building was ablaze, there would be nothing wrong with her blurting out a public alarm during a church meeting, although normally she would have refrained from speaking publicly (1 Cor. 14:34). Is not religious form less important than saving lives?

A Pharisee, however, would value sacred form over all else – no exceptions. We should follow what Scripture teaches, but let us not neglect to display God's gracious character to others when unusual circumstances do arise – in so doing we demonstrate to others that we know more about the Lord than just His name and His teachings.

> I believe that a great number of people are going to die and go to hell because they're counting on their religiosity in the church instead of their relationship with Jesus to get them to heaven. They give lip service to repentance and faith, but they've never been born again.
>
> – Adrian Rogers

Mark Chapter 3

Healing on the Sabbath Controversy (vv. 1-5)

The Lord ceased His dialogue with the Pharisees, but then ventured into "their" synagogue on the following Sabbath day (v. 1; Matt 12:9; Luke 6:1). A week earlier, He had proclaimed that *"the Son of Man was the Lord even of the Sabbath"* (2:28). He, as God, had created the Sabbath for man, and therefore, He was the One who could best explain its meaning and purpose. The Lord Jesus would validate His claim by performing a miracle on the Sabbath, which would also illustrate the purpose the Lord of the Sabbath had for His Sabbath.

There was a man with a withered hand present in the synagogue and the Pharisees were watching the Lord to see if He would heal the man on the Sabbath day (v. 2). Looking for an opportunity to accuse the Lord of wrongdoing, Matthew states that the Pharisees even asked Him, *"Is it lawful to heal on the Sabbath?"* (Matt. 12:10). According to Mark, the Lord asked the man with a withered hand to step forward and then He posed a question to the Pharisees, *"Is it lawful on the Sabbath to do good or to do evil, to save life or to kill?"* (v. 4).

The Pharisees did not answer the Lord's question. It is noted that during the Maccabean revolt in second century B.C. the Jews did engage in warfare on the Sabbath day. The Lord never meant for His people to be slaughtered by invaders if attacked on the Sabbath.

Matthew tells us that the Lord further expounded on His question by pointing out the fact that any one of the Pharisees would rescue one of his sheep if it had fallen into a pit on the Sabbath day (Matt. 12:11). Yet, to God, a man is much more valuable than a sheep; so, it would be *"lawful to do good on the Sabbath"* (Matt. 12:12). Showing compassion and selfless love to others always honors God regardless of what day it is.

The self-righteous, coldhearted attitudes of the Pharisees angered the Lord. According to their oral law, one could not make a sick person better on the Sabbath, as that would be considered work. As Israel's leaders, they were to exemplify God's holy and loving character to the people but were failing miserably to do so. The Lord demonstrated what He had been teaching about the Sabbath and the true nature of God by commanding the man with the withered hand to stretch his hand out. The man obeyed the Lord, and the Lord immediately and fully restored the disabled man's hand (v. 5). There was now no functional difference between either of his hands.

More Miracles Performed by Christ (vv. 6-12)

Rather than praising God for the miracle performed, the Pharisees were enraged that Christ had healed the man on the Sabbath day. The Lord could have healed the man the next day but chose not to. Why should the man suffer his disability even one more day when the Lord had the power to heal the man?

Additionally, the situation provided a perfect opportunity for the Lord to confront the coldhearted attitudes of the Pharisees. Rather than being amazed by the miracle or rejoicing with the healed man, the Pharisees wanted to kill the One that performed the good deed. They began plotting with the Herodians against Him, as to *"how they might destroy Him"* (v. 6).

The Lord knew all about their plans, so He withdrew from the area and continued preaching to the multitudes (v. 7). The Lord withdrew to the Sea of Galilee and a great multitude from Galilee, Jerusalem, Idumea, and even some from as far as Tyre and Sidon followed Him (v. 8). The eager crowd was immense and "pressed about Him" to the extent that the Lord told His disciples to keep a boat ready in case He needed to withdraw from the situation (vv. 9-10).

Mark informs us that when demon-possessed people were brought before the Lord, they fell before Him and shrieked, *"You are the Son of God"* (v. 11). Christ healed all those coming to Him with their infirmities, yet He requested that those healed not publicize what He had done for them (v. 12). Matthew explains why the Lord requested this in verse 17 by quoting Isaiah (Isa. 41:9, 42:1-4). Jesus Christ was God's Servant and their Messiah and, therefore, a Conqueror, but as they had witnessed by His ministry, He was gentle and tenderhearted towards them. He was not seeking fame and honor for Himself, but rather expending Himself to selflessly serve others (Matt. 12:18-21).

The Twelve Are Chosen (vv. 13-21)

The Lord went up on a mountain to pray and called those to Him that He wanted to be His disciples (v. 13). Luke tells us that the Lord prayed throughout the night before commissioning His disciples the next day (Luke 6:12). This highlights the importance of God's people engaging in adequate prayer before making important ministry decisions.

Additionally, Matthew states that the Lord chose His twelve disciples shortly after instructing them to pray that *"the Lord of the harvest would send out laborers into His Harvest"* (Matt. 9:38). The next verse tells us how the Lord answered His disciples' prayers for more laborers in the fields of harvest:

> *And when He had called His twelve disciples to Him, He gave them power over unclean spirits, to cast them out, and to heal all kinds of sickness and all kinds of disease* (Matt. 10:1).

Mark records the same information but adds that the Lord chose the twelve *"that they might be with Him"* while they served Him in gospel ministry (v. 14). Mark again affirms this working relationship after Christ's ascension. while the Lord Jesus would be in heaven during the Church Age, He would be "working with them," speaking of His laborers on earth (16:20). As Moses declared in Exodus 33, if God's people do not have God's presence (His communion and fellowship), what they do is a complete waste of time. Just hours before His crucifixion the Lord told His disciples, *"Without Me you can do nothing"* (John 15:5).

Verse 14 in conjunction with Matthew 9:38 reveals two important truths for us to consider: First, the Lord Jesus is the Lord of the harvest, for He is the one sending and equipping laborers for the work of harvesting souls.

Second, prayer was used to both burden and prepare the disciples to answer the call for needed laborers. They, themselves, were the answer to their own prayers concerning the need for laborers. This shows the transforming power of prayer and that we should be willing to simply pray for what needs we are made aware of without presupposing what God's solution might be. We just might be God's answer to our own prayers also.

Mark lists the names of the twelve apostles that were sent out: *"Simon, to whom He gave the name Peter; James the son of Zebedee and John the brother of James, to whom He gave the name Boanerges, that is, "Sons of Thunder"; Andrew, Philip, Bartholomew, Matthew, Thomas, James the son of Alphaeus, Thaddaeus, Simon the Canaanite; and Judas Iscariot, who also betrayed Him"* (vv. 16-19).

Although it was Andrew who first introduced his brother Peter to the Lord, the inner circle of disciples closest to the Lord later became Peter, James, and John. The Lord referred to the latter two brothers as the "Sons of Thunder." James was the first of the twelve to be martyred in the Church Age (killed by Herod; Acts 12:2). John was the "beloved" disciple and the one to whom the Lord entrusted the care of His mother to (John 19:26). All four men were fishermen by trade before following Christ.

Philip was from Bethsaida and introduced Nathanael (or Bartholomew), the man without guile, to the Lord (John 1:47). Thomas had doubts about Christ's resurrection later, but also declared Christ as Lord and God (John 20:28). Matthew was a former tax collector and likely the wealthiest of the disciples called into ministry; he wrote the Gospel of Matthew. Not much is known about James, the less, the son of Alphaeus; Thaddaeus (also called Judas and Lebbaeus), the son of James (Luke 6:16); Simon, the Canaanite, previously a Jewish Zealot that opposed Roman rule (Luke 6:15). Judas Iscariot betrayed the Lord.

After choosing His disciples, they entered a house to eat bread, but so many people had gathered to see Jesus that it was not possible for them to enjoy a meal together (v. 20). Those who knew Jesus, apparently from Nazareth, tried to rescue Him from the intense situation, saying, *"He is out of His mind"* (v. 21). They were implying that no one in their right mind would want to live under these kinds of circumstances. But the Lord was heavenly-minded, which trumps all earthly-reasoning.

Blasphemy of the Holy Spirit (vv. 22-30)

Not only did the scribes and Pharisees reject Christ's message, but they also accused Him of performing a counterfeit miracle because He was in league with Beelzebub, the ruler of the demons (v. 22). Beelzebub means "Lord of the dung flies." First, the Lord pointed out that such a conclusion was not logical because a kingdom divided against itself cannot be sustained (vv. 23-24). Hence, if Satan casts out Satan, how can his kingdom stand (vv. 25-26)?

Second, the Lord pointed out that Jewish exorcists (the Pharisees' sons, so to speak; Matt. 12:27) claimed to cast out demons. Although the Lord did neither affirm nor deny their assertion, His point was that they too must be in league with Satan, for if the power to cast out demons came from Satan, then whoever exercised that power was under Satan's authority. But the Jewish exorcists would strongly reject such a notion; they believed that God was enabling them to perform exorcisms. This meant that the Jewish exorcists would judge the Pharisees as being inconsistent in their reasoning by concluding that Jesus Christ had cast out demons by Satan's authority. The Lord then states a more logical conclusion: If He was casting out demons by the Spirit of God, then certainly the kingdom of God had come. For the kingdom of God to be powerfully proclaimed by Christ meant that the "strong man" of the house (Satan's authority on earth) must first be constrained (v. 27).

There could be no middle ground in this matter; one must believe who the Lord Jesus proclaimed Himself to be – God's sent Messiah – or reject His claim and remain under Satan's control. There are only two authorities in the world today – God's authority and Satan's rebellious authority, which our Sovereign Creator limits to accomplish His own purposes. Thus, the Lord concluded, *"He who is not with Me is against Me, and he who does not gather with Me scatters abroad"* (Matt. 12:30).

Third, the Lord had a stern message for the Pharisees; they had committed the unpardonable sin: *"Assuredly, I say to you, all sins will be forgiven the sons of men, and whatever blasphemies they may utter; but he who blasphemes against the Holy Spirit never has forgiveness but is subject to eternal condemnation"* (vv. 28-29).

First, notice that there are different forms of sin and blasphemy and that forgiveness for these offenses is possible. Second, a specific sin entitled *"blasphemy against the Holy Spirit"* is unforgivable, and this specific sin relates to a particular age. "In this age" relates to the public ministry in which Christ was presently engaged. "The age to come" relates to His Second Advent to restore Israel and establish His kingdom on earth. In between these ages of Messiah's initial offer and rejection, and second offer and reception, is the Church Age. During the Church Age, Christ is not personally on the earth declaring the "Kingdom Gospel" message to the lost house of Israel and working miracles to authenticate His message. During the Tribulation Period, the kingdom message will be again preached (Matt. 24:14), and Israel shall be converted (Zech. 10:12; Matt. 24:30).

The specific sin that the Pharisees had committed was to ascribe a miracle which Christ had done through the power of the Holy Spirit to

Beelzebub, the prince of the demons (v. 22). They implied that Christ had an unclean spirit and was under demonic control (v. 30).

These hard-hearted, stiff-necked religious leaders had not only rejected the gospel message of Christ and His miracles, but they rendered insults in return for His acts of love and kindness. Because of their intense disbelief which was expressed in disdain for the Person of Christ and the working of the Holy Spirit, they had ruthlessly insulted God. The Pharisees' rejection of Christ was so intense that the Holy Spirit would no longer work with their consciences to lead them to salvation. Without His help, it is impossible for anyone to believe the gospel message (1 Cor. 2:9-13). They were dead in their sins and already condemned. (Everyone is born "condemned already" in Adam; John 3:18.) Though the sin of disbelief still occurs today and keeps people from being saved, this specific unpardonable sin cannot be committed today, for the Lord is in Glory and not before us, pleading, preaching, and doing miracles.

The fact that some still worry about committing the "unpardonable sin" is a good indication that the Spirit of God is still working to bring them to Christ, otherwise there would be no concern about the matter. Thus, the only sin which can be called unforgivable and that is still possible to commit today is the sin of disbelief – rejection of Jesus Christ ensures one's eternal condemnation (John 3:36).

A New Relationship (vv. 31-35)

While the Lord Jesus was still speaking, He was informed by someone in the audience that His mother and brothers had arrived and desired to speak to Him (vv. 31-32). The Lord used this interruption and information to speak of a spiritual union that was more intimate than natural relationships. He asked, *"Who is My mother or My brothers"* (v. 33)? Then, while pointing to His disciples, He answered His own question: *"Here are My mother and My brothers"* (v. 34)! He then clarifies that those who do the will of His Father in heaven are His family (v. 35). Those trusting in Him were His spiritual family forever.

The Lord was not belittling His earthly family or denying His love for them, but rather highlighted that having a spiritual relationship with Him was much more important. Our natural relationships all end with death, but our spiritual union with Christ lasts forever. In Him is life and in His presence unspeakable joy and satisfaction.

Mark Chapter 4

The Sower and the Soils (vv. 1-20)

Because a great multitude had gathered to Him by the sea, the Lord entered a boat, which was pushed out a short distance from shore. He then faced the people on shore and spoke parables to them while sitting in the boat (vv. 1-2). The Lord Jesus intentionally spoke in parables to reveal truth, but in a partially-veiled manner. The parables were not just enjoyable stories but served as a test to the hearers. The casual onlooker, the "window shopper," would hear and not understand, nor would he or she desire any more insight concerning the parable – "thanks for the good story." But those longing to understand the spiritual significance of the parable would seek the Lord for further instruction (vv. 10-12). Yet, those who merely enjoyed the story would go their own way without ever learning God's message to them. Often it was only the Lord's disciples who sought to learn the deeper meaning of His stories and were given understanding of their meanings (v. 34). By design, then, a parable is concealed truth that tests the heart of each one who hears the story.

The Jews were a nation composed of shepherds and farmers. So, when the prophets Hosea (Hos. 10:12-13) and Jeremiah (Jer. 4:3) had sternly warned them centuries earlier to plow up their fallow ground, they understood the analogy. Fallow ground is soil that was once cultivated, but now lies waste and is completely fruitless. The longer it remains uncultivated, the harder it becomes; such is the nature of the human heart that rejects God's Word. For fallow ground to be made profitable again, it must be broken up with a plow; only then can it be planted and made fruitful. The purpose of this Old Testament soil analogy was to call Israel to repentance. The Lord continues that message in the parable of *The Sower and the Soils* (vv. 3-9).

After the multitude departed and the Lord was alone with His disciples, they asked Him about the meaning of the parable (v. 10). The Lord responded to their inquiry by saying:

> *To you it has been given to know the mystery of the kingdom of God;*
> *but to those who are outside, all things come in parables, so that*
> *"Seeing they may see and not perceive, and hearing they may hear and*
> *not understand, lest they should turn, and their sins be forgiven them"*
> (vv. 11-12).

By quoting Isaiah 6:9-10, the Lord Jesus was affirming that He was declaring God's kingdom message to the nation of Israel in such a way that showed that their calloused hearts would not embrace it in faith. If they had been exercised in their minds by Christ's teachings, they would have sought to understand more fully what He was declaring, but they did not. They were satisfied to listen to a story but were not inclined to apply its spiritual implication in a personal way.

However, His disciples did want to understand what the parable of *The Sower and the Soils* meant. The Lord then explained the particulars of the story to them (vv. 13-20).

The ground in which the seed (God's Word) is sown is likened to the various dispositions of the human heart. Four types of "soils" or hearts are identified: the wayside, stony, thorny, and fruitful ground.

The key components of this parable must be properly identified if we are to understand its meaning:

The seed = the Word of God (specifically the Kingdom message).

The sower = Christ primarily.

The soils = various human hearts (i.e., as God knows them).

The birds = Satan's opposition to God's Word being shared.

The sun = persecution and suffering.

The thorns = the influence of humanism and worldly affairs.

The plant = the visible evidence of God's Word at work.

The fruit = the visible evidence of true salvation.

The wayside = someone with no time for or interest in God's Word.

The stony ground = someone emotionally affected by God's Word.

The thorny ground = those who allowed worldliness to negate the Word.

This parable represents the proclamation and offering of the kingdom to Israel by a sower, who primarily represents Christ, but may include John the baptizer also (Matt. 3:2, 4:17). The seed in the parable is God's

Word, which is "living and powerful" (Heb. 4:12). A seed contains life and God's Word offers life to those who will receive it in faith. Specifically, the seed in this parable represents the kingdom message offered by Christ to the Jewish nation; this invitation could not be received without genuine repentance. The various soils represent the spiritual disposition of human hearts that God's message would confront. Only those having a softened and prepared heart received God's message and became fruitful to Him.

The birds depict Satan's adverse efforts to oppose the receipt of God's Word once sown among the populace. Birds are often used in Scripture to metaphorically convey satanic opposition. For example, even after Abram had obeyed God's word and prepared animals and birds for an offering, he still had to drive the unclean birds from devouring his sacrifice until later in the day when God confirmed His covenant with him (Gen. 15). Satan was opposing God's covenant with Abram and thus the forthcoming Messiah that would come through it – the One who would bless all families of the earth (Gen. 12:3). Likewise, in this parable, the birds symbolize Satan's evil influence and operations to oppose the efforts of Messiah to establish His kingdom on earth.

Many have interpreted the visible plant in the parable as a sign of conversion and regeneration, but the Lord clarifies in the explanation that is not the case. What is seen above the ground is a counterfeit life because the plant does not have a root of faith below the ground (i.e., in the heart). Only God sees what is in each of our hearts, that is, what is below the ground in the parable. We can only see the outward manifestation of the heart in visible behavior. The plants in this parable represent the visible evidence that the Word of God has had an impact on a person's heart, but it is not necessarily conversion.

Some people feel conviction and guilt after being confronted with the gospel message and respond by self-reformation, rather than by true repentance and acceptance of Christ. In time, trials (intense sunlight) and the cares of the world (the thorns) reveal the true reality of things – no true conversion (there is no root below ground). In this parable, the plants associated with the stony and thorny ground do not represent true life, but merely an emotional response to God's Word. Only the ground that produced fruit represents a true conversion – there can be no fruitfulness to God unless His seed has produced a root of faith in the human heart.

Previously, the Lord had affirmed that a tree bears fruit according to its character (Matt. 7:17-18). Like trees, people display their spiritual nature by what they do: *"Therefore by their fruits you will know them"* (Matt. 7:20). Only true believers can bear good fruit (i.e., do what God appreciates). This means that at times we may be conned by well-meaning, moral, and Christ-identifying people, but the Lord is not fooled by the facade of an unregenerate person. In fact, the Lord said there are many who will identify with Him but have not trusted Him for salvation; hence, they do not do the will of His Father (Matt. 7:21-23). Clearly, it is possible to know a lot about the Lord and do things in His name without ever being born again. The Lord knows who are truly His and who the counterfeits are. Many identifying with Christ, even calling Him Lord, are not actually saved. The true test of knowing and serving the Lord is found in our desire to do God's will – this is true fruit-bearing. Only those who do the will of God are really His people (Mark 3:35).

The following summarizes the four kinds of soils identified in this parable. The wayside: The heart that has no interest in the things of God and blatantly rejects the gospel message. The Word had no visible influence on the hearer. The stony ground: The heart in which the Word of God did not penetrate deep enough to cause the reality of new birth. These people are mere professors in religious camouflage; they had an emotional response to the gospel message instead of brokenness and repentance before God. A little suffering shows them for who they really are. The thorny ground: The heart in which the Word of God causes the individual to feel guilt and to change his or her conduct through self-effort, but because there is no true conversion, the cares of the world quickly choke out the effect of God's Word in this life. The good ground: The heart that is well-prepared and receives the Word of God by faith alone unto salvation. True salvation is evidenced by fruit-bearing.

The Lamp of Truth (vv. 21-25)

Still speaking to His disciples privately, the Lord affirmed that a lit lamp is set on a stand to illuminate its surroundings (v. 21). For this reason, it would be ridiculous to put a burning lamp under a bed; its light must be seen to be beneficial. Light portrays the meaning of undefiled truth in Scripture: *"God is light and in Him is no darkness at all"* (1 Jn. 1:5).

The Lord then charged them to live out the truth that they had heard from Him (vv. 22-23). To know the truth and intentionally hide it from others would ensure God's displeasure and personal consequences (v.

25). Likewise, those who live according to the truth they have heard will be rewarded with more understanding and opportunities to please God (v. 24). Nothing is hidden from God, and He will parentally judge all offenses against His character and Word which have been revealed to those who are His children. The disciples were thus exhorted to let their lights shine in a world that desperately needs to see Christ in their good works. Daily living out the truth would glorify their Father in heaven.

Mysterious Growth (vv. 26-29)

This parable closely aligns with the Kingdom Parable proclaimed earlier in this chapter – *The Sower and the Soils*. The kingdom of heaven contains the realm of profession: some will hear and receive the Kingdom message, while others will reject it. It is noteworthy that the man sowing the seed is also the one who raises the sickle to gather the harvest into the barn (vv. 26-29).

The key components of this parable are:

The seed = the Word of God (the gospel message).

The sower = Christ primarily (the disciples secondarily).

The ground = lost souls residing in the world.

The seed's mysterious growth = the work of the Holy Spirit.

The harvest = the ingathering of saved souls to heaven.

In the parable of *The Sower and the Soils*, Christ is seen as the primary sower, and indeed, He is the one who will return to harvest those who are His from the earth as inferred in this parable. The Holy Spirit illuminates the minds of those who hear the gospel message so that they may come under conviction for their sin and understand their guilt before God. In this fashion, the Holy Spirit woos condemned sinners to Christ for salvation. Those who repent and respond in faith are regenerated by the Holy Spirit (1 Cor. 6:11; Tit. 3:5) and are waiting to be harvested from the earth by Christ.

While this seems to be the primary meaning of the *Mysterious Growth* parable, the Lord may have told this story to encourage the disciples and future disciples to labor hard for the harvest to come. Perhaps this is why the story is only recorded in Mark's Gospel, which presents the lowly Servant of Jehovah exhausting Himself to serve others. In this view, the sower of the seed (the one preaching that salvation is in Christ) does not know who will believe the message and be spared judgment or who will reject it and remain in their natural condemnation as a descendant of Adam (John 3:18; Rom. 5:12).

The one testifying of Christ to others does not fully understand the work of the Holy Spirit, the process of spiritual growth, nor what it will be like to be with Christ in heaven, yet he or she faithfully shares what they do know and are willing to leave the outcome with God. We can have confidence that when God's Word is shared with others, it will not return void (Isa. 55:11), for His words are *"spirit, and ... life"* (John 6:26).

Only the Holy Spirit can convict people of their sin, and need of righteousness before God (John 16:7-10). Only He can bring them to saving faith and give them the assurance that they are children of God – that is His business (Rom. 8:16). Believers are accountable to be witnesses for Christ in the world (Acts 1:8) and to share the gospel message as they are going from place to place (Matt. 28:19). We must do what we are supposed to do, so that God will do what only He can – save sinners! When the harvest of souls is full and ripe, Christ will come and gather what is His to Himself in heaven (1 Thess. 4:13-18).

The Mustard Seed (vv. 30-34)

In this parable the kingdom of heaven is compared to a mustard seed that quickly grew into an herb and then into a tree that birds could build their nests in (vv. 30-32). The mustard seed would be the smallest seed familiar to the Lord's audience, and represents the humble beginning of the kingdom, when it was relatively small, pure, and fruitful – becoming a fruitful herb as intended. This demonstrated the power of the Holy Spirit to develop and prosper the kingdom through the preaching of the gospel message. This analogy compares well with the first three centuries of the Church Age. Roman oppression during this time had a purifying effect on the Church and resulted in believers taking the message of salvation in Christ alone throughout the empire.

However, the mustard herb continued to grow at a supernatural rate beyond this healthy and fruitful state into a sizable tree which became home to many birds. The evil birds that stole the seed (the Word of God) in the parable of *The Sower and the Soils* (v. 4) find haven in the branches of the tree in this parable. This depicts Satan's evil influences in undermining the message, order, and mission given to the Church originally by Christ. The birds picture the many erroneous religious systems that are associated with Christ's name, but not founded in biblical truth.

Some have suggested that the birds in the branches speak of the kingdom's prosperity, but that is not how the Lord invokes the bird imagery in the kingdom parable series of Matthew 13. An enemy is present in the first four parables and is opposing God's kingdom. It is not until the crowd disperses and Christ is speaking privately with His disciples that the enemy of the kingdom disappears and God's ability to establish it is declared. Given these components, Warren Wiersbe discusses the parable's meaning:

> These facts suggest that the parable teaches an abnormal growth of the kingdom of heaven, one that makes it possible for Satan to work in it. Certainly "Christendom" has become a worldwide power with a complex organization of many branches. What started in a humble manner today boasts of material possessions and political influences.[86]

The tree with its many birds represents the condition of the kingdom of heaven in the later days of the Church Age; this reality may be referred to as Christendom. Christendom has many branches and would obviously include the true Church, but also the cults and various humanized movements that promote what is false and corrupt. In the last days, many will identify with Christ, but deny His deity, His headship (including His order for the Church), and His message of salvation. These religious establishments will deny such scriptural teachings as the Godhead (the Trinity), the eternality of the human soul, and the eternal punishment of the wicked.

Today, much of Christendom embraces false doctrine, and ignores God's expressed requirements for church leaders, roles among genders, and the Great Commission. In summary, Christendom, as pictured in the mustard tree, includes the true Church, but also many religious venues and people who are associated with Christ in name only. Christ has no fellowship with what opposes His authority and rule.

The key components of this parable are:

The mustard seed = the simple but powerful gospel message.

The mustard tree = Christendom.

The birds = Satan's corrupting influence on Christendom.

In Revelation 18:2, unclean birds are confined to a cage before being destroyed. During the Tribulation Period, Satan will work through the Antichrist and demonic deception and power to create an apostate religious system that will be ultimately destroyed. Clearly, in whatever age God's people live, they must avoid religious movements which result in unnatural spiritual unions with the world that deny Christ's headship.

Mark again affirms that Christ taught mainly by employing parables to test the validity of His audience's interest in His message (v. 33). Those who wanted to understand the meaning of His stories received further insight (v. 34).

Power Over the Wind and the Sea (vv. 35-41)

After leaving Peter's home and having a dialogue with three men concerning the cost of discipleship, the Lord entered a boat with His disciples to journey southeastward across the sea to the Gergesenes (Matt. 8:23). Mark informs us that it was evening when they departed Capernaum and that there were other smaller boats following them (vv. 35-36). The Lord went to the stern of the boat and laid down on a pillow and went to sleep (v. 38). As the disciples were rowing, a violent tempest suddenly arose, which caused huge waves to beat against the boat and fill it with water (v. 37).

Can you imagine the life of the Lord Jesus? Day in and day out, at any time of day or night, people were coming to Him with their problems and ailments, while others were continually rejecting His message. No wonder He fell asleep in the stern of a boat and did not wake up when the boat was being tossed to and fro in a violent storm.

The frantic disciples woke the Lord and pleaded with Him to save them, for they were perishing (v. 38). He then stood up and rebuked the wind and the sea, *"Peace, be still!"* and there was a sudden great calm (v. 39). The Lord then admonished His disciples, *"Why are you so fearful? How is it that you have no faith?"* (v. 40). Seeing this powerful feat, the disciples said to themselves, *"Who can this be, that even the winds and the sea obey Him?"* (v. 41).

Obviously, they were still growing in their understanding of who Jesus Christ is. He is the Son of God who created all things and by Him all things consist (John 1:3; Col. 1:17). In this instance, the Lord did not pray to His Father; He merely commanded nature to obey Him and the windstorm and turbulent sea were instantly calmed.

Mark Chapter 5

Power Over the Demons (vv. 1-20)

The Lord Jesus often cast out demons to heal the populace of their physical and mental infirmities and spiritual oppression. In this story, our Lord was willing to sail from the northwest to the southeast shore of the Sea of Galilee with His disciples to meet one demon-possessed man in much turmoil. This was the region of the Gadarenes (Gerasenes). The town of Gadara was about seven miles southeast of the seashore. The Lord teaches us through His actions to go the extra mile to assist those suffering affliction.

Matthew records that there were two "exceedingly fierce" demon-possessed men residing in the tombs near the shoreline (Matt. 8:28). These men were so violent that no one could safely travel through the area. Though there were two possessed men, the story centers around the one called Legion. We are not told if the other man was healed or not.

One of the possessed men immediately came out of the tombs to meet the Lord (v. 2). Luke tells us that he was naked and had been demon-possessed for a long time (Luke 8:27). He had often been shackled and chained but broke his bonds (vv. 3-4; Luke 8:29). Day and night the demoniac was screaming and cutting himself with stones (v. 5). His condition was one of utter misery. After seeing the Lord, he fell before Him and acknowledged His authority as the Son of God (v. 6). The demons speaking through the man were afraid that Christ had come early to render final judgment on them, but that was not the case (v. 7).

Notice that it is the demons that ramble on in the dialogue; the Lord spoke few words. He asked the man, "What is your name?" He responded "Legion" because many demons had entered him (v. 9; Luke 8:30). The Lord also commanded, *"Come out of the man, unclean spirit"* (v. 8). The demons answered the Lord, and yielded to His authority by coming out of the man and entering a large herd of swine (the new host that they had requested; vv. 10-12). The swine then ran violently off a cliff and perished in the sea (v. 13). The enemy often will use the tactic of verbal fogging to avoid accountability, but it does not work with the Lord. An entire legion of demons was cast out of the man.

But why would the Lord grant the demon's request to enter the swine? Scripture is silent on this matter, but William MacDonald offers two possible reasons:

> Why should the Sovereign Lord accede to the request of demons? To understand His action, we must remember two facts. First, demons shun the disembodied state; they want to indwell human beings, or, if that is not possible, animals or other creatures. Second, the purpose of demons is without exception to destroy. If Jesus had simply cast them out of the maniacs, the demons would have been a menace to the other people of the area. By allowing them to go into the swine, He prevented their entering men and women and confined their destructive power to animals. It was not yet time for their final destruction by the Lord.[87]

Additionally, it is observed that the Law deemed swine as unclean animals. The Jews were not to touch or eat, nor offer to the Lord what was unclean (Deut. 14:8). By permitting the demons to go into the swine, which brought about their destruction, the Lord was reproving His countrymen for their disobedience of the Law. The Lord demonstrates His authority over rebel spirits and disobedient men to the glory of God.

When the townsfolk heard of what happened, they came to investigate and found that the previously possessed man was sitting, clothed, and in his right mind. This meant that the one who had accomplished this miracle was more powerful than a multitude of demons and they were afraid; they even asked the Lord to leave the region (vv. 14-16). They did not want to receive the One who had shown Himself more powerful than an entire legion of demons (v. 17)!

Notice that the healed man was clothed. Perhaps a disciple donated clothing, but it seems more likely that Christ crossed the sea with every provision to resolve this man's pain and shame. If we decide to help someone, let us do our best to do the same.

The Lord Jesus is a perfect Gentleman, He will not force Himself on anyone, and so having been asked to leave by the people of the Gadarenes, He entered a boat with His disciples to depart (v. 18). The healed demoniac wanted to go wherever the Lord was going, but He instructed the man to remain in the region and tell family and friends how He had received God's compassion (v. 19). The man did so and proclaimed the incredible miracle throughout the region of Decapolis, and the people marveled at his testimony (v. 20). Those who have experienced God's grace have a story to tell that the unregenerate will never understand, until they, like the demoniac, humble themselves before the Lord Jesus and plead for mercy.

Christ Has Power Over Hemorrhaging and Death (vv. 21-43)

Having crossed back over the Sea of Galilee again, a large crowd quickly assembled shortly after the Lord and His disciples arrived (v. 21). One of the rulers of the synagogue, named Jairus, fell before the Lord and worshipped Him, saying, *"My little daughter lies at the point of death. Come and lay Your hands on her and she will live"* (vv. 22-23). His daughter was in a coma and near death (Luke 8:42). It seems that Jairus believed that his daughter was likely already dead by the time he was able to petition Jesus Christ for help (Matt. 9:18). Thus, Jairus' request was an incredible declaration of faith, as the last resurrection of the dead had not occurred since the days of the prophet Elisha, more than eight centuries previous. The Lord and His disciples agreed to follow Jairus to his home (v. 24).

While en route, a woman who had an ongoing flow of blood for twelve years touched the hem of the Lord's garment to be made well, and she was (vv. 25-29). Luke, the physician, mentions that this woman had spent all her livelihood on physicians, but no one could cure her hemorrhaging, which Mark states was worsening (v. 26; Luke 8:43) – that is, until she came to the Great Physician.

The Lord, knowing that power had come out of Him to accomplish the miracle, did not want the matter of the woman's faith and healing to be a secret, so He asked, *"Who touched My clothes?"* (v. 30). Of course, the disciples did not understand the Lord's question as they were trying to navigate through a large crowd of people as they followed Jairus. But the woman did, and she came trembling and fell at the Lord's feet and publicly confessed to what she had done and why (vv. 32-33). The Lord responded, *"Daughter, your faith has made you well. Go in peace, and be healed of your affliction"* (v. 34). Interestingly, "has made" and "well" in this statement are derived from the same Greek verb *sozo* in the perfect tense. *Sozo* is usually rendered "save" in the New Testament. Literally then, the woman's faith "saved her safe" forever. When Christ heals or saves, a permanent state of physical or spiritual wellness is always received.

True faith is always appreciated by the Lord. Because He chose to handle the situation in this manner, the woman who had been perpetually deemed *unclean* by the Law for years would now be able to resume normal life in Jewish society, for she had been healed and declared "well" by Jesus Christ. This is what Christ came to do: make those declared unclean by the Law, clean before God by grace through faith.

Immediately after this healing, a messenger informed Jairus that his daughter had died and there was no need to trouble *the Teacher* any longer, implying that all was lost (v. 35). Apparently, all attempts to revive her had failed and she was now past any hope of resuscitation. The Lord then encouraged a brokenhearted Jairus with these words, *"Do not be afraid only believe, and she will be made well"* (Luke 8:50).

Sometime later, the Lord arrived at Jairus' home which was crowded with wailing people and hired flute players (v. 38; Matt. 9:23). The Lord said to them, *"Why make this commotion and weep? The child is not dead, but sleeping"* (v. 39). It seems likely that the Lord knew the outcome of what He was about to do and did not want the fame of it to be publicized, so He poetically describes her as merely "sleeping" rather than being permanently dead. Paul also speaks of those who have died in Christ and are awaiting resurrection as being poetically "asleep" (e.g., 1 Thess. 4:13).

The crowd mocked this statement and the Lord responded by putting them all out of the house, especially the noisy, professional mourners (v. 40). The Lord only permitted the girl's parents and Peter, James, and John to accompany Him to where the dead girl was lying (v. 37; Luke 8:51). The Lord took the child's hand and said, *"Talitha, cumi,"* meaning, *"Little girl, I say to you, arise"* (v. 41).

To everyone's amazement, the girl (being about twelve years of age) immediately revived, arose from her bed, and walked about the room (v. 42). The Lord charged those who had observed the miracle to keep it secret and that her parents should give their daughter something to eat (v. 43). Again, the Lord not only resolved the problem (death) but did so in such a way that the girl was not living in a reduced condition, for she could walk about and digest food normally. This is the first recorded resurrection in the New Testament and the fourth in the whole of Scripture.

Mark Chapter 6

The Second Nazareth Visit and Rejection (vv. 1-6)

Luke records Christ's first visit and rejection in His hometown of Nazareth (Luke 4:16-30). On this occasion, the Lord Jesus ventured into a synagogue. He was handed a scroll of Isaiah to read from. After announcing that the Spirit of the Lord was upon Him, He read Isaiah 61 verse 1 and half of verse 2 and then closed the book, returned it to the attendant and sat down. With every eye in the synagogue fixed on Him, the Lord then declared, *"Today this Scripture is fulfilled in your hearing"* (Luke 4:21).

The Jews understood that the Lord was claiming to be the One Isaiah was prophesying of, that is, the Messiah. They became so enraged by His claim that after putting Him out of the synagogue and leading Him out of town, they sought to push Him over a cliff (Luke 4:29). But it was not His time to die, and He walked away through the crowd unharmed.

The Lord did not read the remaining portion of verse 2 or verse 3, as that content pertained to His second advent, when He will return to judge the nations and restore Israel to a proper place of honor: *"And the day of vengeance of our God; to comfort all who mourn, to console those who mourn in Zion..."* (Isa. 61:2-3). For Israel, the Lord's promise to comfort those who mourn will be realized after the Tribulation Period.

A few months later, Matthew and Mark record a second visit to Nazareth by the Lord and His disciples (vv. 1-6; Matt. 13:53-58). This was a bold decision by Christ, as earlier those in Nazareth sought to kill Him for what He taught in the synagogue. But His second visit to Nazareth during His Galilean ministry shows the Lord's compassion and tenacity for reaching the lost sheep of Israel.

On the Sabbath, the Lord returned to the synagogue and taught the people (v. 2). Those listening were astonished at His ability to teach and to do mighty works. The Lord's audience could not reconcile in their minds how a lowly carpenter's son, that they had watched grow up among them, could have such wisdom and ability to teach and to do mighty works. They asked among themselves, "Is this not the son of

Mary, whose brothers are James, Joses, Simon, and Judas and whose sisters are with us also?" (v. 3). God had blessed Mary and Joseph with a large family and the reference is to Jesus' half-brothers and half-sisters through Mary. The people could not see past Christ's upbringing and were thus offended at Him – who are you, a carpenter's son, to teach us anything? They were literally "repelled" by His *words*, His *wisdom*, and His *works*.

The Lord responded to their disdain by saying, *"A prophet is not without honor except in his own country, among his own relatives, and in his own house"* (v. 4). Because of their unbelief (i.e., rejection of the truth), He laid hands on a few sick people to heal them (v. 5). Their rejection of the truth was so profound that the Lord "marveled" at their unbelief (v. 6). Given the words and works that He had declared to His townsfolk, He was bewildered by their hostility. The Lord and His disciples departed Nazareth to continue their Galilean tour, and there is no record that He ever returned there again.

The Twelve Are Sent Throughout Galilee (vv. 7-13)

Matthew informs us that just prior to the disciples being sent throughout Galilee to preach the kingdom message, the Lord had instructed them to pray that *"the Lord of the harvest would send out laborers into His Harvest"* (Matt. 9:38). We now learn how the Lord answered His disciples' prayers for more laborers in the fields of harvest:

> *He called the twelve to Himself, and began to send them out two by two, and gave them power over unclean spirits. He commanded them to take nothing for the journey except a staff – no bag, no bread, no copper in their money belts – but to wear sandals, and not to put on two tunics* (vv. 7-9).

This verse reveals two important truths for us to consider: First, the Lord Jesus is the Lord of the harvest, for He is the one sending and equipping laborers for the work of harvesting souls.

Second, that prayer was used to both burden and prepare the disciples to answer the call for needed laborers. They, themselves, were the answer to their own prayers concerning the need for laborers. This shows the transforming power of prayer and that we should be willing to simply pray for what needs we are made aware of without presupposing what

God's solution might be. We just might be God's answer to our own prayers also.

The Lord not only commissioned His disciples to preach the Kingdom message in Galilee, but also gave them authority over unclean spirits and all kinds of ailments. Whenever the Lord places responsibility, He also fully equips His servants to accomplish all that He desires them to do. The disciples would also go out in pairs to ensure accountability and encouragement for the difficult ministry ahead.

The disciples had been uniquely equipped by the Lord to be His workers in the harvest. Believers today should not think that they have been given the same credentials or calling that the twelve were in the scene before us. Their equipping for the work was unique; their task was to preach the kingdom gospel, and to a specific audience, the lost sheep of Israel in Galilee. Although the Lord has not given His servants today the same specialized ministry of the twelve, He has given each believer a calling and spiritual gift(s) to accomplish it (Eph. 4:11-12).

The Lord told His disciples that their ministry was to be free of charge and that they were to depend on the Lord for their support (vv. 8-9). This would demonstrate that the nature of the kingdom message itself was founded in grace and not the Law. For those who would listen to their message, the disciples were to receive freely their hospitality (v. 10). But for those who rejected their message, they were to shake off the dust of their sandals as a testimony against them and go on to the next town with their message (v. 11).

For those rejecting the disciples' message, the Lord Jesus said that he would be less tolerant of them on judgment day than the wicked cities of Sodom and Gomorrah. How is it possible for the Lord to be more tolerant of wicked cities such as Tyre, Sidon, and Sodom in the day of judgment than the Jewish cities such as Chorazin, Bethsaida, and Capernaum (Matt. 11:20-24)? Because where God permits greater responsibility there will always be greater accountability. The former cities had little revelation of truth to reject (Sodom only had the half-hearted testimony of one carnal believer named Lot), but the latter cities had the Son of God standing in their midst and they rejected His message.

Just as there are different rewards in heaven for faithfulness, there are differing degrees of eternal judgment depending on how much truth was rejected (Luke 10:11-16, 12:41-48, 20:47). Everyone is given some divine truth to consider (e.g., creation demands a Creator, and the human conscience contains moral reckoning), but some receive more evidence and truth to consider; thus, they have more accountability with God.

Given their charge and empowerment, the disciples went out two by two throughout Galilee preaching the gospel of the kingdom which could not be received without repentance (v. 12). As they went, they cast out demons, and healed the sick after anointing them with oil (v. 13).

The Death of John the Baptizer (vv. 14-29)

We now have the story of John the baptizer's murder. Some thought that John was the prophesied return of Elijah or of the Prophet that Moses had foretold would come to Israel in a future day (v. 15). Herod had such high esteem for John that he thought that Jesus of Nazareth had somehow inherited John's power and authority after John had been executed, and in this sense, John had come back from the dead to haunt him (vv. 14, 16).

Herod the Great had at least fourteen children by eight different wives; Antipas and Philip were sons of Herod the Great, but were half-brothers. Herod Antipas apparently had an affair with his brother Herod Philip's wife, Herodias, after Philip settled permanently in Rome. Herodias left Philip and remained with Antipas in Palestine. Antipas divorced his wife (the daughter of Aretas, the king of Petra) to illegally marry his brother Philip's wife, and Herodias divorced her husband, which the Law did not permit. Herodias (the feminine form of Herod) was the granddaughter of Herod the Great, thus a niece to both her husbands, Philip and Antipas.

John rebuked their adultery publicly (v. 18). Although Herod esteemed John as a just and holy man (v. 20), he considered putting John to death to silence his public ridicule of his illicit relationship with Herodias. However, because he feared the people, who believed that John was a prophet, Herod chose to imprison John (v. 17). It is generally believed the John was imprisoned in Herod's royal palace/fortress at Machaerus, which faced Arabia on the southeast border of Herod's domain. Herod had several such residences.

John's imprisonment was unacceptable to Herodias, who had been publicly humiliated by John's rebuke (v. 19). She schemed with her daughter Salome to trick Herod into granting her a request (vv. 21-22). The young girl danced before Herod and his guests on his birthday, which pleased the tetrarch greatly. Herod, with an oath, asked the girl to make a request of Him and he would do it to show his appreciation (v.

23). The girl, following her mother's prompting, asked for John's head on a platter (v. 24). The pompous king had fallen into the feminine trap, and to save face, Herod had John executed (vv. 25-27). His head was brought to Herodias' daughter, who then brought it to her mother (v. 28). John's disciples claimed the prophet's body and buried it, then went and told the Lord Jesus what had happened (v. 29; Matt. 14:12).

The Disciples Return and a Season of Rest (vv. 30-32)

The disciples returned to the Lord from their evangelistic tour in Galilee with an exciting report of their ministry (v. 30). It was at about this time He heard the news of John's death. The Lord told His disciples that it was time to come aside (i.e., time to separate themselves from the crowds and daily ministry) to rest for a while (v. 31).

The Lord teaches us that there should be a legitimate time to grieve the loss of a loved one. Proper grieving requires time away from life's normal responsibilities to reflect and settle one's soul in prayer and reading His Word. The disciples departed in a boat *together* to journey to a deserted place to achieve solitude (v. 32). Notice that they did not isolate from each other during this time. To be free from responsibilities and distractions during the grieving process is important, but isolating from friends and family is dangerous. It is at such times as this that we need our closest friends and family members nearby to anchor our minds in the truth and to weep with us. To give a grieving person a hug from the Lord when the bottom has dropped out of their world is a tremendous blessing.

As we learn in the next verses, the crowds found the Lord and He ministered to them and fed them. Indeed, we should take time to mourn the death of a loved one, but the Lord shows us that there is also a time to get back to serving others.

Five Thousand Are Fed (vv. 33-44)

After an unknown time of solitude, the crowds became aware of their location and sought them (v. 33). When the Lord saw the multitude, He was moved with compassion for them (v. 34). On two different occasions, the Lord Jesus performed miracles to feed the multitudes that had gathered in remote locations to hear His message. Mark records the first event here and the second miracle in chapter 8. The feeding of the five thousand is the only miracle recorded in all four Gospels and signals the conclusion of Christ's two-year Galilean ministry. After this event, the Lord will travel to Phoenicia, Decapolis, Caesarea-Philippi, Judea, Perea, and then back to Jerusalem for His final days of ministry, culminating with His death, burial, and resurrection.

The first feeding miracle occurred in "a deserted place" (vv. 32, 35) that was remotely near Bethsaida according to Luke (Luke 9:10). However, John refers to the location being near Tiberias, a city on the western shore of the Sea of Galilee (John 6:23). Bethsaida is the hometown of Peter, Andrew, and Philip (John 1:44). But there were two towns that went by this name: Bethsaida Galilee (southwest of Tabgha) on the northwest shore of the Sea of Galilee and Bethsaida Julias on the northeast shoreline of the sea. Luke is apparently referring to Bethsaida Galilee as the location of the miracle, which is just north of the area that John identifies for the event. All this to say that the information contained in the Gospels is not sufficient to emphatically identify the exact location of this miracle; we can, however, speculate about its most probable location.

John, an eyewitness of these events, states that the feeding of the 5,000 occurred near Tiberias (John 6:23). The disciples departed from this location in a boat without the Lord and were told by Him to go to Bethsaida (v. 45). If Bethsaida Julias was meant, that would be a nine-mile journey to the northeast directly across the sea at night, which would be a risky venture. John records that the disciples rowed towards Capernaum, which would be in the direction of Bethsaida Galilee (John 6:17). This would be a safer trek northward as the shoreline would remain in sight (John 6:17).

However, a windstorm throughout the night hindered their progress northward until the Lord came to them walking on the sea in the fourth watch. After He entered the boat, He calmed the sea, and instantly moved the boat to a location just southwest of Capernaum (John 6:24), which allowed them to do ministry in Gennesaret the next day (v. 53). This agrees with John's statement that people came in boats from Tiberias to Capernaum looking for Jesus the next day and found Him (John 6:23-24). If the miracle occurred at Bethsaida Galilee, it might be possible for the news to have spread down to the people from Tiberias overnight, but it seems more likely that these seekers from Tiberias had witnessed the miracle themselves and sought Jesus in the most likely place they might find him, Capernaum. Capernaum was the Lord's home base, so to speak, during His Galilean ministry.

After a long day of ministry, the disciples came to the Lord and asked Him to send the people away, so that they could journey to surrounding villages and purchase food for themselves before nightfall overtook them (vv. 35-36). The Lord informed His disciples that there was no need to send the people away, but rather they should feed them (v. 37). John's account affirms that there were neither sufficient funds available, nor nearby resources to feed a crowd of this size. Moreover, the only food that the disciples had found was a boy's sack lunch of two fish and five loaves which Andrew had spied out (v. 38; John 6:9).

The Lord told His disciples to cause the people to sit down in the grass in groups of hundreds and fifties and to bring him the fish and the loaves (vv. 39-40). The Lord shows us the need for good administration to effectively serve others in the best way possible. God is a God of order, not chaos and confusion (1 Cor. 14:33); all that is done in His name should reflect His character.

After receiving what was available, the Lord gave thanks for the fish and the bread, broke the bread, and gave the fragments to the disciples to be passed out to the people (v. 41). After everyone had eaten their fill, there were twelve baskets full of fragments that remained (vv. 42-43). There was a basket for each serving disciple, and each received an abundant portion after their service was completed. This is a wonderful illustration that our serving must precede our reward for serving and it will be far more than we deserve! Additionally, everyone was completely satisfied with the Lord's provision. He fed an estimated 20,000 people (5,000 men, plus women and children; v. 44). The Lord Jesus satisfies all genuine need when we rest in Him. Help may not always come the way we expect it to or when we think it should, but the Lord's provision will never leave us disappointed!

Walking on Water and Calming a Storm (vv. 45-52)

After a long day of ministry, which included feeding a large crowd, it was time for the crowds to disperse. The Lord desired to be alone with His Father, so He told His disciples to enter a boat and cross the sea towards Capernaum (John 6:17). He would send the people away by Himself (vv. 45-47). Just before dark, the Lord saw His disciples in the midst of the sea and struggling to row against a contrary wind (v. 48). The Lord continued praying through the night and in the early dawn hours (the fourth watch was between 3 and 6 a.m.) the Lord came towards them walking on the rough sea (v. 48). John notes that they had rowed only three or four miles total since entering the boat (John 6:19).

Although it was not the Lord's intention, it seemed to the disciples that the Lord was going to pass them by, so they cried out to Him (v. 48). At first, they were terrified by His presence, thinking He was a ghost, but He comforted them with these words: *"Be of good cheer! It is I; do not be afraid"* (v. 50). Peter then said, *"Lord, if it is You, command me to come to You on the water"* (Matt. 14:28). Mark does not record Peter asking the Lord if he could join Him on the sea and then his brief excursion to do so.

The Lord then entered the boat and the impeding wind ceased and the boat was instantly moved across the sea to Capernaum, its intended destination (v. 51; John 6:21). Their half-day arduous trial was over. Mark notes that the disciples were *"greatly amazed ... beyond measure, and marveled"* at this feat. Although they were exhausted from hours of rowing and had not grasped the significance of the miraculous feeding of the 5000 (v. 52), they now humbled themselves before the Lord and worshipped Him, *"Truly you are the Son of God"* (Matt. 14:33).

This text reminds us that the Lord is completely cognizant of where we are at and what we are going through. The disciples were safer in that boat in a raging sea than anywhere else on earth because they were in the will of God. In fact, what they feared most, the sea, is what brought the Lord nearer to them. This is often the case in our own difficulties. The Lord did not force Himself into their hardship until they called out for Him; when they did, they were comforted by His presence and their grueling trial was over. The Lord longs to show Himself strong in our lives, but He will wait to be invited to do so.

Miracles at Gennesaret (vv. 53-56)

Apparently, the Lord conveyed their boat to the shoreline southwest of Capernaum so that they could do ministry in Gennesaret that day (v. 53). Many recognized the Lord, and the news of His arrival quickly spread throughout the region (v. 54). Those with infirmities were brought to Him for healing (v. 55). They had such faith in the Lord's ability that they believed if they merely touched the garment that Jesus was wearing, they would be healed. And as many that did so were *"made perfectly well"* (v. 56). There was no actual power in the garment, but by touching it, they were signifying in whom they were trusting for a miracle.

Mark Chapter 7

God's Commands and Man's Traditions (vv. 1-13)

Mark 6 records that the Lord Jesus was doing ministry in the land of Gennesaret with His disciples. Those in need throughout the region were coming to Him to be healed *"and as many as touched Him were made well"* (6:56). The scribes and Pharisees in Jerusalem heard about what was happening in Gennesaret and journeyed there to question the Lord (v. 1).

These religious leaders were locked into a negative, fault-finding frame of mind. Instead of observing the grace of God at work, all they could see was the disciples eating with unwashed hands (v. 2). The Pharisees immediately challenged the Lord on this matter, *"Why do Your disciples not walk according to the tradition of the elders, but eat bread with unwashed hands?"* (v. 5). All sorts of disabilities were being healed and illnesses cured, but what interested the Pharisees most was that the disciples were not ceremonially washing their hands before they ate bread as required by rabbinical tradition (v. 3).

Mark pauses the narrative in verses 3 and 4 to identify some of the non-biblical traditions that the Pharisees thought were important, such as washing of cups, pitchers, copper vessels, and couches. These man-made rules had nothing to do with maintaining good hygiene or with sanitation, but rather how one must keep ceremonially clean. The Lord's response condemned their cold hearts; they valued their vain traditions over true sincerity before God and the welfare of their countrymen:

Well did Isaiah prophesy of you hypocrites, as it is written: "This people honors Me with their lips, but their heart is far from Me. And in vain they worship Me, teaching as doctrines the commandments of men." For laying aside the commandment of God, you hold the tradition of men – the washing of cups, and many other such things you do" (vv. 6-8).

The Lord then supplied an example of their hypocrisy, *"All too well you reject the commandment of God, that you may keep your tradition"* (v. 9). He then reminded them of the honor one is to have for his or her parents by quoting the fifth of the Ten Commandments (v. 10; Ex. 20:9). Next, the Lord referred to the judgment that the Law required for those who dishonored their parents (Deut. 27:16).

The Lord then provides them an example of how their non-biblical traditions were undermining God's command to honor parents. He refers to their practice of *Corbin* (vv. 11-12). The rabbis taught that if you gave to God the funds required to care for (honor) one's aging parents, that was acceptable to God. William MacDonald describes how the practice of Corbin was abused:

> Suppose that certain Jewish parents were in great need. Their son had money to care for them, but didn't want to do it. All he had to do was say "Corban," implying that his money was dedicated to God or the temple. This relieved him of any further responsibility to support his parents. He might keep the money indefinitely and use it in business. Whether it ever was turned over to the temple was not important.[88]

Corban benefitted those neglecting their parents or Israel's religious leaders, but not neglected aging parents. By negating God's command, this human tradition made God appear as an ogre. How naive to rebuke the disciples for neglecting to wash their hands before they ate when the Pharisees were disregarding God's commands to fill their own coffers.

When human traditions replace God's commands, it is not superior spirituality that is exhibited, but vain piety. Likewise, we should remember that while particulars of our church meetings may change over time, we should never set aside Christ's order for His Church for what seems more profitable or spiritual to us. We are creatures of rote, so let us guard against making our worship a mindless activity; rather, let us refresh the heart of God.

Much of the Old Testament contains the sad history of God's people languishing under human traditions instead of being taught Scripture. Verse 13 offers us a good definition of what "legalism" is: *"Making the word of God of no effect through your tradition which you have handed down."* Whether in Israel previously or in the Church today, there are always consequences when men lord themselves over God's people and burden them with their own rules. Approaching God in other manner than humble sincerity and in obedience to His revealed will is utter vanity. He is not pleased with such religiosity; rather, His wrath is invoked against those offering to Him what He considers putrid.

The Heart Diagnosis (vv. 14-23)

After rebuking the arrogant religiosity of the Pharisees, the Lord offered an axiom of wisdom to the multitude listening to Him: *"There is nothing that enters a man from outside which can defile him; but the things which come out of him, those are the things that defile a man"* (v. 15). The tongue is the tail of the heart that wags out of the mouth. What we say reflects what is in our hearts. It is not what we eat that defiles us, but our words.

Afterwards, Matthew tells us that the disciples came to the Lord privately and told Him that the Pharisees had been offended by His speech (Matt. 15:12). But the Lord was not concerned about their hurt feelings, but rather He affirmed that Israel's spiritually blind leaders and those who followed them would come under God's judgment in a coming day (Matt. 15:13-14).

While in the privacy of a home, the disciples asked the Lord to further explain what He meant about what goes in and out of the mouth (v. 17). Matthew informs us that it was Peter who posed the question. The Lord wondered why Peter did not understand the simple truth that He had stated (v. 18; Matt. 15:16). What one eats goes into the mouth, then passes through the gastrointestinal tract and is then eliminated from the body as waste (v. 19). We are to give thanks to God for the food He provides for us to eat. This activity sanctifies the food we eat to strengthen our bodies to serve the Lord (1 Cor. 10:30-31). However, what one speaks reflects what he or she is thinking about. If carnal or evil thoughts are lurking in our heart, our own speech will inevitably condemn us (vv. 20-22). The Lord then summarized that it is not what is eaten or the eating with unwashed hands that defiles us, but rather our unwholesome speech (v. 23).

The Faith of a Syro-Phoenician Woman (vv. 24-28)

The Lord and His disciples then journeyed northwest to the Mediterranean coastal region of Tyre and Sidon in Phoenicia. As far as we know, this is the only time that the Lord ventured outside of Israel. After arriving there, they entered a home to hopefully remain undetected, but their presence could not be hidden, and people began flocking to see the Jesus of Nazareth (v. 24).

While in Phoenicia, a Greek woman, a Syro-Phoenician by birth, urgently requested that the Lord heal her demon-possessed daughter (v. 25). Matt says that she addressed the Lord Jesus as "Lord, Son of David" (Matt. 15:22). The Lord did not answer her request, but this did not stop her asking for assistance (v. 26). Her ongoing pleading annoyed the disciples, who asked the Lord to send her away (Matt. 15:23). To this request the Lord said, *"I was not sent except to the lost sheep of the house of Israel"* (Matt. 15:24). Mark notes an additional statement by the Lord to the woman, *"Let the children be filled first, for it is not good to take the children's bread and throw it to the little dogs"* (v. 27). By stating this allegory, the Lord Jesus affirmed His heavenly mission to preach the kingdom gospel message to the lost sheep of Israel (the children). The Lord was not sent to preach to the Gentiles (the dogs) at this time.

The Gentile woman understood what the Lord was saying, but added, *"Yes, Lord, yet even the little dogs under the table eat from the children's crumbs"* (v. 28). Concerning the woman's response, Harold Paisley observes:

> The answer of the woman shows her intelligence and faith in God. She is the only person in this Gospel written by Mark who addressed Jesus as Lord. She also accepted His royal rights to refuse her request, but added that even the dogs under their masters' tables may eat of falling crumbs without interfering with the continuance of the meal.[89]

Matthew states that the Lord marveled at her statement and said, *"O woman, great is your faith! Let it be to you as you desire"* (Matt. 15:28). The Lord then assured the woman that her daughter was completely well and the demon residing in her was gone (v. 29). When she returned home, indeed her daughter was well and peacefully lying on the bed (v. 30).

In Christ, Gentiles would become a second benefactor of the New Covenant established with Judah and Israel through Christ's shed blood (Heb. 8:8). Through trusting the gospel message preached in the Church Age, Jews and Gentiles would be fellow members in Christ's Body and fellow heirs to the unconditional blessings God promised to Abraham as obtained in Christ (Gen. 12:3; Eph. 3:6).

The Canaanite woman's description of "little dogs" eating the crumbs of bread that fell from the master's table (i.e., the bread of life that God had provided for the Jewish people to feast on) beautifully conveyed God's plan of saving both Jews and Gentiles in Christ. At this point in His ministry, the Lord Jesus was busy training His disciples, while seeking the lost sheep of Israel to receive Him as their Messiah; His efforts were not directed to the Gentiles. This explains why He performed only two miracles in association with Gentiles. Both healings were performed at a distance on behalf of a Gentile who had great compassion for someone else who was suffering and great faith in the Lord to resolve the issue. The other occurrence is when a centurion showed faith in understanding who Christ was and from where His authority came (Matt. 8:5-13).

The Lord was thrilled by their sincere faith and granted both their requests. Why did the Lord travel outside of Israel to Phoenicia? Perhaps the answer is to merely test the faith of one distressed Canaanite woman. The Lord yearns to demonstrate His compassion and ability to those who will seek Him in faith.

Further Healings in Northern Galilee (vv. 29-37)

After healing the Canaanite mother's daughter, the Lord journeyed southeastward through Decapolis to the Sea of Galilee (v. 31). While journeying, a man who was deaf and had a speech impediment was brought to the Lord for healing (v. 32). He took the man aside and put His fingers in the man's ears and spat and touched the disabled man's tongue (v. 33). Having done this, the Lord looked up to heaven and said, *"Ephphatha,"* which means *"Be opened"* (v. 34).

Immediately, the disabled man could hear properly and speak plainly (v. 35). Again, we see Christ not only repairs what was dysfunctional, but blesses those healed with full functionality afterwards to fully enjoy what God has done for them. The Lord instructed those who had witnessed the miracle to not publicize what had happened, but the people could not be constrained from telling others what they had seen (v. 36). They had been *"astonished beyond measure"* after witnessing the miracle and wanted everyone to know that Jesus of Nazareth, *"has done all things well. He makes both the deaf to hear and the mute to speak"* (v. 37). We enjoy God's peace by learning His character, obeying His Word, trusting in His promises, and resting in His Sovereignty to do all things well!

Mark Chapter 8

Four Thousand Fed (vv. 1-9)

The Lord's preaching and healing ministry in a remote location in Decapolis (on the southeast side of the Sea of Galilee) extended into a third day (vv. 1-2). The Lord Jesus had compassion for the people and told His disciples that He did not want to dismiss them while they were hungry, lest they faint on their journey (v. 3). The disciples concluded that there were no nearby locations to purchase bread for this *"great multitude"* (v. 4). Apparently, they had forgotten how the Lord had previously multiplied a boy's sack lunch and fed 5,000 men, plus women and children.

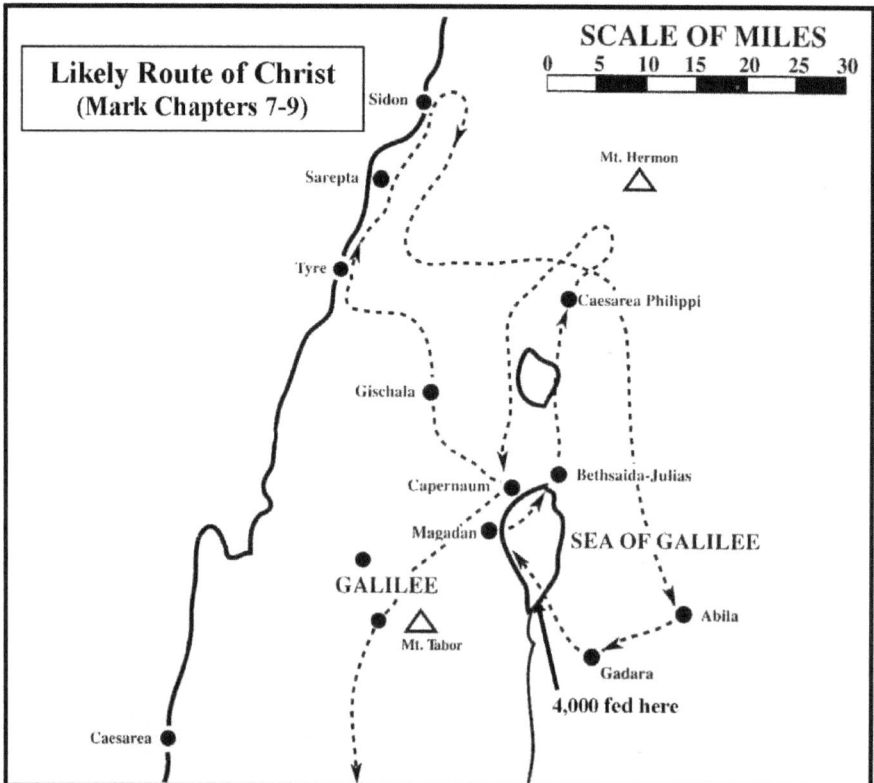

322

The Lord asked His disciples how many loaves of bread they had. They responded, "We have seven loaves and a few little fish" (vv. 5-7). The Lord then commanded all the people to sit down. He then took the loaves and the fish, gave thanks for them, and broke them into small pieces, which He gave to the disciples to be distributed among the people. All the people ate their fill and there were seven large baskets full of leftover fragments (v. 37). Mark then provides the approximate size of the crowd: 4,000 men, plus women and children, perhaps 15,000 people total (v. 9).

Beware of the Leaven of the Pharisees (vv. 10-21)

After everyone had eaten their fill, the Lord dismissed the crowd. Then He got into a boat with His disciples and journeyed to the region of Dalmanutha. Matthew refers to the more specific location of Magdala (or Magadan). Magdala was located about 3 miles north of Tiberias on the western shoreline of the Sea of Galilee.

Not long after the Lord arrived, the Pharisees (Matthew states that the Sadducees were present also) came out to test the Lord by asking Him to show them *"a sign from heaven"* to validate the authority of His ministry (v. 11; Matt. 16:1). All the miracles that Christ did were signs (irrefutable evidence) to Israel that Christ was who He claimed to be – the Messiah. The Lord's preaching and signs composed the kingdom message to the Jews. Though the signs provided proof that Jesus was the Christ, they would prove insufficient to cause the people to trust the Messiah for salvation. *"Without faith it is impossible to please Him [God]"* (Heb. 11:6), and faith requires the soul to venture beyond what the senses can verify.

Previously, the Lord Jesus had stated that it was the unrighteous who wanted to see a "sign or a wonder" to believe in Him. He called these "sign seekers" an evil generation (Matt. 12:38-39). Even those people who had witnessed the miracle of the feeding of the 5,000 were pestering the Lord the very next day: *"What sign will You perform then, that we may see it and believe You?"* (John 6:30). Did they not recall the miracle the day before? Did they not fill their bellies with a boy's multiplied sack lunch? The Israelites saw miracles every day in the wilderness for forty years, yet it did not increase their spirituality – for they constantly murmured against God and His leadership. This shallow spiritual mentality was evident while the Lord Jesus was hanging on the cross:

"Let the Christ, the King of Israel, descend now from the cross, that we ***may see and believe"*** (15:32).

Some of Israel's religious leaders had witnessed the Lord heal people, but now they were asking Him to work some spectacular sign in heaven that they might see and then believe in Him. The Lord sighed deeply and said, *"Assuredly, I say to you, no sign shall be given to this generation"* (v. 12). Matthew records a lengthier dialog at this juncture, in which the Lord offered the Pharisees the sign of Jonah as evidence as to who He was – that is, His death, burial, and resurrection after three days.

Apparently, the disciples were not with the Lord during this interchange with the Pharisees. They may have been purchasing supplies after the long trip north to Sidon, back southeast through Decapolis and then westward across the Sea of Galilee. But the disciples were with the Lord again about the time the Lord was wrapping up His conversation with Israel's religious leaders.

The Lord left the Pharisees and got in a boat with His disciples to cross the sea northward to Bethsaida and Caesarea Philippi (vv. 13, 27). The disciples realized, after rendezvousing with the Lord, that they had forgotten to buy bread (v. 14). There was only one loaf of bread in the boat. The Lord issued a warning to His disciples: *"Take heed and beware of the leaven of the Pharisees and the leaven of Herod"* (v. 15). As leaven is necessary to cause loaves of bread to rise, the disciples believed that the Lord was admonishing them for not buying bread and then warning them not to buy bread from the Pharisees (v. 16).

The disciples' preoccupation with food caused them to completely miss the spiritual lesson that the Lord was referring to. He was not concerned about where their next meal was coming from, but rather the doctrines being taught by Israel's religious leaders (v. 17). The Lord wondered why His disciples were weak in faith: Did they not remember how He had multiplied five loaves and seven loaves of bread on two separate occasions to feed the masses all the bread they could eat (vv. 18-19)? He even quizzed them to see if they remembered that there were twelve full baskets of food fragments remaining afterwards. Rather, His warning was of a spiritual nature and not a rebuke of their negligence.

Leaven, in Scripture, speaks of sin, corruption, or evil doctrine (13:33; 1 Cor. 5:8). Because leaven (yeast) is used in the fermentation process, it is a perfect symbol of decay and corruption, which is why, spiritually speaking, we should not be contaminated by it.

The leaven to be avoided in the believer's life comes in diverse varieties. The Lord Jesus warned His disciples against the influence of humanized traditions that oppose sound doctrine: *"Beware of the leaven of the Pharisees, which is hypocrisy"* (Luke 12:1). Church traditions have caused many professing Christians to ignore Christ's command to remember Him often through the Lord's Supper or to transform the memorial feast into some unscriptural practice. Some, for example, associate the eating of the bread and the drinking of the wine in the Lord's Supper with receiving or maintaining their salvation. This kind of leaven (i.e., false teaching) undermines the gospel message of grace declared repeatedly in the New Testament (e.g., Gal. 1:6-9).

The Lord spoke about the leaven of the Sadducees. The Sadducees were materialists who denied the existence of the supernatural, the spiritual nature of man, and the idea of a future resurrection. In our present day, the ideologies of the Sadducees live on in intellectualism, humanism, higher criticism, post-modernism, and naturalism.

The Lord Jesus also warned His disciples not to be influenced by *"the leaven of Herod"* (v. 15). Herod, a Jew, was in cahoots with the Romans, and was, therefore, a friend of the world (Jas. 4:4). In the case of Herod, and those like him, love for God and His Word had been supplanted by the love for materialism, fame, and political ambition.

A Blind Man Is Healed (vv. 22-26)

Mark provides the account of a healed blind man at Bethsaida. Several individuals brought the blind man to the Lord Jesus and begged Him to touch and heal the blind man (v. 22). This story is unique on several counts.

First, only Mark records the miracle. Second, although the city of Bethsaida was under condemnation for its general rejection of Christ (Matt. 11:21-24), there was still the opportunity for individuals to receive mercy. The city being under judgment probably explains why Christ led the blind man out of town to perform the miracle (v. 23). Third, this is the only miracle that Christ performed in stages, which indicates that there was a spiritual lesson associated with the healing (vv. 24-25). Fourth, the Lord used the unconventional method of spitting on the blind man's eyes and then touching them with His hands to bring about the miracle.

After this procedure occurred, the Lord asked him what he saw. The man said, *"I see men like trees, walking."* The Lord then touched the man's eyes again and afterwards his vision was completely restored. Obviously, the Lord could have healed the blind man instantaneously, but chose not to for a reason. Perhaps He was teaching the disciples, who still lacked much understanding, that spiritual insight would come in time, if they continued to go on with Him in faith. In time, they would no longer know in part or look into a mirror to see the reflection of spiritual things; they would have what was perfect, the inspired Word of God (1 Cor. 13:9-10).

Peter's Confession of Christ (vv. 27-30)

The Lord with His disciples then journeyed to Caesarea Philippi about 25 miles north of the Sea of Galilee (v. 27). After arriving, the Lord Jesus asked His disciples a question: *"Who do men say that I am?"* The disciples responded by saying that some believed that He was John the baptizer, others thought Him to be Elijah, or Jeremiah, or another of the Old Testament prophets (v. 28). While anyone else would have been honored to be considered alongside these great men of faith from the past, these views of Jesus were lacking. He was not Messiah's forerunner prophesied by Isaiah (Isa. 40:3) or just a prophet, but "the Prophet" that Moses prophesied would come to show Israel the way back to God (Deut. 18:15-19). He was God-incarnate, Israel's Messiah, and any other view of Him was deficient and insulting.

Then the Lord asked a more important question, *"But who do you say that I am?"* (v. 29). Peter did not hesitate to answer, *"You are the Christ."* Matthew states that Peter also added *"the Son of the living God"* to his declaration concerning Jesus Christ's full identity (Matt. 16:16). Although Peter was still learning the greatness of His Savior, he did understand that Jesus Christ was the Son of God who had come from heaven to the earth to do His Father's will. The Lord asked His disciples not to publicize this information at that time (v. 30). In His timing, He would fully reveal Himself to the nation of Israel.

There are seven important events pertaining to Christ's ministry that are recorded in all four Gospels: The ministry of John the baptizer as the forerunner of Christ, the feeding of the 5000, Peter's confession of Jesus being the Christ, the Triumphal Entry presentation of Messiah, and the crucifixion, burial, and resurrection of the Lord.

Christ Foretells His death (vv. 31-33)

Often Scripture provides its own outline of a particular passage or book. The phrase *"from that time,"* found only twice in Matthew's Gospel (4:17 and 16:21), properly divides the book into three main sections: *"From that time ... Repent for the Kingdom of heaven is at hand"* (Matt. 4:17). *"From that time forth began Jesus to show unto His disciples, how that He must...suffer"* (Matt. 16:21). Hence, Matthew 1:1 – 4:16 forms an introduction, while Matthew 4:17 – 16:20 presents the Jewish Messiah, and Matthew 16:21 – 28:20 records the rejection of the Jewish Messiah. The last section begins after Peter's confession of Jesus, as Christ and the Son of God, and just prior to the Lord's transfiguration.

It is at this time that the Lord plainly informs His disciples that He must go to Jerusalem and suffer many things by Israel's religious leaders, including being put to death. But this was not the end of the story: He would be raised from the dead on the third day (v. 21).

Peter, who had just declared Christ to be the Son of the living God and had received the keys to the kingdom, took the Lord Jesus aside privately to correct Him, *"Far be it from You, Lord; this shall not happen to You!"* (v. 22). The Father had revealed to Peter who His Son was, but Peter did not understand the Son's mission as God's Lamb of sacrifice for the sin of the world (John 1:29). Peter was now speaking in the ignorance and carnality of the flesh and the Lord rightly rebukes him. What is contrary to God's will is from the devil, so the Lord says to Peter, *"Get behind Me, Satan! You are an offense to Me, for you are not mindful of the things of God, but the things of men"* (v. 23).

There is no doubt that Peter loved the Lord Jesus and did not want Him to suffer any harm, yet He was not speaking for God on this matter. The Lord had already taught His disciples that there was no middle ground in spiritual matters: either we are doing God's will and experiencing His power, or we join ranks with the devil to oppose God (12:30; Mark 9:38-40). This scenario reminds us not to permit natural affections to undermine what Scripture commands us to do or not do.

The Cost of Discipleship (vv. 34-38)

After speaking of what doing God's will would cost Him, the Lord spoke of what following Him would cost the disciples: *"Whoever desires to come after Me, let him deny himself, and take up his cross, and follow Me"* (v. 34). The Lord speaks of three critical mindsets that those identifying with Him must have: self-denial, taking up one's own cross, and following Him.

First, a true disciple of Christ must deny himself. Complete identification with Christ means that we practically reckon who we were in Adam (i.e., in our unregenerate state) as dead and gone, and we are alive in Christ. Paul put the matter this way: *"I have been crucified with Christ; it is no longer I who live, but Christ lives in me; and the life which I now live in the flesh I live by faith in the Son of God, who loved me and gave Himself for me"* (Gal. 2:20; also see Gal. 6:14). The Greek verb rendered "crucified" in this verse has a passive voice and a perfect tense, meaning that God has once and for all carved us out of the world by the cross of His dear Son, and we are now to live for Him. We are one with Christ forever and must seek to live out His life in the way that He desires us to. This new calling precludes self-ambition, self-sufficiency, self-exaltation, and self-gratification (i.e., beyond what has God's approval).

Second, a true disciple must take up his or her cross daily. Anyone being nailed to the cross in ancient days meant that he or she was going to die a slow, agonizing death. Those crucified had nothing on their daily planners for the following week. Dying daily means not my will, but your will be done, Lord. Additionally, when one's hands were nailed to the cross, it made it impossible to grab anything. Bearing one's cross daily means that believers cannot engage in carnal appetites or get sidetracked by worldly pursuits (i.e., grab what is of the world).

Paul identifies what is necessary for Christians to adequately display the name of Christ: *"Let everyone who names the name of Christ depart from iniquity"* (2 Tim. 2:19). Believers cannot pretend to be holy; their conduct will either honor a sin-hating Savior or endorse a Savior-hating system. To declare the name of Christ is a great privilege, but to fully associate with His name is the highest honor. To be identified as a "Christian" is one and the same as acknowledging Christ's call to live as He did – a holy, consecrated life to God.

Accordingly, we come to Christ's cross and leave with our own cross. The cross is a symbol of shame and death, and Christ asks those who believe in Him to follow His selfless example of faithfulness, even unto death. On the night before His crucifixion, the Lord told His disciples that by identifying with Him, they would also experience the world's hatred and persecution (John 15:18-20). The gospel message pleads for the hell-bound sinner to embrace the cross of Christ, and no less so for the heaven-bound saint to take up his or her cross that he or she might enjoy His life now.

Third, a true disciple of Christ must forsake to follow the Lord. Forsaking must occur before following. Otherwise, there are too many anchors to the old life, which will hinder close exposure to the Savior. Our desire to follow Christ is a measure of how much we truly love Him and believe His message. The reason we hold back from being fools for Christ, and thus from seeing the mighty hand of God in our lives, is disbelief – we don't trust God. Through disbelief, the One who was offended for us becomes an offense to us. Those associating with Christ superficially will ultimately find Him loathsome. A true disciple of Christ esteems Him more important than anything this world has to offer, such as: career, wealth, education, prestige, fame, following peers, or just going with the flow of secular thinking.

Many come to Christ's cross for salvation but then neglect to go on with Him and bear their own cross; this is an affront to the discipleship message He taught. The believer was never to flee the cross, but rather is to die daily upon it – only then does his or her life count for eternity (v. 35). Taking up one's cross means that we will follow Christ no matter the personal cost. The Lord Jesus is a perfect gentleman; He will not force us to bear our cross or obey His calling for our lives. However, to ignore His calling is to pursue an existence which has no meaning or no eternal value. Christ likens this ideology to man who gains all the world has to offer, but still loses His own soul in the end (vv. 36-37). What is the profit in that? It is trading brief luxury and sensual pleasure for an eternal abode without God.

May each of us learn the necessity of denying ourselves, taking up our cross, and following the Lord with all our heart. There is a coming day in which all true disciples of Christ will be rewarded for following the Savior (v. 38). For those in the Church Age, this will occur at the Judgment Seat of Christ directly after the Church is raptured from the earth (Rom. 14:10-12; 2 Cor. 5:10).

The Lord suffered much humiliation and shame during His first advent, but when He returns to the earth again, it will be in glory with holy angels to establish His kingdom. For those who were ashamed of Christ and chose not to follow Him, He will be ashamed of them. The only means of avoiding this shame is to continue abiding in Christ now (i.e., enjoying His presence and going on with Him; 1 Jn. 2:28).

Mark Chapter 9

The Transfiguration of Christ (vv. 1-10)

The Lord then said something that certainly perked up the ears of the disciples, *"There are some standing here who shall not taste death till they see the kingdom of God present with power"* (v. 1). Matthew clarifies that this would occur when *"they see the Son of Man coming in His kingdom"* a reference to Christ's second advent to the earth (Matt. 16:28). We learn later that the Lord was primarily speaking of John. As the last living disciple, an elderly John was banished to the isle of Patmos as a Roman prisoner. While there, John witnessed the apocalypse, the revelation of Jesus Christ in various visions. For our benefit, he recorded what he witnessed in heavenly realms. His chronicle of future events has been preserved for us in the book of Revelation.

Six days after the incident in Caesarea Philippi, the Lord took Peter, James, and John up to a high mountain (v. 2). Mount Tabor, about fifteen miles southwest of Tiberias, is the traditional site for Christ's transfiguration, but Scripture is silent on where this event occurred. The Lord and His disciples had been in the region of Decapolis for some time and recently as far north as Caesarea Philippi. This region, loosely considered to be Galilee, boasted many high mountains in which this event may have occurred. Given that the Lord had been in Caesarea Philippi (Matt. 16:28, northeast of Capernaum) and was back in Capernaum directly afterwards (Matt. 17:24), a trip to Mount Tabor (about twenty miles southwest of Capernaum, the opposite direction from Caesarea Philippi) seems unlikely.

Luke infers that the Lord and His three disciples spent the night on the mountain and came down the next day (Luke 9:37). This means that the following events may have occurred during nighttime hours.

When applied metaphorically, mountains in Scripture symbolize governmental authorities or kingdoms. Both Isaiah and Micah foretold of God's glorious mountain on earth, speaking of Messiah's future earthly kingdom (Isa. 2:2; Micah 4:1-3). This future reality is momentarily displayed when the brilliance of Christ's intrinsic glory is revealed on a mountaintop in Galilee. Mark describes the scene: *"He was transfigured before them. His clothes became shining, exceedingly white, like snow, such as no launderer on earth can whiten them"* (vv. 2-3). Matthew states that *"His face shone like the sun"* (Matt. 17:2). One can only imagine the dazzling glory of the Lord on this high, remote mountain and apparently at night.

The Lord Jesus had said, *"There are some standing here who shall not taste death till they see the kingdom of God present with power"* (v. 1). Years later, Peter confirmed what was represented by this incident: *"the power and coming of our Lord Jesus Christ"* – the revealing of *"His majesty"* (2 Pet. 1:16). For a moment the disciples were given a foretaste of the coming kingdom.

Mark then explains that both Moses and Elijah appeared and were talking with the Lord (v. 4). Beholding this sight, Peter suggested to the Lord, *"Rabbi, it is good for us to be here; and let us make here three tabernacles: one for You, one for Moses, and one for Elijah"* (v. 5). But it was not time for the kingdom to be established. Peter's suggestion of erecting three tents showed a lack of discernment for the Lord's proper place in the kingdom. Yet, his unintentional blunder was immediately checked when a sudden, bright cloud overshadowed them and God the Father declared, *"This is My beloved Son. Hear Him!"* (v. 5). Matthew states that the disciples fell to the ground in fear, but the Lord touched them and when they looked up, they only saw the Lord and in His normal appearance (v. 8). There is a glorious earthly kingdom coming in which Jesus Christ will be wonderfully recognized as Son by the Father. He will rule the earth with the full glory, honor, and authority as God's faithful Son.

The Lord asked Peter, James, and John not to reveal what had happened on the mountain until after His resurrection, but the disciples did not understand what *"the rising from the dead"* meant (vv. 9-10). The establishment of His kingdom would occur after His second advent to the earth, but His redemptive work of Calvary was yet unfinished business that must be attended to. Suffering must precede glory!

Elijah Must Come (vv. 11-13)

Having just witnessed a preview of Christ's coming in power and glory, the disciples asked the Lord about the appearance of Messiah's forerunner, Elijah, before the kingdom could be established (v. 11). The prophet Malachi foretold that God would send the prophet Elijah again just prior to the Day of the Lord: *"Behold, I am going to send you Elijah the prophet before the coming of the great and terrible day of the Lord"* (Mal. 4:5).

The Lord confirmed that the spirit of Elijah was in John, who faithfully called that nation to repentance before Christ began His ministry during His first advent (vv. 12-13). Likewise, 144,000 Jews will be sealed and empowered by the Holy Spirit to again preach the kingdom gospel message just before Christ's second advent. Their mission will be similar to Elijah's previous ministry to apostate Israel; it is also possible that Elijah himself will be one of the two powerful witnesses spoken of in Revelation 11:3-14.

F. B. Hole summarizes how Malachi's references to God's messenger (3:1) and to Elijah (4:5) tie together:

> At His first advent the messenger sent in advance was clearly John the Baptist, who prepared the way of the Lord, and came in the spirit and power of Elijah, though not the Elijah of which Malachi 4:5 speaks, for he is to come before the great and dreadful day of the Lord in judgment. John came after the fashion of Elijah, but before the coming of the Messiah in grace, who is the Master, identified here with Jehovah.[90]

Clearly, John the baptizer was not Elijah in person (John 1:21-23), but he was God's messenger (Matt. 3:1) who came in the spirit of Elijah's ministry to call the nation to repentance, hence preparing the way of the Lord. An angel confirmed that this would be the focus of John's ministry even before he was born (Luke 1:17). Then, years later, the Lord Jesus affirmed John's Elijah-like ministry:

> *For all the prophets and the law prophesied until John. And if you are willing to receive it, he is Elijah who is to come. He who has ears to hear, let him hear!* (Matt. 11:13-15).

As in the days of Elijah, Israel did not receive John's message of repentance either. So while John fulfilled the prophecy in the execution of an Elijah-type ministry, it was not successful; therefore Elijah must yet come in such a way that results in national revival of the Jewish nation (Mal. 4:6). Since that will not occur until the Tribulation Period, many believe that Elijah, who did not previously experience death, but must (Heb. 9:27), will be one of the two witnesses for Christ in

Revelation 11. (Perhaps Enoch will be the other for the same reason.) These two men, whoever they are, will preach repentance, will withstand the Antichrist, and will perform great wonders (Rev. 11:1-13).

Whether this will be Elijah himself (as possibly indicated in verse 12), or another who comes like John in the spirit of Elijah's ministry, is debatable. However, the prophecy predicts that Israel will not come to Christ without a supernaturally empowered ministry like Elijah's to call them to repentance. It is with this promise of Christ's coming to judge the wicked, to reward the righteous, and to restore the nation of Israel to Himself that the Old Testament closes. God is not finished with the Jewish nation. Their hope is in Christ, and He is coming in power and in glory. May the Sun of Righteousness rise soon!

Lack of Prayer – Lack of Power (vv. 14-29)

The twelve disciples had returned from preaching the kingdom message throughout Galilee a short time before the events of this chapter (6:30-31). The Lord had given them authority over demons and the power to cure infirmities as they went (Luke 9:1). Immediately after the Lord, Peter, James, and John descended the mountain, they met a large crowd. The scribes were having a dispute with some of Christ's disciples, and many had gathered to listen to the discussion (v. 14). Upon seeing Jesus, the crowd became excited and instantly ran to Him and greeted Him (v. 15).

The Lord asked the scribes what they were discussing with His disciples (v. 16). But just then a man interrupted the conversation by suddenly kneeling before the Lord with an urgent request (v. 17; Matt. 17:14). The man explained that he had a son who suffered terribly because of epileptic fits and that he had brought him to His disciples, but they could not remove the evil spirit from his son to cure him (v. 18).

To have Christ's authority and not reflect His ability in ministry is an offense to the Lord. Accordingly, the Lord publicly chided His disciples for lacking faith to heal the man's son. They were acting like the general Jewish populace, which had been called a *"faithless generation"* (v. 19). The Lord then asked the father to bring his son to Him, which he did. Upon seeing Christ, the boy fell to the ground and began to convulse and foam at the mouth (v. 20).

The Lord asked the father how long his son had suffered with this condition (v. 21). The father answered from childhood and then described how the evil spirit within him had thrown him into the water and into fire to kill him (v. 22). The father then pleaded for the Lord to show compassion by helping them. The Lord responded by saying, *"If you believe, all things are possible to him who believes"* (v. 23). With tears the father of the afflicted son cried out, *"Lord, I believe; help my unbelief!"* (v. 24). The epileptic symptoms were resulting from demon possession, so the Lord rebuked the demon residing within the boy and he was instantly cured (vv. 25-26). The boy was still, and some thought that he had died, but the Lord took him by the hand and lifted him up and the father received his son well (v. 27).

Afterwards, the disciples came to the Lord Jesus privately and asked, *"Why could we not cast it out?"* (v. 28). Matthew informs us that the Lord answered their inquiry by stating that they lacked faith to cast out the demon. Even a little faith in God, as likened to the small size of a mustard seed, can move mountains. Mountains here speak of seemingly insurmountable difficulties in our lives. True faith that discerns the will of God will lay hold of the power of God through prayer and fasting (v. 29; Matt. 17:21).

The Critical Text does not include "and fasting" in verse 29, but the Majority Manuscripts speak of prayer and fasting. Paul would later highlight the importance of prayer and fasting in the Christian experience (Acts 13:2-3, 14:23; 1 Cor. 7:5). This means that prayerless believers will be powerless failures in serving the Lord! The Christian life should be marked by prayer and fasting.

Christ Foretells His Death and Resurrection (vv. 30-32)

While attempting to pass through Galilee to Capernaum undetected, the Lord again reminded His disciples of the sorrow that awaited Him in Jerusalem. The Lord Jesus again affirmed His forthcoming betrayal, death, and resurrection on the third day (v. 31). The disciples did not understand the meaning of the Lord's statement, nor did they want to ask Him about what He meant. Regardless, Matthew says that the disciples were "exceedingly sorrowful" after hearing the Lord's statement (Matt. 17:23).

Humility Is the Secret of Greatness (vv. 33-37)

Apparently, the disciples were having a discussion among themselves while journeying to Capernaum that they did not want the

Lord to be privy to. However, after reaching their destination and entering a house, the Lord asked the disciples what they had been talking about (v. 33). But they kept silent because the dispute had been about who would be the greatest in the kingdom (v. 34). The Lord Jesus knew all about their proud bantering, but quizzed them to invoke guilt for asserting their personal greatness in the kingdom, when the Lord had just told them of His death, which was needful to secure the kingdom. The disciples' dispute revealed what was secretly lurking in their hearts – pride, for *"only by pride comes contention"* (Prov. 13:10).

The Lord sat down and called the twelve disciples to Him. He then told them, *"If anyone desires to be first, he shall be last of all and servant of all"* (v. 35). The Lord then called a little child to Him and set him in the midst of them (v. 36). Evidently, the child came to Him without hesitation, which was the behavior the Lord commended in His lesson. Matthew provides more of the dialogue at this juncture than Mark:

Assuredly, I say to you, unless you are converted and become as little children, you will by no means enter the kingdom of heaven, therefore whoever humbles himself as this little child is the greatest in the kingdom of heaven (Matt. 18:3-4).

Additionally, the Lord told His disciples that *"he who is greatest among you shall be your servant. And whoever exalts himself will be humbled, and he who humbles himself will be exalted"* (Matt. 23:12). The physical kingdom would not be established for some time, but the inward or spiritual realities of the kingdom would be revealed in Spirit-filled believers during the Church Age. This is what the Lord is speaking of now. Greatness is obtained in the kingdom by assuming a humble attitude before others to best serve them: Do we willingly serve others before ourselves? Do we quickly sacrifice our rights for the good of others (1 Cor. 9:19)? Do we serve to insert our personal opinions? Do we desire visibility or recognition for serving? How do we respond when treated like a servant (John 3:29-30)? Do we complain while serving? Do we gloat over our doings? Do we listen or seek to promote ourselves?

In Matthew 18:4, the Lord says that greatness in His kingdom would be achieved by humbling oneself, but in Luke 9, He adds the necessity of demonstrating His love and humility to the lowliest believer. Our esteem for the lowliest believer in the Church shows how much we love the Lord Jesus (25:40). From the parallel account of this incident in Luke, we learn that the disciples had been thinking of their own greatness (Luke 9:46). As a result, they lacked power in the Lord's work, and they lacked wisdom and commitment to properly do what the Lord tasked them to do (Luke 9:40, 54-56).

The Lord used a small child as an object lesson to teach His disciples about having childlike faith in following Him and childlike humility in serving others. Whoever received one of these little children in Christ's name also received Him and His Father who had sent Him (v. 37).

Sectarianism Is Rebuked (vv. 38-41)

John then asked the Lord a question. This is the only time that John is directly quoted by his given name: *"Teacher, we saw someone who does not follow us casting out demons in Your name, and we forbade him because he does not follow us"* (v. 38). But the Lord corrected their behavior, *"Do not forbid him, for no one who works a miracle in My name can soon afterward speak evil of Me. For he who is not against us is on our side"* (vv. 39-40; Luke 11:23).

The Lord admonishes His disciples for their sectarian spirit. They had witnessed someone casting out demons in the Lord's name, and told the man to cease liberating the possessed because he was not specifically associating with Christ, or with them. The man was not teaching false doctrine or doing anything immoral; he just sought to help others and further the cause of Christ.

The Lord told His disciples not to hinder the man, for if he had enough truth and faith in Christ to cast out demons, he was on His side. This meant that the man was confronting Satan and therefore would not be speaking ill of Christ. Anyone believing that Christ was the Son of God was on the right side; they were not working against the Lord.

It is easy for us to think of other believers as "us" and "them" because they do not associate with us or they think differently than we do. Yet, the Lord affirmed the oneness and the equal standing of all believers when He told His disciples, *"For one is your Teacher, the Christ, and you are all brethren"* (Matt. 23:8). Christians are identified by biblical names such as Christians, believers, saints, and brethren. No denominations, cliques, or separate followings should be found in the Body of Christ. Paul asked the Corinthians, who were bestowing special honors to particular preachers instead of following Christ, *"Is Christ divided?"* (1 Cor. 1:13). The act of identifying with anyone or any organization instead of Christ is completely unbiblical. Rather, we should identify with David's thinking, *"I am a companion of all who fear You, and of those who keep Your precepts"* (Ps. 119:63).

In the practical sense, Christian fellowship (i.e., what we share together in the commonwealth of Christ) is dependent on how much we determine we have in common with other believers. While it is true that we will not be able to have the same degree of fellowship with all believers, we should strive to walk as far as we can with all those who have been redeemed by the precious blood of Christ. All that is done in the name of Christ and for the honor of Christ will be rewarded. The Lord even takes note of simple acts of kindness, such as giving a thirsting person a cup of water to drink (v. 41).

Christ Warns of Hell (vv. 42-50)

With the child still in their midst, the Lord warned of the harsh consequences of abusing children, but also extended the application to those who would harm God's children (His people). While living in a sin-cursed world that is plagued with all sorts of evils, offenses to God's children are inevitable. But the Lord warned that it would be much better to suffer in righteousness than to be an agent of evil that offends a child of God (v. 42). Men should take drastic measures to discipline themselves, rather than to tempt a child of God to stumble in their faith and experience God's wrath for doing so.

Whether the offending member is a hand, a foot, or an eye, it would be better to have these removed by a surgeon's scalpel than to permit any member to undermine the work of God in someone else's life (vv. 43-47). The hand speaks of our deeds, the foot – our walk, and the eye – what we crave. A hyperbole is then used to amplify this point: It would be better to endure life without limbs than to be cast into hell with all of them. This statement does not suggest that there will be some without limbs after experiencing bodily resurrection. Rather, the Lord is referring to one's physical condition at the time of death, as determined by the choices we made during our lifetime to harm or to not harm children of the kingdom (i.e., other believers).

Several types of death are spoken of in Scripture, but there are three deaths, or literally, "separations," that are most significant to all mankind. We are all born *spiritually dead*; that is, we are spiritually separated from God. Then, when *physical death* occurs, our soul and spirit separate from our body. If physical death occurs while a person is still spiritually dead, *eternal death* (judgment in hell) is assured. Hebrews 9:27 proclaims, *"It is appointed unto men once to die, but after this the judgment."* The only exception to the above is that perhaps God will demonstrate His grace by applying the blood of Christ to the souls of those who died in the womb or early in life, before they understood the moral law within them and God's solution to their sin problem (2 Sam. 12:23). God calls these young ones "innocent" (Jer. 19:4). But as adults and older children, the unsaved are just one heartbeat, one breath away from sealing an eternal destiny of woe.

If we die without being justified (i.e., receiving forgiveness of your sins and obtaining a righteous standing in Christ), there is no hope for us. Contrary to what some teach, there is no purgatory – those dying without Christ will spend eternity in hell. Christ has already done everything necessary to purge our sins (Heb. 1:3), and rescue us from eternal judgment, but He will not force anyone to go to heaven – it is our choice (2 Pet. 3:9). The Bible vividly describes the ultimate fate of those who reject God's truth. The following are terms used in association with hell (the Lake of Fire):

- *"Shame and everlasting contempt"* (Dan. 12:2)
- *"Everlasting punishment"* (Matt. 25:46)
- *"Weeping and gnashing of teeth"* (Matt. 24:51)
- *"Unquenchable fire"* (Luke 3:17)
- *"Indignation and wrath, tribulation and anguish"* (Rom. 2:8-9)
- *"Their worm does not die* [putrid, endless agony]*"* (Mark 9:44)
- *"Everlasting destruction"* (2 Thess. 1:9)
- *"Eternal fire ... the blackness of darkness forever"* (Jude 7, 13)
- *"Fire is not quenched"* (Mark 9:46)

Revelation 14:10-11 tells us the final, eternal destiny of the sinner: *"He shall be tormented with fire and brimstone ... the smoke of their torment ascended up forever and ever: and they have no rest day or night."* The Bible's teaching of eternal punishment for unforgiven sinners offends people; consequently, many are watering down the truth, teaching that hell is a state of non-existence or quick annihilation. However, misrepresenting the truth to avoid its consequence is never a good idea.

God does not enjoy punishing rebels, but His character demands it. He longs for all men to repent and to turn to Him by faith, as He has said, *"I have no pleasure in the death of the wicked, but that the wicked turn from his way and live"* (Ezek. 33:11). Everlasting "hell fire" was not originally prepared for mankind but, rather, for Satan and other rebellious angels (Matt. 25:41). However, God will use this place of torment to also punish those who reject His only solution for sin – the substitutionary death of His Son.

The Lord concluded His warning of hell by stating that everyone will be seasoned with fire, and every sacrifice will be seasoned with salt (v. 49). Fire in this verse is not specifically hellfire, but the discerning judgment of God, who will both prove the value of the believer's works by fire (1 Cor. 3:11-15) and the worthless deeds of the wicked before they are cast into fire (Rev. 20:11-15). Every sacrifice of the believer seasoned with salt will be found acceptable to God. But salt that has lost its flavor is worthless in seasoning our food. Therefore, the disciples were to maintain a salty testimony for Christ, while maintaining peace with each other (v. 50). Our service to God must be marked by the purity of truth and sacrificial love to properly reveal His character to others.

During the Sermon on the Mount, the Lord, speaking to His disciples, likened their ministry for Him to that of salt: *"You are the salt of the earth"* (Matt. 5:13). Salt is a symbol of purification in Scripture (Num. 18:19). It also symbolized the covenant between God and His people and therefore was required to be added to the burnt offerings on the Bronze Altar. Without salt, sacrifices would not be accepted by the Lord. Salt stands in sharp contrast with leaven, which corrupts and, accordingly, was never permitted on the Bronze Altar. When the salt put on the Levitical offerings was burned, it created billowing white smoke. It was unnoticed until tested by fire and then the evidence of its presence was unmistakable. In this sense, salt speaks of pure, uncompromised truth (e.g., Col. 4:6).

Salt also enhances the flavor of what we eat and serves as a food preservative. Combining all these useful facets of salt, we can understand why the Lord Jesus exhorted His disciples to have a "salty" testimony – declaring preserved truth enhances our testimony. Salt that is no longer salty has no value. A believer who no longer lives to declare the goodness of Christ in word and by deed is become "good for nothing" and his or her testimony will be happily trampled under as meaningless by the children of the devil.

Mark Chapter 10

The first nine chapters of Mark focus on the Lord's ministry in Galilee and Decapolis the previous two and a half years. Neither Matthew, nor Mark, provide details concerning the Lord's Judean ministry from the time of the Feast of Tabernacles (in late September) to the Feast of Dedication celebrated in December. However, Luke dedicates nine chapters of his gospel record to this timeframe (chs. 10-18) and John includes five chapters (chs. 7-11) in his account. The Lord will spend the next four months in Perea and then depart for Jerusalem about a week prior to His passion.

Christ's Teaching on Divorce (vv. 1-12)

We are informed that the Lord ventured south into Judea but remained on the eastern side of the Jordan River in the region of Perea (v. 1). As Mark does not address the Lord's Judean ministry, textually speaking, this journey marks the conclusion of the Lord's ministry in Decapolis, which began in the spring of 29 A.D.

As the Lord trekked southward through Perea, a crowd of people followed Him, and He healed many of their infirmities and taught them (Matt. 19:2). But the Pharisees were also among the multitude. They did not seek to hear Christ's teachings or to be healed by Him. Rather, they came to test Him, hoping to somehow catch Him in His words to accuse Him of wrongdoing.

The Pharisees asked a question which they thought might serve this purpose: *"Is it lawful for a man to divorce his wife?"* (v. 2). The two leading rabbis of this age, Hillel and Shammai, were rival teachers of Jewish tradition. Both lived during the reign of Herod the Great. Hillel was the liberal and taught that a man could end his marriage for any cause (Matt. 19:3). Shammai, the more conservative rabbi, stated that divorce was only permitted for the sin of adultery. All this to say that regardless how the Lord answered this question, some would not be pleased with the answer.

The Lord asked them, *"What did Moses command you?"* (v. 3). They responded by saying that if a bill of divorce was written, then it was permissible to dismiss one's wife (v. 4). But the Lord affirmed that such a provision was only permitted because of the hardness of their hearts. When God instituted marriage, divorce was not an option, but because of sin, God had to put bounds on divorce to limit its destructive nature. The point being that marriage is a union established by divine charter and is not to be tampered with by human enactments such as divorce.

Historically speaking, the Old Testament indicates that children were crucial to Jewish family life. Inheritance and clan leadership were passed down to male children. This is why Elkanah likely married Peninah; Hannah, his first wife, could not bear him children (1 Sam. 1). At this time, men did what was right in their own eyes (Judg. 17:6). Later, kings often had multiple wives to ensure there were plenty of males who could survive, if a rival tried to seize the throne by massacring the kingly line. Though a practical solution from a human perspective, polygamy was not God's intention for marriage.

God instituted His Law with the Israelites to show them that they were inherently sinful, condemned before God, and needed a Savior (Rom. 3:20; Gal. 3:24). The Law put constraints on their sin and warned them against behaviors that displeased God. For example, God's design for marriage did not allow for divorce, but because of the hardness of man's heart, God permitted divorce in the Law with constraints (v. 8). Likewise, polygamy was not God's plan for marriage, but at that time He only warned against it and put constraints on it (Deut. 17:17, 21:15).

However, with the Holy Spirit's coming to indwell believers in the Church Age, the Lord Jesus again confirmed God's original standard for marriage:

> But from the beginning of the creation, God *"made them male and female." "For this reason a man shall leave his father and mother and be joined to his wife, and the two shall become one flesh"; so then they are no longer two, but one flesh. Therefore what God has joined together, let not man separate* (vv. 6-9).

Afterwards, when they had come into a house, the disciples asked the Lord what He meant by His statement to the Pharisees. The Lord told His disciples that unless a marriage covenant is dissolved for the case of adultery (Matt. 5:32, 19:9), any husband marrying another woman commits adultery with her and anyone marrying the illegally divorced wife also becomes an adulterer (vv. 11-12).

Because Matthew is written to a Jewish audience and the exception clause is not found in the parallel accounts in Mark and Luke, some view Matthew's statements relating to the period of purity connected with a Jewish betrothal agreement. This timeframe is bound by the initial marriage betrothal and the physical consummation of the marriage covenant later by the bride and the groom. Mary and Joseph were in this time of purity when the Lord Jesus was conceived in her womb by the power of the Holy Spirit. While this understanding is possible, the Lord does not uphold the Mosaic Law or developed Jewish traditions, but God's design for marriage declared in Eden at the first marriage.

The Lord was affirming God's original order for marriage which was for one biological man and one biological woman to be bound by a marriage covenant until separated by death. Furthermore, the idea of polygamy was not what God intended for marriage. The fact that a man would be disqualified from church leadership if he was a polygamist tells us what marital pattern is important to God. The apostles only had one wife or no wives (1 Cor. 9:5) and those in church leadership or in the office of deacons could not be polygamists (Tit. 1:6; 1 Tim. 3:2, 12). Scripture records no example of any Christian engaging in the practice of polygamy; monogamy, however, is repeatedly shown to be the proper pattern for marriage (Eph. 5:31-33).

Under the Law, adulterers were to be put to death if found guilty of violating the seventh of God's Ten Commandments. This would permit the innocent party to remarry if desired. In the Church Age, we do not put adulterers to death, but the act breaks the marriage covenant, nonetheless. Civil divorce for any other reason than adultery is not biblical. Those who divorce for other reasons and remarry afterwards are guilty of adultery, for the Lord views them as still married to their previous spouse.

Paul presents a high standard for Christians to follow in this matter: remain with your spouse until death ends your marriage covenant, but if living together is not possible, a husband and wife may separate and live in purity, but divorce should not be sought (1 Cor. 7:10-11). Each situation is different, and there may be safety issues or financial concerns that necessitate a civil divorce, but in God's eyes that does not free the husband and wife from their vow to each other and to God. It is important to realize that civil divorce and biblical divorce have different criterion.

Blessing the Children (vv. 13-15)

Little children were being brought to the Lord that He might touch them and pray over them (v. 13). Harold Paisley observes that the episode of parents bringing their children to the Lord to be blessed by Him is in context with the previous subject of divorce: "For it is usually the children who are the innocent and pathetic victims of suffering and loss in such cases. Many have been damaged emotionally for life as a result. This is one of the saddest outcomes of divorce." [91]

The disciples saw this activity as a waste of the Master's time, so they tried to stop the flow of children coming to Him. The Lord responded to their angst by providing an object lesson as to how the lost can enter His kingdom – by exercising childlike faith in Him: *"Let the little children come to Me, and do not forbid them; for of such is the kingdom of God"* (v. 14). Children do not need to become adults to be saved, but adults must have childlike faith to be saved (v. 15).

Accordingly, the Lord continued to lay His hands on the children and bless them (v. 16). As mentioned in the previous chapter, the Lord is not granting these little children access to heaven by touching them and praying for them. There is also no water present in this story, so there was no sprinkling of infants. Nor is there any example of babies being baptized in Scripture. Paul states that trusting the gospel of Christ is what saves a person, and water baptism has nothing to do with salvation (1 Cor. 1:17). Those who are old enough to understand that they have an inherent sin problem, and thus need a Savior, could exercise faith in Christ and be saved by Him (John 3:18). Those too young to understand this were blessed by Christ's presence and may have received His healing and further protection from evil, including demonic forces.

The Rich, Young Ruler (vv. 16-26)

While the Lord was walking on a road in Perea, a rich, young ruler came running after Him. After catching up to the Lord, the young man knelt before Him and asked, *"Good Teacher, what shall I do that I may inherit eternal life?"* (v. 17). Many think that they are good by their own standards of evaluation, but since only God is *good*, the Lord Jesus challenged the young man to think of goodness according to *divine standards* (v. 18). The Lord then used God's Commandments to bypass the intellect to speak to the inquirer's conscience (v. 19).

He referred to the last six of the Ten Commandments (which are manward in application). However, He placed the fifth commandment concerning honoring one's parents behind the ninth, and then represented the tenth, concerning not coveting, by its application of loving one's neighbor as yourself. If you truly love your neighbor, you will selflessly give to your neighbor, not lust for what he has for yourself. Why did the Lord order the commandments in this way? The purpose of the Law is to show us our sin and that we might understand that only God is good (Rom. 3:9-12). The Lord knew all about the sin of this young man, so He placed the most applicable commands last to convict him of what the Lord knew that he had failed to do.

Sadly, the Law did not achieve its intended purpose in the rich, young ruler's heart. Instead of feeling guilt and impending judgment, he declared that he had kept all the commandments that Christ had listed since his youth (i.e., since taking personal responsibility to do so after his Bar Mitzvah; v. 20). Our gracious Lord did not rebuke the young man for his audacious statement, but instead set about to show him who his god really was. After being told that he needed to sell his possessions, give the proceeds to the poor, and follow Christ, the young man departed in sorrow, for he was wealthy (vv. 21-22). Clearly, money was his god; he valued it more than treasure in heaven and following the Lord.

For those of us who have reckoned ourselves as needy sinners and have received the Savior, we can exclaim with David: *"O taste and see that the Lord is good: blessed is the man that trusts in Him"* (Ps. 34:8). Truly, God is good and does good (Ps. 119:68).

After the rich, young ruler departed, the Lord informed His disciples, *"How hard it is for those who have riches to enter the kingdom of God"* (v. 23). The disciples were astonished by this statement, so the Lord repeated it again and then supplied a hyperbolic illustration to accentuate His point (v. 24). *"It is easier for a camel to go through the eye of a needle than for a rich man to enter the kingdom of God"* (v. 25). Some have suggested that this analogy references the act of camels walking on their knees to get under a low archway. However, the Lord's point is not one of difficulty, but impossibility. The Greek word *rhaphidos*, rendered "needle," speaks of a sewing or surgical needle. Luke uses the same description in the parallel account (Luke 18:25). The idea of a large camel fitting through the eye of a surgical needle was impossible. Likewise, anyone trusting in their riches for security or esteeming what they have as more important than pleasing God by doing His will cannot enter into heaven.

Matthew informs us that the disciples were stunned by this statement and asked the Lord, *"Who then can be saved?"* (Matt. 19:25). The Lord responded, *"With men this is impossible, but not with God; for with God all things are possible"* (v. 27). The Lord again emphasizes that in matters of salvation, it is not merely difficult for men to earn heaven by their doings; it is impossible. The work of salvation which God brings about through humble, childlike faith in the Savior is how God ushers redeemed sinners into heaven.

Reward for Faithfulness Now and Later (vv. 27-31)

The Lord Jesus had previously told His disciples of the divisive outcome of gospel preaching: *"Do not think that I came to bring peace on earth. I did not come to bring peace but a sword. For I have come to 'set a man against his father, a daughter against her mother, and a daughter-in-law against her mother-in-law'; and 'a man's enemies will be those of his own household'"* (Matt. 10:34-37). Those who freely chose Christ as Lord and Savior would be isolated and persecuted by those who had not chosen Him (v. 29). This dynamic was exceptionally painful when the division happened within a family. It is evident from Paul's instructions to the saints at Corinth that even marriages were being split apart by the gospel message (1 Cor. 7:12-16).

The rich, young ruler sorrowfully departed from the Lord because he was not willing to part with his wealth to follow Christ. But the opposite was true for the disciples, who had identified with Christ and had been willing to forsake all to follow Him. This prompted Peter to ask the Lord what type of reward they might expect for doing so (v. 28).

The Lord could have responded to Peter's inquiry with a mild rebuke, "How do you know you will have anything in the kingdom?" But He did not. Rather, the Lord then affirmed that they would be highly honored and given authority in His coming kingdom (v. 28). Additionally, they would possess eternal life and even now could expect a hundredfold increase for every relationship severed by the gospel (v. 30).

It is the same for believers today. For every person who persecutes a believer, there will be a hundred more believers to lend him or her a helping hand. Christian love is a powerful weapon against the enemy, for it conveys the reality of the gospel message to the lost. May we all give thanks to the Lord for all the gracious benefits of a loving community of saints during our earthly sojourn. Indeed, rewards will be received at the *Judgment Seat of Christ*, but we can assist each other to be faithful to Christ until that day.

The Lord then reminds His disciples that they must maintain a right attitude in service now to receive His reward later: *"But many who are first will be last, and the last first!"* (v. 31). Believers should consider any personal sacrifices for the kingdom now are merely investment opportunities for eternity.

Christ Predicts His Death Again (vv. 32-34)

The Lord Jesus had concluded His Perean ministry and was beginning His westerly journey to Jerusalem through Jericho (v. 32). He paused with His disciples to speak of forthcoming suffering in Jerusalem.

He knew that He would be betrayed into the hands of Israel's religious leaders, who would condemn Him to death (v. 33). The Lord knew that because the Jews did not have the authority to judicially execute the condemned, He would be given over to the Gentiles (the Romans), who would mock, scourge, and crucify Him (v. 34). But on the third day, He would rise again from the grave.

Christ's Responses to James and John (vv. 35-45)

Matthew informs us that the wife of Zebedee kneeled before the Lord to ask Him a favor. Her sons James and John were with her (vv. 35-36; Matt. 20:20). Mark does not record the presence of the wife of Zebedee, so apparently this was a group request that James and John might sit on either side of Him in His kingdom (v. 37). After hearing her petition, the Lord responded that she did not fully understand the ramifications of her request. So the Lord asked James and John if they were able to drink from the same cup of suffering and undergo the same baptism of sorrow that He was about to undergo (v. 38). They answered, *"We are able."*

The Lord did not deny their intentions of identifying with Him and suffering for doing so, but future reward in the kingdom must be determined by proven faithfulness, not good intentions (vv. 39-40). Time proves the validity of the heart and His Father in heaven knew who would be faithful to live for Christ. These would be rewarded appropriately. Some are sovereignly chosen for specific roles of personal greatness, such as John the baptizer and Mary the mother of Christ, but most will earn greatness in the kingdom through personal faithfulness.

The timing of this request must have somewhat grieved the heart of the Lord. He had just spoken of His future agony and death, but His disciples were thinking about their own glory and not His suffering. Yet, the Lord graciously responded to her request.

However, after the other disciples heard about the request of James and John, they were displeased with the two brothers (v. 41). The Lord then called His disciples together to teach them that true greatness from God's perspective was using authority to humbly serve others (vv. 42-44). The disciples were not to be like the Gentile rulers who lorded their authority and status over others. Rather, they were to follow His example of exercising authority to sacrificially serve others (v. 45).

What the Lord taught in word and deed was counter to the world's philosophies of success. Worldlings will say, "Save your life at all costs," but the Lord taught, "Lose your life to gain one worth living." The world exclaims, "Live for the moment," but Christians are to "live for eternity." Worldlings want to be served by others, but Christ taught His disciples to humble themselves and serve others, for that was the true path to greatness in His kingdom.

Biblical leadership is not one of lordship or heavy-handed tactics of control, but rather is a style that serves God's sheep and upholds them so that they flourish. The Gentile kings were often dictators, who oppressed their subjects, but those who would lead God's people must not do so. Those who love Christ must follow His sacrificial example. Christ stated that He had not come into the world to be served, but rather to die – to give His life as a ransom for those who did not deserve God's favor in any way, shape, or form. If the Lord of Glory can do that for others, should not we be able to serve those who are difficult to serve?

One must be a submitted servant before he or she can be a true leader of others. The Lord Jesus humbled Himself to serve and develop others into profitable leaders. He devoted three-plus years of His life to train twelve men, one of which was a traitor. A true mark of Christlike leadership is the ability to develop greatness in others by serving them.

The Lord's meek and humble character, His compassion for the suffering, and His resolute spirit in the face of opposition invite us to follow His example – He was a true Servant of God. Christ's selfless ministry shows us that true love needs no title to serve, just the power to do so, which is supplied by Him alone. Those who follow His example of selfless service will have the appreciation of the saints now, and will be joyfully honored by the Lord Jesus in the future.

Bartimaeus Receives His Sight (vv. 46-52)

A great multitude of people followed the Lord and His disciples out of Jericho as they journeyed towards Jerusalem (v. 46). (Jerusalem was located about 15 miles west-southwest of Jericho.) Although Mark and Luke record this healing incident, neither mentioned that there were two blind men healed, but Matthew does to uphold his Jewish vantage point of two witnesses. Only Mark supplies the name of the more prominent blind man, Bartimaeus, because of his personal dialogue with the Lord.

Two blind men were sitting on the road out of Jericho and engaged in begging when they heard the commotion. After learning that Jesus was nearing their position, they repeatedly cried out as loudly as they could even after being warned by the crowd to be quiet, *"Have mercy on us, O Lord, Son of David"* (vv. 47-48; Matt. 20:30-31). But the Lord Jesus heard their cries for help and paused to speak to them. Mark records the Lord's conversation with Bartimaeus, the son of Timaeus.

The Lord beckoned those nearby to call the blind man, which they did, saying to him, *"Be of good cheer. Rise, He is calling you"* (v. 49). Bartimaeus immediately threw aside his cloak and started towards the One calling (v. 50). Bartimaeus' name means "son of the unclean." The scene is like the children's game Marco Polo in reverse, in that the Son of David, who sees, is calling (through others) to the Son of the Unclean, who is blind and is calling back. Wherever there is a seeking sinner, there will be a seeking Savior, and those near to Christ have the joy of urging those being called to come and see.

Not only did blind Bartimaeus exhibit faith in Christ by coming to Him when requested, but He also discarded his cloak, perhaps his only possession. This was likely a unique garment that identified him as a blind man and Bartimaeus did not want it to hinder his efforts to come to Christ. By leaving the cloak, he was declaring His faith in Christ to be healed and that He would not be returning to his old lifestyle of begging.

Upon his arrival, the Lord Jesus asked Bartimaeus, *"What do you want Me to do for you?"* (v. 51). He quickly responded that he might gain his sight. The Lord had compassion on both blind men. Matthew tells us that He touched their eyes, and immediately both men gained their sight and followed Him (v. 52; Matt. 20:34).

Mercy; oh, Thou Son of David! Thus, blind Bartimaeus prayed;
Others by Thy word are saved; now to me afford Your aid.
Oh! that all the blind but knew Him and would be advised by me!
Surely would they hasten to Him; He would cause them all to see.

– John Newton

348

Mark Chapter 11

The King's Triumphant Entry Into Jerusalem (vv. 1-11)

The Lord and His disciples traveled towards Jerusalem. John informs us that after departing Perea that the Lord had briefly gone to Jerusalem and then to the wilderness near the city of Ephraim to escape hostility (John 11:54). Now the Lord is returning to Jerusalem for the final time of His earthly ministry, just a few days before His passion.

As the Lord and His disciples drew near the village of Bethphage on the eastern side of Mount Olivet, the Lord sent two of His disciples on a mission (v. 1). They were to go into the nearby village where they would immediately find a tied-up donkey with her colt (v. 2). The disciples were to loosen the donkey and bring both animals to Him. If anyone confronted them for taking the animals, they were to reply, *"The Lord has need of it"* (v. 3). After hearing this, there would not be an objection. Everything occurred just as the Lord said. Although Matthew does not record the protest of the owner, Mark and Luke do, but the owner immediately released the animals into the care of the disciples after hearing that the Lord had need of them (vv. 4-6; Luke 19:33). Matthew notes that Christ was fulfilling Zechariah's prophecy recorded four centuries earlier (Matt. 21:4-5).

On the Sunday just prior to the Lord's crucifixion (John 12:1,12), the Lord Jesus descended the Mount of Olives and entered Jerusalem on the colt of a donkey. Christendom often refers to this event as Palm Sunday, but the scene before us has little to do with palm branches being positioned on the road ahead of the Lord. This was the triumphant entry of Christ into His kingdom's capital.

Kings usually mounted horses in time of war (Rev. 19:11) but rode donkeys in time of peace. At this juncture, the Lord Jesus was offering genuine peace to the nation of Israel, but they must receive it on His terms through repentance and submission.

A large multitude quickly assembled as the Lord descended the Mount of Olives. They laid their clothes and freshly cut palm branches before the colt the Lord was riding on (vv. 7-8). Palm branches were tokens of victory and of peace (Rev. 7:9). The multitude, referring to Psalm 118:25-26, shouted, *"Hosanna! 'Blessed is He who comes in the name of the Lord!'"* (v. 9). In this moment, the Lord Jesus was rightfully declared to be the long-awaited Jewish Messiah.

Psalm 118:25 reads, *"Save now, I pray, O Lord; O Lord, I pray send now prosperity."* The Greek form of the Hebrew *yasha na* (meaning "save now") is "Hosanna." In John's account of this event, he notes that the people called the Lord Jesus, "the King of Israel." This is also how Zechariah identified the one riding on the foal of a donkey. Mark states that the people said, *"Blessed is the kingdom of our father David that comes in the name of the Lord"* (v. 10). All this highlights the intense desire of the Jewish people to be freed from Gentile oppression. They clearly wanted to be immediately liberated from Rome, but not to be saved from their sins. Many shouting "Hosanna" were merely curious seekers who got caught up in the fanfare of the moment without sincerely understanding Christ or His message (John 12:18).

Matthew states that the entire city was moved with wonder and curiosity concerning the One who rode on the colt of the donkey. *"Who is this?"* (Matt. 21:10). Could this be the One prophesied by Zecheriah four centuries earlier? But the far majority believed that Jesus was merely a prophet from Nazareth of Galilee, thus implying that He was not the expected Messiah (Matt. 21:11). Even after three years of preaching the kingdom gospel message throughout Israel, there was still much confusion concerning who Jesus really was.

The Pharisees were greatly agitated by the immense crowd that was shouting "Hosanna" to the One they believed was threatening Judaism (John 12:19). Luke tells us that the Pharisees demanded that Jesus should rebuke His disciples for making such a declaration. But the Lord said to them, *"I tell you that if these should keep silent, the stones would immediately cry out"* (Luke 19:40). However, John notes that he and the other disciples did not understand the significance of Christ's entry into Jerusalem until after His resurrection (John 12:16). For three years Jesus' identity as Israel's Messiah had been kept secret, but now, five days before His crucifixion, His grandeur was to be emphatically publicized. What had been considered dangerous to state earlier was now necessary to boldly publish. Only the Lord Jesus fully understood the significance of the incident. Mark informs us that after entering Jerusalem, the Lord went into the temple and observed all that was going on there. Because the hour was late, He returned to Bethany with His disciples (v. 11).

The Barren Fig Tree (vv. 12-14)

The next morning, the Lord began the trek back to Jerusalem from Bethany (v. 12). Matthew places the incident of the barren fig tree on Tuesday morning, but Mark prefers Monday morning, just prior to the cleansing of the temple. Regardless, the Lord was hungry and sought fruit from a fig tree that was along the roadway (v. 13). Early spring would be an unusual time to look for eatable fruit on a fig tree, but the Lord had a deeper significance to the scene than satisfying His hunger in mind. After seeing that there were only leaves on the tree and no fruit, He cursed the tree in the presence of His disciples, *"Let no one eat fruit from you ever again"* (v. 14). Matthew states that the tree instantly began to wither (Matt. 21:19).

About four months earlier Christ had spoken a parable about an unfruitful fig tree, which represented the fruitless religiosity of Israel at that time (Luke 13:6-9). The Jewish nation is allegorically likened to a foliage trilogy in Scripture: the vine, the fig tree, and the olive tree. Each one represents a distinct aspect of Israel's existence. Israel, as a political reality, is likened to a noble vine (a grape vine; Jer. 8:13), which God planted in the world (Jer. 2:21, 12:10); Israel was to be God's vineyard.

At the end of the Tribulation Period, the refined Jewish nation will receive the Holy Spirit and obtain spiritual life in Christ (Zech. 12:10). The work of the Holy Spirit in Israel is similarly depicted by the oil flowing to a lampstand from the olive tree in Zechariah's vision (Zech. 4:4-7). In this spiritually fruitful state, the Jews will be known as the olive tree which provides a testimony of God's goodness to the entire world (Hos. 14:6; Rom. 11:17-24).

When Israel is spoken of as a fig tree in Scripture, the metaphor relates to Israel's religious veracity, which often was fruitless for God (Jer. 8:13). This reality, including Judaism today, is what the Lord Jesus is addressing in this parable. After preaching the Kingdom message for three-plus years to the lost sheep of Israel, Christ cursed the fruitless fig tree just before His death at Calvary (vv. 18-21). He sought spiritual fruit from the nation of Israel, and none was found. Less than forty years later, Jerusalem and the temple were destroyed, and the Jews have not sacrificed since that time. The Old Covenant was replaced by the New Covenant, sealed with Christ's blood, and God was determined not to allow the Jews to continue in what was now obsolete (Heb. 8:8-13).

One of the signs that the Tribulation Period and the Second Advent of Christ are nearing is that the fig tree (i.e., religious Israel) will again shoot forth leaves after a long winter season of deadness (Luke 21:29-31). Leaves must precede fruit, but the fig tree will bear no fruit until the spiritual rebirth of the nation occurs in the latter days of the Tribulation Period. What might the new leaves speak of? This is likely a reference to the Jews reviving the old sacrificial system during, and perhaps just prior to, the Tribulation Period.

We know from various prophecies that the Antichrist will desecrate the Jewish temple and put a stop to animal sacrifices at the midpoint of the Tribulation Period (Dan. 9:27; Matt. 24:15; 2 Thess. 2:3-7). Hence, logically speaking, a temple will have to be erected and animal sacrifices will have to be reinstituted by that point. The generation that sees this happen will certainly see the coming of the Lord Jesus in His glory (Matt. 24:32-35). But presently, the fig tree, Israel's religious system, is leafless (i.e., no animal sacrifices) and fruitless (void of spiritual vitality).

Christ Cleanses the Temple Again (vv. 15-19)

Mark records that the Lord and His disciples departed from Jerusalem to Bethany after Christ's triumphant entry into Jerusalem and then they returned to Jerusalem the next day, on Monday (vv. 11-12).

Although the Lord Jesus is rarely spoken of in Scripture as being angry, it is evident that His holy anger blazed up on this occasion. After arriving at the temple, He made a scourge to drive the animals and their masters from the temple and He threw over the tables of the moneychangers (v. 15; Matt. 21:12). Harold Paisley summarizes the situation that Christ was correcting:

> The high priest had permitted a market in the court of the Gentiles, for sale of items used in the temple ritual, such as, wine, salt, oil, and birds and animals. There were also moneychangers who produced large revenues, often by fraud. There were those also who carried baggage and merchandise from the markets through the sacred temple area, as a shortcut home. Mark is the only writer who records this added act of irreverence.[92]

These vendors and racketeers had turned the temple, God's house, into a place of commerce and thievery, but the Lord restored it to a house of prayer (v. 16). The Lord then quoted Jeremiah to affirm Israel's offense against God concerning appropriate behavior in the temple, God's house: *"My house shall be called a house of prayer for all nations. But you have made it a den of thieves"* (v. 17). The Lord Jesus cleansed the temple twice, once at the beginning of His earthly ministry (John 2:14-17), and then again, a few days before His death. In both situations, His righteous anger prompted behavior that honored His Father.

Previously, while angry with the Pharisees, the Lord healed a man on the Sabbath day to challenge their shallow spiritual existence (3:5). With utter contempt, He later warned them of impending judgment (Matt. 23:13-36). At other times, the Lord's anger did not result in direct action; instead, He relinquished the offense into His Father's care (Luke 23:34). The Lord shows us that there are times to defer from righteous anger to accomplish a greater good: *"The discretion of a man makes him slow to anger, and his glory is to overlook a transgression"* (Prov. 19:11).

Hearing what Jesus of Nazareth had done in the temple, the scribes and chief priests sought to destroy Him, but because they feared the people, who were astonished at His teaching, Israel's religious leaders did not arrest Christ (v. 18). When evening had come, the Lord departed the temple and again journeyed about two miles east to the village of Bethany and lodged there (v. 19). He would repeat the same trek to Jerusalem and back again on the following day, Tuesday.

The Prayer of Faith (vv. 20-24)

As Christ and His disciples walked back to Jerusalem the next morning, they passed by the fig tree that Christ had cursed the previous day (v. 20). The tree was dried up from its roots. Peter called the Lord's attention to the tree and recalled His judgment upon it (v. 21). The Lord answered the inquiry by affirming that what was declared in the will of God by faith and without doubting could move mountains, let alone wither a tree (vv. 22-23). In a few days, the Lord would be leaving His disciples. He wanted them to understand that through *believing* prayer they would have all the power of heaven to assist them in fulfilling their mission for Him (v. 24).

A Releasing Spirit (vv. 25-26)

The Lord demonstrated in verses 15-18 that our righteous indignation to honor God will be demanded at times. Indignation sacrifices selfish interest to intensely and actively pattern God's own abhorrence of sin.

353

As an example, the Lord "was much displeased" with His disciples for forbidding children to come to Him (10:14). The Greek verb translated "was much displeased" means "to have indignation" towards. The Lord was righteously angry with His disciples.

However, anger is a powerful emotion that we cannot control very long without sinning (Eph. 4:26). If our anger cannot motivate behavior that will serve God or others in profitable way, then we must release the offense to the Lord immediately and extinguish our anger. The word *charizomai* is often rendered "forgiving," as in Ephesians 4:32.

Rather than permitting our bitterness and resentment to destroy us and others, Paul exhorts, "*And be kind to one another, tenderhearted, forgiving one another, even as God in Christ forgave you*" (v. 32). The Greek word *charizomai* is found twenty-four times in the New Testament. It is translated as various forms of "forgive" fourteen times. Interestingly, only two of these fourteen references are found in the Gospels (both are contained in one parable in Luke 7); the remaining occurrences are contained in the Epistles. *Charizomai* means "to bestow a favor unconditionally or to freely give." It expresses the type of unconditional *releasing* attitude a Christian should maintain when offended by others. To freely release the matter means that one does not seek revenge, vengeance or become resentful.

Release determines to not take revenge for an offense but is determined to suffer loss and simply entrust the outcome to the Lord. It waits patiently for the opportunity to extend forgiveness when the offending party confesses sin. Until such time, the matter remains in the background of one's thinking. The main word rendered "forgive" in the Gospels is *aphiemi* and means "let be" (e.g., Luke 23:34). Yet, in the Epistles, we learn how we have been forgiven by God through Christ; thus, we are to immediately release offenses to God, rather than to merely take no action. Then, an unburdened heart can act objectively: How can edify others and uphold God's honor in this hurtful situation?

The mechanics of forgiveness are mainly addressed in the Gospel accounts and are associated with a different Greek word *aphiemi*, which means "to send away" and by implication "let it be – take no action." For example, Matthew 18:15-18 informs us how to go about problem resolution with others, while Luke 17:3 instructs us to not *declare* personal forgiveness until the offending party has repented.

Believers must both release offenses to the Lord when they occur and extend forgiveness to offenders when they have acknowledged their sin and asked to be forgiven (Luke 17:3; Col. 3:13). The Lord Jesus expects us to follow His example of forgiving others; Christians are to be a forgiving people (v. 25; Matt. 18:21-22, 35). Holding on to past offenses and internalizing anger will result in resentment, and eventually bitterness will take root in the heart. Such behavior displeases God and hinders our fellowship with Him (v. 26). An unforgiving spirit presses down on the heart to cause a loss of joy and fellowship with the Lord and His people. We cannot enjoy fellowship with each other unless all parties are in fellowship with the Lord; believers can only share together what they have from the Lord. A believer who does not repent of sin cannot be in fellowship with the Lord. A believer who does not grant forgiveness to another who has confessed his sin cannot be in fellowship with the Lord. Consequently, such individuals cannot enjoy Christian fellowship with any believer until they pattern their behavior after God's own behavior.

The Challenge of the Priests, Scribes, and Elders (vv. 27-33)

The Lord arrived at the temple for *Super Tuesday*. On this day, the Lord would silence multiple challengers, speak three parables to the multitudes, deliver a *woe* message to the Pharisees, and privately teach His disciples about things to come on the Mount of Olives.

The chief priests and Jewish elders were the first to confront the Lord, *"By what authority are you doing these things? And who gave you this authority to do these things?"* (v. 28). The Lord chose to answer their two-part question with a question of His own, which if they answered, then He promised that He would answer their inquiry concerning the origin of His authority (v. 29): The Lord asked them, *"The baptism of John – was it from heaven or from men?"* (v. 30).

The priests discussed that matter and decided that there was no safe answer to the Lord's question. If they said that John's authority came from heaven, then they would be guilty of ignoring His message as the Messiah's forerunner (v. 31). However, if they said that John was not from God, then they feared that the people would revolt against them, because they believed that John was a true prophet of God (v. 32). So, they declined to answer the Lord's question, but their silence affirmed the answer to their own questions to Him. Therefore, the Lord was neither obligated to nor did He need to answer their challenge with a response (v. 33).

Mark Chapter 12

The Landowner and the Wicked Vinedressers (vv. 1-12)

This is the second of three parables spoken together in the temple on the Tuesday before Christ's Crucifixion; Mark only records this parable. In short, a landowner planted a vineyard and leased it to tenants, who would not render to him its fruit and, in fact, the tenants injured or killed the owner's messengers, including his only son, who came to collect what was owed to the landowner. Hence, the tenants would receive the landowner's wrath, who afterwards would lease the vineyard to others.

The nation of Israel, as a political reality, is likened to a noble vine (a grape vine; Jer. 8:13), which God planted in the world. In fact, several Old Testament prophets refer to Israel as God's special vine that He had planted (e.g., Isa. 5:1-7; Ezek. 15:2-4).

The prophet Hosea rebuked Israel because, though it (as a vine) had lush foliage, its fruit was worthless because it was self-produced for itself, and was not from God or for God: *"Israel empties his vine; he brings forth fruit for himself"* (Hos. 10:1). Two centuries later, the prophet Jeremiah told his fellow countrymen that God had planted a beautiful vineyard (speaking of the Jewish nation), but Israel's shepherds had made it desolate (Jer. 12:10). Israel was God's vineyard, but even in Christ's day, because of spiritually corrupt leaders, it was still not fruitful to God.

God repeatedly attempted to restore the vine to a fruitful condition by sending prophets to rebuke Israel's wayward and carnal leaders, but to no avail. Finally, God sent His beloved Son to plead with Israel to repent and be restored to God, but the Jewish nation rejected Him and had Him put to death. As Paul explains to the Ephesians, the offer of grace in Christ has been presented to the Gentiles, who through faith have been brought into the commonwealth of blessing promised to Israel (Eph. 3:2-12). Gentile believers in the "dispensation of the grace of God" (Eph. 3:2) are now bearing spiritual fruit to God. This is what God wanted from Israel, but having rejected Christ, the opportunity was given to those who were not God's covenant people (Rom. 9:25).

The key components of this parable are as follows:

The certain landowner = God.

The vineyard = Israel.

The vinedressers via lease = Israel's leaders.

The servants = the former prophets and John the baptizer.

The Son = the Lord Jesus.

The other vinedressers = Gentiles trusting Christ in the Church Age.

Paul's analogy of the olive tree in Romans 11 parallels Christ's teaching in this parable. In this analogy, the root of the tree is the Abrahamic covenant and the olive tree is Christ: through Him the promises of God will bless Israel, the natural branches. Yet, disbelief leads to rebellion and the loss of God's blessings and fellowship. Willful sin and rebellion will always invoke God's chastening hand. God did to Israel exactly what He told them He would do if His people erred from the Law and abandoned Him (Deut. 28); thus, the natural branches (the Jewish people) were removed from the opportunity to be nationally blessed by God through Christ.

Yet, the analogy shows us that God will restore Israel to Himself. The fact that the Jews (the natural branches) could be, and indeed will be, grafted back into the olive tree indicates that the focus of the illustration is not eternal salvation per se, but rather the blessings that God desires to share with those who exercise faith in Him. Gentile believers (the wild branch) are a second benefactor of the New Covenant and thus are permitted to share in the blessings promised to Israel (Eph. 2:11-3:7). Gentiles are grafted into the olive tree, indicating the blessings of Christ rooted in God's covenant with Abraham. The New Covenant permits individual Jews to be saved now and the Jewish nation to be reconciled to God after the Church Age ends.

However, when Christ spoke this parable, proud Israel was in rebellion against God, His prophets, and His Son, whom they put to death (vv. 6-8). The tenants wanted the inheritance (to control the people and receive their honor and praise) instead of giving it to the rightful owner – God. In Matthew's account, the Lord asked the scribes and Pharisees what should be done with the rebels. They condemned themselves when they adamantly stated that the tenants should be killed for their brutal insolence and the vineyard should be leased to other vinedressers who would render to the owner the fruit of his vineyard (v. 9; Matt. 21:41).

After answering Christ's question correctly, the Lord quoted Psalm 118:22 to affirm that God would provide the Gentiles an opportunity to be tenants of His vineyard to receive the desired fruit He longed for (vv. 10-11). At that time, the Jewish nation had no place for Christ; He was the rejected Stone that God then used as a cornerstone to create the Church (i.e., a Gentile bride for His Son). Those who truly repent and receive Christ alone for salvation (i.e., become broken on the Stone) will be saved and can be fruitful to God (Matt. 21:44). But those who reject Christ will be eternally judged at His second advent to the earth (i.e., they will be crushed to powder by the Stone from heaven; Dan. 2:45).

The scribes and Pharisees were infuriated by this conclusion because it was obvious that Christ was likening them to the proud, murderous tenants who would be destroyed. These religious leaders would have arrested the Lord Jesus but declined to do so for fear of how the crowds listening to Him might respond (v. 12).

The Challenge of the Herodians (vv. 13-17)

On the Tuesday before Christ's crucifixion, the Pharisees, the Sadducees, and the Herodians all challenge His authority. By articulating divine wisdom, the Lord not only stopped the mouths of His objectors, but He also denounced them as corrupt leaders of God's covenant people. These shepherds had not cared for God's sheep in Israel, but rather had led them away from the Lord into a miserable spiritual condition.

The Lord Jesus warned His disciples not to be influenced by *"the leaven of Herod"* and, by implication, others with the same ideology (8:15). Herod Antipas the tetrarch, the infamous son of Herod the Great, was a Jew in cahoots with the Romans, and was, therefore, a friend of the world (Jas. 4:4). In the case of Herod, and those like him, love for God and His Word had been supplanted by the love for materialism, fame, and political ambition. Such individuals are prone to skepticism, immorality, and worldliness, and thus close association with them was to be avoided.

After the Lord spoke *The Marriage Feast* parable, the Pharisees began plotting how they might entangle Jesus in His words (Matt. 22:15). After they devised what they thought would be foolproof questions to accomplish this goal, the Pharisees came with the Herodians to pose their inquiry (v. 13). These two parties were bitter foes, but they had a common enemy, the Lord Jesus, which temporarily caused them to work together. The objective was to dupe Jesus into uttering a political statement against Rome that would then force the Roman authorities to act against Him.

In true political form, the Herodians first complimented the Lord before moving to spring their trap. They claimed that He was a true teacher that taught the way of God accurately despite what men might say about what He taught. Their mistake was thinking that wicked men could ever appeal to the ego of a righteous man. Their praise would not entice the Lord to say something that they wanted to hear; rather their empty praise just revealed the deceit harboring in their hearts.

The question was then posed to the Lord, *"Is it lawful to pay taxes to Caesar, or not?"* (v. 14). If He said "yes," then He would be viewed as affirming Gentile oppression over His countrymen. This position opposed the Abrahamic covenant which promised liberation from Gentile rule. This would be ultimately achieved by the coming Jewish Messiah. Certainly then, if Christ was the Jewish Messiah, He would not endorse paying taxes to Rome. If the Lord said "no" to the question, then He would certainly be arrested by Roman authorities for leading a rebellion against the empire.

But the Lord perceived their wickedness and addressed them as hypocrites for testing Him with such an inquiry (v. 15). How did the Lord answer their question? He said, *"Bring Me a denarius that I may see it"* (v. 15). He was shown a denarius and asked His audience, *"Whose image and inscription is this?"* (v. 16). They responded by saying that it was Caesar's image and inscription on the coin. The Lord then said, *"Render therefore to Caesar that things that are Caesar's, and to God the things that are God's"* (v. 17).

If they were using Roman coinage, then they were admitting that they were under Roman rule. But given the warnings of Moses (e.g., Deut. 28:47-48), Israel would only be under Gentile rule because they had rebelled against Jehovah. So, the Lord was reminding them that they were paying taxes to Rome because they were under the chastening hand of God. When the Lord's oppressors heard His response, they marveled at His wisdom and departed from Him without asking any more questions (Matt. 22:22). He had thwarted their best attempt to hoodwink Him into saying something that would be controversial or dangerous.

The Challenge of the Sadducees (vv. 18-27)

The next group to challenge the Lord's authority was the supernatural-denying Sadducees, a religious sect which formed part of the Jewish judicial court called the Sanhedrin. They did not believe in angels, miracles, or a bodily resurrection (v. 18). These were the liberal theologians of Christ's day, and touted ideologies such as higher-criticism and skepticism that negated the literal interpretation of God's Word.

The Sadducees asked the Lord Jesus about a woman who had been married to seven different men. (She was widowed seven times and never married to more than one man at once, vv. 19-22.) As the Sadducees did not believe in a bodily resurrection, their question to the Lord was clearly a test: *"In the resurrection, when they rise, whose wife will she be? For all seven had her as wife"* (v. 23). The Lord's rebuke of the Sadducees was threefold: they were mistaken, they did not know the Scriptures, and they did not know the power of God (v. 24). They were mistaken, because in the resurrection, people would not be given in marriage, in the same way angels were not given in marriage (v. 25).

Rather than reiterating what they had already rejected, the Lord used the opportunity to affirm the truth of resurrection. The Sadducees did not know the Scripture, for Jehovah was the God of the living (v. 26). They also did not know the power of God, for God was the God of the living, not the dead (v. 27). How could God keep His unconditional covenants with Abraham, Isaac, and Jacob, all of whom had died, unless their souls were eternal, and each would experience a future bodily resurrection?

Contrary to the Mormon and Islamic views of heaven, people in heaven will neither be male nor female, at least in the way we understand the genders to exist today. There will be no marriages (save the Lamb with His saints) or sexual activities in heaven as some world religions tout. The Lord confirmed this truth while responding to a fictitious scenario posed by the Sadducees. Matthew says that those listening to His teaching on this matter were astonished at His wisdom (Matt. 22:33).

Those who experience resurrection will not be gender-significant. They will be like the angels, who are neither male nor female, although when they present themselves in human form to deliver God's messages, they have always appeared as men (e.g., Gen. 18). Male and female genders were God's design to provide complementing companionship in marriage and for the purpose of procreation (Gen. 1:28, 2:18). In heaven, the need for reproduction will be eliminated as everyone will be eternal. Moreover, our communion with God in heaven will far exceed anything we could have ever experienced in an earthly relationship. Accordingly, we will be completely satisfied with being in fellowship with God and desire nothing else, including marital relationships. One of the clear warning signs of a false teaching is the notion that fleshly desires will be satisfied in heaven, or even worse, that such things are a part of some supreme deity's reward system.

The Challenge of the Pharisees (vv. 28-34)

After hearing that the Lord Jesus had silenced the Sadducees, the Pharisees decided it was time for them to confront the Lord with their best test as presented by one of their esteemed lawyers (Matt. 22:34-35). On behalf of the Pharisees, the lawyer asked, *"Which is the first commandment of all?"* (v. 28). In other words, what was the greatest commandment of the Mosaic Law?

The Lord Jesus did not hesitate to answer this important question: *"Hear, O Israel, the Lord our God, the Lord is one"* (v. 29). This was a daily prayer affirmation of the Jewish people. Then the Lord quoted Deuteronomy 10:12, to declare that to love God with all your heart, soul, and mind was the greatest commandment and to love your neighbor as yourself would be the second greatest commandment (vv. 30-31). The Lord then explained that all that was in the Law and declared by the prophets hung on these two commandments (Matt. 22:40). That is, to love God above all and to sacrificially give to others was the basis for all other laws (v. 31).

The scribe-lawyer that was quizzing the Lord said that He had answered correctly (v. 32). He noted that loving God above all, and others as one's own self was considered by God to be more significant than burnt offerings and sacrifices (v. 33). The scribe realized that offerings could not replace the matter of obedience. This correct understanding impressed the Lord Jesus, who said in response: *"You are not far from the kingdom of God"* (v. 34). Afterwards, no one dared test Him with any more questions.

The Lord Challenges the Pharisees (vv. 35-37)

While the Pharisees were still gathered before Him, the Lord asked them some questions from Psalm 110: *"How is it that the scribes say that the Christ is the Son of David? For David himself said by the Holy Spirit: 'The Lord said to my Lord, sit at My right hand, till I make Your enemies Your footstool'"* (vv. 35-36). In Psalm 110, as the writer of Hebrews proclaims (Heb. 1:13), God the Father is speaking to God the Son, whom David calls his "Lord." Given this understanding, the Lord Jesus poses His final question to the Pharisees: How was it possible for David, speaking as inspired by God, to call his Son (his descendant) his "Lord" (v. 37)?

The only logical answer to this question is that David's Son, the future Jewish Messiah, must be both God and a descendant of David. But the Pharisees would not answer this question, for to do so would validate the Lord Jesus' claims as being God's Son and the rightful heir to the throne of David.

The Marks of a Pharisee (vv. 38-40)

Having silenced the Pharisees by His questions concerning David's Son also being his Lord, the Lord Jesus spoke to the multitude (including His disciples) about the hypocrisy of the scribes and the Pharisees. He mentions several of their negative behaviors to show why they had been rejected by God as His shepherds in Israel. The people would be wise to beware of their teaching, for they were prone to self-seeking and self-exalting behavior. Matthew's list of ill behaviors is more extensive than Mark's record.

First, the scribes wore long robes in public to appear pious before the people. They desired others to take note of their outward religiosity and praise them for it (v. 38).

Second, the scribes sought the best seats in the synagogues and at feasts to convey their pompous superiority over the people. What they wore and did in public was for the appreciation of men, rather than by an inward compulsion to please God (v. 39). To appear spiritual to others, they developed practices that went beyond what the Law required.

Third, instead of caring for the poor and especially the widows among them, the scribes took advantage of them for profit (v. 40).

Fourth, the scribes uttered long prayers to appear spiritual to those observing them (v. 40). In their own minds, they were rulers of the people and therefore above them, but as demonstrated by the Good Shepherd, God's idea of a spiritual leader is to humble oneself to serve others, not to honor oneself and neglect caring for others (v. 11; John 10:11).

The Widow's Mites (vv. 41-44)

While still at the temple, the Lord observed how people were contributing their money to the temple treasury (v. 41). Harold Paisley describes the scene for us:

> Along the wall were thirteen copper chests each with a trumpet-like receptacle into which the offerings were dropped. Nine were designated "Jehovah's Offering" and four "The Offering for the Poor." The phrase "sounding the trumpet" was derived from throwing the coins into the receptacle so as to attract attention (Matt. 6:2). Jesus saw many that were rich casting in much.[93]

The rich gave much, but in such a way that others would observe them doing so and honor them for their generosity. They sought the praise of men rather than God's appreciation for a selfless act.

In contrast, the Lord called His disciples' attention to a poor widow who quietly gave to the Lord all she had, two mites (v. 42). A mite (the Greek *Lepta*) was a copper coin of the lowest value in Judea. Mark explains to his Roman audience that the widow cast in two mites, which was worth the same as a Roman *quadron* (or *quadran*) in coinage. Unfortunately, several English translations of this passage compare the widow's two mites to the English penny or farthing, which are virtually worthless in today's economy.

However, if one considers that a *mite* was worth a one hundred and twenty-eighth part of a denarius, a day's wage for a laborer, the value of what the widow gave is more significant. For example, if a laborer today made $20/hour and worked a ten-hour day, that would be a $200 income for the day. One sixty-fourth of that amount would be over $3, which would be the equivalent of what the widow gave to the Lord. It was all she had, but it was not an insignificant gift, and in the Lord's estimation, her giving was priceless.

The Lord told His disciples that from God's perspective, the widow had given more than anyone else. Others had given out of their abundance, but being in poverty, she gave her whole livelihood in faith to God (vv. 43-44). It is one thing to give to the Lord what we will not miss; it is an entirely different matter to have little and give it all to Him. The former behavior is often self-exalting and preserves self-sufficiency, but the latter action reveals what one truly thinks of God.

Mark Chapter 13

The Temple to Be Destroyed (vv. 1-2)

The Tuesday before Calvary (three days prior to the Lord's death) was an incredibly busy day for the Lord Jesus. Besides mastering the verbal challenges of the Herodians, the Sadducees, the Pharisees, the scribes, and a lawyer, He also spoke the "Woe" message to the Pharisees and conveyed several parables. After these events, the Lord departed with His disciples to the Mount of Olives for a time of private ministry. At this time, He proclaimed to them important details concerning the future of Israel and the time of His Second Advent to the earth. Because this teaching was privately given on the Mount of Olives, it is often referred to as "The Olivet Discourse."

As with the "Sermon on the Mount," Matthew records the specific details of this incident more prominently than the other evangelists (Matthew 24 and 25). Both Mark and Luke devote one chapter each to the narration (Mark 13 and Luke 21), while John does not mention the discourse at all. Much of the detail contained in Matthew 25 is completely unique to Matthew.

The Olivet Discourse is *strictly* Jewish, for the Church will already be in heaven before the events of the Tribulation Period begin to unfold. The Olivet Discourse provides escalating signs of the coming Tribulation Period and describes events in the first half, mid, and last half of this horrendous time on earth. Then the Lord spoke of His Second Coming to the earth to judge the wicked.

After departing the temple and arriving on the Mount of Olives, one of the disciples called the Lord's attention to the grandeur of the temple directly west of them across the Kidron Valley (v. 1). The Lord told His disciples that this temple would be completely destroyed; not one stone would remain on another (v. 2). This prophecy was fulfilled when Roman armies under Titus's command destroyed the temple and much of Jerusalem with fire in 70 A.D. The extreme heat crumbled the stones of the temple, but also melted the gold band around the top of the temple.

After the rubble cooled down, Roman soldiers then removed each stone to retrieve the precious metal.

The Beginning of Sorrows: Pre-Tribulation Signs (vv. 3-8)

Having sat down opposite the temple on the Mount of Olives, Christ began to teach His disciples. Peter, James, John, and Andrew asked Him to explain in more detail about the future events He had just alluded to (v. 3). They especially wanted to know, *"What will be the sign of Your coming, and of the end of the age?"* (v. 4; Matt. 24:3).

In response to their inquiry, the Lord identified many signs associated with the coming of the Tribulation Period, the first half of the Tribulation Period, the Abomination of Desolation in the middle of the Tribulation Period, then the Great Tribulation (i.e., the last half of the Tribulation Period), and His second Advent. He desires that Christians in the Church Age, as indicated by the phrase *"the end of the age,"* would not be deceived by false prophets or false Christs (Matt. 24:3).

He first speaks of the Beginning of Sorrows (vv. 5-8). This would be an era marked by specific prophetic fulfillment which would alert the Jews to the forthcoming Tribulation Period. These troubling events are of an escalating nature and are meant primarily to be signs to Israel that the time of *Jacob's Trouble* is nearing. But as the Church will be removed from the earth prior to this seven-year period of Israel's final chastening, believers in the Church Age can be excited about these signs also. However, Christians should remember that there are no signs given to the Church for Christ's imminent return. The rapture of the Church is the next eschatological event on God's calendar.

First, the Lord explains that in the era just prior to the Tribulation Period there would be a dramatic increase in those claiming to be sent from God, especially claiming some type of Messianic authority (v. 6). Many false prophets will rise at this time to confuse and deceive the inhabitants of the earth from believing the truth.

Second, there will be wars and rumors of wars before the Tribulation period (v. 7). The twentieth century saw the first two wars that were worldwide, which ushered in the Nuclear Age and the resulting Cold War – the constant threat of nuclear annihilation. It is not likely that there will be another world war until the Tribulation Period.

Third, nation will rise against nation, and kingdom against kingdom (v. 8). The Greek word rendered "nation" in this verse is *ethnos*, which is the root word for our English word "ethnic." As the Tribulation Period nears, there will be a dramatic increase in ethnic violence. A shift from large numbers of soldiers perishing in warfare to ethnic genocide is likely indicated by this prophecy (see the Matthew 24 discussion for statistics).

Fourth, there will be a dramatic increase in famines, pestilences, and earthquakes in various locations throughout the planet (v. 8). With the rapid rise of expedient transportation in the twentieth century also came the opportunity to rapidly transmit viruses over great distances. Given the earth's growing and mobile population, global pandemics may occur today in days instead of months as in previous centuries. Lastly, the Lord spoke of a time marked by increased earthquakes just prior to the Tribulation Period (see the Matthew 24 discussion for statistics).

The previous, escalating signs prior to the commencement of the Tribulation Period were referred to by the Lord as "the beginning of sorrows" (v. 8). The eschatology timeline presented in Mark 13 is chronological. The Tribulation Period begins in verse 9.

The First Half of the Tribulation Period (vv. 9-13)

The Lord then informed His Jewish brothers that when the time of Jacob's Trouble began, the Jews (the "you") would be hated by the Gentiles (the "they") and be delivered up to tribulation and be killed (v. 9). During the first half of the Tribulation Period, many will be offended by the gospel of the kingdom being preached throughout the world (v. 10). This message will cause much division, betrayal, oppression, and hatred among those living on the earth (v. 11). There will even be a loss of trust in and love for one's own family members (v. 12).

There will be 144,000 divinely chosen and sealed Jewish evangelists that will be preaching the kingdom message throughout the earth at this time (Rev. 7:3-8, 14:1-5). The kingdom message is what Christ preached to Israel initially but was rejected; she was offered a literal, earthly, political kingdom (Matt. 4:17). Today, the Church preaches the gospel of grace: Christ crucified and raised from the dead for our justification. Only believers are tasked by the Lord with sharing this message with the lost (Matt. 28:19-20). There is no example in Scripture of even angels intruding on this responsibility. After the Church Age has concluded, the kingdom message will be preached again in Israel and indeed throughout the world. John foretold that angels would then fly over the earth to publicly declare its validity – the true King is coming to judge; do not worship the Antichrist (Rev. 14:6-12). These gospel distinctions show that Christ's plans for His Church and for restoring Israel are different. The Church has a heavenly citizenship, calling, and inheritance, while Israel has earthly promises and inheritance.

All those who endure through the Tribulation Period and believe that Christ will come to the earth to avenge His name and set up His kingdom will be delivered by Him at His second advent. These individuals will not worship the Antichrist or take his mark (Rev. 13:11-18, 19:20). In fact, a great multitude will not identify with the Antichrist and will be put to death during the Tribulation Period (Rev. 7:9-15). These Tribulation saints will be resurrected to rule and reign with Christ in His earthly kingdom (Rev. 20:4).

Mid-Tribulation: The Abomination of Desolation (vv. 14-18)

The Lord Jesus then referred to Daniel's prophecy concerning the abomination of desolation committed by the Antichrist in the temple of God in Jerusalem (v. 14). Namely, he will stop the Jewish sacrifices and declare himself as God incarnate (2 Thess. 2:4). God moved the prophet Daniel to declare His ultimate timetable for the final restoration of the Jewish nation (Dan. 9:24-27). The prophecy is broken into two major parts: sixty-nine weeks, which consists of two portions of seven weeks and sixty-two weeks, and then the final section of one week. The word translated "week" is literally "seven." But seven what? Based on how the final week is described elsewhere in Scripture, we can conclude that a week is speaking of seven years.

The abomination of desolation committed by the Antichrist (the one who will make a peace covenant with the Jewish nation for one week) occurs in the middle of the week (v. 15; Dan. 8:25, 9:27; 2 Thess. 2:4). But Scripture elsewhere provides the exact timing of this event. It occurs "a time (1), times (2), and half a time (1/2)" after the start of the week of years (Dan. 7:25, 12:7; Rev. 12:14). This three and a half times is also equal to 1260 days (Rev. 12:6) or 42 months (Rev. 13:5). As just witnessed in the fulfillment of Jeremiah's seventy-year prophecy, a Jewish prophetic year in Scripture is consistently 360 days (12 months x 30 days/month = 360 days). Three and a half years would then be equal to 1260 days (3.5 years x 360 days/year = 1260 days). Thus, Daniel's prophecy is unmistakably speaking of seventy weeks of years or, literally, "seventy sevens."

When the abomination of desolation occurs at the midway point in the Tribulation Period, there will also be war in heaven. The archangel Michael, along with his angels, will war against the devil and his fallen angels to constrain evil to the earth (Dan. 12:1; Rev. 12:7-10). Satan, knowing that his time is short, will be enraged and seek to exterminate the Jewish people (Rev. 12:12-15). However, the Lord will preserve and protect a remnant of His covenant people from harm (v. 16; Rev. 12:16-17). The slaughter will be so severe and widespread that the Lord warns His countrymen not to tarry for any reason but to journey to places of hiding in the mountains as quickly as possible (vv. 15-16). The Lord then acknowledged the difficulties of accomplishing this in wintertime, or those who were pregnant or who were caring for young children (vv. 17-18).

The Last Half of the Tribulation Period (vv. 19-23)

While speaking of signs associated with the Great Tribulation (Matt. 24:21), the time when the Antichrist will be gaining followers on the earth and slaughtering those who will not take His mark (v. 19; Rev. 13:15-18), the Lord gave a warning concerning the powerful signs of the Antichrist to deceive the masses (vv. 21-23). The Lord then stated that during this time the slaughter on the earth would be so great that no one would survive the Great Tribulation if it lasted longer than three and a half years (v. 20). But for "the elect's sake" (speaking of the refined Jewish remnant to survive the Tribulation Period), this terrible time would not be permitted to go beyond the appointed time.

In the Tribulation, the beast and the false prophet (with many other deceivers) will be working great signs and wonders to deceive the inhabitants of the world (Rev. 13). The devil is a powerful being that can do what from our lowly vantage point seems impossible. This is why believers are not to trust in their senses, but are to use Scripture to judge all things. The truth is in the whole and if we have rightly divided the Word of Truth and hold it, we will not be deceived. Accordingly, the Lord told the sign-seeking Pharisees that *"An evil and adulterous generation seeks after a sign"* (12:39). Signs (what our senses affirm) can be fabricated by the devil, but God's Word is from Him alone and thus is always truth. The deception at this time will be so powerful that the Lord warned against listening to anything that men proclaimed as truth. Yield to God's Word alone.

GOD'S SALVATION FOR
ISRAEL AND THE CHURCH

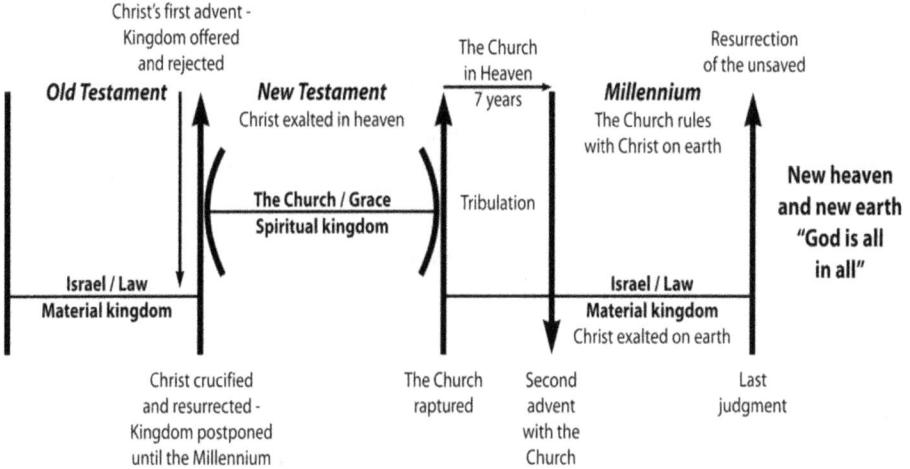

Tribulation Period Ends: Christ's Second Advent (vv. 24-27)

The Tribulation Period concludes with the second advent of Christ to the earth to destroy the Antichrist and liberate surviving Jews in Jerusalem (Zech. 14). This will be a time of great upheaval in heaven and on earth (vv. 24-25). Christ's return will be a visible coming in which the entire world will see the glory of Christ (v. 26; Luke 17:24). Like lightning that flashes across the sky, the Lord's coming will be sudden and visible to all (Matt. 24:27).

When the Jews see Jesus Christ returning to the earth in glory and power, they will mourn as a family would if they had lost their firstborn son or their only son (Zech. 12:10). With Christ's Second Advent to earth, the spiritual blindness of the Jewish nation will come to an end. They will trust in the Lord Jesus Christ, their Messiah, the One they had pierced two thousand years earlier (Zech. 12:10). Although we see that individual Jews in the Old Testament were filled by the Holy Spirit to speak for God or to serve Him (e.g., Ex. 35:30-35; 1 Sam. 10:10), the nation has never been indwelt by the Spirit of God (Zech. 4:4-7). This will not happen until Christ's second coming to the earth (Isa. 59:21).

Immediately after Christ's arrival to the earth, there will be a blast of a trumpet and the angels will gather all of God's covenant people remaining in the world back to the land of Israel (v. 27). The prophet Ezekiel states that the Lord will not leave one Jew anywhere in the world;

all should be brought back to Israel to witness the complete fulfillment of the Abrahamic covenant (Ezek. 39:28-29). Those who hold a Mid-Tribulation Rapture view of the Church point to the Church being taken up to heaven at the trump of 1 Corinthians 15:51-52, which they associate with the last of seven trumpet judgment in Revelation 8-11. However, the seventh trumpet judgments of Revelation 8-11 is not the last trumpet blast to be heard during the Tribulation Period; there is another trump at the end of the Tribulation Period which is used to re-gather all Jews back to Israel (Matt. 24:31).

BIBLE PROPHECY OVERVIEW

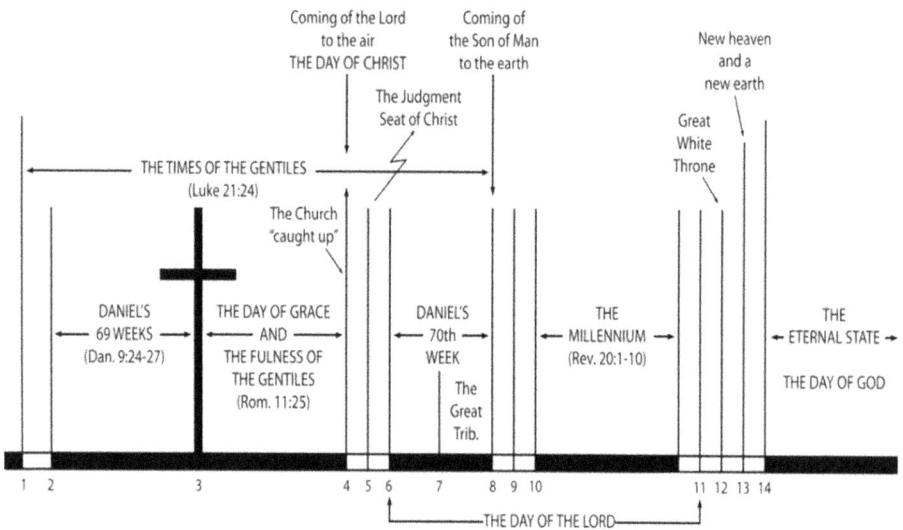

1. The Times of the Gentiles (Jer. 25:1)
2. Decree to rebuild Jerusalem (Neh. 2:1-8)
3. The cross of our Lord Jesus Christ (Luke 23:33)
4. The coming of the Lord to the air (1 Thess. 4:16-17)
5. The Judgment Seat of Christ (2 Cor. 5:10)
6. The 70th week of Daniel's prophecy (Dan. 9:26-27)
7. The Great Tribulation (Matt. 24:21)
8. The coming of the Son of Man (2 Thess. 2:7-8; Matt. 24:30)
9. The judgment of the living nations (Matt. 25:31-33)
10. The Millennium (Rev. 20:4-6)
11. The final rebellion (Rev. 20:7-9)
12. The judgment of the Great White Throne (Rev. 20:11-15)
13. The new heaven and the new earth (Rev. 21:1-5)
14. The eternal state (2 Pet. 1:11; 3:11-12)

The Parable of the Fig Tree (vv. 28-31)

The Lord spoke a prophetic parable concerning the fig tree. The generation that sees the fig tree shoot forth leaves again after being dormant over the winter will see all the things that Christ has just foretold about the Tribulation Period and His second coming to the earth (vv. 28-30). The Lord reminded His disciples that though heaven and earth will pass away, His words were eternal and would come about (v. 35). But what is symbolized by leaves (not fruit) appearing on the fig tree?

As explained in the Mark 11 discussion, the Jewish nation is allegorically likened to a foliage trilogy: the vine, the fig tree, and the olive tree. Each one represents a distinct aspect of the nation's existence. For example, the prophet Jeremiah told his fellow countrymen that God had planted a beautiful vineyard (Israel), but Israel's shepherds had made it desolate (Jer. 12:10). The nation of Israel, as a political reality, is likened to a noble vine (a grape vine; Jer. 8:13), which God planted in the world (Jer. 2:21); Israel was God's vineyard. Jeremiah explains that the destruction of Israel in his day would be like livestock moving freely through God's vineyard and trampling the vines. It would consequently have no productivity, bearing only the fruit of sowing to sin, that is, the thorns of affliction and a harvest of shame (Jer. 12:11-13).

When Israel is spoken of as a fig tree in Scripture, the metaphor relates to the religious element of Israel, which often was fruitless for God (21:19-21; Jer. 8:13). This reality, Judaism today, was identified during one of the events in the life of the Lord Jesus (Luke 13:6-9). After preaching three years to the lost nation of Israel, Christ cursed the fruitless fig tree just before His death at Calvary. Less than forty years later, Jerusalem and the temple were destroyed, and the Jews have not sacrificed since then. The Old Covenant was replaced by the New Covenant, sealed with Christ's blood, and God was determined not to allow the Jews to continue in what was now obsolete.

One of the signs that the Tribulation Period and the Second Advent of Christ are nearing is that the fig tree (i.e., religious Israel) will again shoot forth leaves after a long, winter season of deadness (Luke 21:29-31). Leaves must precede fruit, but the fig tree will bear no fruit until the rebirth of the nation occurs in the latter days of the Tribulation Period. What might the new leaves speak of? This is likely a reference to the Jews reviving the old sacrificial system during, and perhaps just prior to, the Tribulation Period.

We know from various prophecies that the Antichrist will desecrate the Jewish temple and put a stop to animal sacrifices at the midpoint of the Tribulation Period (Dan. 9:27; Matt. 24:15; 2 Thess. 2:3-7). Therefore, logically speaking, a temple will have to be erected and animal sacrifices will have to be reinstituted by that point.

Therefore, we see that, during the Tribulation Period, the Jews will again offer sacrifices under the Levitical system. This reality could commence just prior to the Tribulation period. The Lord Jesus said that the generation permitted to witness this event would also visibly see His coming to the earth in glory (Luke 21:32).

Watchfulness Is Required (vv. 32-37)

Speaking of Christ's second advent and establishing His kingdom on earth, the Lord states that no one knows the day and hour in which that will occur (v. 32). Not even the angels in heaven are let in on this secret; only God the Father had this knowledge. Obviously, as God incarnate, Christ knows all things, but in His humanity, He also learned through experience (e.g., Luke 2:52; Heb. 5:8). Apparently, at this juncture the Jewish Messiah was yet to learn when He would come into His kingdom. This follows the Jewish betrothal and marriage custom of the groom's father directing the timing of when his son would retrieve his espoused wife (from her home). When all accommodations were properly prepared for her, then the father would tell his son to get his wife, and she, not knowing when that might occur, was in a state of watchfulness and readiness (v. 33).

The Lord reiterates this message by telling the parable of The Door Keeper. In the story, Christ is likened to a man traveling far from home who assigns his servants various tasks and tells them to keep busy until he returns (v. 34). There is also a doorkeeper who is appointed to watch over and protect the entrance into the house. Though the master had specifically assigned various tasks, the charge to watch for the master's coming was given to all collectively.

All the Lord's servants are to be alert while faithfully laboring for Him until He returns (vv. 35-36). This means that all believers should be anticipating His imminent return. Some servants, such as church elders, are appointed as doorkeepers of Christ's household. These are to oversee and protect those who are otherwise busy doing their assigned tasks.

Although the Lord had just revealed escalating signs of the coming Tribulation Period and His future return to the earth, these were for Israel, not for the Church. There are no specific prophetic signs given to the Church concerning Christ's coming to the air to snatch His Bride to heaven. The signs that Christ had just mentioned to His disciples would be of great encouragement to the Jewish people suffering under the Antichrist during the Tribulation Period. However, the Church does not know when Christ is returning. His imminent return means that faithful believers should be constantly watching while faithfully serving (v. 37).

Mark Chapter 14

Jewish Leaders Plot Christ's Death (vv. 1-2)

The Passover was two days away and the chief priests and scribes met privately to strategize how they might arrest Jesus of Nazareth through trickery and put Him to death (v. 1). This required careful planning as they feared the people and did not want to cause a riot that might bring the wrath of Rome down on their heads (v. 2).

Christ Anointed for His Burial by Mary (vv. 3-9)

The Lord was in Bethany at the home of a cleansed leper named Simon (v. 3). Matthew and Mark state that this incident occurred on Wednesday, two days before the Passover. The circumstances which John describes are similar, but he places the anointing just prior to Christ's triumphant entry into Jerusalem on Sunday (John 12:1-9). John names the woman who anointed the Lord, Mary (Lazarus' and Martha's sister), but Matthew and Mark do not identify the woman. Matthew and Mark state that the woman anointed the Lord's head (v. 3; Matt. 26:7), while John indicates that Mary anointed the Lord's feet (John 12:3). It is therefore possible that there were two separate anointings by two different women in the final week of the Lord's ministry. However, to simplify the discussion, we will consider both accounts as one incident.

Lazarus, who had been raised from the dead, was sitting with the Lord at a table, while Martha was serving (John 12:2). Their sister Mary arrived with a flask of costly, fragrant oil (v. 3). John tells us that it was a pound of spikenard oil, which was derived from a rare plant in India (John 12:3). She then broke the slender neck of the stone flask and anointed the Lord's head with the expensive ointment. This is a beautiful scene of Christian fellowship, service, and worship before the Lord.

Judas, the betrayer, condemned Mary for her wastefulness, as did some of the other disciples, saying that the oil could have been sold for 300 denarii and the proceeds used to assist the poor (vv. 4-5; John 12:4). But the Lord defended Mary and acknowledged her good work towards Him, *"Let her alone ... She has done a good work for Me"* (v. 6). The

Lord reminded His disciples that the poor would always be with them, but He was about to depart from them (v. 7). Mary had done all that she could to prepare Christ's body for burial ahead of His crucifixion (v. 8). The Lord said that she had kept the spikenard *"for the day of My burial"* (John 12:7). There would be no opportunity to anoint the Lord's body after His death, so she came to do what needed to be done beforehand.

Mary apparently possessed a deeper understanding of what was coming than that of the disciples and she wanted to show her utmost appreciation. She gave her best to the Lord and kept none of the oil for herself. It would be inappropriate to speak of personal cost or limiting gratitude for the One possessing all things and yet was willing to give His life for her to live. John notes that the house was filled with the sweet fragrance of Mary's worship. Genuine, selfless worship will refresh the hearts of all those who love the Lord Jesus. Let us remember that *"Christ came, who is over all, the eternally blessed God"* (Rom. 9:5) and He deserves our best. As a result of her sincere and selfless act towards the Lord Jesus, wherever the gospel was preached, she would be remembered as someone who truly loved the Lord (v. 9).

Judas Agrees to Betray the Lord (vv. 10-11)

Directly after Mary's anointing of the Lord, Judas went to the chief priests to negotiate Christ's betrayal (v. 10). This was likely Wednesday evening. No doubt that Judas, who pilfered the ministry money box (John 12:6), was put out by the terrible waste of the spikenard oil, as he could have secretly profited from its sell. Concerning Judas' treachery John Heading observes:

> If there was worship within, then there was evil and treachery without. Judas is described as "one of the twelve," a unique designation to single out a unique man. In v. 47 he is again described as "one of the twelve," while in John 6:70 the Lord called him "one of you," v. 71 ending with "being one of the twelve." This man "went unto the chief priests." Note the four occasions on which Judas "went." Here he "went" to the chief priests; in John 13:30 he "went" immediately out: and "it was night." In Matt 27:5 he "went and hanged himself." In Acts 1:25 he went "to his own place" as the son of perdition.[94]

The chief priests were delighted with the prospect of secretly arresting Jesus through Judas. Mark does not record the amount of money they paid to Judas, but Matthew does, thirty pieces of silver (Matt.

26:15). The type and amount of currency paid to Christ's betrayer had been foretold four centuries earlier by Zechariah (Zech. 11:12-13). All the scribes had to do to prove that Jesus was not the Messiah was to pay Judas any other amount in any other currency, yet they paid him thirty pieces of silver. But according to Zechariah's prophecy, not only would the Jewish Messiah be betrayed for thirty pieces of silver, but also this money would be returned to the temple and be used to buy a potter's field. Matthew confirms that Judas and the Pharisees fulfilled every detail of this prophecy (Matt. 27:3-10).

Preparation for the Passover Feast (vv. 12-16)

The next day, the first day of the Feast of Unleavened Bread, the day that the Passover lambs were slaughtered in late afternoon, the disciples asked the Lord, *"Where do You want us to go and prepare, that You may eat the Passover?"* (v. 12). The disciples understood that the Lord would be hosting the Passover for them and wanted to get everything ready for the meal later that evening.

The Lord answered their question by instructing them to go into the city and when they saw a man carrying a pitcher, they were to follow him (v. 13). Then they were to say to the master of the house in which the man entered, *"The Teacher says, 'Where is the guest room in which I may eat the Passover with My disciples?'"* (v. 14). Luke and Mark provide the most details concerning the interchange, and both writers tell us that the master of the house showed the disciples a large, furnished, upper room that would be available for the Lord to eat the Passover with His disciples (v. 15; Luke 22:12).

Typically, women retrieved water for the household, so it would be an unusual sight to see a man carrying a pitcher of water. But this would be how the disciples would meet their contact, who then would show them where the Lord wanted to host the Passover meal for His disciples. All was accomplished just as the Lord foretold (v. 16).

The Last Passover Feast (vv. 17-21)

Around sundown on Nisan the fourteenth, the Lord gathered with His disciples to keep the Passover in a large, furnished, upper room (v. 17). After they began eating the Passover feast, the Lord stated that one of them would betray Him (v. 18). The disciples became sorrowful and began asking Him, *"Lord, is it I?"* (v. 19). There is no evidence in

Scripture that Judas ever addressed the Lord Jesus as Lord, but clearly the other disciples did. John records that while leaning on the Lord's breast, He specifically asked the Lord who the betrayer was (John 13:25).

The Lord responded to His question by referring to Psalm 41:9 and saying, *"It is one of the twelve, who dips with Me in the dish"* (v. 20). The Lord added that the betrayer would suffer God's wrath for his evil deed, and it would have been better if he had never been born (v. 21).

On the previous night, Judas had agreed to betray Christ to the chief priests for thirty pieces of silver. The realization that a betrayer sat with Him at the table troubled the Lord's spirit (John 11:33). It was customary for the host to dip a piece of bread in gravy or vinegar and give it to the honored guest (sitting to his left) during the feast. It is likely, given Christ's private charge to Judas, that he occupied this place of honor (John 13:27, 30). Christ gave Judas the sop and thus identified him as the betrayer (John 13:26). John says that Satan entered Judas after he received the sop (John 13:27). Judas then asked the Lord, deceitfully, *"Rabbi, is it I?"* (v. 25). The Lord confirmed that it was and told Judas, *"What you do, do quickly"* (John 13:27). Judas then departed the upper room; the other disciples did not discern what Christ meant by these words. They assumed that Judas, having the purse, was taking care of feast-related matters (John 13:28-29).

The Lord's Supper Is Instituted (vv. 22-26)

Towards the end of the Passover feast, the Lord did something that did not follow the Seder tradition: *"Jesus took bread, blessed and broke it, and gave it to them and said, 'Take, eat; this is My body'"* (v. 22). *"Then He took the cup, and when He had given thanks He gave it to them, and they all drank from it"* (v. 23). As they were drinking from the cup, the Lord explained that the contents of the cup had symbolic significance, *"This is My blood of the new covenant, which is shed for many"* (v. 24). Matthew adds why Christ's blood was shed, *"for the remission of sins"* (Matt. 26:28).

The Greek root verb for "blessed" in verse 22 is *eulogeo* and means "to speak well of something," that is, to give praise for or to bless something, in a religious sense. In the parallel account, Luke says that the Lord "gave thanks" for the bread (Luke 22:19). The Lord was not putting some spiritual blessing on the bread that would then be internalized when eaten by the disciples. Rather, He was following His normal practice of giving thanks to God for the food about to be eaten.

Likewise, the Lord "gave thanks" for the contents of the cup before passing it to His disciples to drink. The contents of the cup symbolized His blood necessary to secure the new covenant between God and Israel (Heb. 8:8). The Greek root verb *eucharisteo* is rendered *"when He had given thanks"* (v. 23). In the Roman Catholic church, the eucharist (or holy communion) that members consume after being blessed by a priest is taught to no longer be bread and wine, but the literal body and blood of Christ. But the Lord was merely providing two symbols for believers to regularly use to remember Him and His sacrifice.

Paul later reiterates the words of the Lord on this occasion to the Corinthians: *" 'Take, eat; this is My body which is broken for you; do this in remembrance of Me.' In the same manner He also took the cup after supper, saying, 'This cup is the new covenant in My blood. This do, as often as you drink it, in remembrance of Me'"* (1 Cor. 11:24-25). "As often as" means every time it is kept. Believers are to keep the Lord's Supper often, in the way specified, but no specific regularity was stated. The first Lord's Supper was not held in a church building; in fact, the Church did not exist at that time. The first Christians obeyed the Lord's command by continuing steadfastly in the breaking of the bread (Acts 2:42), and they did so often from house to house (Acts 2:46). Christians were meeting informally and often to remember the Lord (not just on Sundays or as a local assembly).

Years later, the practice of the local church gathering together on Sundays to break bread became the standard pattern of the Church. For example, on one occasion, Paul waited a week in Troas to break bread with the saints there on Sunday (Acts 20:7). However, because Paul preached long, they actually did not break bread until the wee hours on Monday morning and that was completely acceptable.

To summarize, *the commands* for the Lord's Supper are to do it often and to preserve its protocol and purpose. The *developed pattern* of the Church was that saints gathered together in local assemblies each Sunday to break bread together. The latter point is a scriptural observation, which means there is no prohibition in Scripture preventing saints from remembering the Lord on other days of the week or in smaller groups. While following the scriptural pattern is safe for guiding our behavior, not following what is observed should never negate what is commanded. So, no matter what our circumstances might be, let us follow the Lord's command and remember Him the best possible way that we can!

The Lord Jesus did not drink from the cup that He passed to the disciples, but He promised to drink it with His disciples at a future day in His Father's kingdom (v. 25). By drinking the contents of the cup, the disciples were accepting the full test to be faithful to Christ. They were following Christ's example of drinking down to the dregs the cup of wrath to be received from His Father at Calvary.

Having instituted the Lord's Supper on the eve of His crucifixion, Mark records that the Lord sang a hymn with His disciples before departing to the Mount of Olives (v. 26). If following the Jewish tradition, this hymn would have been the final song in the Jewish *Hallel* – Psalm 118. This song celebrates God's patient faithfulness to Israel, and previews a future day when Israel will be restored to God and honored by all nations. Fittingly, it is also the final Messianic poem in the book of Psalms. The psalmist concludes by requesting continued salvation and prosperity for the people at the hand of the one who *"comes in the name of the Lord"* (Ps. 118:25-29). Because this psalm was sung at Passover, its lyrics would have been on the minds of the people when Christ entered Jerusalem on what is commonly referred to as Palm Sunday. Thus, it was no accident that the psalm was openly shouted by the people when the Lord descended the Mount of Olives into Jerusalem a few days before His crucifixion: *"Blessed is He who comes in the name of the Lord"* (Ps. 118:26). Jesus Christ is the one who comes in the name of the Lord, offering life and blessing.

Psalm 118:22 is quoted several times in the New Testament, where it is evident the reference to the rejected Cornerstone relates to Israel's refusal of Jesus Christ as their Messiah. The psalmist says, *"this is the day which the Lord has made"* (Ps. 118:24). The Lord Jesus Himself acknowledged that this verse spoke of Him (21:42; Luke 20:17), as did the apostles (Eph. 2:20; 1 Pet. 2:6-7). After being rejected by the Jewish nation, the Lord suffered and died at Calvary and was resurrected to the highest station in heaven, and in a future day He will return to the earth to establish His throne as Israel's King.

The Hebrew word *yowm*, normally translated as "day," appears frequently in the Old Testament; however, only about twenty times is it used in the Hebrew expression that correlates to the English phrase, "on that day" or "this is the day." In Psalm 118:24, the specific day referred to had been marked on God's calendar since before the foundations of the world were laid – it would be the day in which propitiation for humanity's sins would be offered by His own Son (Heb. 2:9; 1 Jn. 2:2).

If following the Jewish tradition, it seems likely that the Lord with His disciples sang of this special day, just hours before Calvary.

It is hard to imagine what thoughts went through our Savior's mind when He with His disciples sang Psalm 118 at the conclusion of the first Lord's Supper. The day that the Lord had made was the day that redeeming blood was to flow from Immanuel's veins to ensure the redemption of all those trusting in His message of salvation. Animal sacrifices were bound by a cord on the north side of the Bronze Altar before their throats were slit and the blood was collected and applied to its horns or poured out at its base. Incredibly, the psalmist wrote of this spectacular day:

> **The stone which the builders rejected** *has become the chief cornerstone.* **This was the Lord's doing**; *it is marvelous in our eyes.* **This is the day the Lord has made**; *we will rejoice and be glad in it* (Ps. 118:22-24).

> **Blessed is he who comes in the name of the Lord!** *We have blessed you from the house of the Lord. God is the Lord, and He has given us light;* **bind the sacrifice with cords to the horns of the altar** (Ps. 118:26-27).

After rehearsing in song with His disciples what was about to happen to Him at the cross, the Lord then expressed His resolve to honor God: *"You are my God, and I will praise You; You are my God, I will exalt You"* (Ps. 118:28). And the Lord Jesus did just that!

Ironically, the Church often sings the latter portion of this Psalm as a praise chorus, without regarding its proper context. In other words, we are applying a different meaning to it than what the Holy Spirit intended. While it is true that the Lord is sovereign over each of our days, the focus of our joy is not *our day*, but *the day* Christ was rejected of men and judged by God for our sins. The content of this psalm is a capstone on the revelation of all the fullness of Christ and His work mentioned in the other Messianic Psalms. May we treasure the full value God breathed into the text of Psalm 118 three thousand years ago and, like the psalmist, let us rejoice and be glad in what God has accomplished through Christ!

Christ Foretells of Peter's Denials (vv. 27-31)

According to John, after the Lord Jesus instituted His remembrance feast, the Lord informed His disciples that He would soon be leaving them (John 13:36-38). It was at this juncture that the Lord quoted Zechariah 13:7 to inform His disciples that they would all scatter from Him that night (v. 27). God was about to strike His Shepherd with a sword at Calvary and all the disciples would stumble before the Lord because of it. But the Lord then promised that after His resurrection He would see them again in Galilee (v. 28).

Peter specifically asked where the Lord was going (John 13:36). The Lord answered his question by saying that where He was going Peter could not follow Him then, but implied that he would later. Christ was going to the cross and then on to heaven. Peter would do the same in about thirty-five years.

Peter then declared his allegiance to the Lord and that he would follow Him now even if all others stumbled at Him (v. 29). But the Lord informed Peter that before the early morning watch was over (known by the cock's crowing), he would have denied Him three times (v. 30; John 13: 38). Peter responded to this statement, *"If I have to die with You, I will not deny You!"* (v. 31). The other disciples also affirmed the same allegiance to the Lord. In a few hours their self-confidence would be shown to be futile in comparison to the Lord's words.

Luke also records Peter's willingness to die with the Lord (Luke 22:49-50). John states that the Lord then warned Peter with a question, *"Will you lay down your life for My sake?"* (John 13:38). In a short time, Peter would learn just how weak his flesh was in serving Christ. The Roman division of the night was four three-hour watches. The watch from midnight to 3:00 a.m. was the first crowing and the watch from 3:00 a.m. to 6:00 a.m. was the second crowing.[95] Mark was likely speaking of both watches (v. 30), while Matthew only identifies the second watch. The idea being that before dawn Peter would deny the Lord three times, and the roosters crowing would remind Peter of the Lord's prediction.

Christ in the Garden of Gethsemane (vv. 32-42)

After leaving the upper room, the Lord and His disciples meandered through the streets of Jerusalem, trekked eastward across the Kidron brook and up the Mount of Olives to the Garden of Gethsemane, a place the Lord often resided with His disciples. He asked His disciples to sit in a particular place and then He went a little farther into the garden with Peter, James, and John (vv. 32-33).

It was at this juncture that the Lord informed the three disciples with Him that His soul was *"exceeding sorrowful, even to death"* (v. 34). He then asked them to stay with Him and watch with Him while He prayed. The Lord then went a little farther and fell on His face and prayed, *"Abba, Father, all things are possible for You. Take this cup away from Me; nevertheless, not what I will, but what You will"* (v. 36). Luke says that *"being in agony, He prayed more earnestly"* (Luke 22:44).

A similar scene is recorded in Matthew, but not in John, who presents Christ in His deity. Thus, there is not one word in John's account about Christ's anguish of soul or perspiration while praying in Gethsemane, but Luke writes, *"Then His sweat became like great drops of blood falling down to the ground"* (Luke 22:44). These statements describe the Son of Man as the Man of Sorrows. John is the only one to present the heavenly view of that night; thus, he highlights Christ's great expectation of being received into heaven, regaining His glory, and being with His Father forevermore (John 13:1, 17:1-5).

The Lord returned to find Peter, James, and John sleeping. At the most critical moment in the Lord's ministry, even His closest friends were not there for Him. He said to them, *"Simon, are you sleeping? Could you not watch one hour?"* (v. 37). He then exhorted them to watch and pray lest they be given over to temptation (solicitations to do evil). But the Lord also acknowledged what Paul later confirmed in his own life: None of us can do what pleases God in the power of the flesh (v. 38; Rom. 7:15-18). Peter had claimed to be the tough guy that would never deny the Lord, but when the Lord needed him most, he was sleepy.

A second time the Lord departed from the three disciples to privately pray with His Father as before, *"O My Father, if this cup cannot pass away from Me unless I drink it, Your will be done"* (Matt. 26:42). After a while, the Lord returned to where Peter, James, and John were and found them sleeping again, *"for their eyes were heavy"* (v. 40). Matthew states that the Lord understood their weariness and therefore did not wake them again. However, Mark indicates that the disciples were stirred from their slumber by the Lord's presence but did not say anything. Despite being disappointed, the Lord's compassionate grace amid human failure is astounding.

The Lord returned to His previous place to continue praying as He did before (Matt. 26:44). There is no evidence in Scripture that the Lord slept at all the night before His passion. His human soul was "exceedingly sorrowful," so He spent the night preparing His disciples for what was coming and in prayer. Luke, who upholds the humanity of Christ in his gospel account, informs us that angels ministered to Christ in the garden. None of the other writers mention that detail.

The Lord returned to His sleeping disciples a third time and aroused them because the hour had now come for Him to be betrayed *"into the hands of sinners"* (v. 41). But prayer had accomplished its work, despite the previous anxiety of His human soul; the Lord declared that He would continue to please His Father no matter the personal cost to Himself: *"Rise, let us be going. See, My betrayer is at hand"* (v. 42).

Christ's Betrayal and Arrest (vv. 43-52)

While the Lord was speaking, His betrayer arrived in Gethsemane. Judas knew the place that the Lord often resided with His disciples, and he had led a great multitude having clubs, torches, and swords to that location, with the Jewish leaders also (v. 43). Why so many people to arrest someone that had never hurt anyone? Apparently, Christ's arrestors thought that He would be hiding, and they would have to search him out. The moon would have been full at the Pascal feast, so there would have been plenty of light to find a hiding Jesus. But John states that seeing His arrestors approaching Him, He stepped forward and asked them who they were looking for (John 18:4). The Lord Jesus already knew what was going to happen to Him at Calvary and did not resist being arrested, though He had the power to do so.

Judas had told the mob that he was leading, *"Whomever I kiss, He is the one; seize Him and lead Him away safely"* (v. 44). He then immediately went up to the Lord and said, *"Rabbi, Rabbi!"* and kissed Him. In Matthew's account of this incident, Judas said "Greetings Rabbi" when betraying the Lord (Matt. 26:46). The Greek verb for "greetings" is in the present tense, indicating that Judas likely spoke to the Lord more than once (and likely kissed Him repeatedly) to ensure that everyone knew who should be arrested. Kenneth Wuest's *Expanded Translation of the New Testament* renders what Judas did this way: "He [Judas] embraced Him and kissed him tenderly and again and again."

How did the Lord respond to such blatant betrayal? Matthew states that He said to Judas, *"Friend, why have you come?"* (Matt. 26:50). Mark leaves this detail out of his record. Fully knowing what Judas was doing, our Savior still extended kindness and compassion to Judas. Although under Satan's control, the Lord still felt it was necessary to appeal to Judas' conscience one last time. When it seems like everything around you is dark and evil, remember individual souls still need to be reached by compassion and with the truth. But Judas did not respond to the Lord's tenderness; rather, the Lord was arrested. John says that they first bound the Lord before taking Him away (John 18:12).

As Christ's arrestors stepped forward, Peter drew his sword and was ready to face down a band of soldiers to protect His Lord (vv. 46-47). Peter struck one of the high priest's servants named Malchus and sliced off his ear. The Lord Jesus told Peter to put his sword away, lest he perish by it, and then He repaired the damage that Peter's sword did to Malchus' ear (Matt. 26:52; John 18:10-11). Peter needed to learn that the Lord did not want Peter to die once to serve Him, but to die daily to self to live for Him. It is easier to swing a sword while opposing God's will than to fully rest in the Lord and remain in God's will.

The Lord then reminded Peter that everything that was happening was under His control and fulfilling Scripture (Matt. 26:54). If He needed protection, He could request that His Father send twelve legions of angels to assist Him (Matt. 26:53). That would be between 36,000 and 72,000 angelic warriors – no human agency would survive such an angelic force.

The Lord's response to those arresting Him was noteworthy (vv. 48-49). He clearly states the facts to appeal directly to the consciences of those arresting Him: "I was with you daily in the temple without any expression of hostility; why then are you coming against Me now with clubs and swords?" "What have I done that now justifies you treating Me like a robber?" The Lord does not try to escape what He knows is necessary, but He still has a compassionate heart towards those under the enemy's control. He chooses to reason with them, not attack or retaliate against them in any way.

Indeed, the situation was being incited by wickedness in high places, yet the Lord's compassion for those individuals under its influence is paramount. Additionally, He told His arrestors that all that was happening was to fulfill what the prophets had foretold, as recorded in Scripture (v. 49). Then, as the Lord had previously predicted in the upper room, all His disciples forsook Him and fled (v. 50). It is here that we learn that a young John Mark was present with the Lord and His disciples in the Garden of Gethsemane. When the soldiers tried to apprehend him, he escaped arrest, but left the linen cloak that was covering his naked body behind (vv. 51-52).

Why did the Jewish leaders want to arrest Jesus in the middle of the night and in a private place, like Gethsemane? The Roman historian Tacitus stated that Jerusalem's population was 600,000 when Rome assaulted the city in 70 A.D. Yet, this number seems high as compared with archeological information relating to that timeframe. Examining this evidence, Geva offers a minimal estimate of the city's population to be 20,000 at this time.[96] Others, such as Wikinson[97] and Broshi,[98] put the population of Jerusalem in 70 A.D. to be between 70,000 and 80,000 persons. Though estimates vary, it seems likely that Jerusalem's population at the time of Christ's crucifixion was likely between 50,000 and 80,000 people. However, during religious festivals this number often increased three- to fourfold.

The Jewish leaders knew the possibility of social unrest was high at such times and even a riot was a distinct possibility. Because the Pharisees feared the people (for many had high thoughts of Jesus), and of Roman repercussions for a riot, they chose to arrest Jesus of Nazareth in a private place, which the betrayal of Judas made possible.

Christ's Religious Trials (vv. 53-65)

The Lord would endure three religious trials and three civil trials in less than nine hours. Quirinius, the governor of Syria, appointed Annas as the Jewish high priest in 6 A.D. However, the Romans did not want a long-standing high priest. Limiting the high priest's tenure would reduce the priest's sway among the people. So Annas had been replaced in 15 A.D. by Valerius Gratus, procurator of Judea, and then each of his five sons were appointed the high priest and then Caiaphas, his son-in-law.[99] Luke confirms that both Annas and Caiaphas were high priests currently (Luke 3:2). From the Jewish perspective, Annas was the true high priest, though Caiaphas was the acknowledged leader to pacify Roman rule.

John states that Christ first appeared before Annas and then was interrogated by a larger gathering of Jewish leaders with Caiaphas present (v. 57; John 18:13). Interestingly, night gatherings of the Sanhedrin for a capital trial were illegal.[100] The introduction of false witnesses at the trial and the declaring of a verdict before the trial commenced were also forbidden (John 7:51). As F. B. Hole observes, the worst part was not the presence of false witnesses, but that Israel's leaders, who were to represent God's justice – sought false witnesses:

The mob delivered Him to the leaders of Israel, and these men, who claimed to represent God, had thrown away any pretense of seeking righteousness. We are not told that they were *misled* into accepting false evidence, nor that they were *tempted* into receiving it because it was thrust upon them. No, it says, they *"sought* false witness against Jesus, to put Him to death."* They SOUGHT it. Has there ever, we wonder, been another trial upon this earth where the judges started by hunting for liars, that they might condemn the accused? Thus, it was here; and in the presence of it, Jesus held His peace. Judgment being utterly divorced from righteousness, He met them with a dignity that was Divine, and He only spoke to affirm His Christhood, His Sonship, and to affirm His coming glory as the Son of Man.[101]

Moreover, the Defendant was not permitted any time to prepare His case. This was a sham trial from start to finish, and one that violated Sanhedrin protocol. At first light, the Lord would be brought before the full Sanhedrin to determine how He should be put to death. Peter followed the Lord at a distance, but after arriving at the high priest's courtyard, he sat down to see what would happen and warmed himself by a fire with Caiaphas' servants (v. 54). John tells us that he spoke on Peter's behalf so that he would be permitted into the courtyard area.

The chief priests and elders were soliciting false witnesses to testify against Christ before Caiaphas, so they could put Him to death, but initially they could not find two that agreed (vv. 55-56). Finally, they found two witnesses that agreed that the Lord Jesus had said, *"I will destroy this temple made with hands, and within three days I will build another made without hands"* (vv. 57-58). But even the testimony of these two witnesses was proven not to be consistent (v. 59). Not having any credible witnesses, Caiaphas stood up and asked the Lord to answer this charge, but He said nothing (v. 60).

Then Caiaphas, being the high priest, put Christ under oath to implore Him to answer whether He was the Christ, the Son of God (v. 61; Matt. 26:63)! Under the Mosaic Law, the Lord Jesus would bear guilt if He did not answer the high priest who put Him under oath (Lev. 5:1). The Lord's response affirmed that He was the Christ, the Son of God, but Israel's leaders would see Him no more until He returned from heaven in power and glory to establish His kingdom (v. 62).

After hearing the Lord's statement, Caiaphas tore his priestly apparel, which was forbidden by the Law, for such was considered holy before the Lord (v. 63; Lev. 21:10). Caiaphas declared that the Lord

Jesus spoke blasphemy and that there was no need of further witnesses, for they had heard the offense themselves. His constituents agreed saying, *"He is deserving of death"* (v. 64). In a fit of rage, they spit in Christ's face and struck Him with their fists. As He was being beaten, they mocked His testimony by saying, *"Prophesy to us, Christ! Who is the one who struck You?"* (v. 65; Matt. 26:68). Considering that He could have quickly ended all their lives, the Lord demonstrated incredible restraint in not swiftly judging His oppressors. *"In Him all things consist"* (Col. 1:17). The Lord Jesus maintained the molecular integrity of the very human fists that were causing Him so much pain!

Peter Denies the Lord (vv. 66-72)

While Peter was sitting outside in the lower courtyard with others by a fire, a servant girl saw him and said, *"You also were with Jesus of Nazareth"* (vv. 66-67). Peter utterly denied this assertion in front of everyone (v. 68). Strike one. Whether or not Peter heard the warning, we do not know, but Mark states that a rooster crowed after his first denial. Apparently, Peter became uncomfortable with his surroundings and ventured towards the porch by the courtyard gateway.

A little later, another servant girl saw him and stated that he was one of them that had been with Jesus (v. 69). Matthew states that Peter promptly replied, *"I do not know the Man!"* (Matt. 26:73). Mark simply records that Peter denied the Lord again (v. 70). Strike two. So far, the tough fisherman has been taken down by two girls. A while later Peter was challenged by those waiting on the outcome of the trial, *"Surely you also are one of them, for you are a Galilean, and your speech shows it"* (v. 70). Peter, while cursing and swearing, adamantly declared, *"I do not know this Man of whom you speak!"* (v. 71). Strike three.

No sooner had the words departed Peter's lips, when he heard the rooster crow. It was normal for roosters to crow in the fourth watch (3 a.m. to 6 a.m.) and Mark notes that the rooster had sounded the warning alarm more than once, but it was now that Peter recognized it and remembered the Lord's prediction that *"Before the rooster crows twice, you will deny Me three times"* (v. 72). Luke states that at this moment Peter's eyes and the Lord's eyes briefly met (Luke 22:61). It was a sorrowful look that Peter would never forget. The defeated fisherman immediately went out of the courtyard and wept bitterly.

Mark Chapter 15

Christ Before the Sanhedrin (v. 1)

The full Jewish Sanhedrin gathered at first light to determine *how* they should put Jesus to death (v. 1). He had already been found guilty and deemed worthy of execution by the high priest and some of the Sanhedrin (Matt. 26:66). The Romans did not permit the Jews to execute anyone according to their laws and tradition, so if Christ was to be executed, He must be taken to the Roman governor of the region, Pontius Pilate (John 18:31), which they did immediately.

Christ Before Pilate (vv. 2-5)

The Lord Jesus was brought before the Roman Governor of Judea, Pilate, to be questioned. It did not take the Sanhedrin long to decide Jesus' fate for when He arrived at the Praetorium, it was still early morning (John 18:28). The chief priests and elders informed Pilate that Jesus was subverting the nation by denying that the Jews should pay Caesar tribute and by claiming Himself to be King instead of Caesar (Luke 23:2). Pontius Pilate then interrogated the Lord to discern if these charges of sedition were legitimate.

Pontus Pilate asked Jesus if He was *"the King of the Jews"* (v. 2). The Lord affirmed that what he had asked was correct. John records a lengthier dialogue between Pilate and the Lord Jesus. John tells us that Pilate was also told by Jesus Christ that though He was a king, His kingdom was not of this world; if it were, His servants would have fought for Him, and the Jews would not have arrested Him (John 18:36).

While before Pilate, the chief priests and Jewish elders accused Jesus of many things, but Christ did not defend Himself, even when Pilate extended an opportunity for Him to do so (vv. 3-5). Pilate marveled greatly at the Lord Jesus' restraint, and Luke tells us that he told the Jewish leaders, *"I find no fault in this Man"* (Luke 23:4). This may have been the first time, that Pilate had an accused offender at his judgment seat that made no effort to defend himself.

Mark does not refer to Christ's second civil trial before Herod, but Matthew and Luke do. According to Luke, after Pilate proclaimed Christ's innocence, the Jewish elders became fiercer in their accusations of Jesus, saying that He was a Galilean and had incited trouble from Galilee to Judea (Luke 23:5). After hearing this, Pilate sent Jesus to Herod to be examined. Galilee was Herod's jurisdiction as a tetrarch, and he was in Jerusalem at that time for the feast (Luke 23:7). This was Christ's second civil trial. Although Herod asked Jesus many questions, the Lord answered him nothing. After Herod's soldiers had mocked and abused the Lord Jesus, Herod sent Him back to Pilate.

Barabbas or Jesus of Nazareth? (vv. 6-15)

There were likely between 150,000 to 300,000 people in Jerusalem for the Passover Feast. The potential for a riot was high and Pilate wanted to avoid that scenario, lest he be called to Rome and questioned by Caesar for the uprising. To encourage a peaceful situation, it was Pilate's custom to pardon a Jewish prisoner of the people's choosing during the feast (vv. 6-7). The people were also expecting Pilate to do this, as he had done previously (v. 8). As an attempt to release Jesus, Pilate offered the Jewish assembly a choice of whom he would pardon. They could choose to free Jesus of Nazareth, "the King of the Jews," or a notorious prisoner, Barabbas, who had been found guilty of inciting rebellion in Jerusalem and of murder (v. 9).

The Roman governor chose to contrast the worst convicted criminal available to him with an accused Man that, in his judgment, was completely innocent, to highlight the motive of why the Jewish leaders were indicting Jesus – their envy (v. 10). The chief priests stirred up the people to demand Barabbas' release (v. 11).

Pilate was unable to persuade the Jews to turn from their bloodthirsty intentions. They wanted Barabbas released and Christ crucified (vv. 12-13). Pilate again asserted that Jesus had done nothing worthy of death, but the crowd cried out the more, *"Crucify Him"* (v. 14). Fearing that a riot might ensue, Matthew tells us that Pilate washed his hands in a basin and proclaimed, *"I am innocent of the blood of this just Person. You see to it"* (Matt. 27:24). The Jewish crowd answered, *"His blood be on us and on our children"* (Matt. 27:25). In effect, they had put themselves under a blood curse for condemning a righteous man to death (Acts 2:23, 3:14-15, 5:28). The Jewish nation had no idea the centuries of pain and sorrow that would result from this proclamation. But the consequences of cutting off their Messiah were foretold by the prophet Daniel long ago: War and desolations would be determined against them until the end of the Tribulation Period, when, by grace, the blood of expiation will erase the blood of the curse (Dan. 9:24-27). The Jews crucified God's incarnate Son and their Messiah.

Pilate then released the notable murderer Barabbas and had Christ scourged before He was to be crucified (v. 15). Perhaps Pilate thought that by having Christ severely whipped, the hostile horde might then show Him sympathy and His life would be spared. But the Jewish crowd had no sympathy for Jesus Christ. To prevent an uprising in a city likely having four times its normal population because of the Passover, Pilate sentenced Christ to death by crucifixion.

A common punishment under the Law and practiced in both the Old and New Testaments by the Jews was that of scourging (Lev. 19:20). According to Deuteronomy 25:1-3, up to forty stripes could be administered, but to ensure compliance with the Law, the Jews limited themselves to "forty stripes minus one" or *thirty-nine* stripes (2 Cor. 11:24). However, there were no such limitations of abuse during a Roman scourging, which typically preceded public executions to speed up the dying process of crucifixion.

The Roman whip did much more than put stripes on the condemned; it was designed to rip the flesh wide open. A Roman flogging resulted in deep lacerations which exposed muscles and caused excessive bleeding. Church historian Eusebius of Caesarea recounts the horror of a Roman scourging: "For they say that the bystanders were struck with amazement when they saw them lacerated with scourges even to the innermost veins and arteries, so that the hidden inward parts of the body, both their bowels and their members, were exposed to view."[102] The term "half-dead" was commonly associated with a Roman scourging, as many who endured its wrath died afterwards. But the idea was to stop the beating before death to permit the victim to undergo public crucifixion.

Isaiah foretold that the Messiah, God's Servant, would be faithful to live out what He was asked to do no matter the personal cost to Himself. In the prophecy, the Servant conveys His determination to expend Himself on Israel's behalf (and on ours too) despite the human brutality and divine judgment He knew He would suffer:

I gave My back to those who struck Me, and My cheeks to those who plucked out the beard; I did not hide My face from shame and spitting.

389

> *For the Lord God will help Me; therefore, I will not be disgraced; therefore, I have set My face like a flint, and I know that I will not be ashamed* (Isa. 50:6-7).

This prophecy tells us that Christ knew beforehand that He would be scourged, beaten in the face, and spat on. Mark records the direct fulfillment of these prophecies in his gospel account (14:65, 15:19, 24). Thankfully, two thousand years ago, the Lord Jesus did not enter into His rest until He had secured ours, through the shedding of His own blood. We worship a brave, tenacious, and sacrificial Savior!

Christ Stripped, Mocked, and Beaten (vv. 16-21)

In the previous hours, the Lord Jesus has been abused by the servants of the chief priests and by Herod's men. He has already received many blows from human fists. After being scourged, Matthew informs us that the Lord was taken into the Roman Praetorium, and an entire garrison of soldiers gathered to have sport with Him (v. 16). They stripped Him of His clothes and put a purple (or scarlet) robe or cloak on Him, which likely revealed His nakedness (v. 17). Scarlet and purple were colors of royalty. They twisted a crown of thorns and placed it on His head and put a hollow reed in his right hand (Matt. 27:29).

Being adorned with a mock robe, crown, and scepter, the Roman soldiers then bowed the knee to Jesus and declared their mock worship of Him, *"Hail, king of the Jews!"* (v. 18). The Lord had been rejected and abused by the Jewish authorities; now the Gentiles also were guilty of disdaining the Savior. They spit on Him and then took the reed out of His hand and beat the crown of thorns into His brow with it (v. 19).

Afterwards, the soldiers put His own clothes on the Lord and led Him away to be crucified (v. 20). In His physically weakened state, the Lord was not able to bear His own cross (bar or beam) on His shoulder, which was estimated to weigh between 75 and 125 pounds. The Romans compelled Simon from Cyrene to bear Christ's cross to the place of public execution (vv. 21-22).

Jesus Christ Is Crucified (vv. 22-32)

The Lord Jesus was brought to Golgotha, the "Place of the Skull," to be crucified (v. 22). John Heading describes the meaning of Golgotha and what it symbolized:

Golgotha and the corresponding Roman name Calvary (Luke 23:33) both mean "skull" – hence Matthew's interpretation "a place of a skull." Various reasons have been suggested why the place had this name; for example, because the shape of the place resembled a skull. Typically, however, the name speaks of the apex of human wisdom, for those who crucified the Lord of glory possessed this wisdom, the opposite to the wisdom of God (1 Cor. 2:6-8). It speaks of the unsanctified intelligence of men who still reject Christ in unbelief.[103]

Before the nails were driven through His wrists to the cross bar, Christ was offered wine mingled with gall (a narcotic to numb the senses to reduce pain), but after tasting the mixture, He would not drink it (v. 23). The Roman soldiers then stripped the Lord of His clothes and crucified Him at the third hour (9 a.m.; v. 25). They cast lots for His outer garment that was woven without seam and tore his inner garment into four pieces, so that each soldier would receive a portion (v. 24).

After the soldiers had crucified two condemned men on either side of the Lord, they placed a placard over the Lord's head that read *"This is Jesus the King of the Jews,"* and then they sat down to watch over the pitiful sight (vv. 26-27). Both Luke and John document that the superscription hanging above the Lord's head was written in Greek, Latin, and Hebrew. As Luke is an appeal to humanity and John is writing to the whole world, it makes sense that the use of all three languages was recorded by these two evangelists. If Matthew had written concerning this detail, perhaps he would have only focused on the Hebrew language. Likewise, Mark would have likely referred to the language of the Roman Empire, Latin.

Those passing by blasphemed Him, the chief priests mocked Him, and even both robbers initially reviled him (vv. 29-32). They quoted back to the Lord Jesus His own words to cast doubt on their validity, given His circumstances. Let us see You build the temple in three days now! If You are the Son of God and the King of Israel, prove it by saving Yourself! If God was really Your Father, He would deliver You from this crisis!

Victory in Death (vv. 33-41)

Matthew and Mark do not record any of the Lord's statements or intercession during His first three hours on the cross. Mark states that at the sixth hour (noon in Roman time) until the ninth hour (3 p.m.) there was an intense darkness *"over all the land"* (v. 33). The judgment of human sin was a private matter between the Son and God the Father; nothing would be permitted to intrude into the work of eternal propitiation.

After suffering for three hours in darkness, the Lord cried out with a loud voice, saying, *"Eloi, Eloi, lama, sabachthani?"* meaning *"My God, My God, why have You forsaken Me?"* (v. 34). The English expression "loud voice" is derived from the Greek *megas phone*. A megaphone effectively amplifies sound for all to hear. Some standing by thought that Jesus was calling for Elijah to assist Him (v. 35). One of them immediately got up and filled a sponge with sour wine and placed it on a reed and lifted it up to the Lord to drink from it (v. 36). However, the other onlookers rebuked the actions of this man, and said to leave Jesus alone to see whether Elijah would come to assist Him.

After finishing the required suffering for all human sin (Heb. 2:9; 1 Jn. 2:2), the Lord Jesus *"cried out again with a loud voice, and breathed His last"* (v. 50). Matthew states that He willingly yielded up His spirit at this moment. "Loud voice" is again derived from the Greek phrase *megas phone*. What did the Lord cry out with a loud voice? John tells us what the Lord said, before commending His spirit into His Father's care: *"It is finished!"* (John 19:30). John uses the perfect tense verb *teleo* to declare that what Christ had just accomplished at Calvary could never be undone – it was an eternal propitiatory and redemptive work. Afterwards, there would never be another offering for the offense or damages of human sin (Heb. 9:28, 10:12-14).

While the Lord Jesus was hanging from a cross, He was fully aware and in complete control of His situation. He astutely fulfilled every Old Testament prophecy so there would be no question that He was Israel's promised Messiah. For example, just before His death, the Lord quoted Psalm 22:1 with a shrill cry: *"My God, My God, why have You forsaken Me?"* (Matt. 27:45-46). The Lord affirmed that while He was being our Sin-bearer, fellowship with His Father was severed. The Lord also wanted to ensure that Psalm 22 would be associated with His redemptive work.

Just after Christ gave up His spirit, the inner veil of the temple (a sixty-foot-tall hanging tapestry) was torn from top to bottom (v. 38). Matthew also tells us that there was a great earthquake causing rocks to split at this juncture (Matt. 27:51). Jewish tradition upholds that the temple veil was as thick as a man's hand and was so heavy that it took

300 priests to manipulate.[104] Albert Edersheim affirms this description to be correct.[105] The point being that tearing the veil from the top downward while it was hanging in the temple was an impossibility, humanly speaking.

In the Old Testament, access to God was limited. Only the high priest could enter the Most Holy Place of the tabernacle and temple once a year on the Day of Atonement, and he did so with trepidation and not without the blood of a goat and a bull. After the completion of Christ's work at Calvary, the inner veil of the temple was rent from top to bottom to illustrate that through Christ, God could have full fellowship with man and man could have full access to God.

When the centurion who was overseeing Christ's crucifixion saw all that had happened, he and those with him feared greatly, saying, *"Truly this man was the Son of God!"* (v. 39). The three hours of intense darkness, the Savior uttering gracious intercession for His oppressors, the rent veil in the temple, and the great earthquake convinced them that Christ was who He proclaimed to be.

Mark then notes that many of the women who had served Christ during His three-plus-year ministry were watching from afar (vv. 40-41). Among these were Mary Magdalene, Mary the mother of James the less, and Salome, the mother of James and John.

The Body of Christ Is Buried (vv. 42-47)

A rich man named Joseph from Arimathea was a disciple of Christ and asked Pilate for the body of Jesus (v. 43). After verifying that Jesus of Nazareth was dead, Pilate granted his request (vv. 44-45). He brought a hundred pounds of myrrh and aloes to the tomb (John 19:39).

With Sabbath only minutes away, Joseph and Nicodemus quickly wrapped Jesus' body with the spices in strips of clean linen (John 19:40). Then both men placed the Lord's body in Joseph's own tomb hewn out of rock (v. 46; John 19:42). This new tomb was in a garden near the crucifixion site (John 19:41). After placing the body in the tomb, Joseph and Nicodemus sealed it with a large rolling stone and departed.

The two Marys before mentioned observed where Christ's body was placed and then came to the tomb Sunday morning to properly prepare the body after the Sabbath had concluded (v. 47). Mark does not record the details of the sealing of Christ's tomb or the Roman guard that was posted to prevent anyone from opening the tomb until after the third day.

Mark Chapter 16

Christ's Resurrection (vv. 1-14)

While there is some debate as to whether Christ was crucified on Thursday or Friday, the Scripture clearly informs us that He experienced resurrection early on Sunday morning. Mark had noted that Mary Magdalene and Mary the mother of James the less observed where the body of Christ was entombed. Now that the Sabbath had passed, they and other women were going to the tomb at the earliest possible moment to properly prepare the Lord's body for burial (vv. 1-2).

Matthew states that the Marys were en route to the tomb at the starting of dawn. Mark's account has three women coming to the tomb at the rising of the sun. John states that Mary Magdalene came to the tomb when it was yet dark (John 20:1). Luke mentions at least five women that came early to the tomb (Luke 24:10). Putting the accounts together, we have various women arriving at the tomb early Sunday morning at various times. Since the women were coming from Bethany, and perhaps Jerusalem, it would have taken some time to get to the tomb. Some arrived in predawn darkness, while others arrived at sunrise.

Mark informs us that the women were wondering among themselves, *"Who will roll away the stone from the door of the tomb for us?"* (v. 3). Clearly, they knew that the stone blocking the entrance to the tomb was too heavy for them to move. This also indicates that the opening into the tomb was sizable. When the women arrived at the tomb, they were surprised to see that the "very large" stone blocking the tomb's entrance had been rolled away (v. 4).

Matthew informs us what happened just prior to the women arriving at Christ's tomb; an angel from heaven descended from heaven and rolled away the stone sealing the tomb and then sat on it (Matt. 28:2). This feat was accompanied by a great earthquake. The countenance of the angel was like lightning and his clothing as white as snow (Matt. 28:3). The guards were terrified at the angel's presence and fell to the ground like dead men (Matt. 28:4).

The women entered the tomb and were alarmed to see a young man in a long white robe sitting on the right side (v. 5). The angel spoke to them, saying, *"Do not be alarmed. You seek Jesus of Nazareth, who was crucified. He is risen! He is not here. See the place where they laid Him. But go, tell His disciples – and Peter – that He is going before you into Galilee; there you will see Him, as He said to you"* (vv. 5-6).

The women departed the tomb in different directions to accomplish their task (v. 8). Matthew states that the risen Savior appeared to some of them and said, "Rejoice!" The women immediately fell to the ground at His feet to worship Him (Matt. 28:9). The Lord comforted them and then instructed the women to complete the task that the angel had given them to do. It is noted that Matthew and Mark describe one angel speaking to the women, while Luke and John state that two angels were in the tomb. We may conclude that, indeed, there were two angels in or at the tomb, but only one served as the spokesman.

It is important to realize that each Gospel writer presents Christ from a different perspective. If all the writers gave exactly the same story, same order, same details, we would immediately become suspicious that the records were the copies of a single account. But because some events are recorded in some Gospels and not others, we have proof of multiple accounts and not one story repeated. For example, only Matthew records Christ's first appearance to the women, while only Luke records the events transpiring on the Emmaus Road. Luke does not record Mary Magdalene's visit to the tomb. Only John and Luke record Christ's appearance in the upper room on resurrection day to His fearful and grief-stricken disciples. Given all the information recorded in the Gospels, there is a reasonable construction of all that took place on resurrection morning without contradiction.

New Testament Scripture confirms at least ten separate post-resurrection appearances of Christ prior to His ascension. Five of these incidents occurred on the day of Christ's resurrection. None of the Gospel writers record all of these appearances. As previously noted in Matthew 28 comments, this is the most likely order of Christ's post-resurrection appearances to those loved by Him:

First, to Mary Magdalene after telling Peter and John that Christ had arisen and having returned to the tomb (v. 9; John 20:11-18).

Second, to women returning from the tomb after they had heard the angel's declaration and instructions (Matt. 28:8-10). These women had apparently departed the tomb after Mary Magdalene had left.

Third, to Peter to deal with his sin of denial privately and to restore him (Luke 24:34; 1 Cor. 15:5). Peter's sin would be publicly dealt with later (John 21).

Fourth, to the two disciples on the Emmaus Road (vv. 12-13; Luke 24:13-32). Christ became known to them in the breaking of the bread.

Fifth, to ten of His disciples, plus others, who were together behind locked doors listening to the men who had walked with Christ on the Emmaus Road (Luke 24:36-43). Thomas was not present. Initially the disciples did not believe the testimony of Mary or the two on the road to Emmaus, but after Christ appeared to ten of His disciples – all doubt concerning His resurrection was gone (vv. 11-14).

Sixth, to the disciples, with Thomas present (John 20:26-31).

Seventh, to seven disciples who had fished all night on the Sea of Galilee (John 21). The Lord cooked them breakfast.

Eighth, to the apostles and above 500 brethren (1 Cor. 15:6). It seems likely that this event coincides with Matthew's account but may refer to a separate post-resurrection experience, such as Christ's ascension (vv. 16-20).

Ninth, to Christ's half-brother James, which led to his conversion as well as of His other half-siblings (1 Cor. 15:7; Acts 1:14). The timing of this resurrection appearance is unknown.

Tenth, to the disciples and many other followers on Mount Olivet before ascending into Heaven forty days after His resurrection.

Jesus Christ declared to the Pharisees that His resurrection would prove that He was the Son of God (Matt. 12:39-40; Rom. 1:4). Jesus Christ, the only begotten Son of God, was the firstfruits of eternal resurrection and is now with His Father in heaven (Heb. 1:5; Rev. 3:21). The doctrine of Christ's resurrection is essential to the Christian faith and the evidence for the resurrection of Jesus Christ is overwhelming!

The Great Commission (vv. 15-18)

In just fourteen verses, Mark introduced the Lord Jesus as the Son of God and expedited Him into active ministry as the Servant of Jehovah.

And Jesus Christ steadily worked until they nailed His worn out and beaten body to a cross. However, as the risen Savior, His work on earth would continue in His disciples after His ascension into heaven. Hence, on the day of His ascension, the Lord again issued the Great Commission decree that He had previously given to His disciples on a mountain in Galilee (Matt. 28:18-20). They were to go unto all the world and preach the gospel to every creature (i.e., person; v. 15).

Those who, after hearing the gospel message, respond with repentance and confess Christ publicly through water baptism will be saved (v. 16). Those who reject the gospel message will retain the guilt of their sins and remain condemned before God (John 3:18).

While both these statements are true, Mark does not address a third possible group of people: Those who have believed on Christ for salvation but have not been baptized. There are about one hundred verses in the New Testament that clearly state that salvation is gained through faith in Christ alone (e.g., John 3:16, 18, 36, 5:25, 6:47; Rom. 10:9, Eph. 2:8-9; Tit. 3:5). Furthermore, Paul declared that water baptism was not part of the gospel message and therefore baptism cannot save anyone (1 Cor. 1:17). Salvation is obtained by faith alone, but Paul also told the saints at Rome that *"with the heart one believes unto righteousness, and with the mouth confession is made unto salvation"* (Rom. 10:10). In other words, if someone is truly saved, they will want to publicly profess Christ and therefore follow the Lord's command to be baptized in His name. In this way baptism does not save, but it demonstrates the reality of salvation (Jas. 2:17).

Having confirmed their authority to preach the message of salvation to the world, the Lord then informed His disciples that He would be giving them authority to work spectacular miracles, speak in tongues, and heal the sick. These signs would confirm that the message they were proclaiming was His message to the world and that the apostles were an extension of His authority (Acts 2:16-22).

Christ's Ascension (vv. 19-20)

Mark then concludes His Gospel by describing the ascension of the Lord Jesus Christ back to heaven. Mark is careful to uphold his gospel theme, Christ – the lowly Servant of Jehovah, even to the very last verse:

> So then, after the Lord had spoken to them, He was received up into heaven, and sat down at the right hand of God. And they went out and

preached everywhere, **the Lord working with them** *and confirming the word through the accompanying signs. Amen* (Mark 16:19-20).

Verse 19 records the ascension of the Lord Jesus back into heaven, thus, a splendid climax to conclude Mark's story. However, that was not all that the Holy Spirit had in mind, for He inspired Mark to add one more verse. In doing so, every disciple since that day understands that Christ, though in heaven, continues to labor with them. In Matthew, Christ's authority in directing the disciples is prominent throughout: *"Jesus sent them forth." "He commanded them," "go not,"* and *"but go."* Mark, however, alludes to an aspect of the Commission which Matthew does not: *"the Lord working with them."*

We do not labor for the kingdom alone or in vain, for it is Christ's work, and He labors with us to accomplish it – we are His eyes to discern the needs of others and His hands to serve them. Paul enlightened the believers at Corinth that *"we are laborers together with God"* (1 Cor. 3:9; KJV). Christ labored with His disciples after commissioning them, and He still labors with His saints today.

With earnest gratefulness and loving appreciation, God the Father proclaimed to the far reaches of creation itself, "Behold My Servant!" His meek and humble character, His compassion for the suffering, and His resolute spirit in the face of opposition invite us to follow His example and to be true "servants of God." True love needs no title to serve, just the power of humility to do so.

There are many of us that are willing to do great things for the Lord, but few of us are willing to do little things.

– D. L. Moody

How comforting it is, in view of that inevitable scrutiny of our poor works, to learn that in His patient love He is so leading us and working in us now that He can then find something in it all for which to praise us.

– C. I. Scofield

Endnotes

1 C. I. Scofield, *The New Scofield Study Bible* (Oxford University Press, New York; 1967), p. 987

2 Samuel Ridout, *The Serious Christian* (Books for Christians, Charlotte, NC; no date), p. 24

3 Arthur Pink, *Why Four Gospels?* (Scripture Truth Book Co., Fincastle, VA; no date), pp. 162-163

4 J. H. Thayer, *Thayer's Greek Lexicon* (Biblesoft; 2000), electronic database

5 James Strong, *New Exhaustive Strong's Numbers and Concordance With Expanded Greek-Hebrew Dictionary* (Biblesoft and International Bible Translators, Inc.; 1994)

6 Louis A Barbieri, Jr., *The Bible Knowledge Commentary: Matthew* (Victor Books, Wheaton, IL; 1983), p. 15

7 C. I. Scofield, *The New Scofield Study Bible* (Oxford University Press, New York; 1967), p. 994; Note 3

8 William MacDonald, *Here's the Difference* (Gospel Folio Press, Port Colburne, ON; 1999), pp. 119-120

9 L. Laurenson, *Classic Christian Commentary* (Books for Christians, Charlotte, NC; no date) p. 44

10 Louis A. Barbieri, Jr., *The Bible Knowledge Commentary* by Dallas Seminary (Victor Books, Wheaton, IL; 1983), p. 18

11 Donald A. Hagner, *World Biblical Commentary: Matthew 1-13* (Zondervan, Grand Rapids, MI; 2015), p. 37.

12 Raymond Brown, *Birth of the Messiah* (Yale University Press; New Haven, CT; 1999), pp. 204-205

13 John Heading, *What the Bible Teaches: Matthew and Mark* (John Ritchie; 2000), pp. 54–55

14 William MacDonald, op. cit., p. 1208

15 Louis A. Barbieri, Jr., op. cit., p. 23

16 F. B. Hole, Matthew Chapter 4 (STEM Publishing); https://stempublishing.com/authors/hole/NT/MATTHEW.html

17 Arthur Pink, op. cit., pp. 109-110

18 C. I. Scofield, op. cit., p. 994, note 3

19 Arthur Pink, op. cit., pp. 45-46

20 W. T. P. Wolston, Chapter 22: *The Beatitudes* (STEM Publishing); https://www.stempublishing.com/authors/wolston/HAND322.html

21 H. A. Ironside, *Isaiah* – Revised Edition (Loizeaux, Neptune, NJ; 2000), p. 255

22 William MacDonald, op. cit., p. 1217

23 John Phillips, *Exploring the Gospel of Matthew: An Expository Commentary* (Kregel Pub., Grand Rapids, MI; 1999), p. 95

[24] Lawrence O. Richards, *The Teacher's Commentary* (Victor Books, Wheaton, IL; 1987), p 547

[25] Edythe Draper, *Draper's Quotations From the Christian World* (Tyndale House Publishers Inc., Wheaton, IL – electronic copy)

[26] William MacDonald, op. cit., p. 1227

[27] C. H. Mackintosh, *Genesis to Deuteronomy* (Loizeaux Brothers, Inc., Neptune, NJ; 1972), p. 458

[28] William MacDonald, op. cit., p. 1229

[29] A. C. Gaebelein, *The Gospel of Matthew* (Loizeaux Bros., NY; 1910), p. 420

[30] William MacDonald, op. cit., p. 1233

[31] David Brown, A. R. Fausset, and Robert Jamieson, *A Commentary, Critical, Experimental, and Practical, on the Old and New Testaments: Matthew–John*, vol. V (William Collins, Sons, & Company, Limited, London; Glasgow), p. 56

[32] William MacDonald, op. cit., p. 1237

[33] J. G. Bellett, Matthew Chapter 10 (STEM Publishing) https://stempublishing.com/authors/bellett/evang3.html#a2

[34] Warren W. Wiersbe, *The Bible Exposition Commentary*, Vol. 1 (Victor Books, Wheaton, IL; 1996), p. 37

[35] Edythe Draper, op. cit.

[36] Warren Wiersbe, *Be Joyful: A New Testament Study – Philippians* (Victor Books, Wheaton, Il; 1996 – electronic copy)

[37] F. B. Hole, op. cit., Matt. 10

[38] Edythe Draper, op. cit.

[39] Arthur Pink, op. cit., pp. 46-47

[40] William MacDonald, op. cit., p. 1394

[41] John Heading, op. cit., p. 166

[42] William MacDonald, op. cit., p. 2080

[43] Willaim MacDonald, op. cit. p. 1252

[44] Warren Wiersbe, op. cit., p. 46

[45] Warren Wiersbe, op. cit., p. 46

[46] Warren Wiersbe, op. cit., p. 53

[47] John Phillips, op. cit. p. 55

[48] Randy P. Amos, *The Church* (Henrietta, NY); no date

[49] F. B. Hole, *Malachi*, STEM Publishing, Mal. 3: http://stempublishing.com/authors/hole/Zion/Malachi.html

[50] Mishnah: *Shekalim* 1:1

[51] Laurence Laurenson, op. cit., Matt. 17

[52] Willaim MacDonald, op. cit. p. 1272

[53] William MacDonald, op. cit., p. 1274

[54] John Heading, op. cit., p. 283

[55] J. J. Stubbs, *What the Bible Teaches – Zechariah* (John Ritchie LTD, Kilmarnock, Scotland; 2015), Zech. 11:8

[56] William MacDonald, op. cit., pp. 1288–1289

[57] J. G. Bellett, op. cit., Matt.23

[58] *Divine Principle*, pp. 368-369, 520

59 Guichaoua, André, *Journal of Genocide Research* (2 January 2020): *"Counting the Rwandan Victims of War and Genocide: Concluding Reflections"*; (22: 125–141)

60 Vejl Lorens, adapted from "Civina odbrana" (Vojnoizdavacki i novinski centar, Beograd, 1991), p. 30

61 WFP, "Famine Intervention" (Feb. 15, 2021)

62 WHO (July 24, 2024)

63 IDS, "Famine in the Twentieth Century" (Feb. 16, 1993)

64 USGS, "Why Are We Having So Many Earthquakes" (https://www.usgs.gov/faqs; accessed Jan 4, 2025)

65 USGS, "Does Fracking Cause Earthquakes?" (https://www.usgs.gov/faqs; accessed Jan 4, 2025)

66 Prophecy News, "Temple Institute Performs 'Educational Passover Sacrifice" by Chris Perver; April 10, 2012, http://www.prophecynews.co.uk/index.php/temple-mount/1919-temple-institute-performs-educational-passover-sacrifice

67 Louis A. Barbieri, Jr., op. cit., p. 79

68 William Kelly, *Lectures on the Gospel of Matthew*: Chapter 25 (STEM Publishing) https://stempublishing.com/authors/kelly/2Newtest/MATT_PT2.html#a25

69 John Heading, op. cit., p. 357

70 Hillel Geva, *"Jerusalem's Population in Antiquity: A Minimalist View"* (Tel Aviv, 42:2; 2013), pp. 131-160

71 John Wilkinson, *"Ancient Jerusalem, Its Water Supply and Population"* (PEFQS 106; 1974), pp. 33–51

72 Magen Broshi, *"Estimating the Population of Ancient Jerusalem"* (BAR 4:02; June 1978)

73 Edwin Blum, *The Bible Knowledge Commentary* by Dallas Seminary (Victor Books, Wheaton, IL; 1983), p. 335

74 Mishnah (Sanhedrin 4.1)%

75 F. B. Hole, op. cit., Matt. 26

76 Laurence Laurenson, op. cit., Matt. 26

77 J. J. Stubbs, op. cit., Zech. 11:13

78 *Ecclesiastical History*, Book 4, chp. 15

79 John Heading, op. cit., p. 393

80 Herbert Danby translator, *The Mishnah*, p 161, par 5

81 Alfred Edersheim, *The Life and Times of Jesus the Messiah* (Hendrickson Pub., US; 1993) bk. 5; chp. 15; p. 894

82 Dr. Howard Taylor, *Spiritual Secret of Hudson Taylor* (Whitaker House, New Kensington, PA; 1996), p. 368

83 Warren Wiersbe, op. cit., p. 416

84 Hamilton Smith, *Classic Christian Commentary – Matthew* (Books for Christians, Charlotte, NC; no date), pp. 1-3

85 Arthur Pink, op. cit., p. 75

86 Warren Wiersbe, op. cit., p. 46

87 William MacDonald, op. cit., p. 1233

88 William MacDonald, op. cit., p. 1337

89 Harold S. Paisley, *What the Bible Teaches: Matthew and Mark* (John Ritchie, 2000), p. 489.
90 F. B. Hole, op. cit., Mal. 3
91 Harold Paisley, op. cit., p. 514
92 Harold Paisley, op. cit., p. 526
93 Harold Paisley, op. cit., p. 538
94 John Heading, op. cit., p. 357
95 M. G. Easton, *Easton's Bible Dictionary* (Harper & Brothers Pub, NY; 1893), p. 152
96 Hillel Geva, op. cit. pp. 131-160
97 John Wilkinson, op. cit., pp. 33–51
98 Magen Broshi, op. cit.
99 Edwin Blum, op. cit., p. 335
100 Mishnah (Sanhedrin 4.1)%
101 F. B. Hole, op. cit., Matt. 26
102 *Ecclesiastical History*, Book 4, chp. 15
103 John Heading, op. cit., p. 393
104 Herbert Danby translator, *The Mishnah*, p 161, par 5
105 Alfred Edersheim, op. cit., p. 894

www.ingramcontent.com/pod-product-compliance
Lightning Source LLC
Chambersburg PA
CBHW052028090426
42739CB00010B/1820